INSIDE SPETSNAZ

INSIDE SPETSNAZ

Soviet Special Operations
A Critical Analysis

Kirsten Amundsen William H. Burgess III John J. Dziak
James F. Gebhardt David C. Isby Owen A. Lock
John H. Merritt Jim Shortt Robert D. Smith

Edited by Maj. William H. Burgess III
Foreword by Gen. Robert C. Kingston (USA, Ret.)

PRESIDIO

The individual views expressed in this book are those of the authors and should not be construed as representing positions of the United States Government, any part thereof, or of any government or commercial organization with which the authors are affiliated.

Published by Presidio Press
31 Pamaron Way
Novato, CA 94949

Distributed in Great Britain by
Greenhill Books
Park House, 1 Russell Gardens
London NW11 9NN

Library of Congress Cataloging-in-Publication Data

Inside spetsnaz: Soviet special operations: a critical
  analysis / Kirsten Amundsen . . . [et al.]: foreword by Robert C.
  Kingston: William H. Burgess III, editor.
      p.   cm.
  Includes bibliographical references.
  ISBN 0-89141-339-1
  1. Special forces (Military science)—Soviet Union. I. Amundsen,
Kirsten. II. Burgess, William H., 1952- .
UA776.S64I57   1989
355.3'5—dc20   89-23025
                                                           CIP

Illustrated by Larry A. Fourmet

Printed in the United States of America

For Collette

Behold! human beings living in an underground den. . . .
Like ourselves . . . they see only their own shadows, or the
shadows of another, which the fire throws on the opposite
wall of the cave.

Plato's Allegory of the Cave
The Republic, Book VII

Contents

Foreword   ix
    GEN. Robert C. Kingston (USA, Ret.)

Acknowledgements   xi

Introduction   xiii

Abbreviations   xvii

Glossary   xix

Chapter 1   **Assessing Spetsnaz**
                  William H. Burgess III   1

Chapter 2   **Western Misperceptions**
                  Robert D. Smith   17

Chapter 3   **Historical Precedents**
                  Dr. John J. Dziak   29

Chapter 4   **The Spanish Civil War**
                  Owen A. Lock   47

Chapter 5   **Spetsnaz Engineers in the
                  Great Patriotic War: An Overview**
                  William H. Burgess III   71

Chapter 6   **The Far North Origin of Naval Spetsnaz**
                  James F. Gebhardt
                  and William H. Burgess III   81

Chapter 7   **The Arctic: Petsamo-Kirkenes,**
             7 to 30 October 1944
             James F. Gebhardt   113

Chapter 8   **Manchuria, 1945**
             William H. Burgess III
             and James F. Gebhardt   135

Chapter 9   **Spetsnaz and Soviet Far North Strategy**
             Kirsten Amundsen   159

Chapter 10   **Prague to Kabul**
             John H. Merritt   181

Chapter 11   **Afghanistan**
             David C. Isby   203

Chapter 12   **Spetsnaz and the Deep Operation**
             William H. Burgess III   221

Chapter 13   **Organization, Capabilities**
             and Countermeasures
             Jim Shortt   237

Chapter 14   **Conclusions**
             William H. Burgess III   257

About the Authors   260
Appendix: The Players   263
Bibliography   277
Index   302

Foreword

This book is a unique open-source study of the oft-discussed but little understood subject of Soviet special operations and *spetsnaz* forces. The contributors are specialists in military and historical analysis who have a knowledge of Russian and experience in special operations and intelligence. They deftly define Soviet special operations by analyzing the combat record, doctrine, and evolution of *spetsnaz* from varying perspectives, and use their aggregate information and skill to produce a very insightful volume.

A major contribution of this volume is that it informs and does not alarm: Various myths and legends attributed to *spetsnaz* in open literature in the West are put in perspective and hard, historical facts are emphasized. A wide array of original Soviet sources are used, many of which are virtually unknown in the West. In some cases, contributors have also yielded differing insights in their analyses of the same sources. The result is a revealing expose and assessment of how and why the Soviets have mounted special operations and employed special forces from the time of the Bolshevik uprising to the present.

I recommend this work to serious students of Soviet military affairs because it significantly advances public knowledge in several crucial areas: in particular, the complexity of Soviet military thought, the underlying organizations that control special operations and special operations forces, and under whose policies, direction and command these forces operate. This volume also offers several technical and operational lessons for Western nations in their conduct of special operations.

The book should clear the air, stimulate critical analysis, and impose some intellectual discipline on the discussion of Soviet special operations capabilities. It will answer basic questions about the past, present and likely future of such capabilities, and will provide a reliable baseline for further study. It is a valuable window through which the reader may understand an important element of the Soviet political-military power continuum.

Gen. Robert C. Kingston (USA, Ret.)
Alexandria, Virginia

Acknowledgements

From inception to completion of this arduous project I was blessed to have the generous support of many dedicated professionals, kind friends, and my family. Each of the contributors brought a unique perspective to the study, and added immensely to the quality of each other's work through rigorous review and candid criticism of innumerable drafts, an experience all treated with utmost professionalism, patience and good humor.

Many others, far and wide, were indispensable to the effort of putting the book together. Dr. George Tanham of the Rand Corporation and John M. Collins of the Library of Congress gave encouragement and some key insights when the book proposal was being put together. Ms. Dorothy E. Nicolosi of the National Strategic Information Center, Inc. granted permission to use much of the material that appears in Dr. Jack Dziak's chapter. Mr. Don McKeon and Ms. Jaime Welch-Donahue each provided keen advice as to form and style when the manuscript was in its embryonic stages. Dr. Robert C. Suggs provided constant encouragement and advice throughout the project, and was especially helpful with those parts of the book dealing with naval *spetsnaz*.

Dr. Graham H. Turbiville and others on the staff of the Soviet Army Studies Office at Fort Leavenworth provided voluminous documents and translations, without which this book would be much leaner. My friend and mentor, Col. Scott Crerar (USA, Ret.), faithfully read and fully commented on key portions of the manuscript, and despite often being inundated by successive drafts, redrafts and telephone calls, always came through with advice that kept the project on track.

Capt. Mark G. Perry, my close friend in the 6th Infantry Division (Light), carefully read and provided incisive comments on the drafts of several chapters, and never uttered a complaint when I brought the manuscript along during our twenty-one-day bear hunt on Kodiak Island. Ms. Adele Horwitz, Editor-in-Chief of Presidio Press is commended for her patience and grace in the face of my initial manuscript, and for her immense skill in guiding the manuscript from the initial draft through completion.

Special praise is owed to my wife, Collette, and to my children, Bill and Alison, who kept me emotionally and intellectually energized during the project, but who set reasonable limits on my divergence from normal family routine.

WHB III

Introduction

In preparing this book, the contributors have strived to lay a cornerstone for others to build on. This book is perhaps the most extensively researched open-source Western study of Soviet special operations, and yet merely scratches the surface: for every question answered, a hundred more remain. If it accomplishes nothing else, this book should underscore the need for detailed critical case studies of all aspects of Soviet special operations history since the dawn of the Soviet state.

A true definition of *spetsnaz*, in the sense of Soviet commando forces, is difficult to pin down. In general, six criteria must be met for a force to be considered as *spetsnaz*: (1) a specialized mission, e.g., ground reconnaissance to operational depths in the enemy rear; (2) a unique organization and/or unusual equipment; (3) high political reliability; (4) extraordinary selection and training; (5) unusually high level subordination; and (6) utility at all levels of conflict and war.

James F. Gebhardt, one of the contributors, suggests a seventh criterion for some *spetsnaz* units: lineage to earlier *spetsnaz* formations. He also suggests the following litmus test for identifying *spetsnaz* units from historical records:

1. **NAME:** Does the name of the unit contain any of the following elements (in Russian)?
   Ground: *spetsialnogo naznacheniya* — special designation/purpose
   osobogo naznacheniya — special designation/purpose
   otdel'nyi — separate, independent

Naval: *razvedyvatel'nyi otriad shtaba* (xxx) *flota* — reconnaissance detachment of headquarters (named) fleet

2. **PERSONNEL SELECTION AND TRAINING:** Does the text contain references to special selection of personnel? Physical and political screening? Segregation of unit and personnel in barracks? In training? What kind of training was conducted? Is there emphasis on demolition skills, reconnaissance, land navigation, physical and mental endurance, recognition of enemy equipment and personnel, and/or employment of enemy weapons? Look at unit training tasks as well as individual training tasks.

3. **SUBORDINATION OF UNIT:** To what level of command was the unit subordinated? *Spetsnaz* organizations were most frequently subordinated to STAVKA or Front. Look for indications of operational subordination which may deviate from standard, e.g., STAVKA on occasion allocated a *spetsnaz* formation to Front for use in a particular situation. Fleet *spetsnaz* units were sometimes subordinated to a defensive region (*oboronitel'nyi raion*) for an operation.

4. **MISSIONS:** What kind of missions did the organization perform? Look for special operations: deep raids, reconnaissance, partisan support, prisoner snatches, assassinations, and the like.

5. **HISTORY:** What is known about the unit's history? Does this history reflect a track record of special operations? If World War II German microfilm records are available, see how the Germans describe the unit or operation.

6. **PERSONALITIES:** Record all names associated with the unit or operation. Do these names appear in other Soviet sources in association with special operations? Look for Heroes of the Soviet Union and check their official biographies.

The Soviets have learned a lot about special operations over the decades, and have retained many of these lessons from one conflict to the next. History has taught the Soviets that simplicity, political reliability, physical and mental toughness, good security, and adaptability are essential to success in special operations. One result is that *spetsnaz* will adapt their organization, equipment, and tactics to their combat environment (though not always readily or without difficulties). Unilateral direct action special operations forces were used to seize Kabul; two years later, *spetsnaz* were reintroduced to Afghanistan after conversion to motorized special counterinsurgency infantry. The hiatus was perhaps because the war had become too "politicized," even by Soviet standards, but it may also illustrate a gap between Soviet doctrine and battlefield application.

History has favored the use of *spetsnaz*. For example, during World War II the Soviets did better with small airborne and amphibious diversionary (*spetsnaz*) groups than with large, conventional airborne operations (e.g., the disastrous Vyaz'ma operation in January 1942).* *Spetsnaz* have proved capable of operating in extremely harsh climates, where conventional forces could not operate, as when *spetsnaz* were used during World War II to collect intelligence and conduct direct action raids in northern Norway in winter.

Historically, *spetsnaz* have been resourceful, but not elaborate, in utilizing various modes of transport to get to or from, and be resupplied within, their areas of operations. Such modes have included foot, truck, submarine, small surface craft, float plane, and parachute. Their range, even when on foot, is impressive. During World War II, there were many instances of *spetsnaz* patrols covering more than two hundred kilometers round-trip on foot.

Spetsnaz operations behind enemy lines have also historically emphasized the integration of language skills sufficient for quick exploitation of prisoners, documents, and communications. Interestingly, there are examples on record where the linguist assigned to a deep-strike *spetsnaz* mission was female. While most *spetsnaz* units may have only a rudimentary foreign language capability, *spetsnaz* signals intelligence (SIGINT) detachments operating behind enemy lines generally may have skills sufficient for at least basic field analysis of intercepted voice communications.

The Soviets have also historically integrated politically reliable foreign nationals in their special operations structures. This was demonstrated to a great extent during the Spanish Civil War, and by the utilization of Spanish Communist expatriates in the Soviet Army afterward. This may also be demonstrated to a similar degree by the use of Afghan Communist expatriates after the fall of the pro-Soviet regime in Afghanistan.

One of the more interesting features of Soviet special operations is that *spetsnaz* detachments have often been accompanied on their missions by senior intelligence or engineering officers of the rank of major through

---

*See, Lt. Col. David M. Glantz, *The Soviet Airborne Experience* (Fort Leavenworth, KS: U.S. Army Command and General Staff College, November 1984).

lieutenant general. Most of the time these escorts appear to have been conventional officers tapped for special occasions. Sometimes, however, they were special operators. Their duties appear to have mostly entailed technical supervision of the operation, the conduct of extremely sensitive political and intelligence sub-missions, liaison with conventional forces, and provision of the rank needed for particular tasks.

Soviet *spetsnaz* troops are politically reliable, physically tough, technically competent, security-conscious professional soldiers. They are among the first troops the Soviets commit to combat. In the case of Afghanistan, they were among the last to leave the battlefield. They are certain to play an important role in the next Soviet armed conflict.

The bulk of Soviet special operations capabilities, however, is in units not seen as bona fide "special forces" by many in the West: the VDV airborne divisions, air assault brigades, airborne naval infantry, and the like. Historically, the Soviets have tailored existing organizations or created new formations to deal with battlefield demands for special operations. There are two main strands in the evolution of Soviet special operations forces: state security and the military. There are two military strands: intelligence and combat engineering. The combat engineer strain in the *spetsnaz* bloodline, in particular, has been almost completely overlooked in the contemporary literature. In fact, operational-level (Army and Front) combat engineer formations may represent a latent *spetsnaz* deep operation capability.

No attempt was made in the preparation of this book to forge consensus positions, or to utter the last word on the subject of Soviet special operations. Although there is wide agreement among the contributors on many aspects, the differing backgrounds and approaches of the contributors have necessarily led in some instances to different interpretations of the available evidence. The book should, nevertheless, provide a focus on Soviet special operations and contribute to public understanding of a subject that will command increasing attention through the end of this century.

William H. Burgess III
1 May 1989

Abbreviations

BMD – Boevaia Mashina Desantnika (Airborne Combat Assault Vehicle)

CAA – Combined Arms Army

Cheka – (Also VChKa) Vserossiyskaya Chrezvychaynaya Komissiya po bor'be s Kontrrevolyutsiyey i sabotazhem (All Russian Extraordinary Commission to Combat Counterrevolution and Sabotage)

ChON – Chasti Osobogo Naznacheniya (Detachments of Special Designation)

Comintern – Communist International

CPSU – Communist Party of the Soviet Union

C3I – Command, Control, Communications and Intelligence

DRA – Democratic Republic of Afghanistan (former name of the Republic of Afghanistan)

GPU – Gosudarstvennoye Politicheskoye Upravleniye (Main Political Directorate of the Army and Navy)

GRU – Glavnoye Razvedyvatelnoye Upravleniye (Main Intelligence Directorate of the General Staff)

GSFG – Group of Soviet Forces Germany

GUGB – Glavnoye Upravleniye Gosudarstvennoye Bezopasnosti (Chief Directorate, or Main Administration, of State Security of the NKVD)

GUKR – Glavnoye Upravleniye Kontrrazvedki (Main Administration for Counterintelligence)

IPB – Intelligence Preparation of the Battlefield

I&W – Indications and Warning

KGB – Komitet Gosudarstvennoi Bezopasnosti (Committee for State Security)

KHAD – Khidamate Aetilaati Daulati (State Information Service of the Republic of Afghanistan)

km – kilometer(s)

Komsomol – Youth Organization of the CPSU

LOC – Line(s) of Communication

MGB – Ministerstvo Gosudarstvennoye Bezopasnosti (Ministry of State Security)

mm – millimeter(s)

MOD – Ministry of Defense

MRD – Motorized Rifle Division

MSR – Main Supply Route

MSS – Mission Support Site

MVD – Ministerstvo Vnutrennikh Del (Ministry of Internal Affairs)

MZD – Mina zamedlennogo deystviya (delayed-action mine)

NKO – Narodnyy Komissariat Oborony (People's Commissariat of Defense)

NKVD – Narodnyy Komissariat Vnutrennikh Del (People's Commissariat of Internal Affairs)

NS – New Style, or Gregorian Calendar

OB – Order of Battle

OGBM – Otdelnyy gvardeyeskiy batal'on minerov (Guards battalion of *miners*)

OGPU – Obyedinennoy Gosudarstvennoye Politicheskoye Upravleniye (Unified State Political Directorate)

OMG – Operational Maneuver Group

OPSEC – Operational Security

Osnaz – (Also OSNAZ) Osobogo Naznacheniya (Special Designation). Also osoboye naznacheniye (nominative case).

Politburo – Politicheskoye Buro (the chief political and executive committee of the CPSU)

POW – (also PW) Prisoner of War

PSYOP – Psychological Operations

RA – Republic of Afghanistan

REC – Radioelectronic Combat

RKP(b) – Rossiyskaya komunisticheskaya partiya (bolshevikov) Russian Communist Party (Bolsheviks)

SIGINT – Signals Intelligence

SLOC – Sea Line(s) of Communication

SMERSH – Smert' Shpionam ("Death to Spies," Soviet Armed Forces Counterintelligence Directorate, 1943–46)

SO – Special Operations

SOF – Special Operations Forces

Sovnarkom – Sovet Narodnykh Komissarov (Council of People's Commissars)

Spetsnaz – (Also SPETSNAZ) voiska spetsialnogo naznacheniya (troops of special designation/purpose) .

Stavka – (Also STAVKA) General headquarters (of the VGK)

TA – Tank Army

TD – Tank Division

TsK KPSS – Central Committee, Communist Party of the Soviet Union

TV – Teatr Voeny (Theater of War)

TVD – Teatr Voennykh Deistviy (Theater of Military Actions)

UFO – Unidentified Flying Object

USSR – Union of Soviet Socialist Republics

VDV – Vozdushno-Desantniye Voiska (Airborne Forces of the General Staff)

VGK – Stavka Verkhovnoe Glavnokomandovaniye (Supreme High Command)

VSN – Voiska Spetsialnogo Naznachenya (Forces of Special Designation)

Glossary

aktivnyye akty—direct actions

aktivnyye meropriyatiya—active measures

basmachi—bandits; a pejorative Soviet term for Moslem rebels in Soviet Central Asia and Afghanistan; occasionally used in place of "dushman"

brigada—an independent command, brought together for a special task

chast'—unit; [voinskaya chast'] administrative, line, and supply unit (yedinitsa) of the [branches] of troops, which has a number and banner, e.g., a regiment, separate battalion (batal'on), and troop organizations equal to them; pl. "chasti"

commandon—commando; Afghan *mujahideen* term for Soviet special forces

desant—assault team, assault party, or assault operation (e.g., airborne, amphibious, soldiers riding on the backs of tanks, and the like)

dushman—bandit; pejorative term for an Afghan antigovernment rebel

glavnoye komandovaniye—high command

glubokii boi—deep battle

gulag—Soviet state security prison system

initsiyativa nakazyvaetsya—"initiative is punishable"

iskatelia—personnel involved in long range reconnaissance patrol (LRRP) operations

karavan okhotniki—caravan hunters; personnel involved in special interdiction operations against *mujahideen* lines of communication in Afghanistan

kholodniye oruzhiye—"cold weapons," including the shtyk (bayonet), entrenching tool (shantsevaya lopata) and knife (nozh)

kombrig—brigade commander

kursanti—officer cadets

maskirovka—deception, camouflage, OPSEC

miner—demolitions expert; pl. "minery"

minerov dobrovotsev—*miner* volunteer

minery gvardeiskie—guards *miners* (guards demolition experts)

mokrie dela—"wet affairs"

nachal'nik razvedki—intelligence chief

oblast—region or province

operativnyi desant—operational-level assault force or assault

operativnoye ob'yedineniye—large-scale formation of various *soyedineniye* of the branches of troops, which is temporary in composition and is intended to conduct operations in a war

osobogo naznacheniya—special designation; abb. "osnaz"

ostrov—island

otdel—department or section

otdel diversii—diversionary department

podrazdeleniye—troop unit of permanent organization and homogenous composition, which unit forms a larger podrazdeleniye or a chast'; generally thought of in terms of battalion down to platoon

razvedchiki—personnel involved in reconnaissance; regimental or divisional scouts or intelligence soldiers; s. "razvedchik"

razvedyvatel'no-diversionnyia otriad—diversionary detachments

razvedivatel'nye otriadi—reconnaissance detachments

razvedka—intelligence, reconnaissance, surveillance and other activities associated with the collection and processing of information about actual or potential enemies

reydovaya rota—regimental or divisional reconnaissance company

reydoviki—foreign raiders or commandos; often erroneously used in Western sources for *spetsnaz* conscripts.

rezident—KGB station chief

rezidentura—complement of KGB agents operating abroad in a given city or geographical area

rukopashnyi boi—hand-to-hand combat (generic term)

ryukzak bolshoi—large rucksack

samo-oborona bez oruzhiya—Soviet combat without weapons; the unarmed combat section of rukopashnyi boi; abb. "sambo"

shapka-ushanka—standard Soviet military winter cap with ear flaps

soyedineniye—combination; "soyedineniye voyskovoye" is a combination of several chast' of one or various branches of troops into a permanent organization (division, brigade, or corps), headed by a command and a staff and including chast' and podrazdeleniye of auxiliary troops and services necessary for combat operations.

spetsialnaya razvedka—special reconnaissance

starshina—noncommissioned officer

strategicheskii desant—strategic assault force or assault operation

takticheskii desant—tactical assault force or assault operation

telniashka—blue and white T-shirt worn by Soviet naval infantry, airborne, air assault and *spetsnaz* troops

voiska spetsialnogo naznacheniya—troops of special designation; abb. "spetsnaz"

vysotniki—foreign career-term military special operations personnel; special operations personnel inserted by high altitude low opening (HALO) or high altitude high opening (HAHO) parachuting; often used erroneously in Western sources for career-term *spetsnaz*

zakhvatchiki—personnel involved in prisoner-taking operations

zampolit—political officer

CHAPTER 1

Assessing Spetsnaz

William H. Burgess III

Spetsnaz are mostly unilateral direct action forces integrated with the intelligence functions of the KGB and the GRU, both of which have their own special operations forces (SOF). The logical consistency of associating special forces with intelligence is contained in the Soviet military concept *razvedka*:[1] a seamless web of intelligence, reconnaissance, surveillance, and other activities associated with the collection and processing of information about actual or potential enemies. But *spetsnaz* are more than long-range scouts, for they can also be used in direct action raids and demolition missions, to seize critical facilities in a *coup de main*, to supplant a victim's political-military power, to negotiate garrison surrenders in the enemy rear, and for other purposes.

The lineage of Soviet special forces is Janus-faced, half rooted in the military and half in state security.* The military lineage is also split, between intelligence and assault combat engineering. The earliest use of Soviet SOF may have been employment of special "Red" cavalry for operations in the enemy rear, and the organization of Communist-led *chasti osobogo naznacheniya* (detachments of special designation, or ChON) in industrial areas in spring 1918.[2] In 1920, "insurgency" Cossack cavalry, Red Polish cavalry in Polish uniform, and special diversionary/insurgency

---

*Some analysts divide the lineage into thirds between the military, state security, and internal security components.

combined-arms battalions operated behind Polish lines with some success.[3] In mid-1919 a precursor of the KGB, the Cheka,[4] expanded and reinvigorated ChON into assault forces of the territorial units of the Red Army.[5] ChON detachments saw considerable action in the Russian civil war and in the suppression of the Moslem *basmachi* (bandits) up to 1925, when ChON was disbanded and its resources turned over to the Red Army.

The USSR pioneered the development of airborne special forces. As early as 1927, small airborne detachments were used against the *basmachi* in Central Asia.[6] In 1929, an Afghan incursion into Tadzhikistan "was repulsed thanks to the surprise insertion of a small but heavily armed paratroop force."[7] In 1930, Aleksandr N. Lapchinskiy[8] referred to the airlanding of individuals (possibly espionage agents) "in the enemy disposition" during the First World War, and to a 1920s airlanding of a fifteen-man reconnaissance detachment in three airplanes behind a force of *basmachi* in the Saksaul bush country. In 1931, according to a White Russian source, "fifteen parachutists with a machine gun landed in the rear of a large band of Basmach bandits in Central Asia and successfully carried out their mission."[9]

The interest of Marshal Mikhail N. Tukhachevskiy in the potential of parachute forces in the 1920s led to the first organized field exercises of small-unit airborne concepts in 1928.[10] In 1930, the first regular airborne units were created and in August and September the Soviets conducted their first field exercises involving the parachute insertion of small (11- to 12-man) diversionary units behind enemy lines.[11] By 1931, Soviet airborne forces were dedicated to disorganization of the enemy rear to operational depths, interruption of enemy command and control, and destruction of enemy air and naval bases.

With the successful suppression of its major domestic enemies, Soviet special operations (SO) from the early 1930s until the beginning of World War II focussed on the disruption and elimination of anti-Soviet activities abroad. The lead went to the Cheka which in 1936 created an Administration for Special Tasks to kill or kidnap enemies outside the USSR. Assassinations, abductions, and other covert and clandestine activities eventually rendered most targets ineffective or under Soviet control.[12] During the Spanish civil war, NKVD[13] and GRU operators engaged in a variety of terrorist, sabotage, and guerrilla activities behind Nationalist and Republican lines. The Finns allege that during the 1939–1940 Winter War the Soviets parachuted *desants* of Finnish-speaking Inkeris behind Finnish lines.[14] A GRU veteran of the Spanish civil war, General Khadzhi-Umar

Mamsurov, also made an unsuccessful attempt to employ a fifty-man special forces unit in the Winter War on prisoner-snatching operations, "the first prewar instance of an identified Soviet military entity with responsibility for diversionary (that is special operations) activity."[15]

During the Great Patriotic War (World War II), the Soviets gained considerable experience with the use of a wide variety of initially ad hoc Chekist, GRU, assault combat engineer[16] and naval special reconnaissance SOF in unilateral missions and partisan support and control operations in hostile, denied, and contested territories.[17] The varied conceptual forerunners of modern *spetsnaz*, "recce-diversionary brigades," NKVD "special groups" (which ultimately became the NKVD Separate Motorized Rifle Special Purpose Brigade),[18] "guards battalions of miners,"[19] and the Reconnaissance Detachment of Headquarters, Northern Fleet[20] were employed on the Western Front and Far North as early as summer 1941.[21] During the Manchurian Campaign, the Soviets used assault engineer *spetsnaz* battalions to seize the approaches to critical tunnels in the opening phase of the campaign, airlanded assault detachments deep in the enemy rear (at major Manchurian cities, on South Sakhalin Island and on the Kurile Islands chain) to seize critical installations and force the surrender of enemy garrisons after the Japanese capitulation, and in between employed the Pacific Fleet's *osnaz* reconnaissance detachment to seize port facilities, conduct "reconnaissance by battle," and provide security for Soviet agent-handlers during clandestine meetings along the northeastern coast of Korea.

Immediately after World War II, the Soviets apparently disbanded their *spetsnaz* formations and gave the primary rear-area diversionary mission to their conventional airborne formations. Sometime in the mid- to late-1950s, however, the Soviets created separate, permanent structures for SOF and institutionalized a rough division of labor between the KGB and the GRU. The former focusses on strategic social, economic, and political targets and the latter conducts special reconnaissance for operational and tactical objectives.

There is little published about modern KGB *spetsnaz* other than that they comprise a small core cadre of professionals aided by up to several hundred support personnel, including clandestine agents.[22] Organized under Department Eight, hidden within Directorate S (Illegals), KGB special forces undertake relatively few, carefully selected operations under conditions of extreme security. Examples include strategic sabotage and *mokrie dela* ("wet affairs") such as the physical elimination of key enemy personnel, including national or regional political leaders (e.g., the murder of Afghanistan's President Amin).[23]

Spetsnaz and SO-capable formations are reported in virtually every armed forces echelon below the Main Military Council in peacetime and the Headquarters of the Supreme High Command (Stavka) in war time. GRU *spetsnaz* may have served as the vanguard of the 103rd Guards Airborne Division in the seizure of Prague Airport in 1968. One Western source claims special forces teams have deployed to South Vietnam to field test the SVD Dragunov sniper rifle.[24] In Afghanistan, GRU and KGB special forces played key roles in the assassination of President Hafizullah Amin of Afghanistan during the assault on the presidential residence[25] and seizure of the Kabul airport in December 1979. *Spetsnaz* have been used to "stiffen" the militia of the Republic of Afghanistan (RA) and have engaged in various unilateral direct action operations against the *mujahideen* resistance.[26] *Spetsnaz* have also allegedly been cadre for training foreign terrorists and ideological mercenaries for over two decades.

Soviet tactical and operational special reconnaissance operations described in open literature include: acquisition, capture, and/or neutralization of equipment, installations, personnel, and documents in accordance with preset target priorities; deception (*maskirovka*); area reconnaissance, including signals intelligence (SIGINT); point reconnaissance; pathfinder operations for the airborne insertion or airlanding of larger conventional formations; employment of terminal guidance devices in support of air and missile strikes; and special weapons delivery.[27]

Mythology

The Western press has also reported several submarine and swimmer incursions, and perhaps land penetrations, with possible SOF involvement into Scandinavian,[28] Japanese,[29] Filipino[30] and American territorial waters since 1980. However, most reports of land penetrations by *spetsnaz* must be viewed with considerable skepticism. This is especially so in the case of Alaska, where widely-held beliefs in Soviet special forces incursions have not held up under close examination.[31] Nonetheless, many of these stories are unquestioningly repeated, and often shamelessly embellished in the open media as factual, confirmed data.[32] The analogy with the unidentified flying object (UFO) mania that spread throughout the U.S. in the 1950s and 1960s is remarkable.

More insidious contamination of the open-source data base comes from specious stories and analyses with apparent credibility enhanced by the credentials of the "experts" who write them and the reputation of their publishers. When the media uses such sources to "frame" the *spetsnaz* story, otherwise sane persons can make strange and even preposterous statements. For example, Mr. Yossef Bodansky claimed in the 25 January 1986 edition of *Jane's Defence Weekly*, that:

> The Soviet Union has maintained a secret detachment of female Spetsnaz special forces in the area of Britain's Greenham Common Air Base since the deployment of U.S. Air Force land based Tomahawk cruise missiles there in December 1983. Soviet defectors have disclosed that three to six trained agents . . . infiltrated women's protest groups at Greenham Common and were "present at all times." . . . Defectors and informants have given details to *Jane's Defence Weekly*. They are not being identified because they fear their lives are at stake. . . . After extensive inquiries in Washington, London and Greenham Common, *JDW* can exclusively reveal that . . . there has been a regular rotation of agents to enable a large number to gain field experience. . . . The women agents are trained . . . to attack the missile sites under war or surprise conditions in a pre-emptive strike. They will act as 'beacons' for other Spetsnaz and airborne troops who would be used to attack the missiles in war.

Usually, such stories are accepted at face value and become ingrained in the folklore of *spetsnaz*. Bodansky's story, however, was investigated by James Adams of the *Sunday Times* (London), who wrote:[33]

> Exhaustive inquiries in Europe and the United States suggest that this report was wrong. Allied intelligence has no evidence to suggest that any Spetsnaz forces have been based at Greenham or at any other Cruise missile base.

Organization and Capabilities

Contemporary Western assessments of Soviet special forces organizations and capabilities vary widely,[34] with many estimates extrapolated from other estimates without revalidation of old sources. There *is* a lack of original open-source material on contemporary *spetsnaz* operations. There are no known public reports of bona fide Soviet special forces operators defecting to another country, or being captured in battle, and revealing their experiences firsthand. Afghan guerrillas who have attempted to capture *spetsnaz* have told the author stories of such soldiers committing individual and group suicide[35] to avoid being taken. There is, however, an abundance of open-source Soviet material covering *spetsnaz* operations from the civil war through the Great Patriotic War, but most Westerners who write about *spetsnaz* either do not know of this information or decline to use it.

Most *spetsnaz* are two-year conscripts, specially selected on induction for their political reliability, athletic ability, intelligence, motivation, and paramilitary skills acquired prior to call-up. The majority of *spetsnaz*, the conscripts, are reported to be similar in capabilities to U.S. Army Rangers. A minority of long-term professionals seem to make up the core of most *spetsnaz* units. These professional cadre are believed similar in many aspects to U.S. Army Special Forces or the British Special Air Service.

Soviet special forces have historically demonstrated flexible task organization into forces of less than a dozen up to several hundred personnel, often involving conventional infantry weapons systems not normally associated in the West with SO.[36] Afghan guerrillas have told the author over the past several years that *spetsnaz* encountered were seldom fewer than forty or fifty in number and usually twice that, and that they often employ BMD infantry fighting vehicles lifted into otherwise inaccessible ambush positions by Mi-8 HIP helicopters. These sources also say that their SOF adversaries are distinctive because they employ good individual camouflage, are in excellent physical condition, and often carry body armor and much unusual equipment. Special equipment carried includes silenced 7.62mm Kalashnikov AKM assault rifles (many with 100-round drum magazines and night vision or telescopic sights), silenced pistols, BG-15 grenade launchers, RPG-22 rocket-propelled grenade launchers, fighting knives, night vision goggles, burst-capable radios and small seismic and electromagnetic sensors to detect movement outside their positions and along ambush trails. Although doctrinally designed for small-unit SO in Europe, Soviet SOF have adapted to an environment lacking cover, concealment, indigenous support, or critical point targets capable of being destroyed in surgical operations (e.g., radars and command posts), and where the enemy knows the terrain, is elusive, and presents mostly area targets such as caravans and troop columns.

The Soviets strive to win their wars in the initial phase, placing great reliance on surprise at the tactical, operational, and strategic levels.[37]

They place great reliance on special forces to exploit operational and strategic surprise in the initial and subsequent phases of war. Thus, Soviet SO capabilities should be examined closely. Doctrinal strength, however, should not be confused with operational strength. It is unlikely that undermanned and underequipped Soviet formations in low-priority regions have full-up SOF. It is more likely that, consistent with the overall trend in the allocation of manpower and equipment to Soviet armed forces, those formations most likely to go to war have the most complete SO capabilities, while the remainder have only a residual capability.[38]

Although *spetsnaz* give the Soviets a powerful military capability, there are flaws in this capability. For example, a given society can by definition produce only a finite number of "elite" fighting personnel, at best a tiny minority even among those otherwise qualified for military service. There is also a limit to the capabilities that can be developed in a two-year draftee (three years in the case of the navy), even if the draftee is brighter than average and prior to induction underwent extensive paramilitary training (such as in marksmanship and free-fall parachuting) while in high school.

Introductory training in SO capabilities attributed to the Soviets would take many months, even under the most ambitious and efficient training regimen.[39] Rudimentary cross-training and language training further decreases potential time available to deploy such a soldier. Giving large numbers of SOF training in the advanced, often esoteric, skills associated with their missions would be daunting in terms of time, logistics, quality control, and operational security. Although the Soviets have always shown a willingness to devote tremendous resources to meet military requirements, they have also shown a tendency to stick to the basics in developing mission capabilities.

Soviet SOF are by definition products of their own societies, and can be expected to exhibit the basic strengths and weaknesses of the wider population from which they are drawn. Alcoholism, known to be rampant in the Soviet military, perhaps blunts to a degree the effectiveness and efficiency of *spetsnaz* and their associated support troops (although elite units may have less of a problem than regular units). Also at issue is the presence, or not, of non-Slavs in *spetsnaz*. One theory is that security and effectiveness within these formations is enhanced by the virtual absence of non-Slavs. A competing theory is that *spetsnaz* contain a variety of ethnic Germans, Japanese, Koreans, Iranians, Spaniards, Afghans, and other nationalities to aid operations in the rear areas of their enemies, according to the geographic orientation of the formation to which they are assigned. The truth is likely somewhere in the middle, with ethnic Slavs predominating and highly-motivated minority individuals, including displaced communist sympathizers from abroad and their progeny, making up a small portion of *spetsnaz*. This would reduce barriers of language, nationality, and culture that would otherwise lessen effectiveness, while facilitating selected covert operations.[40]

Assuming that most of their basic impediments could be overcome to some degree, there are serious questions about the ability of the Soviets to effectively employ all but a fraction of their SO capability within a given scenario. The essence of effective SO is surprise, the ability to catch the enemy unaware at a time and place most advantageous to the attacker. Soviet war-fighting stresses strategic surprise and rapid victory. The combat preparation for all but a small percentage of the alleged active service *spetsnaz*, including intensified training, logistical buildup, and associated communications activity, runs a substantial risk of compromise through detection by hostile intelligence services. If, indeed, sizeable portions of Soviet SO capability are among the reserves, risks of compromise and loss of the element of surprise are marginally compounded by the necessity of mobilization.

Beyond getting ready to fight, there are substantial problems associated with deployment into hostile enemy rear areas. Multiple legal entries individually under diplomatic cover weeks or months prior to hostilities, and in small groups disguised as tourists or businessmen via commercial transportation just before hostilities break out, can prove complicated and difficult to coordinate. The Soviets have nothing comparable, at this point, to the U.S. MC-130E/H Combat Talon penetrator aircraft[41] for long-range, high-speed covert infiltration of action elements or support agents. Their large long-range helicopter fleet is relatively unsophisticated in equipment and crew training. Alternate modes of infiltration open to *spetsnaz* are either slow, imprecise in getting the forces on target, extremely dangerous, easily overloaded, or a combination of these factors. It would be, for example, very risky for SOF to attempt massive, covert, pre-hostility infiltration and target acquisition into Western Europe by ship, rail, air, or on foot. Any combination of security force vigilance, individual Soviet error, or accident could cause such an operation to quickly unravel and compromise Soviet national intentions.

Large-scale infiltration *after* the outbreak of hostilities would face similar and perhaps more serious risks. A moderate level of infiltration in the narrow gap between surprise invasion by conventional forces and organized resistance to the invasion offers the greatest promise for success. An associated problem in the utilization of large numbers of *spetsnaz* over wide geographic areas is that of synchronization: It would be a herculean task to coordinate the simultaneous employment of more than a fraction of Soviet SOF with the actions of conventional forces, while still maintaining the element of surprise.

Once on the ground, it is debatable just how well Soviet SOF can operate in a fluid and very lethal environment. An important factor in successful SO is the ability to adjust rapidly to unforeseen circumstances and continue the mission. Soviet battlefield doctrine generally does not stress flexibility at the tactical level. Indeed, totalitarian societies such as the Soviet Union perhaps do not foster the kind of individualistic risk-taking that permits soldiers to seize the initiative even when at variance with prior commands from a higher authority that does not have as accurate a picture of the battlefield. Furthermore, the Soviets will likely face the same difficulties in radio communications as are often experienced by their Western counterparts, resulting in less-than-ideal command, control, and intelligence reporting on the battlefield.

Even supposing that a special forces element reaches its objective, its success is far from guaranteed. A lone guard who does what he is trained to do, or the "concerned citizen" who dutifully reports something out of the ordinary to an alert police force, can destroy what would otherwise be a decisive advantage on the side of the attacker.

Conclusion

Rather than accept the alarmists' perspective, military planners should exercise moderation. To panic and pull troops off the line during perceived *spetsnaz* emergencies will aid long-term Soviet goals more than enhance security. A streamlined and effective Indications and Warning (I & W) system, backing up a quick, flexible, integrated, and redundant command, control, communications, and intelligence (C3I) apparatus, and alert personnel trained in common tasks and practicing aggressive patrolling and other actions to minimize the element of surprise, are the most effective bulwark against SO, Soviet or otherwise.

The outcome of the rear battle will be ruled by the quality, as well as quantity, of Western response. Comprehensive pre-hostility intelligence preparation of the battlefield (IPB), integrating realistic threat appraisals, is a basic necessity. Relying on the IPB effort, an operational plan is required which advances the goals of observing and reporting all movement, and denying the threat a place to hide, set up a mission support site (MSS) or the like. Such a plan should employ professional rear-area security forces reinforced as needed by homeguards of the young, old, and frail. Massive popular participation in watching, reporting, guarding, and defending closely linked to light, rapidly-deployable mobile hunter forces will present an effective bulwark against the threat. It will be sufficient if the first waves of SOF are exhausted by this less than Olympian opposition, as neither the pool of qualified Soviet personnel nor training time will permit their replacement. Planners should, however, expect some losses to SO, including a few of spectacular proportions, in spite of defensive preparations.[42]

A clearing of the air as regards the Soviet special operations capabilities is in order. There needs to be a "defining of the level of ignorance" with regard to fact and source by sorting out the true facts from the pseudofacts which have gained acceptance by successive uncritical repetition. The Soviet special operations data base needs to be expanded through greater exploitation of open Soviet sources. The facts should then be matched against those essential questions about Soviet *spetsnaz* capabilities that must be accurately answered for effective countermeasures to be developed. The gap between what we do in fact know about *spetsnaz* and what we need to know should then frame subsequent research and debate. It is at that point that the myth of *spetsnaz* will be cut down to size.

Notes

1. *Razvedka* is an element of the wider Soviet concept of *activnyye meropriyatiya* (active measures), which embraces overt, covert, and clandestine political influence operations, propaganda, manipulation of foreign political parties and subnational groups, economic warfare, terrorism, and so in the Western sense. Soviet *razvedka* places more emphasis on direct human observation and less on technical intelligence collection means (radars and sensors) than Western military intelligence does. Col. William V. Kennedy, Dr. David Baker, Col. Richard S. Friedman, and Lt. Col. David Miller, *The Intelligence War* (London: Salamander Books, Ltd., 1983); Brig. Gen. Shelford Bidwell, et al., *Russian Military Power* (New York: St. Martin's Press, Inc., 1980).

2. "Units of Special Designation (1917–1925)," *Voenno istoricheskii zhurnal*, 4/1969, 106–112, trans. James F. Gebhardt.

3. For a discussion of the use of White and Red Russian cavalry during the revolution and civil war, see Pulk. Marjana Kukiela, *Studja Taktyczne: z historji wojen polskich 1918–1921* (Tactical Studies: The History of the Polish Army, 1918–1921) (Warsaw: Wojskowy Instytut Naukowo-Wydawniczy, 1923 and 1925): vol. 2, 104–105, vol. 5, 20, and vol. 9, 4 and 5, trans. Ronald D. Kolenda; John Ellis, *Cavalry: The History of Mounted Warfare* (New York: G. P. Putnam's Sons, 1978): 178–181; and Edgar O'Ballance, *The Red Army* (New York: Frederick A. Praeger, 1964): 67–68, 78–83.

4. All-Russia Extraordinary Commission for Fighting Counter-Revolution and Sabotage.

5. "Detachments of special assignment," *Chasti osobogo naznacheniya*. See, Oliver H. Radkey, *The Unknown Civil War In Soviet Russia* (Stanford CA: Hoover Institute Press, Stanford University, 1976); John J. Dziak, "The Soviet Approach to Special Operations," *Special Operations In U.S. Strategy* (Washington DC: U.S. Government Printing Office, 1984): 98; id., *Chekisty: A History of the KGB* (Lexington MA: Lexington Books, 1988): 35.

6. Raymond L. Garthoff, *Soviet Military Doctrine* (Glencoe IL: The Free Press, 1953): 351.

7. Chris Bellamy, "Red Star in the West: Marshal Tukhachevskiy and East-West Exchanges on the Art of War," *Royal United Services Journal*, December 1987, 63–73, citing V. F. Margelov, I. I. Lisov, Ya. P. Samoylenko, and V. I. Ivonin, *Sovetskiye vozdushno desantnye: voyenno-istoricheskiy ocherk* (Soviet Airborne Forces: A Military-Historical Outline) (Moscow: Voyenizdat, 1980).

8. A. N. Lapchinskiy, "Airborne Landings," *Voyna i Revolyutsiya* (War and Revolution) (1930), Book 6, as printed in A. B. Kadishev, ed., *Voprosy Taktiki v Sovetskikh Trudakh 1917–1940* (Questions of tactics in Soviet military works 1917–1940) (Moscow: Voyenizdat, 1970): 348–354, excerpts, in Harriet Fast Scott and William F. Scott, *The Soviet Art of War* (Boulder CO: Westview Press, 1982): 64.

9. Capt. Sergei N. Kournakoff, *Russia's Fighting Forces* (New York: International Publishers, 1942).

10. Bellamy, 66.

11. Lt. Col. David M. Glantz, *The Soviet Airborne Experience*, Combat Studies Institute Research Survey Number 4 (Fort Leavenworth KS: U.S. Army Command and General Staff College, November 1984); Marshall Lee Miller, "Airborne Warfare: A Concept the USSR Can Actually Claim It Invented First," *Armed Forces Journal International*, October 1986, 48–51.

12. Dziak, *Chekisty*, 39–50.

13. *Narodnyy Komissariat Vnutrennikh Del*, People's Commissariat of Internal Affairs.

14. Allen F. Chew, *The White Death* (East Lansing MI: Michigan State University Press): 13–14.

15. Dziak, *Chekisty*, 115.

16. S. Kh. Aganov, ed., *Inzhenernye voiska sovetskogo armii 1918–1945* (Moscow: Voyenizdat, 1985): 459–463, trans. James F. Gebhardt.

17. Department of the Army Pamphlet 20-240, *Rear Area Security in Russia: The Soviet Second Front Behind the German Lines* (Washington DC, 31 July 1951); Garthoff, 391–409; Edgar M. Howell, *The Soviet Partisan Movement, 1941–1944*, Department of the Army Pamphlet 20-244 (Washington DC: 30 August 1956); Dziak, *Chekisty*, 114–120.

18. F. L. Kurlat and L. A. Studnikov, "Brigada osobogo naznacheniia" (Special Purpose Brigade), *Voprosy istorii*, September 1982, 95–104; Lt. Col. (res.) D. Rostovtsev, "Athletes in War," *Soviet Military Review*, 4/1981.

19. Aganov.

20. See, M. A. Babikov, *Otriad osobogo naznacheniya* (Special Purpose Detachment) (Moscow: "Sovetskaia Rossiia," 1986); id., *Letom sorok pervogo* (The Summer of '41) (Moscow: "Sovetskaia Rossiia," 1980).

21. C. N. Donnelly, "Operations in the Enemy Rear: Soviet Doctrine and Tactics," *International Defense Review*, 1/1980, 35–41; Rostovtsev, 62–63.

22. John Barron, *KGB: The Secret Works of the Soviet Secret Agents* (New York: Bantam Books, 1974); id., "Double Agents in a Secret War," *Reader's Digest*, May 1985, 181–182, 184–186, 188, 190.

23. Dziak, *Chekisty*, 162–163.

24. F. C. Brown, "Soviet Cong: Ivan in Indochina," *Soldier of Fortune*, November 1985, 70–74. Note that this account is not supported by other sources.

25. A joint KGB-GRU operation in which an MVD major general and the colonel in charge of the KGB special operations school at Balishika were killed in action.

26. See, Yossef Bodansky, "Soviet net closes in on Afghan resistance," *Jane's Defence Weekly*, 2 August 1986, 173, 175–176; Edward Giradet, "Afghan Trek," *The Christian Science Monitor*, 5 December 1984, 30–31; id., "Afghanistan: Soviets get tougher," ibid., 27 December 1985, 1, 8; id., "Afghan guerrilla leader: Soviets have made significant changes in tactics," ibid., 31 December 1985, 7, 8; id., "Behind new Soviet tactics in Afghanistan," *U.S. News & World Report*, 20 January 1986, 30–31; David C. Isby, "Spetznatz [sic] Suppressor Captured in Afghanistan," *Soldier of Fortune Magazine*, August 1984, 70–71, 92, 94, 96; id., "Spetsnaz in Afghanistan: Soviet Special Operations Forces in Action," MS, March 1985; id., "Soviet Special Forces in Afghanistan, 1979–1985," MS, May 1985; id., "The Better Hammer: Soviet Special Operations Forces and Tactics in Afghanistan 1979–86," MS, c. August 1986; id., "Soviet Special Operations Forces And The War In Afghanistan: Organization and Capabilities For Combat," *Special Forces*, December 1987, 34–38.

27. C. J. Dick, "Catching NATO Unawares: Soviet Army surprise and deception techniques," *International Defense Review*, 1/1986, 21–26; Donnelly, "The Development of Soviet Military Doctrine," ibid., 12/1981, 1589–1596; id., "Operations in the Enemy Rear: Soviet Doctrine and Tactics," ibid., 1/1980, 35–41.

28. Carl Bildt, "Submarine Incursions: Sweden fights back," *Jane's Naval Review* (London: Jane's Publishing Company, Ltd., 1985): 135–141; Juris Kaza, "Sweden targets mystery frogmen off coast," *The Christian Science Monitor*, 1 February 1984, 1, 10; id., "Foreign sub still eludes Sweden's net," ibid., 7 March 1984, 7; id., "Sweden's hunt for underwater intruders begins to come under political attack," ibid., 13 March 1984, 16; id., "Can Swedes keep subs at bay?" ibid., 14 May 1984, 13; Erik Lettlander, "Sweden's report on submarine incursions names no names," ibid., 23 December 1983, 10; Tomas Ries, "Soviet Submarines in Sweden: Psychological Warfare in the Nordic Region?" *International Defense Review*, 6/1984, 695–696; Suvorov, "Soviet special forces at work in the Baltic?" *Jane's Naval Review* (London: Jane's Defence Publishers, Ltd., 1985): 142–149.

29. Stephen V. Cole, ed., *For Your Eyes Only*, 146, 1 September 1986.

30. "Soviet Break-Ins?" *Newsweek*, 9 November 1987, 6; "Magazine reports Soviet intruders at Navy base," *Anchorage Daily News*, 2 November 1987, A3.

31. See, David Hulen, "Some wonder if Soviet troops occasionally visit St. Lawrence," *Anchorage Daily News*, 23 December 1987, 1, A8; John Quinley, "Soviets sighted on St. Lawrence Island," *Anchorage Times*, 11 February 1988, B1, B3; and Kaza, "Swedish worry over Soviet submarines resurfaces,"

9; Bernard E. Trainor, "Eskimo Guards on Alert Off Siberia," *The New York Times*, 20 February 1988, P1.

32. For examples of the more preposterous Soviet special forces stories see, Bodansky, "Soviet Spetsnaz at Greenham," *Jane's Defence Weekly*, 25 January 1986, 83; Paul Bedard, "On Siberian Border, Eskimo Scouts Search For Clues Of Soviet Plans To Invade Alaska," *Defense Week*, 8 September 1987, 8–9; Neil C. Livingstone and M. K. Pilgrim, "Spetsnaz Invades America," *Soldier of Fortune*, January 1988, 56–61; Quinley, B1, B3; UPI, "Soviet soldiers detected on remote Alaskan island," *New Haven Register*, 11 February 1988, 24; R. Cort Kirkwood, "Soviet Sabotage and Assassination Teams Operate in America," *Conservative Digest*, April 1988, 71–80; "Increased Spetsnaz Incursions Into USA," *Special Forces*, August 1988, 4; Peter A. Iseman, "Lifting the Ice Curtain," *The New York Times Magazine*, 23 October 1988, 48–51, 59–62; Tom Bates, "Red Rumors Rising: SOF Staffer Teams With Eskimo Scouts to Track Soviet Spetsnaz in Alaska," *Soldier of Fortune*, January 1989, 50–59, 93–94, 96–101.

33. James Adams, "Special Forces In America: The Day Before," *Orbis*, Spring 1988, 199–215, at 201.

34. See, Stephen Seth Beitler, *Spetsnaz: The Soviet Union's Special Operations Forces* (Washington DC: Defense Intelligence College, June 1985) (Defense Technical Information Center #AD-A169 710); Robert S. Boyd, "SPETSNAZ: Soviet Innovation in Special Forces," *Air University Review*, November-December 1986, 63–69; Lt. Col. David A. Burtt, II, *Soviet Use of Spetznaz [sic] Forces* (Maxwell AFB AL: Air War College, Air University, March 1986) (DTIC #ADA177911); Angelo Codevilla, "The Challenge of Special Operations," *Journal of Defense & Diplomacy*, June 1985, 18–27; John M. Collins, *Green Berets, SEALs & Spetsnaz: U.S. & Soviet Special Military Operations* (Washington DC: Pergamon-Brassey's, 1987); Dziak, "The Soviet Approach to Special Operations," 95–120; James Hansen, "Soviet Vanguard Forces – Spetsnaz," *National Defense*, March 1986, 28–32, 36–37; Ross Kelly, "Spetsnaz: Special Operations Forces of the USSR," *Defense & Foreign Affairs*, December 1984, 28–29; id., "Soviet Low-Intensity Operations: Moving to Center Stage," ibid., January 1985, 28–29, 37; Lt. Cmdr. David R. Kohler, "Spetsnaz," *US Naval Institute Proceedings*, August 1987, 47–54; Walter N. Lang, Peter Eliot, and Keith Maguire, *The World's Elite Forces* (New York: Military Press, 1987); Livingstone and Pilgrim, 56–61; Drew Middleton, "Russia's 'Twilight' War Poses Greatest Threat," *The Salt Lake Tribune*, 29 March 1985, A15; Steven J. Zaloga and James Loop, *Soviet Bloc Elite Forces* (London: Osprey Publishing, Ltd., 1985).

35. A practice also shared by their North Korean counterparts when cornered by the South Koreans.

36. The "conventionalized" nature of the 22d Spetsnaz Battalion in Afghanistan is seen in John Barron, "Ambush at Silk Gorge," *Reader's Digest*, February 1988, 74–78.
37. P. H. Vigor, *Soviet Blitzkrieg Theory* (New York: St. Martin's Press, 1983): 1–9, 144–166.
38. U.S. Army Field Manual 100-2-2, *The Soviet Army: Specialized Warfare and Rear Area Support* (Washington DC: Headquarters, Department of the Army, 16 July 1984): chapters 2, 3, and 5; *Russian Military Power*; *The Soviet Battlefield Development Plan* 1, "Soviet General Doctrine For War" (U.S. Army Intelligence Agency Intelligence and Threat Analysis Center, Department of the Army, June 1987); Casper W. Weinberger, *Soviet Military Power 1986* (Washington DC: U.S. Government Printing Office, March 1986); id., *Soviet Military Power 1987* (Washington DC: U.S. Government Printing Office, March 1987).
39. "Greenham defences 'copied for Spetsnaz training,'" *Jane's Defence Weekly*, 25 January 1986, 84; Bodansky and Louis Rees, "Unraveling the Soviet Terrorist Web," reprinted in *Current News*, Special Edition No. 1472, Denise Brown, ed. (Washington DC: Department of Defense News Clipping and Analysis Service, August 5, 1986): 32–36.
40. Maj. J. Kazokins, RA, "Nationality in the Soviet Army," *Royal United Services Institute Journal*, December 1985, 27–34; Joseph C. Brandt, "Soviet Military Grapples With the Language of Command," *Armed Forces Journal International*, July 1988, 38, 41.
41. William B. Scott, "Combat Talon 2 Completes First Flight of Development Program," *Aviation Week & Space Technology*, 18 January 1988, 36–37.
42. See, U.S. Army Field Circular 100-20, *Low Intensity Conflict* (Fort Leavenworth KS: U.S. Army Command and General Staff College, 30 May 1986).

CHAPTER 2
Western Misperceptions

Robert D. Smith

A calculated appreciation of Soviet special operations forces (SOF, commonly referred to as *spetsnaz*) is nearly impossible in light of Soviet secrecy, deception and disinformation, and Western mythology, analytical mirror-imaging, media speculation and oversimplification. Nonetheless, this chapter describes some of the basic structural flaws in Western perceptions of Soviet SOF and proposes corrective action.

In the media and in private among some analysts of military affairs Soviet SOF have an almost mystical aura, though there is disagreement among the experts. Pundits of military affairs disagree on which Soviet organizations control SOF, different priorities are assigned to SOF missions, and there is considerable disagreement on what Soviet SOF actually are. Such forces and operations are rarely discussed within the context of the Soviet strategic operation or even within the context of *spetsnaz*'s own organizational capabilities or requirements. Although the U.S. intelligence community has a more realistic view of Soviet SOF capabilities, the open press with its misleading or misunderstood reporting and generally shallow analysis have provided the public with few facts, but much in the way of fiction, speculation, hyperbole, and oversimplification.

Examples of widely-held and oft-repeated misperceptions, myths and distortions about *spetsnaz* having no factual basis include:

—The Russian term *spetsnaz* is the linguistic equivalent of "special forces" in the sense of Western commando forces;

- Soviet SOF routinely conduct cross-border training and reconnaissance missions in Alaska;
- Female *spetsnaz* have been permanently stationed outside key NATO military installations;
- Up to twenty thousand *spetsnaz* soldiers disguised as truck drivers and seamen are roaming Europe collecting intelligence;
- *Spetsnaz* caches containing inflatable boats, chemical protective masks, food, and radios have been discovered in Alaska and Canada;
- An officer of the Alaska Army National Guard "Eskimo Scouts" was murdered by *spetsnaz* intruders;
- The body of a *spetsnaz* SCUBA diver once washed up on an Alaska beach; and
- *Spetsnaz* comprise a substantial portion of the Combined Olympics Team of the Soviet Union.

Outright refutation of these legends is impossible: there is just too little authoritative information available. Consequently, the issue devolves into reinterpretation of the "evidence." The nature of press coverage of Soviet SOF has compounded the challenge by regularly failing to disclose such basic details as names of sources (the ubiquitous "highly placed government official" is often the best the reader gets), dates or locations.[1] Prejudices among Western opinion leaders, policy-makers and pseudo-experts that favor worst-case Soviet threats also tend to foster perceptions of *spetsnaz* omnipotence.

Some in the West believe it analytically naive to downplay *spetsnaz* capabilities, and warn that the "prudent military planner" must be prepared to counter *any* potential Soviet SOF capability. The prudent military planner, one must assume, has the assets to counter all 211 Soviet divisions[2] and the full spectrum of *spetsnaz* capabilities. Such a planner does not exist in NATO or anywhere else threatened by the Soviets. To properly assess the threat, one must define what *spetsnaz* units are (and what they are not), examine their missions, and scrutinize Western reporting on these matters.

Identification

The term "SOF" provides an immediate basis for misunderstanding. In the West, SOF include a variety of antiterrorist units, special police or internal security forces, counterinsurgency units, and other units with unusual specialization. The Soviets, on the other hand, use the phrase "special designation" (*spetsialnogo naznacheniya*) to describe several types of formations, including special engineer formations, armored trains, special radio-technical units, as well as experimental formations.[3] Compounding Western confusion, the Soviets designate certain combat service support units as "special troops."

For the purposes of this chapter, *spetsnaz* are defined as military units with highly specialized training, e.g., in parachuting, SCUBA and other insertion skills, and in mission skills such as long-range communications, reconnaissance, survival and close-quarter combat. These units are intended to conduct autonomous operations in the enemy's rear area against targets of strategic or operational (as in operational art) significance. Their missions can include reconnaissance, raiding, assassination, abduction, sabotage, and the formation and training of partisan or insurgent forces. Generally, *spetsnaz* operate covertly in units smaller than company size (less than one hundred soldiers), most often in platoon, squad, or team strength (as few as a half-dozen soldiers).

Four Soviet organizations have the capability and charter for conducting operational/strategic operations in the enemy's rear area. The Soviet armed forces have three of these organizations: "Troops of Special Purpose" (*Voiska spetsialnogo naznacheniya*, more commonly known by the Russian acronym *spetsnaz*), airborne divisions, and air assault troops. The Committee for State Security (KGB) controls a fourth organization, Directorate S, Department 8 of the First Chief Directorate.[4] Out of the three Soviet military organizations with SOF operations capabilities, only *spetsnaz* is dedicated to this mission. Airborne and air assault units are primarily intended for overt operations at battalion strength or greater once they are deployed into the enemy's rear area.

The KGB's Directorate S, Department 8 is responsible for covert operations from which the Soviets wish to hide their association. This directorate targets civilian populations and governments to create panic, disrupt government functions, and destroy key utilities and production facilities. Although these forces pose a wartime threat to NATO, the depth at which they operate make them more of a concern for counterintelligence personnel, police and internal security forces such as the West German *Bundesgrenzschutz*, than a concern of military forces.[5]

Due to size and specialization, *spetsnaz* stands at the pinnacle of Soviet SOF operations capability. It poses the largest, best trained, and most militarily significant threat to NATO rear areas and deserves the most scrutiny.

Some Soviet organizations have predecessors that performed SOF operations. During various wars and campaigns, the predecessors of the KGB and the Ministry of Internal Affairs (MVD) participated in partisan operations. This has caused some Western scholars to erroneously project a potential wartime SOF capability in non-*spetsnaz* organizations.[6] Presently, the KGB maintains a military border guard force that has been reported to be conducting "special operations" to protect Tadzhikistan from Afghan *mujahideen* raids.[7] Such operations, more accurately described as tactical raiding, are well within the border guards' organizational charter, but pose no threat to NATO or other Western nations. The MVD has a large paramilitary force to protect internal installations, perform convoy duties and, during war, provide rear area security, guard prisoners of war (POWs) and maintain order.[8] During the 1979 invasion of Afghanistan, the First Deputy Minister of Internal Affairs, Lt. Gen. Viktor S. Paputin[9] was killed. Although some insinuate from this episode that MVD troops could be part of the *spetsnaz* advance guard, this is unlikely. It is more likely that MVD troops, if any were in Kabul (there is no evidence of such a presence), were there to guard POWs and key installations. In an invasion of the Soviet Union, KGB and MVD forces could threaten enemy rear operations on Soviet soil, but projecting these forces into foreign countries as SOF is implausible. These troops do not have the mission, equipment, or training necessary to attack enemy rear areas other than those immediately adjacent to the Soviet Union.

Missions

Spetsnaz's mission is to conduct "special reconnaissance" (*spetsialnaya razvedka*), defined in the Soviet *Encyclopedic Military Dictionary* as:

> (Foreign Term) A type of reconnaissance conducted with the goal of undermining the political, economic, and military potential and morale of a probable or actual enemy. Principal tasks: to obtain information concerning economic and military installation; destruction or neutralization of these installations; the organization of sabotage and diversionary-terrorist acts; training of rebels and others. It is organized by military and civilian intelligence services and conducted by the forces of agent reconnaissance and troops of special purpose.[10]

Many *spetsnaz*-enamored Westerners accept this definition as dogma on Soviet SOF missions. They ignore the caveat "foreign term," which could make the definition apply to Western (and not necessarily Soviet) missions. Even when the definition does apply to the Soviets, too many Westerners erroneously translate a doctrinal desire into a confirmed capability. The Soviets are known for making doctrinal prescriptions in lieu of or in advance of practical application.

Despite superficial similarities between *spetsnaz* and some Western SOF units, *spetsnaz* are quite different and can only be properly understood within the context of their Soviet military environment and Soviet military thought. A *spetsnaz* unit is controlled by the intelligence staff of the Front, Fleet, or Army headquarters to which it is subordinate. A common misperception is that *spetsnaz* is under the direct control of the Main Intelligence Directorate (*Glavnoye Razvedyvatelnoye Upravleniye*, or GRU) of the Soviet General Staff. As with any other Soviet unit, the higher levels of command could task a Front or Army level *spetsnaz* unit to perform a particular mission. However, the majority of *spetsnaz* missions are in support of the field commander to which the *spetsnaz* unit is assigned.[11]

Many Westerners also fixate on the diversionary and sabotage portions of *spetsnaz*'s mission, overlooking the primary missions of target acquisition and information collection. Many authors, particularly "Viktor Suvorov," muddle the distinctions between these missions.

Sources

Open media discussion of *spetsnaz* capabilities varies from excellent to absurd. In government, academic, and media circles, the trend is toward complacency and reinforcement of error and away from critical analysis and correction. *Spetsnaz* are routinely described in pejorative terms as "cutthroats" who "murder" their victims and so on. The "experts" on Soviet SOF tend to be generalists who cannot comprehend the nuances of Soviet special operations and make objective evaluations, and few resources are devoted to following the relatively complex and minuscule story of *spetsnaz* than to the larger and simpler stories relating to nuclear arms and conventional general purpose forces. Overall, the treatment of *spetsnaz* is shallow.

A wide variety of journalists, military officers, civil servants, government contractors, academics, and Soviet defectors contribute articles on *spetsnaz*. Each writes with his own latent agenda and assumptions and exhibits common logical fallacies or assumptions. For example, alleged sightings by local natives of unidentified divers, swimmers, boats, ships, airplanes, and so on are often reported along the northwest coast of Alaska. Ignoring less glamorous but more plausible explanations for such sightings (e.g., activities of poachers,[12] bootleggers, drug runners, fishermen on unauthorized shore leave, and so on), and in the absence of objectively verifiable supporting evidence, members of the media have attributed such events to Soviet SOF[13] despite repeated official post-inquiry denials.

For example, Lt. Gen. Herbert R. Temple, Jr., Chief of the National Guard Bureau, visited Alaska in February 1988 and flatly denied there was any evidence of actual Soviet intrusions into Alaskan territory.[14] This denial is echoed by Maj. Gen. John W. Schaeffer, Adjutant General of the Alaska National Guard. Major General Schaeffer has also stated that, to his knowledge, his Eskimo Scouts "have never found [Soviet] caches of any kind. Period." He also flatly denies that any Scout has been killed by intruding *spetsnaz*, and states that M. K. Pilgrim and Neil C. Livingstone, in an article alleging such a murder and other *spetsnaz* activities in Alaska,[15] "took some liberties to come to some conclusions, that we do not have the information to back up."[16] Nonetheless, uncritical reporting has turned local myths into accepted truths that contaminate Western data and skew perceptions of Soviet SOF.

Many writers have built "Soviet invasion" stories out of unusual but otherwise benign events. The *spetsnaz* invasion of remote northwest Alaska is currently in vogue.[17] The press highlights "discoveries" of an occasional raft, civilian decontamination kit, batteries and "transmitters" of Soviet origin among jetsam and flotsam on Alaska beaches as "evidence" of Soviet *spetsnaz* incursions. Such analyses are shallow and transparent. Given that a fundamental rule of covert operations is to leave no trace behind, the existence of this garbage suggests sources other than military reconnaissance. Yet, in favor of sensationalism (and sales) over accuracy, many reporters have skirted the obvious fact that local ocean currents regularly propel garbage from the Soviet Union (and many other nations) onto U.S. shores. Ominous interpretations are added to the garbage to make "news": Commercial sonobuoys become nefarious "Soviet transmitters." A distressed inflatable raft that washed up on the beach, buried in the sand during a storm, and subsequently uncovered by shifting sands becomes a "*spetsnaz* cache." A battery salvaged from a sonobuoy by a local citizen and subsequently discarded at the end of a dirt runway becomes evidence of a covert SOF airlanding.

In fact, journalists generally provide the most inaccurate reports on *spetsnaz* activities. Even the prestige press can blunder. The *Wall Street Journal*[18] reported that between eight thousand and twenty thousand *spetsnaz* soldiers are roaming throughout Western Europe collecting intelligence while posing as truck drivers and seamen, and that 10 percent of this force is composed of East Germans. These figures are a preposterous 53 to 133 percent of total estimated *spetsnaz* strength, including forces in Afghanistan.[19] Furthermore, the overwhelming majority of *spetsnaz* soldiers are drafted Soviet nationals. The Russians do not induct East Germans into the Soviet Army.

The media have been lazy and gullible in their treatment of the *spetsnaz* story. One of the best illustrations of press failings in this regard is their overreliance on a GRU defector who, under the pseudonym "Viktor Suvorov," has written a series of controversial "insider" books and articles on Soviet conventional forces,[20] military intelligence,[21] and *spetsnaz*.[22] The problem with Suvorov is that while his personal remembrances are somewhat accurate (although Dimitri Simes[23] has called one of his books "the functional equivalent of consumer fraud"), he lacks general credibility because of a tendency to make all events fit into his rather sinister view of Soviet aims. He is the only author writing on *spetsnaz* who claims firsthand knowledge of their operations from a Soviet perspective, who received *spetsnaz* training and evaluated a *spetsnaz* unit, but was never actually a *spetsnaz* officer. His "authoritative" books are largely anecdotes, philosophical monologues, and diatribes that do not attribute facts appearing in open-source Soviet publications. As Lawrence Goodrich of *The Christian Science Monitor* puts it, "there is no need for the paranoia that a literal acceptance of Suvorov's anecdotally supported analysis would engender."[24] If those who liberally quote his thoughts would stop and think, they would readily see the inadequacies of his writings.

The confluence of speculation, misinterpretation, threat-hyping, and uncritical acceptance of *spetsnaz* myths occasionally yields threat scenarios of intense emotional impact that depict a naive Western alliance at the mercy of a handful of *spetsnaz* supermen.[25] These scenarios usually speculate that the irrepressibly evil Soviets are plotting to conduct blitzkrieg against NATO. According to the Soviet plan, large numbers of *spetsnaz* surreptitiously enter western Europe prior to hostilities, assassinate European leaders, interfere with European mobilization and destroy NATO's ability to launch a nuclear strike or conduct a credible defense.

These scenarios juxtapose monolithic Soviet aggressiveness and *spetsnaz* omnipotence with NATO incompetence in an emotional appeal to the reader's personal fear of inadequate peacetime security practices. They generally overlook:

1. The size of the target set that the *spetsnaz* force must attack (e.g., to "destroy" NATO command and control) is massive.
2. *Spetsnaz* formations have very large numbers of eighteen- to twenty-year-old two-year draftees who generally lack credible foreign language skills or high levels of technical proficiency and who would be conspicuous in prewar Western nations.
3. In times of severe East-West tension, customs police and border guards would increase vigilance.
4. So many of these teams would be killed, captured, or forced to evade prior to their targeting windows that it is quite possible the Soviets would be unable to inflict significant damage with their SOF.
5. The early capture of these *spetsnaz* soldiers could key their intended Western victims to when, where, and how the Soviets would attack, and would galvanize Western defenses with a clear and present danger.
6. Soviet political leaders trying to avoid war will likely not permit premature border crossings by *spetsnaz*, and will withhold such authority until the last minute.

Prescription for the Future

The problem with the way the "experts" have treated the issue of Soviet SOF comes down to intellectual inadequacy. With scant exception, reasonable standards of scientific, intellectual, or intelligence analysis have not been applied. Insufficient attention is paid to bona fide historical data and too much weight has been given to the wrong kind of evidence. Rumor has been rationalized into fact and given enhanced credibility through uncritical repetition. Pundits who prefer to play it safe and authors searching for sensation have chosen to err on the side of expanding the threat and scaring the public.

Overestimation of *spetsnaz* capabilities can divert public attention and funds away from larger and more significant defense issues. There is also the long-term risk that cynicism will set in and cause one to ignore or disbelieve when real evidence of *spetsnaz* activities presents itself. *Spetsnaz* reconnaissance and special operations *are* a real danger to the West and should not be ignored, but Western reaction must be tempered.

The problem will probably never go away. Nonetheless, it can be minimized by heightened consciousness among the public, the media, and the self-professed experts. The public must demand solid, objective analysis from the experts and accurate and verifiable media reporting on this issue. It is reasonable, after all, to seek corroborating evidence before retelling a story that is ludicrous, or at least suspect, on its face. All who write on the subject must be aware of the independent variables that will affect their treatment of the subject, and be cautious not to echo rumors and unfounded opinions in order to have enough spectacular news to warrant publication. Authors who wildly speculate and hype the threat should be challenged at every opportunity to either prove their assertions or publicly retract them. Those who deliberately pander falsehood should have their intellectual dishonesty publicly exposed and be driven from the public forum. The alternative is continued unpreparedness to meet the challenges of Soviet SOF.

Notes

1. See, for example, Neil C. Livingstone, and M. K. Pilgrim, "Spetsnaz Invades America," *Soldier of Fortune*, January 1988, 56–61, and Paul Bedard, "On Siberian Border, Eskimo Scouts Search for Clues of Soviet Plans to Invade Alaska," *Defense Week*, 8 September 1987, 8–9.
2. *Soviet Military Power: An Assessment of the Threat, 1988* (Washington DC: U.S. Government Printing Office, 1988).
3. Maj. James Holcomb, Jr., *Soviet Special Operations: The Legacy of the Great Patriotic War* (Fort Leavenworth KS: Soviet Army Studies Office, April 1987): 3.
4. John J. Dziak, *Chekisty: A History of the KGB* (Lexington MA: Lexington Books, 1988): 162–163.
5. Ibid., 71.
6. See, John M. Collins, *Green Berets, SEALs & Spetsnaz: U.S. & Soviet Special Military Operations* (Washington DC: Pergamon-Brassey's, 1987).
7. "Foreign Report," *The Economist*, 21 December 1982, 1–2.
8. Harriet Fast Scott and William F. Scott, *The Armed Forces of the Soviet Union* (Boulder CO: Westview Press, 1984): 238–239.
9. David Binder, "U.S. Links Afghan Events and Soviet General's Death," *The New York Times*, 3 February 1980.
10. Marshal of the Soviet Union Sergei F. Akhromeyev, *Sovetskaia voennaia entsiklopedicheskii slovar'* (Soviet Military Encyclopedic Dictionary) (Moscow: Voyenizdat, 1986): 698.
11. Robert S. Boyd, "SPETSNAZ: Soviet Innovation in Special Forces," *Air University Review*, November-December 1986, 64.
12. Organized poaching is a major problem in Alaska, and accounts for a number of mysterious aircraft and watercraft sightings all across the state. See Craig Medred, "Investigation Draws Bead on Alaska Guide," *Anchorage Daily News*, 27 February 1988, B1, B3.
13. See, for example, Bedard, op. cit.; Livingstone and Pilgrim, op. cit.; (UPI) "Soviet Soldiers Detected on Remote Alaskan Island," *New Haven Register*, 11 February 1988, 24; R. Cort Kirkwood, "Soviet Sabotage and Assassination Teams Operate In America," *Conservative Digest*, April 1988, 71–80; "Increased Spetznaz [sic] Incursions Into USA," *Special Forces*, August 1988, 4; Peter A. Iseman, "Lifting the Ice Curtain," *The New York Times Magazine*, 23 October 1988, 48–51, 59–62; Tom Bates, "Red Rumors Rising: SOF Staffer Teams With Eskimo Scouts to Track Soviet Spetsnaz In Alaska," *Soldier of Fortune*, January 1988, 50–59, 93–94, 96–101. An example of critical assessment of the SOF story in the media is David Hulen, "Some Wonder if Soviet Troops Occasionally Visit St. Lawrence," *Anchorage Daily News*, 23 December 1987, 1, A8, which explores a number of alternative theories

to explain reports of mysterious intruders on St. Lawrence Island in the Bering Sea between Alaska and Siberia.

14. Lt. Gen. Herbert R. Temple, Jr., interview, "Newsmakers," WTUU, Channel 2, Anchorage, 15 February 1988.
15. Livingstone and Pilgrim, op. cit.
16. "Pride of the Guard," *Soldier of Fortune*, January 1989, 54–55.
17. Livingstone and Pilgrim, op. cit.; Bedard, op. cit.; and Kirkwood, op. cit. See also, James Adams, "Special Forces in America: The Day Before," *ORBIS*, Spring 1988, 199–215.
18. Victoria Pope with a contribution by Marcus W. Brauchli, "Soviet-Bloc Troops Prowl in West Europe: Spetsnaz Commandos Are Said to Spy by the Thousands," *The Wall Street Journal*, 7 March 1988, 14.
19. Boyd, 64.
20. See, Viktor Suvorov, *The Liberators: My Life In The Soviet Army* (New York: W. W. Norton & Company, 1981); and id., *Inside the Soviet Army* (New York: Macmillan Publishing Co., Inc., 1982).
21. See, Viktor Suvorov, *Inside Soviet Military Intelligence* (New York: Macmillan Publishing Co., Inc., 1984); and id., *Inside the Aquarium: The Making of a Top Soviet Spy* (New York: Macmillan Publishing Co., Inc., 1986).
22. See, Viktor Suvorov, "Spetsnaz: The Soviet Union's Special Forces," *International Defence Review*, 9/1983, 1209–1216; id., "Soviet Special Forces At Work in the Baltic?" *Jane's Naval Review* (London: Jane's Defence Publishers, Ltd., 1985): 142–149; and id., *SPETSNAZ: The Story of the Soviet SAS* (London: Hamish Hamilton, 1987).
23. Dimitri Simes, review of *Inside the Aquarium*, by Viktor Suvorov, *The Washington Post*, 11 May 1986. *Aquarium* and Suvorov's recent *SPETSNAZ: The Inside Story of the Soviet Special Forces* (New York: W. W. Norton & Company, 1988) are especially unreliable, and more akin to a Le Carré novel than a historical record.
24. Lawrence Goodrich, review of *Spetsnaz: The Inside Story of the Soviet Special Forces*, by Viktor Suvorov, *The Christian Science Monitor*, 19 December 1988, 18.
25. Capt. Erin E. Campbell, "The Soviet SPETSNAZ Threat to NATO," *Airpower Journal*, Summer 1988, 61; Livingstone and Pilgrim, op. cit.

CHAPTER 3
Historical Precedents

Dr. John J. Dziak

Specialized military/security units have been a common feature of the Soviet system from its inception. Beginning with the Latvian riflemen, followed shortly by VChKa combat detachments, the Communist Party has always seen fit to maintain discrete units of politically reliable troops to carry out sensitive assignments that, for a variety of reasons, it chose not to entrust to regular military formations. To this day, special troop units associated with the intelligence and security services of the USSR occupy a unique position relative to the Party. Such an association is a constant of Soviet history.

On 20 December 1917 (NS), within weeks of its seizure of power, the Council of People's Commissars (Sovnarkom) issued the protocol creating the All-Russian Extraordinary Commission to Combat Counterrevolution and Sabotage,[1] a secret police that has since become an export commodity for repressive revolutionary regimes throughout the world. It quickly became known by its acronym, VChKa or Cheka. Among the initial tasks set out for the Cheka was:

> Organization to comprise an information department; an organizational department to organize the struggle with counterrevolution throughout Russia; *and a fighting department to conduct operational action* [emphasis added].[2]

29

In June 1918, Feliks Edmundovich Dzerzhinskiy gave an interview to the Moscow correspondent of Maxim Gorky's newpaper, *Novava zhizn'* (New Life), in which the head of the Cheka stated:

> We represent in ourselves organized terror—this must be said very clearly— such terror is now very necessary in the conditions we are living through in a time of revolution.
>
> Our task is the struggle with the enemies of Soviet power. We are ter- rorizing the enemies of Soviet power in order to strangle crimes in their germ.[3]

This last item espoused "preemptive counterintelligence." Later refined by Stalin, it gave state security the precedent for targeting those who had the *potential* for opposition and set the tone for future operations undertaken by the special designation forces of state security and select elements of the military.

Thus, the birth of the idea and need for specialized, elite Soviet units coincided with the creation of an extra-legal security service designed to protect and promote the monopoly position of the Communist Party and its claims to exclusive power. From the start, then, Soviet special opera- tions units bore a character unlike the later special forces of Western parliamentary democracies. Soviet special forces missions, offshoots of the broader purpose of state security, would result in organizational con- figurations and operational experiences alien to Western practice. If we were to look for analogues to this Soviet tradition, the SS of Nazi Ger- many, with its sundry special units fulfilling Party missions, would be more appropriate both politically and operationally. The rest of this chap- ter chronicles these unique roots and precedents of today's KGB and GRU special purpose forces.

Chekist Special Operations

At first, the paramount mission of Soviet special operations units was the preservation of the minority Bolshevik faction's monopoly of political power. Though the major fronts of the Civil War were secured by the Red Army by fall 1920, the requirement for Cheka "extraordinary measures" did not abate, despite internal Party pressures from some quarters to limit the scope of the Cheka's authority. There also were persistent rebellious movements among the peasantry and various national minorities, which picked up strength in the winter of 1920–21. These were abetted by the demobilization of the Red Army, itself a peasant conscript force, which pumped large numbers of men back into the restive countryside. The Party had little choice in this decision in view of the raging famine and a thoroughly wrecked economy; in some respects internal ferment in 1921 was far more threatening to the survival of Bolshevism than the Whites, Poles, and foreign armies had been collectively.

The tendency to form elite units from broader categories of existing specialized forces was evident as early as mid-1919, when a separate structure of Party troops called "Detachments of Special Purposes" (*Chasti Osobogo Naznacheniya* or ChON) were created following a Central Committee resolution.[4] Various categories of elite Cheka troops had been created even earlier in the Civil War. With their comrades in ChON detachments they were engaged in doing what they were created for—fighting insurrections from whatever quarter these emerged. By 1921 there were approximately 137,000 Cheka troops along with 94,000 Frontier troops under Cheka control.[5] Such special Cheka and ChON troops played a prominent role in crushing the Kronstadt uprising in March 1921, when the rebels were subdued as viciously as any losing White Army in the Civil War. Selected Party cadres, Red Army units, and special Cheka forces, with blocking units of Cheka machine gunners at their backs to discourage retreat or desertion, made several unsuccessful assaults across the ice before the rebels were smashed. Survivors were either shot outright or perished later in northern camps. Several thousand escaped to Finland. Many of these, in response to a Bolshevik offer of amnesty, returned to Russia only to be shipped off to Cheka camps and death.[6]

Special units formed by the Cheka during the Civil War were later institutionalized as standing units subordinate to state security under its various titles (Cheka, GPU, OGPU, GUGB, NKVD, etc.). Thus, by the time the Party embarked on its "second revolution" in the late 1920s–early 1930s with collectivization and industrialization, there were several categories of specialized troops subordinate to state security, comprising Frontier Troops, Internal Troops, and specialized state security formations such as the OGPU's Dzerzhinskiy Division.

With the passing of the more serious internal threats to Party rule following the Bolshevik victory in the Civil War, the Party's use of these forces took a different direction. During collectivization, the expropriation of the *kulaks* (landed peasantry) was beyond the ability of party activists. Similarly, an operation of such high political sensitivity could not be exclusively entrusted to the Red Army, whose conscript base was drawn from the peasantry. The campaign against the *kulaks* was thus augmented and in many cases conducted by special units such as the Dzerzhinskiy Division, which served as the Party's cutting edge for the imposition of its radical programs.[7] Even Soviet sympathizers relayed accounts of OGPU troops surrounding villages and firing indiscriminately into crowds of peasants.[8]

In another kind of special operation, the OGPU prosecuted counter-guerrilla operations against Moslem "Basmachi" insurgents in Soviet Central Asia, who had been resisting Soviet rule since 1918, through the 1920s and into the early 1930s.[9] A special force, the Khorezm Group, had to be created in the Central Asian Military District as late as August 1931, when "the situation became complicated"[10] (meaning the insurgents were defeating Soviet forces!). In addition to regular military and aviation units, the Khorezm Group comprised special OGPU cavalry and artillery units plus mechanized detachments of the Dzerzhinskiy Division. A Western account claims that the 63d OGPU Division was involved in the recapture of Krasnovodsk in June 1931, which had been taken by the rebels in the previous month.[11] In effect, the operation was a precursor to World War II and contemporary combined-arms operations in which elite *spetsnaz*[12] detachments conducted specialized actions not entrusted to the regular military. An operational style was forged which gave such special troops a certain primacy of mission over the Red Army, particularly when Party control in a given region was in jeopardy.

The Cheka and its early successors also engaged in extensive penetration, provocation, deception, and other related operational counterintelligence initiatives. What are now known variously as "active measures" (*aktivnyye meropriyatiya*), disinformation, and *maskirovka* (roughly speaking, military deception in its totality) appeared in a stylized Russian and Soviet operational vocabulary used in the integration of varied state security operational initiatives. In the first several decades of state security history active measures included "wet affairs." "Wet affairs" were part of the operational argot for assassinations, kidnappings, sabotage, and the like, especially after the creation in 1936 of NKVD chief Nikolay I. Yezhov's Administration for Special Tasks, which set mobile killer teams loose against White officers, defectors, the exiled Leon Trotsky and his followers, and other "enemies" outside of the USSR.

Organization for Direct Action (Wet Affairs) in Soviet State Security[13]	
Pre-1936	Foreign Department (INO), with tasking and oversight from Stalin and/or his personal secretariat
1936–1941	Administration for Special Tasks, NKVD
1941–1946	Fourth Directorate (Partisans), NKVD
1946–1953	Spets Byuro No. 1, NKGB-MGB
1953–1954	Ninth Section, First Chief Directorate, MVD
1954–late 1960s	Department 13, First Chief Directorate, KGB
Late 1960s–early 1970s	Department V, First Chief Directorate, KGB
Early 1970s–Present	Department 8, Directorate S (Illegals), First Chief Directorate, KGB

Indeed, the hallmark of state security special operations outside the USSR during this time and into World War II and the postwar years was precisely such activity. Yezhov's killer teams in the late 1930s seemed to roam at will in the U.S., Western Europe, and especially Spain. Such actions carried over into the postwar years with an apparent increase in tempo and even outlasted the death of Stalin when some of the more notorious assassinations and kidnappings generated headlines throughout the West. The institutional focal point for these acts, beginning with Yezhov's Administration for Special Tasks, consistently remained with state security although numerous name changes of the overseeing unit tended to mask organizational responsibility and, at times, culpability. The line remains unbroken into the late 1980s. "Wet affairs" apparently no longer is the operative term: "Direct action" is.

Regular Army Special Operations

As for special purpose forces in the regular Soviet military between the Revolution and the outbreak of World War II, the record is not quite as clear. In the heyday of the Comintern and especially after the Sixth Comintern Congress in 1928, Moscow assumed that until the USSR was strong enough to help propel the world revolutionary process, it would be endangered by a capitalist encirclement determined to crush Soviet communism in its formative stages. It was against such a political background that Soviet military theorists conceived ways of linking Soviet military operations with insurrections by workers in capitalist countries. Such linkages with the enemies' rear areas were not really unique, since they fed on the earlier experiences of the Russian Civil War. Flushed with victory over a variety of internal foes and so-called "interventionalists," Civil War heroes such as the future Marshal Mikhail Tukhachevskiy saw the Red Army as an exporter of revolution, capable of aiding and abetting insurrections in the capitalist countries as well as their restive colonies. Indeed, following the failure of revolutions in the industrial West, Moscow placed great emphasis on the colonies as the new and vulnerable rear of capitalism.

A principal beneficiary of Stalin's frenetic industrialization program was the Soviet military, which, in addition to its concentration on traditional combat arms, conducted ambitious experiments with new military concepts and structures, such as the world's first airborne forces. The first parachute detachments appeared in 1929[14] and by the early 1930s were taking part in field exercises. While such forces were primarily intended to destroy the enemy in his entire depth in conjunction with long-range armor units, other purposes of a more clearly political nature were envisioned by such leaders as Tukhachevskiy. Part of Tukhachevskiy's concept of the "nonstop" offensive involved the advancing Red Army linking up with a rebellious proletariat during the process of liberation.[15] The main body of airborne forces, operating in advance of the Red Army, would employ Special Purpose battalions trained to conduct special operations in foreign environments. Their missions, in addition to linkage with insurgent workers, apparently included direct action against enemy leadership and facilities. By 1938 the Red Army had five airborne corps, four in the western USSR and one in the Far East. Each corps had three airborne brigades and one or two Special Purpose battalions.

How these unique forces might have been used in the kinds of operations conceived by Tukhachevskiy cannot be determined. Tukhachevskiy and many of those responsible for the new concepts and organizational developments in the Red Army in the late 1920s and 1930s were eliminated during the purges of 1937–38. Imagination and initiative were not qualities to be touted by the survivors. In the early stages of the German invasion in 1941, the bulk of the airborne elements were destroyed fighting as infantry, along with most of the special purpose battalions. While an unbroken link between these battalions and some of the contemporary *spetsnaz* forces of the USSR cannot be established, the former may at least be viewed as a conceptual forerunner.

Spain and Finland

The experiences in Spain* and Finland immediately before World War II strongly influenced Soviet partisan actions against the Germans. During the Spanish Civil War of 1936–39 concurrent NKVD and Military Intelligence (after 1943 known as the GRU) terrorist and guerrilla activities were carried out on Stalin's orders behind Nationalist *and* Republican lines. Aleksander Orlov, who became NKVD rezident, or chief, in Spain, tells us that the Politburo selected him for that post on the basis of his having fought in the Russian Revolution and having knowledge of guerrilla warfare.[16] Actual NKVD sabotage and guerrilla operations behind Nationalist lines were controlled by Leonid Eitingon (alias General Kotov), who was Orlov's assistant in Spain.[17] Eitingon then applied that experience in running partisan operations in the USSR during the war under Gen. Pavel Sudoplatov. They were both imprisoned in the purge of Beria's lieutenants after Stalin's death.

To head the Soviet military aid effort in support of the Republicans Stalin dispatched Yan Berzin, the recent Chief of Military Intelligence. Berzin was given the following tasks by Stalin: to help in the defense of Madrid with Soviet advisors, armor, and aircraft; and to advise the Republican General Staff on operational planning. In addition, Berzin also provided leaders/advisors to Spanish commando and guerrilla groups operating behind Nationalist lines. One such officer was Khadzhi-Umar Mamsurov (discussed, infra) who, in addition to helping prepare Madrid for the Nationalist siege, was to form a stay-behind guerrilla operation in the event of a Nationalist seizure of the city.[18] Another officer under Berzin and, hence, GRU subordination, was one Artur Sprogis whom Berzin had known earlier in the USSR. Sprogis was attached as advisor to a Republican guerrilla group in southern Spain, experience he put to good use in World War II in the partisan movement in Byelorussia and Latvia.[19] Numerous other military officers who served in Spain were not

---

*See chapter 4, "The Spanish Civil War."

so fortunate; they either fell at the hands of the NKVD there or, like Berzin, were recalled to Moscow and disappeared in the purges.

Orlov, who until his defection in 1938 headed the NKVD presence in Spain, has stressed how critical direct action commando/guerrilla operations were to regular military operations in Spain.[20] He characterizes sabotage and guerrilla warfare as the "eighth line of activity of KGB intelligence."[21]

Berzin necessarily had to work closely with Orlov's and Eitingon's large NKVD contingent, which in turn conducted special operations that included, among other things, spiriting Spain's gold reserves to Russia and liquidating Trotskyites, anarchists, and other "enemies." The NKVD also maintained its own network of informants among Berzin's entourage, a practice maintained to this day by the KGB in its penetration of the GRU and the Soviet military in general. Berzin was recalled to Moscow in June 1937, and disappeared soon thereafter, a victim of the Great Terror. His NKVD counterpart, Orlov, defected to the West in 1938 when he received a summons to "confer" with a Party official on a Soviet ship in Belgium. He knew it was time to disappear.

The Soviet experience in the Spanish Civil War is worth studying because it highlights the main Soviet principles in planning and executing special operations. Above all, these principles included secrecy and compartmentalization of small elite groups for conducting delicate political-military operations such as the transport of the Spanish gold. Spain also provides early evidence of the role of military intelligence (GRU) in planning and commanding special operations, the access of the GRU to regular military personnel in carrying out its mission, and GRU involvement in military assistance groups. Spain also illustrates the working relationships between military intelligence and state security (NKVD), with their separate yet parallel and sometimes redundant operations. It demonstrates the clearly superior position of state security in terms of access to the political leadership. And it points up the strong rivalry and hostility between the two, a situation especially owing to the penetration of military intelligence by state security. Though nearly five decades have passed, some of these same principles, attitudes, and practices characterize contemporary Soviet approaches to special operations.

Another intelligence officer from the GRU who developed guerrilla experience in Spain was Maj. (later General) Khadzhi-Umar Mamsurov.[22] He and other GRU officers led special units fighting with the Republican XIV Special Corps, carrying out attacks on the transportation and communications networks in the Nationalist rear areas. Mamsurov later surfaced in Finland during the Winter War of 1939–1940. He brought a special designation unit (*spetsnaz*) of about fifty men to the front in an effort to capture Finnish soldiers for intelligence purposes and thus gain a certain psychological redress for the severe defeats inflicted on the Soviet giant by the tiny Finnish army. As with overall Soviet military performance in this war, Mamsurov's operation was a failure. What is significant about this particular experience is that it was the first prewar instance other than in Spain of an identified Soviet military entity with responsibility for diversionary (that is, special operations) activity. Mamsurov's unit was subordinated to the Fifth Department (*Otdel*) of the GRU and was openly referred to as the *Otdel Diversii* (Diversionary Department).[23] Penkovskiy in the early 1960s revealed that the Fifth Department had been elevated to the Fifth Directorate (diversion and sabotage) and that General Mamsurov had risen to become one of two deputies to GRU chief Ivan Serov.[24] More recent defector information shows that the Fifth Directorate of the GRU still has line responsibility, through a dedicated *spetsnaz* department, for controlling standing GRU *spetsnaz* brigades posted in the USSR, Eastern Europe, and Afghanistan.[25]

World War II

As noted earlier, Tukhachevskiy's Special Purpose battalions and regular airborne forces were expended in infantry operations during the early days of the German invasion in 1941. Attempts to reestablish regular airborne forces for special operations with GRU participation were abandoned because of the logistical problems in maintaining such units behind German lines.

However, specialized state security forces (NKVD, NKGB, and "SMERSH," the Armed Forces Counterintelligence Directorate) were expanded into the hundreds of thousands to ensure the loyalty of the military, to prevent "unauthorized" retreats, and to serve as special shock units (and even armies). As the war progressed in Moscow's favor, they were also intended to serve as the Party's "action arm" for reimposing Party control in the reconquered territories and for imposing communism in newly annexed territories and in Eastern Europe.[26]

On the special operations front, the Central Committee of the Communist Party of the Soviet Union (CPSU) authorized a "Central Staff of the Partisan Movement" for conducting guerrilla, espionage, sabotage, and assassination operations behind German lines. Forces involved were drawn from the NKVD, the GRU, and GUKR-NKO, or SMERSH, the latter headed by NKGB General Viktor Abakumov, who reported directly to Stalin. Central political control was, therefore, an operational reality.

Moreover, the thorough permeation of partisan detachments by NKVD and SMERSH personnel ensured that state security retained critical operational leverage, despite the military focus required by coordination between Red Army operations and partisan activities.[27] At any rate, day-to-day partisan operations were in the hands of state security Gen. Maj. Pavel Sudoplatov, known as the "master of special detachments" in the German rear areas. His deputy was Leonid Eitingon, the NKVD guerrilla warfare overseer in Spain and the mastermind behind Trotsky's murder.

Soviet partisan operations served as the major formative laboratory for subsequent Soviet state security and military structures for running or supporting postwar diversionary (including terrorist) and guerrilla movements. Although the Central Staff of the Partisan Movement under the Supreme High Command (Stavka) had been organized under General P. K. Ponomarenko, Party and state security cadres were the actual controlling elements. The announced purpose of the partisan movement was the harassment of the German rear areas, but the real objective was to reintroduce Party control in occupied territories. Many of these actions involved deceptions and provocations to surface and eliminate real and potential opponents to the reimposition of Soviet rule. They also involved the neutralization and compromise of non-Soviet resistance and partisan groups. A major means for accomplishing all this was the provocation of terror and German counterterror with the ultimate objective of both intimidating and infuriating the local population.[28]

Organizationally, partisan operations were structured as follows:[29]

Central Staff of the Partisan Movement under the Supreme High Command (also known as the Partisan Directorate). Technically, all partisan units not directly under the control of the NKVD-NKGB or the GRU — essentially "civilian" partisan units — were controlled and coordinated by the Partisan Directorate, itself subordinate to the Party. It was, however, heavily staffed by the NKVD-NKGB. From 1942 to 1944 it was directed by General P. K. Ponomarenko.

NKVD-NKGB. The following types of units have been identified as being subordinated first to the NKVD (until 1943), and then to the NKVD and NKGB (after 1943). After 1943 it is difficult to sort out the exact operational subordination.

Partisan Units. These were specially organized units operating independently or in coordination with other partisan units; they also organized and trained additional partisan units. As the war progressed, these units operated in Eastern and Central Europe in advance of the Red Army. Men from these units operated with communist partisan detachments in German-occupied countries of northern and western Europe as well.

Spetsnaz Units. The term *spetsnaz* (*chasti spetsial'nogo naznacheniya*) is occasionally used to designate particular NKVD-NKGB units operating in the German rear. They appear to have been employed mainly for independent operations although on occasion they did work with other partisan units. They were used to eliminate collaborators, propagandize the local population, conduct intelligence gathering and counterintelligence operations, and generally serve as enforcers of Party control. They also conducted operations against the Germans.

Extermination Battalions. These units were formed in the initial days of the war, and operated in both the German and Soviet rear areas. Operations included actions against German agents and German special units, Soviet deserters, dissidents, nationalists, and other persons or groups deemed as "anti-Soviet" or not behind the war effort. They may have come from the NKVD *Osnaz*[30] divisions, but this is unclear.

Special Detachments. These units spanned a wide range of size and composition, and included such entities as radio intercept units, agent communications units, radio disinformation teams, parachutist "reception committees," "hit" teams, and positive intelligence collection teams.

Hunter Units. These were designated to mop up nationalist and other anti-Soviet activities, as well as Nazi stragglers in recently occupied territory. These units may have been successor units to the early extermination battalions.

Special Assault Divisions. Such units were of very large, division-plus, size and were formed toward the end of the war to combat Ukrainian nationalists and Polish, Lithuanian, Estonian, and Latvian guerrillas. One of these was identified under General Kobulov's command (Kobulov was one of Beria's lieutenants). Such divisions may have been formed from the large pool of state security *Osnaz* and Border Troops divisions.

Singleton Operations. Individual special detachment members — Party and Komsomol personnel, and politically reliable local inhabitants — were used to carry out clandestine activities such as agent servicing, intelligence collection, and courier service. Additionally, hundreds of state security officer personnel were sent into the German rear to take over command and commissar positions in partisan units comprising non-NKVD-NKGB personnel. This was a means of strengthening Party control over the partisan movement. Personnel from "uncontrolled" units frequently wound up in the Gulag when their regions were reoccupied by the Red Army. The system brooked no independence.

NKVD Internal Security (Osnaz Divisions). These divisions operated mostly in the Soviet rear, but they did conduct counterinsurgency and counterguerrilla operations against anti-Soviet elements. However, they contributed thousands of snipers to the regular military and to partisan detachments.

GRU. The following units operated under military intelligence control and drew their personnel from the ground, naval, and air forces of the regular Soviet armed forces.

Partisan Units. These consisted of specially organized teams inserted to operate as partisans in the same fashion as the NKVD-NKGB partisan detachments. General Mamsurov, of Spanish and Finnish reputation, evidently continued his diversionary activities in this category of operations.

Special Detachments. As with state security, a variety of apparently GRU-subordinated special units surface in the literature. These often appear to be specially configured teams for intelligence collection (including prisoner snatching) against specific targets or for surveillance of enemy activities in a narrowly defined geographic area. Such teams were landed from Soviet submarines in Norway and Poland to observe Nazi shipping in support of Soviet submarine operations from 1943 on. These were Soviet variants of "coastwatchers," so to speak.

Singleton Operations. GRU activities of this type tended to mirror those of state security; but they were more focussed on military targets.

Coordination, command, and control over these diffuse entities were not easily accomplished. The confused Soviet response to German invasion was reflected in the partisan movement. Units were slapped together and thrown in with little regard for standardization, efficacy of mission, redundancy, or human cost. The initial objective was to do something, anything, to stem the German advance and prevent the Soviet system from collapsing. Hence the need to foster the image of Party presence in occupied areas.

Nominally, the Party exercised control over all partisan operations. In practice, it was state security that provided the abiding presence. Feuds between the military and state security were not uncommon and it was to resolve these that the Central Staff of the Partisan Movement was created. This was a move not unlike the creation of SMERSH, that is, the joining of several organizations in a supra-institutional body (in this case the Stavka) to rise above the fray in pursuit of broader national objectives. But as with SMERSH, state security still played the prominent role. Throughout the war state security maintained tight control over its many partisan or related activities, even running them directly from Moscow Center, without coordinating with its own district or regional echelons. For instance there were cases of radio disinformation operations, based on turned German agents, run from Moscow Center. Their broadcasts were picked up by local NKVD radio intercept units that could not break the ciphers, unaware that the radio traffic came from Moscow in the first place.

As the tide of war on the Eastern front turned and the German retreat speeded up, Moscow increased the insertion of special units in the enemy rear. For instance, NKVD partisan units went into Czechoslovakia ahead of the Red Army, and played a major role in precipitating the Slovak uprising. When the uprising was smashed by the Germans, the Soviets had fewer potential opponents to worry them when they foisted a communist government on that country. Soviet-trained teams of Bulgarians and Rumanians were inserted by submarine in both nations prior to the arrival of the Red Army and helped to coordinate the imposition of communist rule there. In Norway, special reconnaissance units involved in military operations there during the war were also laying the groundwork for subversive actions after the war, conducting recruitment for espionage and covert action agents.[31]

At the end of the war, Moscow was busy with securing its newly seized territories and reestablishing Soviet rule in areas occupied by Germany.

Violent nationalist guerrilla movements had risen throughout the Baltic republics, the western Ukraine, and in Poland and Slovakia. Moscow made extensive use of NKVD-NKGB hunter/extermination units and the special counterguerrilla division of NKVD created and commanded by Beria's associate, General Kobulov. A former KGB officer and member of this unit states that this division went directly from Yalta (where its members provided security for the Yalta Conference) to western Ukraine and western Byelorussia. Fighting continued for this division until 1947, when the division was disbanded. However, operations against Ukrainian guerrillas continued into the early 1950s.[32]

Prominent among state security officals involved in all aspects of the partisan-counterinsurgency experience during and immediately after the war were Merkulov (NKGB), Kobulov (NKVD), and Serov, who served under Kobulov. Sudoplatov worked for both Merkulov and Kobulov. Serving under him was the organizer of Trotsky's murder, Leonid Eitingon, alias General Kotov. Sudoplatov and Eitingon had the task, under the newly minted MGB after the war, of setting up a covert state security diversionary infrastructure for operations against the new NATO alliance. All of these men were arrested following the downfall of Beria, Sudoplatov and Eitingon being fortunate enough to receive only prison terms. Their colleagues were executed. Despite their unceremonious exits, they were the men who built the organizational and operational framework for contemporary KGB and GRU direct-action, special operations activities. In a certain sense, the road to Afghanistan in the 1980s led from the partisan experience during World War II, the Spanish Civil War, and ultimately the anti-Basmachi campaigns of the 1920s–1930s.

Conclusions

The Soviets view their partisan experiences in Spain and World War II as highly effective unconventional adjuncts to the regular military campaigns of these conflicts.[33] The partisan experience also had a profound impact on subsequent Soviet planning and organization for special operations against the United States following Germany's defeat. The Ministry of State Security (MGB) carefully drew upon the talents of officers who served in Sudoplatov's and Eitingon's "special detachments" to help build an in-place underground infrastructure "to establish combat operations for weakening the network of military bases of the American command in

Europe."[34] However, the bulk of this activity was probably vested in the "executive action," or "wet affairs," element of the MGB's First Chief Directorate (Foreign Operations). That was in keeping with the powerful personalities involved, especially Eitingon who, by all accounts, was a Stalin favorite because of the Trotsky operation.

Little information is available relating to militarily-connected *spetsnaz* elements in the immediate postwar years. While it is true that the airborne forces were reconstituted in the Moscow area, it is not known if the new divisions included "special designation" units under GRU or airborne subordination. Most "direct action" operations in the postwar era seemed to focus on KGB kidnappings and assassinations directed against defectors, emigres, and anti-Soviet opponents throughout Europe. Until the late Khrushchev and early Brezhnev period, little open evidence surfaced indicating an increased GRU/military role in the field of special operations. But once the Soviet military began to manifest a newfound ability to project beyond the Soviet heartland, GRU *spetsnaz* forces began surfacing. And in Afghanistan, they came into their own.

Notes

1. For the actual protocol, see G. A. Belov, et al., eds., *Iz istorii vserossiyskoy chrezvychaynoy komissii 1917-1921gg. Sbornik dokumentov* (Moscow: Gospolitizdat, 1958): 78; Mervyn Matthews, ed., *Soviet Government: A Selection of Official Documents on Internal Policies* (New York: Taplinger Publishing Co., 1974): 237-238.

2. S. K. Tsvigun et al., *V. I. Lenin i VChK: Sbornik dokumentov (1919-1922 gg.)* (Moscow: Politizdat, 1975): 36-37.

3. From the Bertram Wolfe Collection, Hoover Archives, Box 110, file 110-2, p. 4 of *Novaya zhizn'.*

4. P. G. Sofinov, *Ocherki istorii Vserossiyskoy chrezvychaynoy komissiy (1917-1922gg.)* (Moscow: Gospolitizdat, 1960): 152; See also I. G. Bewlikov, et al., *Imeni Dzerzhinskogo* (Moscow: Voyenizdat, 1976): 5-36.

5. MID Report from Riga, Latvia, No. 02021, 23 September 1921 (20037-10084/5), National Archives, RG165.

6. George Leggett, *The Cheka: Lenin's Political Police* (Oxford: Oxford University Press, 1981): 328.

7. Belikov, 46-50.

8. Isaac Deutscher, *Stalin: A Political Biography* (New York: Vintage Books, 1962): 325.

9. "Basmachi," or bandits, was a Soviet term of opprobrium. The insurgents labeled themselves "Beklar Hareketi," or Freeman's Movement.

10. Belikov, 58-61.

11. Martha B. Olcott, "The Basmachi or Freeman's Revolt in Turkestan 1918-1924," *Soviet Studies*, July 1981, 362.

12. Short for *spets*ialnogo *naz*nacheniya, or "special designation."

13. From John J. Dziak, *Chekisty: A History of the KGB* (Lexington MA: Lexington Books, 1988): 177.

14. John Erickson, *The Soviet High Command* (London: St. Martin's Press, 1962): 327.

15. Erickson, 351.

16. FBI Memorandum, June 6, 1954, SAC New York to Director, FBI, Ref. Aleksandr Orlov's evaluation of Walter Krivitsky's *In Stalin's Secret Service.*

17. Senate Committee on the Judiciary, *The Legacy of Alexander Orlov*, 93rd Cong., 1st sess. (Washington DC: U.S. Government Printing Office, 1973): 25, 70, 75.

18. Polina Mamsurov, "Boyevoye zadaniye," in S. M. Aleksandrovsky, et al., *My — Internatsionalisty* (Moscow: Politizdat, 1975): 54-55.

19. *Voyennyy Entsiklopedicheskiy Slovar'* (Moscow: Voyenizdat, 1983): 700.

20. Aleksandr Orlov, *Handbook of Intelligence and Guerrilla Warfare* (Ann Arbor: University of Michigan Press, 1963): 164-183.

21. Orlov, 38.
22. Mamsurov, 46–58.
23. Interview with Ismail Akhmedov, former GRU officer, June 1985.
24. Oleg Penkovskiy, *The Penkovskiy Papers*, trans. Peter Deriabin (Garden City, NY: Doubleday & Company, Inc., 1965): 69–70.
25. Viktor Suvorov, *Inside Soviet Military Intelligence* (New York: Macmillan Publishing Co., Inc., 1984): 136–140.
26. The bulk of the material on World War II is drawn from John J. Dziak, *Chekisty*, chapter 6.
27. Kurt DeWitt, "The Role of Partisans in Soviet Intelligence," *War Documentation Project*, Research Study No. 6, Vol. 1 (Maxwell AFB AL: Air Research and Development Command, 1954): passim.
28. An excellent analysis of these aspects of partisan war is found in Walter Goerlitz, *Der zweite Weltkrieg, 1939–1945* (Stuttgart: Steingrubon-Verlag, 1952): 57–71.
29. This section is drawn from the following works: P. A. Aleksandrov, et al., eds., *Partiya voglave narodnoy bor'by v tylu vraga, 1941–1944* (Moscow: Izdatel'stvo "Mysl'," 1976); I. G. Belikov, et al., *Imeni Dzerzhinskogo* (Moscow: Voyenizdat, 1976); A. Emelyanov, *Sovietskiye podvodnye lodki v Velikoi otechestvennoi Voine* (Moscow: Voyenizdat, 1981); V. Endzheyak and A. Kuznetsov, *Osobaya partizansko-diversionnaya* (Kiev: Politizdat Ukrainiy, 1977); A. L. Manayenkov, et al., eds., *Partizanskie formirovaniya Belorussii v gody Velikoy Otechestvonnoy, 1941–1944* (Minsk: Izdatel'stvo "Belarus," 1983); A. Fyodorov, *The Underground R. C. Carries On.* 2 vols. (Moscow: Foreign Language Publishing House, 1949–1950); Abwehr (Ostfront), *Organisation und Aufgaben des sowjetischen Geheimdienstes im Operationsgebiet der Ostfront, 1944* (Abwehr manual from German archives, declassified 15 August 1946); DeWitt, *The Role of Partisans*; N. F. Yudin, *Pervaya partizanskaya* (Moscow: Izdatel'stvo "Moskoviskiy Rabochiy," 1983); Raymond L. Garthoff, *Soviet Military Doctrine* (Glencoe IL: The Free Press, 1953): 391–409.
30. Short for *oso*bogo *naz*nacheniya, or "special designation."
31. See, Robert C. Suggs, "Soviet Subs in Scandinavia: 1930 to 1945," *Proceedings of the United States Naval Institute*, March 1986, 100–106.
32. Discussion with Ilya Dzirkvelov, June 1986.
33. Pospelov, et al., *The Great Patriotic War of the Soviet Union, 1941–45* (Moscow: Progress Publishers, 1974): 459.
34. Nikolai Khokhlov, *In the Name of Conscience* (New York: McKay, 1959): 127. Khokhlov served under Sudoplatov in World War II and subsequently moved into MGB "wet affairs" activities in Western Europe.

CHAPTER 4
The Spanish Civil War

Owen A. Lock

In the summer of 1936 a great civil war engulfed Spain, pitting Generalis-simo Francisco Franco and his Falange Nationalist rebels against the dem-ocratic left-wing Republican government. Foreign intervention immedi-ately cast an international complexion on the war, which ultimately served as a precursor to World War II. Mussolini's Italian infantry and Hitler's German airmen and tankers aided the Nationalists. Stalin's Soviet officers and technicians, reinforced and aided by the Communist movement's "international brigades," took up the Loyalist Republican cause.

A brutal fratricide, the war was punctuated by gross atrocities such as the 1937 destruction by aerial bombardment from German and Italian air-craft of the Basque town of Guernica. The war also introduced the world to the German concept of *blitzkrieg* (lightning war), the use of massed armor as the spearpoint in combined arms offensives. Less well known, but of immense relevance to the course of the war and to later conflicts, is the manner in which the conflict served as a laboratory in the develop-ment and validation of Soviet state security and military special operations concepts and *spetsnaz* (commando forces) to conduct such operations. While to some it may seem anachronistic to apply the term *spetsnaz* to Republican units in the Spanish Civil War, that is the Soviet usage.[1]

The Soviet special operations effort in Spain was an advanced program of covert and clandestine direct action sabotage, partisan (guerrilla) war-fare, and *razvedka* (intelligence operations) that foreshadowed subse-

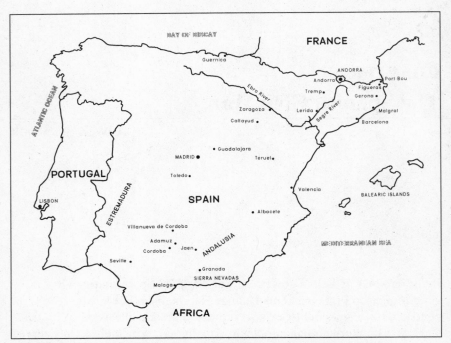

Figure 1. Spain, including principal localities of *spetsnaz* activities.

quent Soviet special operations during World War II, the Czechoslovakia and Afghanistan interventions, and other conflicts. The Soviets dispatched many of their most experienced special operations personnel to Spain to make the program work. Moreover, key Soviet *spetsnaz* in Spain who also survived Stalin's purges went on to play crucial roles in the ongoing evolution of Soviet special operations capabilities. Several amassed more than thirty years' service in special operations, an impressive indicator of Soviet special operations institutional memory and experience.

As events unfolded in the summer of 1936, the Soviets accurately predicted that special operations and other forms of unconventional warfare would play an important role in the fight for Spain. As early as 20 July 1936, the Soviet Politburo decided that experience in guerrilla warfare would be a prerequisite for the position of senior state security (KGB) advisor to the embattled Republican government.[2] The Politburo's early emphasis on the importance of guerrilla warfare in Spain apparently was

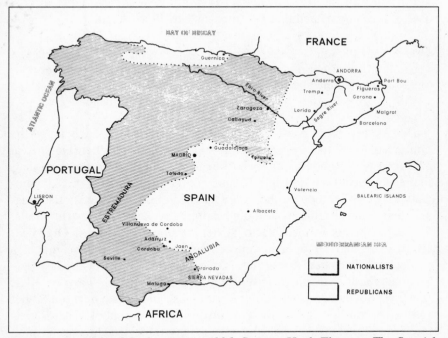

Figure 2. Division of Spain, August 1936. Source: Hugh Thomas, *The Spanish Civil War* (New York: Harper & Row, 1977): 402.

not, however, merely to aid the Spanish Republic to prosecute the war. According to KGB Gen. Alexander Orlov, one of his assignments as KGB chief (*rezident*) in Spain was to provide for a revolt by the workers, "should that tactic seem necessary,"[3] i.e., to prepare for the possibility of seizing control of the Republic, presumably with the intent of creating a Soviet-model client state. By October 1936, just weeks after the KGB chief's arrival in Spain, Soviet advisors began urging the Republicans to form *spetsnaz* units to support friendly guerrilla bands with weapons and training.

At first the Republicans were reluctant to parcel out slim resources to what they viewed as small and unimportant units. Eventually, probably by late November 1936, the Republicans gave in to Soviet pressure and provided some assets, though the Soviets may not have waited for formal permission to begin setting up such units. As Anna Kornilovna Starinov, the translator of the first *otriad spetsialnogo naznacheniya* (special purpose or *spetsnaz* detachment) formed in late 1936 stated:

> There weren't even quarters; the staffs of the Republican Army didn't believe in the effectiveness of partisan warfare. We had to waste a lot of effort before getting and preparing cadres for these new and little known affairs. [4]

Despite the initial resistance, the Soviets successfully encouraged the Republican Army to form *spetsnaz* groups and conduct offensive special operations within months after the war broke out. Within the first year, separate multinational *spetsnaz* detachments comprising hundreds of commandos were operating in the Valencia-Catalonia, Andalusia, Estremadura, and Madrid regions. Although nominally Republican Army units, these detachments were de facto Soviet *spetsnaz* formations. Organization, training, and deployment followed the Soviet model and the guidance or direction of resident Soviet advisors. Moreover, most of the key personnel in these detachments were active-duty Soviet military or KGB personnel, Soviet citizens or emigres, the offspring of one or more Soviet parents, or non-Soviet Communists of the Moscow school. The Soviets exercised indirect operational control of at least three detachments through their advisors and agents, while the fourth was directly controlled by the KGB and had a Soviet commander. By the fall of 1937, these detachments had been expanded and consolidated under a new headquarters, the "14th Special Corps."

Command and Control

Existing information implies very confused Soviet lines of communication between KGB headquarters, the staff of the 14th (after it was formed), and the individual *spetsnaz* detachments. Personnel turbulence in the Soviet military attache's office and in the independent military mission, and in the KGB mission, competition between the KGB and military intelligence (GRU), and the backdrop of Stalin's purges, created a near-constant state of uncertainty.

From about October 1936 through late 1937, the Soviet military attache to the Republican government was Vladimir Yefimovich Gorev. [5] As a military attache and part of the Soviet diplomatic mission to the

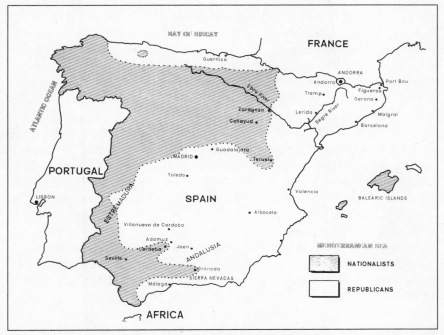

Figure 3. Division of Spain, March 1937. Source: Hugh Thomas, op. cit., 605.

Republic of Spain, although nominally subordinate to the Soviet ambassador, Gorev would normally have received his instructions from GRU headquarters in Moscow. Gorev was an experienced military advisor (he spent several years in China) and agent handler (he was Whittaker Chambers' first control). After the Republican government abandoned besieged Madrid for Valencia on 6 November 1936, most of the Soviet advisors also relocated to Valencia. However, by 15 November, Gorev had returned to Madrid to direct its defense and orchestrate much of the military activity of the Republican forces.[6]

From March 1924 until April 1935, the GRU was headed by an experienced underground worker and former high-ranking KGB military counterintelligence officer named Peter Kyuzis, who is best known as "Yan Karlovich Berzin." In April 1935 Berzin was reassigned to a staff position (probably chief of staff) under the commander of the Soviet Red Banner Far Eastern Army (OKDVA). After the Spanish Civil War began in July

1936, Berzin was given the cover name "General Grishin" and appointed head of the Soviet military mission to Spain. He first took up residence in Madrid, then (in early November) followed the Republican government's stampede to Valencia. Berzin had at least one *spetsnaz* unit under his personal control, advised by Artur Karlovich Sprogis, an experienced operations officer who had commanded a Soviet border guard detachment.[7] In addition, he may have controlled the detachment led by Mamsurov, discussed infra.

After Berzin's recall to the Soviet Union in late May or early June 1937, Gen. Grigoriy Mikhailovich Shtern (Stern) became chief of the military mission. Early in 1938, Shtern was replaced by his deputy, Gen. Kuzma Maksimovich Kachanov.[8] On or about 6 February 1939, Kachanov crossed into France with the bulk of the Soviet advisors, as the Republican effort finally collapsed.[9]

In addition to his personal staff and the "legal" military-intelligence organization in Spain (Gorev's staff), Berzin also enjoyed the assistance of a powerful KGB presence from the very beginning. Its chief, Alexander Orlov, arrived in September 1936 to advise the Republican government on matters of intelligence, counterintelligence and guerrilla warfare,[10] while at the same time seeing to the disposition of arms shipments from the Soviet Union and ensuring that Soviet advisors neither annoyed the Spanish nor strayed.[11] The chief of *spetsnaz* forces in Spain, however, was Leonid Andreyevich Eitingon, a senior KGB officer who had other duties as well (chiefly espionage). Eitingon operated in Spain under the cover name "General Kotov" (and possibly "General Ivon") and reported to Orlov.[12]

The Formation of Spetsnaz

Orlov's first deputy (executive officer), Eitingon, was charged with immediate supervision of commando operations during the war.[13] As Orlov put it:

> The experience gained by the Soviet guerrilla troops in the [1920] Russo-Polish War became the cornerstone of Soviet guerrilla science of the future. Sixteen years later, in 1936, during the Spanish Civil War, the former commander of the Soviet guerrilla troops in the Russo-Polish War was sent by the Russian Politburo to Spain, where he organized and directed for the

Republican government of Spain guerrilla detachments which operated in the rear of Franco's forces. [14]

Orlov's Senate testimony makes clearer that he was "the former commander of the Soviet guerrilla troops in the Russo-Polish war," sent to Spain. Eitingon also brought experience in espionage accumulated in Manchuria, Turkey and Greece, [15] which he broadened during the Spanish Civil War by running agents in and out of France. [16] Somewhere between Eitingon and the individual *spetsnaz* detachments falling under his sway were Lev Ozolin (cover named "Kraft") in Barcelona, [17] and Grigoriy Sergeyevich Syroezhkin, a highly-decorated long-time KGB officer who specialized in paramilitary counterintelligence operations.

Eitingon began by organizing two schools, one near Madrid and another in Benimamet, near Valencia. [18] According to Orlov, each of these "saboteur schools" trained about two hundred men. Later, four more schools were organized, one near Barcelona having as many as six hundred students. Those selected for commando duty were:

> Trained principally in various kinds of demolition work, high-grade marksmanship, elementary guerrilla tactics (raids and ambushes), map reading, living off the land, and long marches with loads up to 25 pounds.* On graduation, each trainee had to be able to plan and execute the demolition (on contact or by remote control) of various types of bridges, railway tracks, and power lines, and to mine roads. [19]

Given that Republican Spain was reeling, the program of instruction could have taken less than one week. After the formation of the Republic's 14th Special Corps the training period lasted six to eight weeks. By comparison, the World War II partisan curriculum established on the Western Front in July 1941 by a Soviet veteran *spetsnaz* advisor from Spain, Col. Ilya Grigorevich Starinov, just three weeks after the Germans invaded their Soviet allies, at first lasted three to five days. The course taught mining and demolition, topography, intelligence/scouting operations, partisan tactics, marksmanship and weapons maintenance, field sanitation, and other subjects. Subsequently the duration of the course was extended to as long as ten days. [20]

---

*Orlov may have meant kilograms: About fifty-five pounds would be a good load for such commandos.

Levant-Catalonia

Shortly after the Republican government moved to Valencia in early November 1936, I. G. Starinov was assigned as a trainer/advisor to the very first formal *spetsnaz* detachment of the Spanish Civil War.[21] Starinov was briefed by Berzin, who found much need for improvement in the organization of Republican forces: The Spanish Army had neither clear structure nor unity of command, and consisted of separate detachments that were subordinate to various parties and committees.[22] Among other failings, many of the line units did not conduct reconnaissance.[23]

Initially, Starinov was assigned to train five men who seemed dedicated to the Republic but unsuited to the physical demands of guerrilla warfare. The five selectees had thought they were to be used as agents behind the lines and were very upset at learning what was in store for them. After Starinov complained of the men's condition to his immediate Soviet superior,[24] a "General Ivon," and the matter was taken up with the general secretary of the Communist Party of Spain, twelve combat veterans headed by a thirty-eight-year-old cavalry officer, Capt. Domingo Ungria, were assigned to the unit. Subsequently, the detachment was provided with a truck, five automobiles, and a house at Benimamet in the suburbs of Valencia which, inter alia, was used as a sabotage school and center to develop tactics and techniques of partisan warfare.[25]

By December 1936 the detachment had eighteen effectives, and a test mission against Teruel (one hundred kilometers from Valencia) was run in the latter half of that month using twelve men, Starinov and his female interpreter, and six men held in reserve. As a reflection of the state of command in the Spanish Republic at the time, the local commander could offer neither guides nor intelligence on what enemy forces might be in the area.[26] As well, he thought the twelve *spetsnaz* could destroy *all* telephone and telegraph lines within an area fifteen to twenty kilometers north of Teruel, capture a "tongue," as well as interrupt road and railway transport between Teruel and Calatayud!

The detachment carried knives, pistols, and one light machine gun, and had their dynamite in rucksacks. The terrain was hilly and the men were not accustomed to moving at night. They reached the main highway at 0300 hours. The group was there divided in half, one team to mine telephone poles and a highway bridge and the other to mine nearby railroad tracks. The demolitions went off as planned, and the group returned to friendly lines by dawn.[27]

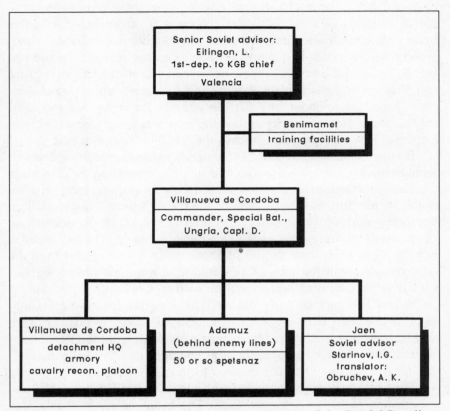

Figure 4. Hypothetical organization and subordination of the Special Battalion, March 1936.

Ungria's group conducted several more operations behind enemy lines along the Teruel front before being sent to Albacete, headquarters of the International Brigade, on the southern front in January 1937. There the detachment filled out to about one hundred personnel, picking up about twenty Interbrigadists, including Poles, Yugoslavs, Bulgarians, Czechs, Slovaks, Germans, Austrians, Italians, Finns, Frenchmen, and an American named "Aleks" (possibly Alex Kunslich or Cunslich, a major and one of the only three Americans in the 14th, who was subsequently captured by Franco's forces and shot).[28]

To minimize the risks of being fired on by friendly forces, as well as by enemy forces, when crossing the lines between the armies, by the middle of February 1937 Ungria's detachment was organizing clandestine bases behind Franco's lines. Supplies and munitions (primarily explosives) could be stored in quantity at these bases and personnel could rest between missions. The first of these bases was in an abandoned olive grove and olive oil processing plant about twelve kilometers northwest of Adamuz. From there, about fifty partisans conducted ambushes and raids behind enemy lines. Security around the base was closely observed, and a reserve base was prepared in case the first was compromised.[29]

Between January and April 1937, Ungria's *spetsnaz* groups were tasked with destroying railway and automobile tunnels, organizing the disruption of military formations, demolition of enemy road transport, incapacitation of enemy aircraft, and destruction of the enemy's means of production. Separate groups moved sympathizers prepared to aid in the destruction of important military objectives behind enemy lines.[30] On one night in late February 1937, three groups of about ten men each staged from the Adamuz base with the mission of derailing a train and destroying two small but high railroad bridges on the road to Cordoba.

In late February or early March 1937, Ungria's forces successfully ambushed a train carrying a large number of Italian troops. For that action, Ungria was called to report personally to Chief of the Republican General Staff Vicente Rojo, the unit was upgraded to a "special battalion," and Ungria became "Jefe del batalion especial."[31]

The new battalion was provided with a battalion staff, whose chief was a Yugoslav (Serb) major named Ilich. The battalion was probably also provided with a new senior advisor, Khadzhi-Umar Dzhiorovich Mamsurov. In late April 1937 the *spetsnaz* bases in Jaen, Villanueva de Cordoba, and the clandestine one in Adamuz[32] were visited by Gay Lazarevich Tumanyan and Mamsurov. Tumanyan departed for Moscow several weeks later, on 2 May 1937, but Mamsurov remained as senior advisor to the 14th until late summer 1937.[33]

According to Starinov, in the spring of 1937 the new special battalion had three bases on Republican soil: Jaen, Villanueva de Cordoba, and Valencia (Benimamet).* At this time, Benimamet housed the training facil-

---

*I. G. Starinov does not mention Vasilevskiy's detachment in Las Vegas, either because he did not know of it, because it was not considered part of the special battalion, or because of security considerations.

ities for all new *spetsnaz* as well as the main workshops for the assembly of mines, grenades, and other devices. Mines and grenades were also assembled, and new types developed, at the workshop in Jaen.[34] By April 1937 Ungria had also created a *spetsnaz* cavalry platoon at Villanueva de Cordoba.[35]

An interesting aside to the story of the Ungria detachment is the relationship between Mamsurov and writer Ernest Hemingway, then working in Spain. According to Mrs. Mamsurov, her husband met with Hemingway for three days in a row during 1937, from about 1800 hours until after midnight, describing diversionary groups in Estremadura and the people in them, without naming individuals. Soviet sources claim this to be the information Hemingway used as the basis for commando operations portrayed so well in *For Whom the Bell Tolls*. Although most Soviet Bloc commentators treat this as an attempt to use a sympathetic newsman to sway world opinion in favor of the Republican struggle, Lev Petrovich Vasilevskiy, former commander of the Madrid *spetsnaz* detachment, was critical:

> One of the comrades acting parallel to us but not subordinate to Grigoriy Syroezhkin, also led a group [on missions] in the rear of Franco's forces and said something of it to [Ernest] Hemingway, to whom he had been introduced by Mikhail Koltsov and Ilya Ehrenberg, who were then in Spain. Later, in his memoirs, Ehrenberg wrote that this Soviet comrade served as Hemingway's model for the main hero of his novel, *For Whom the Bell Tolls*. Grigoriy [Syroezhkin] not only did not approve of such conversations with journalists, he categorically forbade anything to be said about our marches in the enemy's rear.[36]

The Central Front

In February or March 1937, about the time Ungria's unit was being upgraded to a "special battalion," Vasilevskiy arrived in Spain and was recruited by Senior Advisor Syroezhkin to command a *spetsnaz* unit stationed in the Las Vegas area, near Madrid. Probably in early March 1937, Vasilevskiy was accompanied by Syroezhkin to the detachment's headquarters, two dilapidated houses. The unit then had about 150 men (growing to 160 by July), largely Andalusian farm laborers, three or more Soviet advisors, and a Soviet commander (Vasilevskiy). At some time it acquired a Spanish commissar named Galarsa Peregrin. Of the known *spetsnaz* units formed during the Spanish Civil War this detachment was unique for having a Soviet officer as its commander.

The remainder of the detachment's personnel was "Internationalist": Bulgarians, Germans, Frenchmen, Englishmen, Americans, Canadians, and three Latvians. "All were Communists who had left their homelands," Vasilevskiy says, "via the underground."[37] One advisor who had preceded Vasilevskiy to the unit was Aleksandr Rabtsevich, who was "already experienced in partisan and underground operations by the time of the Russo-Polish War of 1920." Other advisors who were associated with Vasilevskiy's unit were Kirill Orlovskiy,[38] Capt. Stepan Glushko,[39] and Pavel Boyarskiy.[40]

According to Vasilevskiy, in early 1937 the Republican command had already improved somewhat from the state described by Berzin in late 1936, but it still exercised no direct supervision of the Soviet *spetsnaz* advisors:

> At that time [February-March 1937], the situation in Spain on the Republican side was reminiscent of that [in the Soviet Union] at the beginning of 1918. A regular army had been formed. Instead of uncoordinated detachments and columns, brigades and divisions already existed, but their commanders were frequently not subordinated to the high command, and were still following the dictates of political leaders [rather than those of their higher headquarters]. Because of this circumstance, the influence of the anarchists was increased. Staffs composed by the regular army were undermanned and did not take full advantage of their rights. Thus our diversionary detachment in Madrid was only formally subordinate to General Miaja, the commander of the Central, or Madrid, Front: neither the general nor his staff gave us assignments, being satisfied with the data we obtained from the enemy [on our own initiative]. Consequently we had complete freedom of action in the choice of direction and time of dispatch of our groups to the enemy's rear. Thus, it fell to me to choose the direction of my first march [with my group].[41]

Andalusia

During the difficult days of November or December 1936, Artur Sprogis was assigned by Yan Berzin to accompany Mamsurov to Madrid to

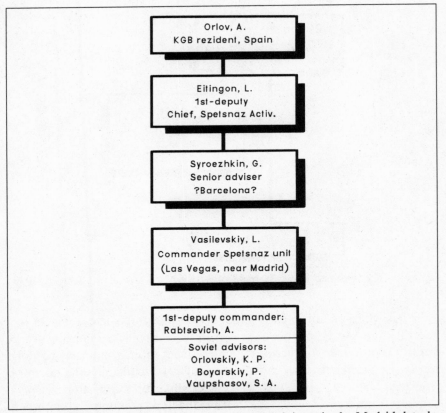

Figure 5. Chain of command for Soviet *spetsnaz* advisors in the Madrid detachment, March 1937.

strengthen the hard-pressed city's defenses. But before Sprogis and Mamsurov could depart, Sprogis was hastily reassigned to advise guerrillas defending Malaga, in the south of Spain. Berzin asked I. G. Starinov to explain to Sprogis how to improvise explosives and detonators from commonly available materials, which suggests that Sprogis may have been weak in this area. Sent with a radioman and a translator (probably Regina Tsitron),[42] Sprogis advised a guerrilla band under the command of Jose Munoz Gomez that mined roads and bridges along the approaches to Malaga from Granada, destroying five bridges from 25 January to 4 February 1937.[43]

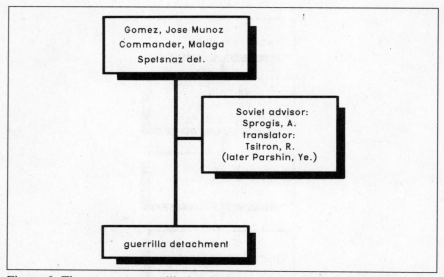

Figure 6. The *spetsnaz* guerrilla band of Jose Munoz Gomez in January 1937.

After Malaga's fall in early February 1937, Sprogis and a unit of the guerrillas he had helped to train served as a mobile commando group directly subordinate to Berzin, the chief Soviet military advisor, fighting across the Sierra Nevadas and the Andalusian Mountains, and north of Granada.[44] Sprogis's unit was also responsible for the destruction of a number of trains, and he is said to have undertaken extremely important assignments during the Nationalists' general attack on Madrid, when the Seville-Toledo road had been cut and the Italian Expeditionary Corps was thrown at Guadalajara.

In May 1937, fearing that Franco's forces were massing for a possible attack along that section of the Madrid front through which passed the railway to Guadalajara, Berzin ordered reconnaissance forces on the Madrid front, presumably the newly formed *spetsnaz* detachment commanded by Vasilevskiy, to capture a live prisoner for interrogation. After a week's fruitless wait, Berzin assigned Sprogis's unit to the task, which was successfully carried out with a five-man team deployed at night several kilometers across enemy lines. This was the last assignment Sprogis personally received from Berzin before the latter's departure for the Soviet Union in late May or very early June 1937.[45] In addition to Sprogis's group, Nikolay Prokopyuk worked with a *spetsnaz* detachment in Andalusia, but little is known of it except that Prokopyuk was a welcome, if tight-lipped, visitor at Vasilevskiy's headquarters in Las Vegas.[46]

Estremadura

In early 1937, sometime before the end of April, Khadzhi Mamsurov led a group operating behind Franco's lines[47] in Estremadura.[48] Little is reliably known about its size, its operations, or what happened to the unit after Mamsurov became senior advisor to Domingo Ungria, commander of the Special Battalion, in April 1937 (see, infra).

Creation of the 14th Special Corps

In the fall of 1937 all Spanish Republican units that fought behind enemy lines were incorporated into the 14th Special Corps (also known in some sources as the "14th Partisan Corps," "14th Spetscorps," and possibly "Special 14th Corps, Partisan"). In Mrs. Starinov's account, the 14th was established by the high command of the Republican Army in the fall of 1937 as an umbrella organization to unite "all forces acting in the rear of the enemy,"[49] probably a month or two after Mamsurov's recall to the Soviet Union.[50] Korenevskiy and Sgibnev, however, laid the creation of the 14th at Berzin's feet:

> The centralization and planned utilization of partisan forces [within a single command] was Berzin's idea, and as strikes in the enemy's rear became more powerful because of it, the coordination [of the activity] of regular units with the soldiers of "the little war" became possible. Remember how Hemingway in his novel *For Whom the Bell Tolls* has General Goltz order the partisan Robert Jordan not only to blow up a bridge but to do it "at exactly the indicated hour based on the time designated for the attack [by the regular infantry]."[51]

Berzin had rotated back to the Soviet Union in late May or early June, where he was reinstalled as head of the GRU, so Sprogis's detachment could have been made available to the 14th.[52] If Mrs. Starinov's statement that the 14th was established in the fall of 1937 is correct, then the first senior advisor to the 14th was Soviet Army *Kombrig* (Brigadier General) Khristofor Intovich Salnyn. In March or April 1938, Salnyn was recalled to the Soviet Union, arriving in April. He was purged not long thereafter.[53] Salnyn was replaced by Nikolay Kirillovich Patrakhaltsev, who was followed in May or June 1938 by Vasily Avramovich Troyan.[54]

In March 1938, when Troyan arrived in the headquarters of the 14th at Pins del Valles (in Catalonia, near Barcelona), he found the 14th was commanded by Lieutenant Colonel Ungria. The chief of staff was probably still Major Ilich. The headquarters itself consisted of two buildings, one called "Casa Roja" (for the color of its bricks) or "Chapayev" (after a military commander who fell during the Russian Civil War), and a two-story gray building.[55] Casa Roja was used by Interbrigadists (possibly officers only)[56] and Soviet advisors resting after missions, while the other building housed teams resting after missions, the Soviet senior advisor, and possibly the 14th's staff.[57]

At its height, the 14th consisted of four divisions, each of which had three or four "brigades" (akin to Soviet detachments) of 150 to 200 men. One division was stationed in Catalonia (northeast Spain), and Patrakhaltsev assigned Troyan to a detachment on the right flank of the Catalonian front, near Tremp.[58] Not much else is known about that particular division, except that one of its detachments had a waystation in a small villa in the town of Malgrat.[59] The 14th's three other divisions were distributed throughout the central zone, assigned to Andalusia, Estremadura, and the central front. They had the bulk of the Soviet advisors then present in the 14th: Andrey Emil'ev, Aleksandr Kononenko, and Grigoriy Kharitonenko (possibly a cover name for Grigoriy Syroezhkin).[60]

By the second half of July 1938, the 14th was preparing for the Ebro offensive, which began 25 July.[61] The night before the attack, Ungria, Troyan, and his interpreter were at the headquarters of one of the participating corps, coordinating *spetsnaz* support and seeing to the proper distribution of intelligence gathered by the 14th. During the Ebro campaign, the Republican Army commander Juan Modesto and the commanders of the two corps — especially Enrique Lister — made frequent requests for the 14th to carry out diversionary activities behind Franco's lines:

> Numerous groups, detachments, and even whole brigades were dispatched to [the enemy's rear]. They carried out diversionary activities on railways and roads, attacked staffs, depots, and other military objectives, [and] cut

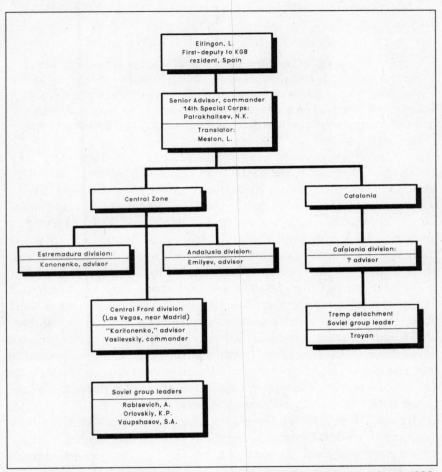

Figure 7. Soviet personnel associated with the 14th Special Corps in March 1938.

communications. As a result, parts of rail lines, particularly that running between Saragosa and Lerida, were paralyzed. Using contact-detonated and delayed-action mines, the partisans derailed trains and made roads impassable. Mines were placed around sharp bends along roads. Diversionary activities carried out in the mountains were particularly successful: cars, trucks, busses, etc. not destroyed by the explosion itself were nevertheless hurled into space by its force.[62]

Describing the heated activity of the 14th during the Ebro campaign, Troyan notes:

From the beginning of the Ebro operation all work of the commander of the 14th Special Corps and me, as senior advisor, was turned to the brigades and detachments. We worked out an original shuttle schedule: some groups and detachments left on assignment, others returned. We gained experience in preparing personnel and in the conduct of military operations, nevertheless there were difficulties.[63]

By November 1938, the Republican forces had retreated across the Ebro and the Segre, taking up defensive positions in Catalonia. What occupied the 14th between November 1938 and January 1939 is not known. But on 24 January Troyan was ordered to Barcelona, which expected an imminent attack from Franco's forces. Troyan and Major Ilich arrived in Barcelona that evening and found that all services had already been evacuated except for a small group of advisors led by General Kachanov.[64]

After reporting to the staff of General Kachanov, Troyan and Ilich went to the 14th's headquarters at Pins del Valles, where documents were destroyed and the sole detachment remaining at the site (about 180 men) was readied for the retreat to Gerona.[65] On 25 January, Troyan, the Soviet advisor group, and the Catalonian *spetsnaz* detachment began to retreat northeast along the road from Barcelona to Figueras. Though the advisors' flight was slowed by refugees, it was aided for three days by the apparent lack of pursuit by Franco's forces.

By early February, the Soviets had reached Gerona. On 5 February they were briefed by General Kachanov to wear civilian clothes and have their foreign passports the next morning for the crossover into France through the railway tunnel at Port Bou. As a last mission, Troyan's brigade was tasked to destroy the large quantities of munitions and supplies at the Port Bou railroad station while Franco's forces occupied the town and battles raged in the streets. Perhaps because of the surprise appearance of Franco's forces in Gerona and the consequent fighting, the route from Gerona to Port Bou took three days to traverse.[66]

When Port Bou was finally reached, the Soviets found that the hundreds of tons of munitions and supplies stored there could not be destroyed because of the large numbers of nearby refugees. Instead, during the night of 8 February, two special divisions (that from Pins del Valles, nine men of Vasilevskiy's unit, and, possibly, that from Tremp)[67] guarded the pas-

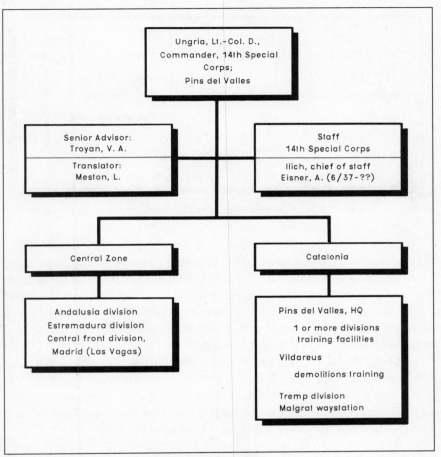

Figure 8. The 14th Special Corps in June 1938.

sage of the Soviet advisors and remains of the Republican forces as they passed through the tunnel and into history.[68]

Post-War Activities

After evading capture by Franco's forces, many commandos of the 14th fled to France and were interned there. Of those who managed to escape

Advisor	Dates
Eitingon, L. A.	September 1936 to February 8 or 9, 1939
Syroezhkin, G. S.	Late 1936 to December 1938
Mamsurov, Kh.-U. Dzh.	April 1937 to late summer 1937
Salnyn, K. I.	Late summer 1937 to March 1938
Patrakhaltsev, N. K.	March 1938 to June 1938
Troyan V. A.	June 1938 to February 9, 1938
Vaupshasov, S. A.	January 1939 to March 1939

Figure 9. Senior Soviet advisors to the 14th Special Corps and its predecessors.

Franco, many took part in guerrilla activities "in a number of countries, particularly Yugoslavia, Italy and Poland," against the Germans after World War II began in 1939. In mid-1942 the 14th is said to have reformed under the leadership of Antonio Buitrago to fight the Germans on French territory. Buitrago, however, was fatally wounded shortly thereafter and command was assumed by Jesus Rios.[69]

During World War II, more than three hundred Spanish veterans of the 14th served under Col. I. G. Starinov in the Operational Training Center of the Western Front and in the 5th Separate Spetsnaz Engineer Brigade of the Soviet Army. Still other veterans served in Allied organizations such as the American Office of Strategic Services (OSS).

Conclusion

The Soviets throw away nothing that works. Although the Republican cause lost Spain, the Soviets gained much experience in the war that stood the Soviet Union in good stead for many years afterward. Although they were not neophytes as they went into the conflict, the Soviets were able to experiment with and validate (or invalidate) their concepts of special operations and partisan warfare. At the same time, the Soviets displayed behavior that is instructive to those who study the pattern of Soviet operations then and now.

Then, as now, political reliability is the *sine qua non* of Soviet special operations. With very few exceptions, all of the personnel associated with the Soviet special operations program in Spain were committed Communists with intense loyalty to the Soviet Union. The extensive use of Communist foreign nationals ("interbrigadists") of intense ideological commitment further illustrates this point.

As is also the case today, the KGB had overall control of those special operations external to the Soviet Union, short of general war conditions. KGB control assured all undertakings supported the strategic political goals of the Soviet Politburo, and that all players were intimidated or otherwise insulated against political "contamination." Overall KGB control also favored a degree of unity of command of Soviet assets in Spain and a good measure of operational security (OPSEC).

Comparatively senior and highly skilled staff officers were directly involved in *spetsnaz* activities in Spain and most *spetsnaz* missions were operational, as is contemporary Soviet practice: deep reconnaissance, direct-action sabotage, prisoner snatching, and provocations. OPSEC within the detachments was also fairly good, with the possible notable exception of Mamsurov's discourses with Hemingway, despite the mix of people from diverse cultures and backgrounds. As a result, the *spetsnaz* normally enjoyed the element of surprise and were able to undertake operational missions such as airbase demolition raids with an economy of force.

Despite their best efforts, the Soviet side lost in Spain as it is now doing fifty years later in Afghanistan. In Spain, as in Afghanistan, however, it is naive to conclude that *spetsnaz* were an irrelevancy. Though the strategic correlation of forces ultimately swung decisively in favor of the Nationalists, the operational intelligence gathered by the *spetsnaz* and the punishment they inflicted on the Nationalists gave the Republicans much more breathing room, and a longer life, than they would otherwise have enjoyed.

Notes

1. See Anna Kornilovna Starinov, "V tylu y myatezhnikov," (In the Rebel's Rear), in Sofya Aleksandrovsky, et al., comps., *My—Internatsionalisty* (We Are Internationalists) (Moscow: Politizdat, 1975): 104.
2. FBI letter from SAC New York to Director FBI (105-22869), June 1954, 5. This letter consists of an interrogator's summaries of Alexander Orlov's replies to questions about statements in Krivitsky's *In Stalin's Secret Service*. Generally, the questions concerned the Spanish civil war and the part Krivitsky alleged Orlov played in it.
3. FBI letter, 5; John Dziak, *Chekisty: A History of the KGB* (New York: Ivy Books, 1988): 101.
4. A. K. Starinov, 104.
5. Alexander Orlov, *The Secret History of Stalin's Crimes* (New York: Random House, 1953): 235–236; V. I. Adriashenko, "Na severe" (In the North), in Aleksandrovskiy, et al., comps., *My—Internatsionalisty*, 172; Nadezhda and Maya Ulanovskiy, *Istoriya odnoy semi* (One Family's Story) (New York: Chalidze Publications, 1982): 101; E. L. Volf, "Nezabymoye," ("The Unforgettable"), in *My—Internatsionalisty*, 188–189.
6. Lewis Fischer, *Men and Politics: An Autobiography* (New York: Duell, Sloan and Pierce, 1941): 135, 395; Ovidiy Gertsovich Savich, *Dva goda v Ispanii* (Two Years in Spain), 4th ed. (Moscow: Sovetskiy Pisatel', 1981): 140.
7. E. Vorobyev, "Starik i ego ucheniki" (The Old Man and His Students), in I. Vasilevich, comp. *Vernost' Dolgu* (Faithfulness to Duty) (Moscow: Voyenizdat, 1985): 32.
8. I. N. Goffe, "Pod Teruehlem" (At Teruel), in *My—Internatsionalisty*, 233.
9. Vasiliy Avramovich Troyan, "Chetyrnadtsatyy spetsial'nyy" (The 14th Special Corps), in *My—Internatsionalisty*, 252.
10. Orlov, *The Secret History*, x.
11. FBI letter, 5.
12. Ilya Grigorevich Starinov, *Miny zhut svoego chasa* (The Mines Await Their Hour) (Moscow: Voyenizdat, 1964): 76.
13. Orlov, *The Secret History*, x.
14. Orlov, *The Handbook of Intelligence and Guerrilla Warfare* (Ann Arbor: University of Michigan Press, 1963): 172.
15. Georges A. Agabekov, *OGPU: The Secret Russian Terror* (New York: Brentanos, 1931): 207–208.
16. Nikolai I. Khokhlov, *In The Name of Conscience* (London: Muller, 1960): 42.
17. Lev Petrovich Vasilevskiy, *Ispanskaya khronika grigoriy grande* (The Spanish Chronicle of Gregory Grande) (Moscow: Molodaya Gvardiya, 1974): 163.
18. I. G. Starinov, at 77–79, claims the real impetus for the schools came from him.

19. Orlov, *Handbook*, 172.
20. A. T. Kuzmin, et al., *Vsenarodnaya bor'ba v Belorussii protiy nemetsko-fashistikh zakhvatchikov v gody velikoy otechestvennoy voyny* (The National Battle in Belorussia Against The Fascist German Bandits During World War II), vol. 1 (Minsk: Belarus', 1983): 107.
21. A. K. Starinov, 104.
22. I. G. Starinov, 76.
23. Ibid., 84.
24. Ibid., 77–79.
25. A. K. Starinov, 105; Orlov, *Handbook*, 172; I. G. Starinov, 79.
26. I. G. Starinov, 84–86.
27. Ibid., 85–87.
28. Ibid., 101; Arthur H. Landis, *The Abraham Lincoln Brigade* (New York: The Citadel Press, 1967): 135.
29. A. K. Starinov, 109–111.
30. I. G. Starinov, 106.
31. A. K. Starinov, 112–113.
32. I. G. Starinov, 132.
33. A. Eisner, cited in M. Korenevskiy and A. Sgibnev, "Zhizn' i podvig Khristofor Salnynya" (The Life and Exploits of Christopher Salnyn), in *Vernost' Dolgu*, 408.
34. I. G. Starinov, 130.
35. Ibid., 132.
36. Ibid., 76–77.
37. Vasilevskiy, 22.
38. Ibid., 22.
39. Orlov, *Handbook*, 177–178.
40. Vasilevskiy, 45–46. Boyarskiy apparently returned to the Soviet Union in late December 1937 or early 1938.
41. Ibid., 24.
42. Vorobyev, 32–33; I. G. Starinov, 76.
43. Vorobyev, 56.
44. Ibid., 27–30.
45. Ibid., 73–74.
46. Vasilevskiy, 54.
47. Ibid., 52.
48. P. Mamsurov, 55.
49. A. K. Starinov, 114.
50. Korenevskiy and Sgibnev, 408, citing A. Eisner, who was on the staff of the 14th, have Mamsurov departing Spain in late summer of 1937.
51. Ibid., 409.

52. V. Serebryannikov, "Gotovyy byt' ryadovym" (Ready to Serve as a Private), *Kommunist*, 17/1979: 113; Orlov, *The Secret History*, 238; Korenevskiy and Sgibnev, 408.
53. Korenevskiy and Sgibnev, 407; Pavel I. Goldshteyn, *Tochka opory* (Jerusalem: MS, 1982): 1, 14.
54. Troyan, 244.
55. Ibid., 244–245.
56. Ibid., 242.
57. Ibid.
58. Ibid., 243.
59. Vasilevskiy, 189.
60. Troyan, 243.
61. Ibid., 246–247.
62. Ibid., 248–249.
63. Ibid., 250.
64. Ibid.
65. Ibid.
66. Ibid., 251–252.
67. Ibid., 253; Vasilevskiy, 214.
68. Troyan, 253–254.
69. A. K. Starinov, 115.

CHAPTER 5
Spetsnaz Engineers in the Great Patriotic War: An Overview

William H. Burgess III

The doctrinal lineage of modern *spetsnaz* has many roots. Most famous among its ancestors are the special designation forces of Soviet state security (NKVD/KGB) and military intelligence (GRU) which saw action in the Russian Civil War, the 1920 Russo-Polish War, the Spanish Civil War, and the Great Patriotic War (World War II). Often overlooked is the strong strain of combat assault engineering in the *spetsnaz* bloodline.

Rear area engineer *razvedka* (reconnaissance) and demolition operations at the tactical and operational levels of war are longstanding aspects of Soviet military doctrine and practice.[1] Such activities are part of the Soviet Army's long history of innovation and specialization to meet battlefield engineering demands. Faced with unique engineering requirements, the Soviets have often tailored existing organizations or created entirely new formations as the situation dictated.

In the late 1920s, for example, the Ukrainian Military District organized a special partisan task force charged with the demolition of critical facilities and commodities along the border with Poland and Rumania as a wartime contingency. According to one of the members of this force, Ilya Grigorevich Starinov,[2] the task force was responsible for development of demolition technology (possibly including some form of barrier penetration study), establishing contingency caches of explosives, and training special teams to carry out demolition tasks. Primary targets of these teams were the key points and rolling stock of the Soviet rail system, their objective being to deny use of this system to an invading enemy.

According to Starinov, more than sixty such demolition teams with an average strength of twenty-three persons each (including some females) were trained, involving approximately 1,400 personnel. Every demolitions expert (*miner*) was also a parachutist, radio operator, and master of camouflage (*maskirovka*).[3] In fall 1932 Starinov and some of his personnel jumped into the Leningrad Military District on an exercise to demonstrate their skill in operations in the enemy rear. Their missison was to

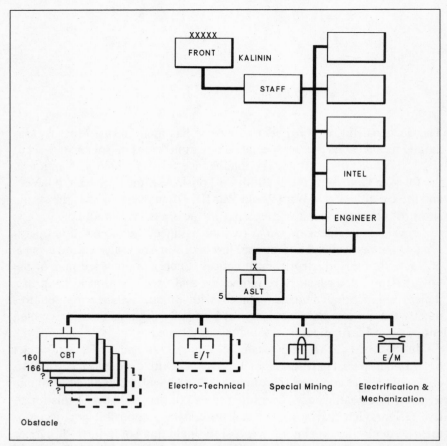

Figure 1. Possible organization and subordination of the 5th Separate Spetsnaz Engineer Brigade.

capture a headquarters and destroy transportation facilities. They placed ten mines on a ten-kilometer stretch of track (one mine blew up under the wheels of a commuter train before they could remove it), caused a panic in a village with the detonation of three incendiary practice mines, and generally created a stir in the exercise headquarters. At one point, Starinov was personally ejected from the exercise, but he was subsequently reinstated.[4]

Although primarily an engineering effort, this program was closely related to the GRU's creation of special partisan cadre who would conduct "stay behind" operations in the enemy rear in the event of invasion. Gradually, however, the threat of foreign invasion subsided, conventional "deep battle" theorists replaced the advocates of partisan warfare as primary defense of the Russian Revolution, and Starinov and his fellow demolitionists were absorbed into the Red Army. However, the partisan program was destroyed, and most of the personnel associated with it were killed, during Stalin's purges in the late 1930s,[5] possibly because Stalin feared the program was a threat to his own regime.

Engineer Spetsnaz in Combat

Nonetheless, Starinov (as a Military Engineer, 3rd class) and others with backgrounds in special operations demolitions did see action during the Spanish Civil War of 1936–1939, when their skills were employed in the 14th Special Corps and its predecessor units. The Soviets made good use of the combat engineer skills of veterans of the 14th. In July 1941, shortly after the outbreak of war with Germany, Colonel Starinov and other Spanish Civil War *spetsnaz* combat engineering veterans established and ran the GRU's Operations Training Center of the Western Front, a main GRU sabotage school. In April 1942, Starinov and other Spanish Civil War veterans were also instrumental in creating the first major *spetsnaz* engineer unit of the war, the 5th Separate Spetsnaz Engineer Brigade.[6]

Throughout the war, *spetsnaz* combat engineer units made significant contributions to delaying and blocking enemy advances, defeating fortified enemy positions, disrupting the movement of enemy reserves, and diverting front-line troops to rear area security through missions conducted in enemy rear areas. Most were committed at the operational level to improving defensive belts around critical terrain features and population centers during the German offensives at the beginning of the war, and in penetrating and clearing enemy fortified zones when the Soviets went on the counteroffensive. The 5th Brigade and similar units made use of such advanced demolition and barrier technology as remote-controlled and command-detonated mine fields, electrified wire barriers, and the like.[7] According to Col. A. A. Soskov, depending on their size, these *spetsnaz* engineer brigades could emplace between twenty thousand and thirty-five thousand antitank mines, or open 135 to 190 pathways through enemy mixed mine fields, in twelve hours.[8]

At the outset of World War II, small groups of *miners* (demolition experts) were created from standing engineer units for reconnaissance and "diversionary" activities against fortifications and lines of communication (LOCs) in the enemy rear.[9] By mid-1942, such units were active on all Soviet fronts. In the offensive in the Moscow area, reconnaissance-*miner* detachments of three to five men each were created in all combat engineer and engineer battalions. These detachments were sent into enemy rear areas on missions lasting several days, demolishing bridges and roadbeds on highways and railroads, destroying enemy equipment, killing enemy soldiers, and collecting engineer information and other intelligence. In February 1942, for example, *miners* of the Western Front destroyed five bridges and planted 720 mines in the enemy rear.

In June 1942, the 160th and 166th Engineer Obstacle Battalions of the 5th Brigade, then commanded by Col. F. B. Ab, were assigned activities in the enemy rear on the Kalinin Front. In all, 159 teams from the 160th and 166th were sent into the enemy rear, where they blew up thirty-two enemy trains, five railroad and highway bridges, thirty-two automobiles, and an ammunition dump, and killed more than six hundred enemy soldiers.

Guards Miners

Soviet effectiveness in reconnaissance and diversion against enemy LOCs and fortifications increased with the August 1942 creation by edict of the People's Commissariat of Defense of the USSR of specially trained separate guards battalions of *miners* (*otdelnyy gvardeyskiy batal'on minerov*, abbreviated OGBM). By October 1942, there was one such battalion in every operational Front and one brigade in Stavka reserve.[10] The utilization of such battalions in the enemy rear was controlled from the headquarters of the chief of engineer troops of each Front, which closely coordinated such activities with the headquarters of the partisans of the *oblast* (republic) on whose territory the Front was operating. In the years 1943–1944, guards *miners* derailed five hundred seventy-six trains and five armored trains, blew up approximately three hundred tanks and self-propelled guns, six hundred fifty wheeled vehicles and armored cars, more than three hundred rail and highway bridges, and killed or wounded thousands of enemy soldiers.[11]

OGBM troops were selected on the basis of devotion to the Motherland (political reliability), moral courage, valor, and physical endurance. Most, if not all, OGBM troops were Communists or Komsomolists, aged eighteen to thirty years, and sportsmen or hunters. Enlisted troops were trained in the use of Soviet and German demolitions. OGBM troops were also trained in parachuting, the use of a map and compass, and terrain orientation.

The main mode of employment of OGBM assets was to infiltrate small groups into several sectors of the enemy rear for simultaneous strikes on enemy LOCs in support of offensive action by conventional Soviet formations. Once given their mission, these groups would normally cross the front lines at night, through gaps and junctions of enemy units. Sometimes, they were delivered to the enemy rear by transport aircraft, the chosen landing zone being about fifteen kilometers from the objective.

OGBM *miners* usually operated with partisans. They trained the partisans in demolitions and targeting, and gave them demolition supplies. The partisans, in turn, provided the *miners* with area and target intelligence, and information and guidance for the approach to targets. Occasionally, partisans provided security for the *miners* when they were placing their charges.

Most OGBM demolitions were emplaced at night. Delayed action mines (*mina zamedlennogo deystviya*, or MZD) were often used, because of their strong psychological impact on the enemy. According to S. Kh. Aganov,[12] these mines were often used to deny enemy use of several sections of a rail line, and to force the enemy to build bypasses.

In preparation for the Smolensk offensive at the end of July 1943, nine groups totalling 316 men from the 5th Brigade and the 10th OGBM were inserted by airplane into the enemy rear to simultaneously destroy enemy rail lines to a depth of three hundred kilometers on order from the commander of the Kalinin Front. After the order was given, the *miners* blew up more than 3,500 rails with an aggregate length of seven hundred kilometers, seriously disrupting the movement of enemy reserves and significantly aiding the Soviet offensive.

On the night of 11 March 1943, a twenty-three-man platoon of the 9th OGBM of the Northwestern Front, commanded by Lt. I. P. Kovalev, was parachuted into the enemy rear in an area thirty kilometers northwest of Novorzhev. On the ground, the *miners* made contact with the 1st Partisan Regiment of the 3rd Partisan Brigade. The *miners* and partisans went into action on 17 March, conducting four demolition operations on railroads and highways on that day. Over the next seven months, until 16 October, the *miners* derailed sixteen military trainloads of men and equipment, and destroyed seventeen bridges, more than eight thousand linear meters of track bed, nearly fifteen hundred meters of telephone wire, several dozen motor vehicles, two tanks, an armored car, eight truckloads of ammunition, and, with the partisans, killed approximately five hundred enemy soldiers. In one of the operations with the partisans providing security, the OGBM troops on 24 August destroyed the fifty-six-meter-long railroad bridge across the Keb' River with four fifty-kilogram explosive charges placed under the bridge piers, cutting that rail line for several days. For his actions in this period, Kovalev was named Hero of the Soviet Union, and all soldiers and sergeants in his platoon were awarded the Order of the Patriotic War or the Red Star.

OGBM troops were also used as tank destroyers on LOCs in the immediate enemy rear. In the July 1943 fighting in the Kursk Salient, for example, the 1st Guards Special Purpose Engineer Brigade was credited with destroying 140 German tanks and self-propelled guns, and inflicting up to 2,500 German casualties.[13] The 13th OGBM operated this way in the vicinity of Bogodukhov and Akhturka in August 1943. During the Kiev operation, forty-seven tank destroyer teams of the 13th operated in the enemy rear. In two years of combat, the teams of the 13th destroyed 93 tanks, 11 self-propelled guns, 214 automobiles, 9 large trains, and 4 bridges and killed more than 2,000 Germans.[14]

Petsamo-Kirkenes

During the preparatory period of the October 7 to 30, 1944, Petsamo-Kirkenes Operation to clear the Germans from the approaches to Murmansk, the headquarters of engineer troops of the Karelian Front planned operations in the enemy rear by three detachments from the 6th OGBM and the 222d Motorized Assault Combat Engineer Battalion of the 20th Motorized Assault Combat Engineer Brigade (one of five motorized engineer brigades under the chiefs of the engineer troops of the various Fronts). The first detachment, 133 men from the 6th OGBM in two companies, went into the enemy rear on 18 September. The two remaining detachments, 108 men from the 222d, and 49 men from the 6th OGBM, went in on 2 October. Several hours before the beginning of the offensive, the detachments received the order by radio to go into action. Over the course of fifteen days, the detachments conducted reconnaissance and demolition operations, destroying 20.6 kilometers of telephone wire, eleven bridges and several score trucks, killing 452 Germans and capturing forty-five, and suffering only eight wounded in action. In Aganov's estimation, these *spetsnaz* engineer activities made the success of the 14th Army possible. About half of the men who operated in the enemy rear were decorated with awards and medals for their exemplary fulfillment of their mission.

The Far East

As the war with Germany drew to a close, *spetsnaz* engineers were redeployed to the Far East in preparation for the Manchurian campaign against the Japanese.[15] Among the units transferred was the 20th Brigade, which was assigned to the 1st Far Eastern Front. The first operational combat mission of the 20th was the seizure and neutralization of the defenses of a complex of three railroad tunnels near Suifenho. The tunnels were located one to three kilometers from the Sino-Soviet border, were on the avenue of advance of the 5th Army, and could not be bypassed.

The Japanese defenses were attacked in the predawn hours of 9 August by two detachments of the 20th. Each detachment comprised one assault battalion, one company of flame throwers, two platoons of submachine-gunners, and a group of artillery observers. These detachments were also supported by an armored train and two battalions of Front artillery. By morning on 9 August, the detachments had defeated the Japanese defenses, permitting the forward detachment of the 187th Rifle Division to capture the tunnels intact and secure entry of the 5th Army into the Manchurian heartland.

Subsequent to the Suifenho operation, and after the Japanese capitulation, special detachments of the 20th were airlanded more than 250 kilo-

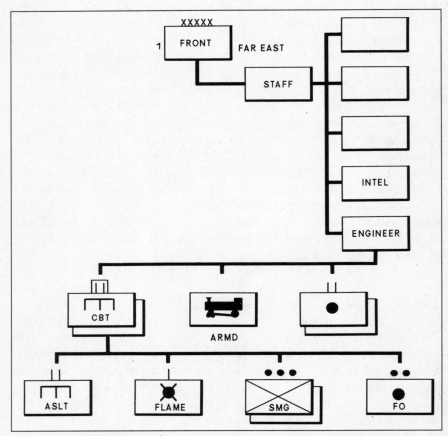

Figure 2. Possible organization and subordination of the Suifenho tunnels *spetsnaz* detachments.

meters into hostile territory at Harbin (120 men on 18 August) and Kirin (150 men on 19 August) to accompany Front plenipotentiaries who negotiated the surrender of Japanese garrisons there. These detachments, for the most part made up of men who had fought in the Suifenho operation, took the Japanese defenders by surprise. On landing, as negotiations progressed, they quickly captured key bridges, rail yards, radio stations, telephone and telegraph offices, banks and other critical installations to prevent destruction or removal by the Japanese. The assault force landing at Harbin also captured Kwantung Army chief of staff General Hata and several other senior Japanese officers.

Conclusions

Spetsnaz combat engineer capabilities as they existed over forty years ago played an important role in the theory and practice of deep battle against the Germans. Moreover, the spirit of this capability remains, as seen in the continued Soviet emphasis at operational and tactical levels on engineer *razvedka* and direct action to help commanders see and shape the battlefield.

Based on their past performance, it can be argued that current Soviet engineer units at operational echelons may present at least a latent *spetsnaz* "deep operation" capability that has been largely overlooked. It could mean that the Soviet Army has the potential, through augmentation and supplementary selection and training, to rapidly reform ostensibly conventional, frontline units into forces for deep raiding and reconnaissance. If so, this would represent an economical and operationally secure way for the Soviets to quickly expand and modify their *spetsnaz* capabilities to meet specific contingencies. Whether or not it is the Soviet intent to maintain a latent engineer *spetsnaz* capability, the deep operation potential of Soviet combat engineer units must be recognized.

Notes

1. See Col. David M. Glantz, *Soviet Operational Intelligence in the Kursk Operation (July 1943)* (Fort Leavenworth KS: Soviet Army Studies Office, August 1988): 6, 7, 18, 21, 22, 28, 31.

2. Information about Starinov is derived from Ilya Grigorevich Starinov, *Miny zhut svoego chasa* (The Mines Await Their Hour) (Moscow: Voyenizdat, 1964): 76, trans. Owen A. Lock and James F. Gebhardt.

3. Ibid., 34.

4. Ibid., 41–42.

5. Ibid., 157.

6. Col. A. A. Soskov, "Sovershenstovovanie organizatsionnoy struktury inhenernykh vovsk v gody velikoy otechestvennoy" (Improvements in the Organization of Engineering Troops During World War II), *Voenno-istoricheskiy zhurnal*, 12/1985, 66 and 68 (table), trans. Owen A. Lock.

7. Ibid.

8. Ibid.

9. Most of the information in this chapter on *miners* is derived from the following translations by James F. Gebhardt: S. Kh. Aganov, ed., *Inzhenernyye voyska sovetskoy armii 1918–1945* (Engineer Troops of the Soviet Army 1918–1945) (Moscow: Voyenizdat, 1985): 459–463; Arkadii F. Khrenov, *Mostu k pobede* (Bridges to Victory) (Moscow: Voyenizdat, 1982): 336–344; V. F. Margelov, et al., *Sovetskie vozdushno-desantnye: voenno-istoricheskii ocherk* (Soviet Airborne Assault Forces: A Military-Historical Outline) (Moscow: Voyenizdat, 1986): 296–299; Kirill A. Meretskov, *Na sluzhbe narody* (In Service to the People) (Moscow: Voyenizdat, 1983): 391, 411, 413; and N. P. Suntsov et al., *Krasnoznamennyi dal 'nevostochnui: istoriia krasnoznamennogo dal 'nevostochnogo voennogo okruga* (Red Banner Far East: The History of the Red Banner Far East Military District) (Moscow: Voyenizdat, 1985): 202.

10. *Sovetskaia voennaia entsiklopedia* (Soviet Military Encyclopedia) 5 (Moscow: Voyenizdat, 1978): 290.

11. Ibid.

12. Aganov, 460.

13. Lt. Gen. M. Kushnikov, "Toilers in the War," *Voennii Vestik*, 5/1985, 78–81 (undated English translation).

14. Aganov, 462.

15. Information on engineer *spetsnaz* activities in the Far East is derived from Khrenov, Meretskov, Margelov, and Suntsov, ops. cit.

CHAPTER 6
The Far North Origin of Naval Spetsnaz[1]

James F. Gebhardt
William H. Burgess III

There is a large body of historical materials on the World War II special operations in two of the four Soviet fleets (the Northern and the Pacific): contemporary Soviet press accounts, German war diary entries, postwar memoirs, official histories, monographs, and many other secondary sources. Using as many of these sources as are available, this chapter explores the development of *spetsnaz* in the Northern Fleet and describes the repertoire of their actions against the Germans in the Far North from 1941 to 1944. It concludes with an analytical summary establishing these forces as a legitimate precursor of present-day Soviet naval *spetsnaz*.

The Soviets have a long history of clandestine and covert special operations in the Far North countries of Finland, Sweden, and Norway. The beginning of the current Soviet special operations capabilities in the area may have been in short-range submarine reconnaissance operations believed to have been undertaken along the Barents Sea coasts of Finland and Norway during the mid-1930s, and similar reconnaissance conducted in the Baltic Sea by then, if not earlier, against Sweden and Finland.[2] Although not clearly established, ground reconnaissance and/or the dropping off or recovery of agents may have occurred on at least some of these voyages.

The alleged first wartime employment of the Soviet *spetsnaz* in the Far North occurred during the 1939 to 1940 Winter War with Finland, at a point when such capabilities were relatively primitive. During the war, the Finns feared the threat of fifth column traitors (which, to Stalin's dismay, never materialized) and occasional enemy agents. The Finns also allege that the Soviets parachuted "descanti" (*desanti*), or assault teams of Finnish-speaking Soviet Inkeris (a tribe from near Leningrad) behind Finnish lines. The effect of such operations was limited, although rumor of them did cause Field Marshal Carl Gustav Emil Mannerheim to consent to the presence of a small personal bodyguard at his headquarters.[3] It is also alleged that Gen. Khadzhi-Umar Mamsurov, a distinguished GRU officer with substantial special operations experience in the Spanish Civil War, brought a *spetsnaz* unit of about fifty men to the front in an effort to capture Finnish soldiers for intelligence purposes. Mamsurov's operation apparently also failed.[4]

Early Development in the Northern Fleet

At the very beginning of the Soviet-German war, Fleet Admiral A. G. Golovko, Commander of the Northern Fleet, urgently needed immediate intelligence on German land forces in northern Norway and Finland. Starting only ninety kilometers west of the fleet main base at Poliarnyi (north of Murmansk) a German corps-sized force had begun a land offensive on 29 June 1941 to capture Murmansk, the principal Soviet industrial and port city in the region.[5] Admiral Golovko was concerned lest an element split off from the offensive to attack his naval base overland, from the west. He was not sure that Soviet Army ground forces defending Murmansk could halt the Germans, nor did he believe he could depend on Army intelligence sources for his daily estimates of enemy locations, capabilities, and intentions.

The Northern Fleet also had a forward base on the northern side of Srednyi Peninsula, only thirty kilometers by sea from the German-controlled port of Petsamo. Although Soviet naval ground forces blocked the landward approaches to this base at the narrow Srednyi Isthmus, there was a possibility that the Germans would launch amphibious operations against Srednyi or Rybachii peninsulas, or against Soviet territory farther to the east. Such operations could be launched from Vardo and Vadso on the nearby Varanger Peninsula, as well as from Kirkenes or Petsamo. German air units based at Kirkenes and two forward airfields were also within striking range of Poliarnyi and Murmansk. Thus, Golovko needed his own ground reconnaissance force.

Figure 1. The countries of the Far North.

With these problems in mind, in the first days of the German offensive Golovko met with his intelligence staff and assigned tasks which they worked into a collection plan.[6] The area of most immediate concern was the coastline on the left flank of the German offensive. The second area of interest was the German corps rear area, particularly headquarters and lines of communication (LOCs). The third area of interest was Finnish and Norwegian ports where the Germans could be gathering the forces necessary for amphibious operations.

The chief of the intelligence section of the Fleet was Captain 3rd Rank (0–4 equivalent) P. A. Vizgin, who had served in the same capacity under

Golovko when the latter commanded the Amur River Flotilla.[7] Among Vizgin's subordinates were a major, four lieutenants, and an undisclosed number of enlisted men, all too few for the immediate assigned tasks. As all incoming personnel were being assigned to ships and other combat units, the decision was made to recruit volunteers from several sources, including the commercial fleet in Murmansk, civilian and Fleet athletic and sports clubs, and the group of Norwegian Communists living in the Murmansk area who had fled the 9 April 1940 German occupation of Norway.

The Fleet Chief of Staff, Admiral Kucherov, approved the collection plan, and on 5 July 1941 Admiral Golovko authorized the formation of a ground reconnaissance detachment with an initial fill of sixty-five to seventy.[8] The detachment's first complement was recruited from among the Fleet's athletes. To aid in the selection process, Vizgin and Major L. V. Dobrotin (Vizgin's deputy and a decorated cavalryman in World War I) sought the assistance of the Fleet physical training director, Captain Domozhirov, who personally knew all the leading athletes. They emphasized to him that they needed two platoons of men, seventy in all, and particularly wanted Communists and Komsomolists. At the urging of Vizgin and Dobrotin, Domozhirov joined the detachment and became its trainer and leader.

The detachment's first barracks was with the submarine brigade in Poliarnyi, where they would be "cut off from unnecessary eyes."[9] Training began immediately, with the urgency of impending combat deployment. The detachment was assigned its first combat mission just a week later, to reconnoiter the coastline east of Srednyi Isthmus and determine if the Germans had occupied positions along the southern shore of Motovskii Bay. The detachment departed Poliarnyi in two wooden fishing boats at 2300 on 13 July. Some wore army uniforms, some had gymnastic accessories, riding breeches or bell bottoms, quilted sweaters, and rucksacks on their backs. Most had helmets, but many kept their sailor caps on instead. Most of them had semiautomatic rifles and carried pouches with ammunition and grenades. As would become characteristic of Soviet *spetsnaz* operational security (OPSEC), the group was told that it was going on a special mission for the Fleet, but that they would not be told where they were going and what they would be doing until they got to the target.[10]

The detachment split into two groups, one-third and two-thirds. Both groups went ashore and penetrated into their assigned sectors. Senior

Lieutenant Lebedev's men found the road leading east from Titovka flanked by overhead telephone wires. After observing the road for three hours and seeing nothing, they pulled down the wire, pushed over several poles, and left, covering a total distance of fifty kilometers. Both groups were picked up and returned to base on 16 July. They reported to Golovko that the Germans were only sending small reconnaissance parties to the north of Titovka Road, and then only two to three kilometers.

The detachment quickly reached its initial strength goal of seventy men, and acquired a *zampolit* (political officer). The new deputy commander was Intendant 3rd Rank N. A. Inzartsev, who was previously the chief of the athletic department of the Fleet submarine force.[11] Among the personnel recruited to the detachment during this period were Viktor N. Leonov, who would later become its commander,[12] and Olga Paraeva, a female medic and Finnish interpreter.[13]

While this force trained for and conducted operations in the German tactical depth, Vizgin's staff prepared other smaller groups for deeper penetrations. Vizgin reported to Golovko the readiness of a group of seven men to reconnoiter the Kirkenes area, and Arctic Ocean Highway (German *Eismeerstrasse*, the road from Rovaniemi to Petsamo). He also had a group of eighteen Norwegians training for operations in Norway.[14]

In the detachment's second operation, on 19 July, twenty-five men landed from a single boat near the mouth of the Litsa River.[15] Part of the group was to reconnoiter the German encampment at Titovka, while the remainder was to attack a strongpoint and capture a prisoner. Both groups were to return to the landing site in three days. Twenty men moved off to the northwest where several hours later they engaged a German outpost, killed more than a dozen Germans, and searched the rucksacks and pockets of the dead. Three men in the group were killed and others wounded, but they returned to the shore with a prisoner. The five-man patrol to Titovka returned late, reporting that they did not reach their objective because of German activity.

Several more such operations followed and after these initial successes, the detachment suffered a major defeat in August. While returning from a successful raid on a Finnish army position near Cape Pikshuev,[16] the detachment was caught in the open sea and strafed by six German fighters. Eight men were killed and thirty wounded, over half the detachment's total strength including some of its most experienced leaders.[17] With Admiral Golovko's support, however, the detachment was reconstituted by mid-August. Among the new personnel was one Lieutenant F.

Nikolaev, who had served in a ski detachment during the 1939–1940 Winter War against Finland. Nikolaev, an accomplished skier, was ordered to establish a ski training program for the detachment and was sent to Leningrad to recruit other skiers and obtain the needed special equipment.[18]

Training of the newly-arrived personnel included day and night movement techniques in the peculiar terrain of the area, camouflage and concealment skills, the crossing of water obstacles, weapons handling, cross-country skiing, parachuting,[19] and reconnaissance-related skills. The approach of winter necessitated a search for clothing and footwear appropriate for the harsh climate. The items finally adopted reflected careful consultations with local reindeer herders and cross-country ski clubs. These items were light, warm, durable, and would protect not only men on the move, but also wounded personnel being carried in litters or on sleds.

In late August to early September the detachment attempted to mount an operation in cooperation with an Army reconnaissance element against the German airfield at Luostari. The Army reconnaissance force was as poorly prepared as the naval force was well prepared: The Army detachment had been organized less than a week. Men had been taken from jails in Murmansk, and promised exculpation of their guilt for participation in this mission. There were only two Communists and seven Komsomolists among the more than eighty men. Operations security was very poor within the Army group, and their physical conditioning was not adequate for the task. Despite all these problems, the joint force managed to reach pre-positioned supplies, penetrate on foot into the objective area, and was only eight to ten kilometers from the airfield when one of the Army personnel deserted. Having lost the element of surprise, the commander of the composite force ordered withdrawal and return to base.[20] Although not all joint operations conducted with Army or naval infantry forces ended in this manner, henceforth the Fleet reconnaissance detachment preferred to operate independently.

The German offensive was still moving southeastward and by the end of August had penetrated to within forty-five kilometers of Murmansk and only fifty kilometers due west of Poliarnyi.[21] In response to this immediate threat, Admiral Golovko committed his untested 12th Naval Infantry Brigade. To fill some of the lower-level leadership positions with combat-experienced personnel, Golovko ordered Vizgin to provide eighty to ninety of his men. Vizgin was able to hold back only his ski detachments and the groups being prepared for insertion into Norway.[22]

As the German offensive spent itself against hastily formed and committed Soviet formations, Golovko and Vizgin planned the subsequent operations of the reconnaissance detachment. In September Golovko acquired a renewed interest in German activities in their Norwegian bases. Although the men who had been siphoned off to the naval infantry did not return, the detachment was reconstituted a second time and readied for new missions. Golovko promised Vizgin a pair of dedicated patrol torpedo boats for insertions and extractions, and also ordered Vizgin to develop a relationship with air units which would provide aircraft for jumping, and for delivering food and ammunition. Vizgin requested and received permission to plan also for the use of submarines.[23]

In September two small reconnaissance groups went out to determine the utility of land routes into and out of Norway should bad weather prevent the use of sea routes. One group, including three Norwegians, was inserted by an amphibious aircraft onto a lake from where they walked into the area between Nikel and Luostari and back out again. Their journey lasted ten days and covered three hundred kilometers. The other group reconnoitered the zone closer to the seacoast, marching nearly two hundred kilometers in a week.

The first insertion of Soviet special operations forces into the Varanger Peninsula occurred in late September 1941.[24] This force had two missions: (1) to determine the location, strength, and activities of German garrisons between Vardo and Vadso,[25] and (2) to establish contact with the Norwegian resistance as part of a plan of regional intelligence activities.[26] Although led by a Soviet lieutenant, half of the eighteen-man group were Norwegians. They boarded a submarine in Poliarnyi and proceeded toward their landing site at Langbunes, twenty kilometers south of Vardo. On 26 September, the group went ashore by rubber boat without incident, and remained in the German rear area until 15 November, continuously moving about the eastern portion of Varanger Peninsula to gain information and avoid capture. They reported their positions and activities by radio, made numerous contacts with Norwegian civilians, and on more than one occasion had to shoot their way clear of danger. Tight German population control measures prevented them from establishing contacts with the resistance, but they did learn much about the several small local German garrisons. Part of the group returned to Soviet control by fishing boat on 22 October, and the remainder were resupplied by air after that and picked up by a submarine on 15 November.

Long-Range Reconnaissance in Norway

A conclusion drawn from the September-November 1941 operation on Varanger Peninsula was that a protracted, Soviet-sponsored partisan struggle there was not feasible. There was little cover or concealment, all the populated areas were concentrated along the coastline where the Germans could maintain tight observation and control, and the population base was too small to absorb strangers. The alternative to a partisan effort was special operations in the form of small groups of two or three men inserted into the Varanger Peninsula to monitor and report on German naval traffic. Targeting data thus obtained would then be used to vector naval air and submarine forces.[27]

The Soviets were aided by the presence in Murmansk of many Norwegian refugees who had fled the German occupation of their country in 1940. Many, but not all, of these Norwegians were communists and were thus politically reliable. Many were also experienced watermen who knew the coastal areas of Varanger Peninsula and other areas very well: From the small fishing village of Kiberg alone, forty-eight men went to the Soviet Union during the war. Many Norwegians came back to their home areas during the war as part of the Soviet coastwatching effort. For example, in October 1943 the Soviet submarine S-55 (skippered by Capt. 3rd Rank L. M. Sushkin) put ashore a three-man team at the foot of Hesten Cliff, just north of Bakfjord. The team was comprised of two Russians, Pavel Bogdanov and radioman Nikolai Sisov, and was led by Norwegian Arnulf Mathisen, a native of Kiberg. The team made daily contact with their Poliarnyi base, reporting on the ships coming through Rolvsoy Sound. They were extracted by an unidentified submarine in February 1944, but this did not end Soviet contact with the region: In 1948 Sisov returned to Bakfjord in a small boat to take Selmer Nilsen (subsequently arrested as a Soviet spy in connection with the May 1960 shooting down of Francis Gary Powers' U2) by force to the Soviet Union for espionage training.[28]

Late in 1941, Captain 3rd Rank Vizgin reported the preparation of five teams, each consisting of two Norwegians and one Soviet radio operator.[29] The commander of this group was Senior Lieutenant P. G. Sutiagin, and his political officer was a female, Krymova.[30] It was planned to deploy the first team in late December or early January, and the second team a few weeks later. Although the initial deployment areas were along the north coast of the Varanger Peninsula, Vizgin hoped to be placing

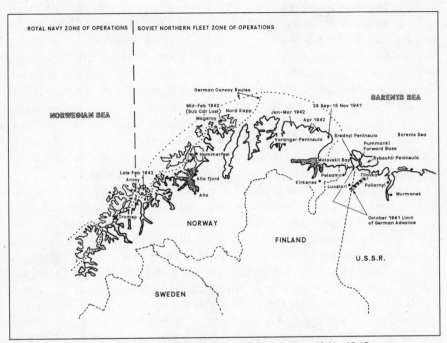

ROYAL NAVY ZONE OF OPERATIONS | SOVIET NORTHERN FLEET ZONE OF OPERATIONS

Figure 2. Naval *spetsnaz* operational areas in Norway, 1941–1942.

teams near Nordkapp (North Cape) and Tromso in February. Thus, the Fleet intelligence staff could monitor German shipping along its entire route from the west coast of Norway into and out of Kirkenes, the main logistics base for German ground forces in the Murmansk area. In order to assure reliable radio communications, Vizgin requested from the Fleet Chief of Staff the establishment of a separate communications center, manned around the clock, for monitoring operations of these groups. The Chief of Staff also assured Vizgin of close air support, and the placing of reconnaissance specialists on ships.[31] The latter resulted in the inclusion in submarine crews of personnel specially trained for inserting and extracting reconnaissance teams by rubber boat, operations often accompanied by the platoon leader.

In early January 1942 the first team was inserted into the northern coast of Varanger Peninsula by submarine S-101, near Cape Nalneset (between Tanafjord and Kongsofjord).[32] This group operated in the area between Berlevag and Cape Nalneset for two and a half months, reporting on German naval traffic and the activities of the local garrison. They maintained limited contacts with sympathetic local Norwegians from whom they obtained information about German population control measures, local military construction, and Soviet air operations against Kirkenes. They communicated regularly with their base, sometimes three times in a twenty-four-hour period, and listened to reports given by other coast-watching teams. By the end of March, however, their provisions were exhausted and they were in danger of exposure due to lengthening days. On 29 March they were alerted that a submarine was enroute to pick them up, and a few days later they were delivered to their base.

Not all attempts to land reconnaissance teams in Norway were successful. On 14 February, a submarine approached Mageroy Island (ten kilometers southwest of Nordkapp) and after careful periscope reconnaissance of the landing area surfaced to commence the landing operation.[33] While small boats were taking the reconnaissance team to shore, strong winds and currents pushed the submarine inshore, endangering it. The commander made another attempt to approach the shore to put off the team's supplies, without success. For three nights the submarine remained in the area, while a storm raged. On the night of 18 February it returned to the landing area, on the surface, only to discover German patrol vessels. During the ensuing crash dive, the submarine commander was left wounded on the conning tower, and was later believed to have been captured alive by the Germans. On shore, meanwhile, three men of the reconnaissance team and two sailors were left without food, special winter clothing, and other items of equipment necessary for their mission.[34]

Three days later, another team was lost in a similar incident.[35] A submarine was inserting them into Arnoy Island, northeast of Tromso, on 21 February 1942. Encountering problems with high seas and winds, it managed to land the two Norwegians, but not the Soviet radio operator. Although some weeks later these two Norwegians linked up with another team on the Varanger Peninsula, the two incidents together clearly indicated the need for better training of submarine crews and reconnaissance teams in small boat handling.

The next reported insertion of a team into Norway was on 4 April 1942, just a day after the extraction of the team from Nalneset. Submarine M–173 landed three men on the southeast shore of Syltefjord.[36] This team ranged east and west along the coast between Kiberg and Hamningberg, maintaining limited contacts with Norwegian sympathizers. In early

May the two Norwegians who had been stranded on Arnoy in February joined them and passed all the information they had gathered about German activities in the Tromso area to their base by radio. The group remained in this area until sometime in the early autumn of 1942, resupplied periodically by air. Soviet sources credit them with providing information that led to the sinking of nine German transports.[37]

Although the insertions of these three-man reconnaissance teams continued through the remainder of 1942 and 1943,[38] the only reference to another specific operation in Soviet sources is in the early spring of 1944.[39] A three-man team parachuted into Varanger and survived nine months on the run, enduring the elements, hunger, and German patrols vectored by radio direction-finding teams. They were extracted by submarine from Varanger in the fall of 1944, with a German dog-equipped patrol in hot pursuit.

Raids Into the Enemy Tactical and Operational Depth

By late September 1941 the front had stabilized in the vicinity of the Litsa River, some forty-five to fifty kilometers northwest of Murmansk. Vizgin used this time to build up the strength of his reconnaissance detachment and to train them. Intendant 3rd Rank Inzartsev had been promoted to captain and made commander of the detachment. Responding to requests for assistance from the 14th Army, Golovko authorized Vizgin to conduct a joint raid on German positions in the Titovka area.[40] On the night of 24 October a composite force of over one hundred men landed from small subchasers along the south shore of Motovskii Bay. They found a German garrison near the Titovka settlement and attacked it, setting fire to a number of vehicles, a gasoline storage tank, and ammunition stocks.[41] They returned to the pickup point on the morning of 25 October where four small boats extracted them.

During the winter of 1941–1942, the detachment made several unsuccessful attempts to go ashore from submarines between Rybachii Peninsula and Kirkenes.[42] The Germans had too many shore batteries, listening posts, and searchlight positions. Frequent winter storms and rough seas further complicated the Soviet effort. Unable to approach German installations from seaward, the detachment went to ground.

In November 1941 another attempt was made to reconnoiter the Luostari airfield, this time by the detachment's ski teams.[43] They were to examine the approaches to the airfield, and discern the nature of its defensive system. If all went well, the ground force would initiate an attack, followed by airstrikes by Fleet aviation units.[44] The ski group was accompanied in the initial leg of its march by reindeer pulling sleds carrying ammunition, heavy machine guns, and extra provisions. On 11 November they left Soviet lines, and a few days later crossed the Titovka River south of Lake Chapr. On 14 November they reached the target and conducted detailed reconnaissance, including the drawing of sketches of airfield defenses and installations. On 15 November they began the seven-day trek back to friendly lines, carrying one of their men who had suffered an accute attack of appendicitis. It was probably this circumstance that caused the cancellation of the joint air and ground attack.

While the ski troops were reconnoitering the airfield, Captain Inzartsev led a platoon-strength group on a mission to locate a German strongpoint overlooking the mouth of the Litsa River.[45] The group landed from two small subchasers, moved up into the snow-covered hills, and after some hours of movement, followed a telephone wire to a German guardpost. Without carefully observing the surrounding landscape, they attacked the guard and an adjacent shelter. Several other Germans returned fire from nearby positions, forcing Inzartsev and his men to make a hasty retreat to the shore. They had located the German position, but at the price of four dead.

Some time later, the Army informed them of a captured Finnish lieutenant who was willing to lead a patrol to an unoccupied "winterized" German strongpoint.[46] Vizgin sent seventy men on two boats from Poliarnyi to Cape Pikshuev, accompanied by an Army detachment with the Finnish officer and an interpreter. Delayed by a winter storm, the composite detachment arrived at their target area on the second day and moved directly from shore to the strongpoint. There, buried under the snow, they found two small antitank guns with over three hundred shells, other weapons and ammunition, and over seven kilometers of telephone wire in rolls. They moved all the captured materiel to shore, and then to their base. The detachment now had enemy guns and ammunition for use in operations behind German lines.[47]

In January 1942 a group of twenty-five men attempted to penetrate into the Nikel area, the site of an important mine and airfield, seventy kilometers behind the frontline and over fifty kilometers from the coast.[48] Golovko was not eager to permit an operation so far inland, but allowed it to go ahead only because the Army requested assistance. The mission was to determine how much ore was being extracted, and by what routes, means, and schedule it was being taken to Kirkenes for loading onto ships. The one-way distance to the objective area was over one hundred fifty kilometers on extremely difficult terrain, in the coldest month of winter. Accompanied by reindeer pulling sleds, the group departed Soviet lines on 4 January in temperatures below −30 degrees C (−22 degrees F). To avoid observation by German aircraft, they at first planned to move only at night. But the patrol leader soon discovered that the men could not lie still for long periods of time without suffering from frostbite, and so they moved during the day as well. It was during one of these daylight movements that a flight of German aircraft observed and strafed them, wounding ten men. The group was forced to return to base.

Also in January, another group from the detachment made an unobserved approach to a German position north of the Litsa River. Although the Soviets were numerically inferior to the German force, they had the element of surprise. Captain Inzartsev was unable, however, to convince the senior officer, a member of Vizgin's staff, to permit an attack or even an attempt to capture a prisoner. In the after-action review that followed, Admiral Golovko expressed strong displeasure with the planning and leadership of both. At his direction, younger and more experienced political officers were sought to accompany future patrols, and Vizgin's staff officer was reprimanded and prohibited from participation in subsequent missions.

In late January several unsuccessful attempts were made to insert two patrols along the coast between Petsamofjord and Kirkenes.[49] These groups contained both experienced and new personnel, some armed with German weapons. But they were unable to get ashore, being driven off either by high seas or alert German shore battery crews.

At the end of February 1942, nearly three months had passed since the detachment had taken a detailed inventory of German activity on the south shore of Motovskii Bay. On 3 March three small subchasers departed Poliarnyi, arriving in the landing area near Cape Pikshuev late that night.[50] One platoon went ashore to clear the immediate area, while the remainder of the force waited on the boats. When the lead platoon reached the rocky plateau above the landing site, it made contact with a German outpost of undetermined strength. The Soviet force quickly put the Germans to flight, while another platoon rushed from the boat to their aid. The Soviets quickly gathered up the documents from several German bodies, and took with them back to the boat a wounded German soldier, who soon died. Vizgin was himself present on one of the subchasers, and after consultation with the platoon leaders decided not to continue the operation. The element of surprise had been lost, and pursuit of the small German force could result in unnecessary casualties.

Another patrol of one to two platoons went to the same area on 13 March on two subchasers.[51] Sometime after midnight one group was put ashore south of Cape Pikshuev. Another dozen men were landed at Cape Mogil'nyi, to the west. A storm quickly obscured the entire area, preventing any kind of signal communications between the forces ashore and the boats. The leader of the smaller of the two forces, moving by dead reckoning in a blinding snowstorm, halted his men in what he believed would be a safe shelter. At dawn, however, with the storm subsided, the group found themselves in the middle of a German position that contained approximately ten shelters.

The Soviet scouts lay in the snow the entire day observing the activities of this heretofore unknown German position. German aircraft enroute to bomb the Rybachii Peninsula flew low overhead twice. German soldiers were constructing fortifications with rocks, apparently developing the position into a strongpoint. After dark, the naval scouts quietly moved back toward their landing site, pulling behind them on a makeshift sled one of their men who had suffered frostbite. After waiting some three hours, they were picked up. Unable to find the other patrol, at dawn the boat commander returned to base.

Several unsuccessful attempts were made over the next five days to extract the remaining patrol, some being turned back by stormy seas, and another by German shelling and strafing. Golovko ordered Vizgin personally to lead the search. On the sixth recovery sortie, late on the evening of 19 March, Vizgin with two boats and naval air support extracted the patrol. Five of the men were taken straight from the dock to the hospital with serious frostbite. The group had for six days contended with the weather, German ground troops, and periodic air searches. Their provisions ran out on 15 March, but they found a large codfish on the shore and ate it. Late on 18 March they observed a thirty-five-man German search party, and the next morning German artillery began to fire methodically into the area. German ground forces, supported by aircraft, were closing in on them from two directions. As they were about to be overrun, Soviet aircraft arrived on the scene and suppressed the German pursuers. The exhausted patrol was safely extracted.

The next major combat activity of the detachment was a landing in

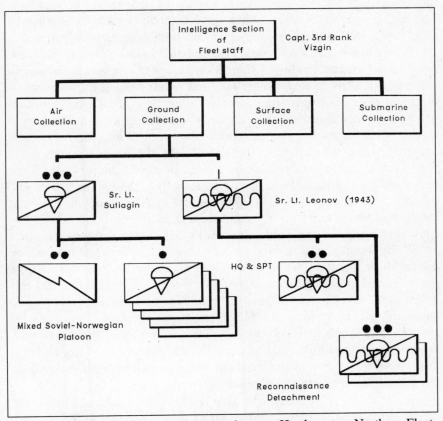

Figure 3. Organization for ground reconnaissance, Headquarters Northern Fleet, 1942–44.

support of the Soviet spring offensive, 28 April to 13 May 1942.[52] On 26 April, the reconnaissance detachment was subordinated to the commander, 12th Naval Infantry Brigade, to support his unit's landing on the German-held coast west of Cape Pikshuev. The mission of the detachment was to attack and seize a German outpost on Hill 415.3, and hold it until receipt of further orders.[53] Their landing was purposely timed to distract the attention of the German defenders for the main landing area of the larger brigade to the east. To Captain 2d Rank Inzartsev's regret, all the planning for this operation had been done in the headquarters of the naval infantry brigade without consultation with the reconnaissance detachment. The brigade communications officer gave Inzartsev an abbreviated list of code words to be used in communications with brigade headquarters.

Two platoons and a command group boarded small subchasers on the evening of 27 April, landing at Cape Mogil'nyi at midnight. German mortar fire greeted them at the shoreline, one round passing through one of the boats above the waterline. Soviet artillery from Rybachii Peninsula conducted counterfires, enabling the detachment to get ashore. They made contact with German troops as soon as they moved into the rocky hills above the shore. Attacking from opposite flanks, the Soviet platoons drove the German company-size force back, and occupied the position. They had already suffered casualties, and were behind their time schedule.

The Soviets continued to move southeastward, while the German infantry followed them on a parallel course. Fourteen hours later, they were within sight of their objective, Hill 415.3. Outmaneuvering another attack, the naval scouts arrived at their objective which was manned by a handful of Germans with a machine gun. They quickly occupied the position, and awaited further orders. The German company that had followed them invested the slopes of the hilltop, looking for some way to attack the Soviet position. The Germans set up three machine guns for support, and began to climb the hill. The scouts drove them back with their own rifle and machine-gun fire. The remainder of the day and that night were quiet. But in the morning, the size of the German force on the slopes below them had doubled.

To the east of this action, the 12th Naval Infantry Brigade had come ashore unopposed, having found an undefended approach to the German defensive positions. By the morning of 29 April, a naval infantry battalion was in position three to four kilometers southwest of the reconnaissance detachment, on a lower hill. Inzartsev could observe Germans encircling the naval infantry, but he was unable to contact either the battalion or brigade headquarters. The German force around his own position continued to grow, now reaching battalion strength. If the scouts were going to help the naval infantry battalion break encirclement, they would first have to break out themselves.

Meanwhile, the scouts began to suffer from the cold. Their boots and clothing were still wet from the landing, and the temperature hovered around freezing. There was no cover on the hilltop from the cold wind. The Germans continued to probe the Soviet defenses from all sides, seeking a way to the top. Twelve separate attacks were beaten back. For

another night Inzartsev and his men sat on the hilltop, still without communication with brigade headquarters. On 30 April he ordered his men
to conserve ammunition. A third night passed. Their water consumed, the
men began to eat snow, which fell intermittently. Between snow squalls,
the sun shone brightly, causing snow blindness.

On the fifth day, Inzartsev sent Viktor Leonov with two men to establish contact with the naval infantry battalion and seek their fire support
for an attempt to break through the German encirclement. The battalion
commander received permission from his brigade to send a rifle and a
mortar platoon over to Hill 415.3 to reinforce the scouts, but a breakout
maneuver was forbidden. With the help of these reinforcements, the
reconnaissance detachment held Hill 415.3 until 4 May, when they finally
were ordered to withdraw. Of the seventy men who landed ashore on 27
April, ten were healthy, two were dead, two were wounded, and the
remainder were suffering from frostbite and/or snow blindness.

In early summer 1942, the detachment conducted another patrol to the
Luostari airfield to observe German activity there and determine the
nature of its defenses.[54] The four-hundred-kilometer round trip was
figured to take three weeks. Each of the fifty men carried his own supplies,
and also common items such as extra ammunition discs, radios, and batteries. Five radio operators accompanied this patrol, far more than
normal.

The detachment walked for several days, crossed the Titovka and Petsamo rivers, photographed and noted locations of suitable fording sites.
When they finally arrived at an observation position near the airfield, they
drew sketches of it and took more photographs. Six days later the scouts
crossed back into Soviet positions where they reorganized for a brief
excursion to Lake Chapr. Part of the detachment took all the remaining
supplies for the new mission, and the remainder returned to base.

The patrol to Lake Chapr was brief, lasting three to four days. The
group found evidence of German patrolling activity, but no positions or
forces until they reached Hill 374 (Bolshoi Karikvaivash). There they
noted a German observation position of at least half a dozen men. This
patrol also returned safely.

Several changes greeted them. Their barracks had been bombed, and
several men killed or wounded. Lieutenant Colonel Dobrotin and Captain
Inzartsev were leaving for new assignments. Their new commander was
immediately unpopular with the men. A few scouts were taken to the naval
infantry, several men were transferred out due to their injuries or wounds,

and three others went away to attend short courses. Another wave of new volunteers arrived.

In September 1942 the detachment was once again subordinated to a naval infantry force for an operation.[55] Two platoons, fifty men in all, were to accompany two companies of naval infantry and a platoon of sappers from the Rybachii Peninsula to the south shore of Motovskii Bay, lead them to the German strongpoint at Cape Mogil'nyi, then return to shore. The mission did not appear difficult, and many of the scouts knew the terrain in that area well from earlier operations. At dawn the composite force was to return to Rybachii.

At midnight, as the boats carrying the reconnaissance detachment approached the shore west of Cape Pikshuev, machine-gun and mortar fire fell around them. The boat commanders returned fire and put the force ashore. A short distance away the naval infantry also disembarked. Coordination between the two forces was poor. Two hours after landing, with no orders from the naval infantry company commander, the reconnaissance detachment commander decided to press on to the objective. After an hour of marching they made contact with the captain commanding the naval infantry and one company, the other company having become lost.

Behind schedule, the naval infantry captain ordered the composite detachment to move forward, scouts leading, without an advance guard. At sunrise, they were still moving. The scouts separated from the main body again to attack the objective from another flank. As they approached the German strongpoint through a defile, the reconnaissance detachment fell under heavy machine-gun and mortar fire. Several men were wounded or pinned down in the first volleys, and the detachment was split into small groups. Part of the detachment moved back to shore, carrying their wounded commander, and other men reached the shore singly or in small groups. Led by Leonov, by skillful maneuver the remaining fifteen scouts consolidated and organized a defense, vainly waiting for help from the naval infantry. Soviet artillery from Rybachii Peninsula fired over four hundred shells, but none landed on the Germans. One of the scouts lost his nerve and blew himself up with a grenade. A German aircraft flew overhead, but the scouts did not fire at it.

At nightfall, Leonov prepared his group to break out. Leaving seven dead and carrying their wounded, they moved by rushes toward the shore, covering themselves with small arms fire and grenades. By dawn they reached the point where they had landed but found no boats. Falling snow obscured their view of the sea. Twice boats approached their position and then turned away. Finally two boats approached, one laid a smoke screen, and the other rushed in to extract the scouts. Other members of the detachment, pulled off the shore at other points, were already on board. The boats returned them to Poliarnyi.

At the ensuing after-action review by the Fleet military council, it was revealed that the naval infantry captain had led his unit in headlong flight to the shore as soon as the first shot was fired by the Germans. The military council delivered him over to a tribunal. A few days later, Admiral Nikolaev decorated several men of the reconnaissance detachment and at the same ceremony appointed Leonov a junior lieutenant.[56]

Raids on Varanger

In the spring of 1943, the reconnaissance detachment moved to the Solovetskii Islands in the White Sea to train for combat actions on the Varanger Peninsula.[57] The organizer and supervisor of this training was Lieutenant Sutiagin, the platoon leader of the mixed Norwegian-Soviet platoon. The recent infusion of many new personnel into the detachment necessitated training in landing operations in addition to instruction on the language, customs, and terrain of the new area of operations.

The first operation into Varanger was a futile effort to execute a night ambush on the coast road between Vardo and Vadso.[58] There was no vehicular or foot traffic, and the detachment returned to base empty-handed. Vizgin relieved the detachment commander and appointed Leonov, by this time the *zampolit*, as the new commander. He gave Leonov and Sutiagin three days to prepare for another landing. Together the two leaders planned a different approach to the task.

In a preliminary raid, Leonov and six men went ashore on the small island of Lille Ekkeroya, twenty kilometers east of Vadso, and captured the lighthouse operator.[59] Returning to base, Sutiagin interrogated him and learned the pattern of German traffic along the road. Several days later, about half the detachment returned to the peninsula and landed just after nightfall. Deployed along the road in three groups, they ambushed a column of German vehicles, destroying many by small arms fire and grenades. Three prisoners were captured and taken back to base.

Other successful raids into Varanger followed. In December 1943, the detachment landed near Cape Kvalneset, thirty kilometers southwest of Vardo.[60] They climbed up the steep coastal escarpment to the road above, and came out near a small cottage. Here they killed two German guards and captured six others who were inside drinking. Later interrogation of these Germans revealed information concerning an incident involving a Soviet submarine that had entered Batsfjord.

In February 1944 the detachment conducted a raid on a German shore battery guarding Batsfjord, located midway along the northern shore of Varanger Peninsula.[61] Although the plan was to land in Makkaursandfjord to the southeast and attack the German position from the rear, the patrol torpedo boat was turned back by the fire, and then signal-light interrogation of a German shore observation post. Leonov and Shabalin, the boat commander, agreed upon another approach, and turned the vessel to the west, toward Batsfjord. Ignoring the signals of the German observation post, the torpedo boat slipped quietly into the fjord and landed the detachment on a deserted shore, less than two kilometers from the small settlement of Batsfjord. Leonov divided his detachment into an assault group and a support group, and moved to the village to capture prisoners. Shabalin followed them with his boat, hugging the shoreline. The scouts returned to the waiting boat with two German sailors bound and gagged. Shabalin guided his torpedo boat out into the open sea, and by dawn returned the detachment with its prisoners to base.

Another similar raid was less successful. A group on two patrol torpedo boats approached a Norwegian fjord entrance during a storm, and made its way past the German light post by imitative deception.[62] When the two boats reached the landing site, Leonov and his main force moved to the shore in small boats without difficulty. The support group and communications cell on the other torpedo boat, however, did not organize themselves properly for a rapid landing. As a result, one of the assault team leaders was left on the shoreline with the radio operators, while the main force was executing the raid on the nearby small German garrison. The stranded team leader moved forward alone, seeking to rejoin his unit. The main force completed its mission, called the boats forward to pick them up, and the entire force departed the area. The team leader was lost, not only because he had sought to catch up to his men, but also because his absence was not reported prior to departure from the area.

Occasionally, a raiding force was not able to reach the objective area because of action at sea enroute. In one such occurrence, Shabalin with two patrol torpedo boats was delivering Leonov to the Varanger Peninsula.[63] They came upon a well-escorted German convoy, and in the ensuing sea battle one of Leonov's men was killed. Although the Germans lost two ships to Soviet torpedoes, the reconnaissance mission was scrubbed and Shabalin returned to the forward base at Pummanki.

In another similar incident, the detachment was returning from a successful raid on Varanger when it encountered a German convoy.[64] The smoke-discharging apparatus on the deck of one of the patrol torpedo boats was struck by a shell, igniting the device and threatening the safety of the boat. Two nearby scouts, risking their own lives, were able to tear the apparatus away from its mountings and push it overboard. One of the men later died as a result of the burns he received, and the other had to be transferred to the Black Sea Fleet, away from the cold northern climate. Despite these occasional setbacks, the detachment conducted several more raids along the Varanger coastline through the spring of 1944, each time returning with extra "passengers,"[65] and concluded major operations in the Far North with two strike operations in the October 1944 Petsamo-Kirkenes Operation.

Just two days after the Soviet capture of Kirkenes, Leonov's detachment conducted its final operation in Norway.[66] A reconnaissance party of ten men parachuted into the hills southwest of Vardo on the night of 27 October, but was scattered by strong winds. Radio contact with that group was immediately lost. On 29 October three survivors of the ill-fated jump reached Soviet-controlled ports by motorboat. On the night of 30 October, the remainder of Leonov's detachment went ashore at Cape Langbunes, twenty kilometers southwest of Vardo. They quickly established contact with the survivors of the parachute jump, and through conversations with civilians determined that the Germans had already fled the area. On the basis of this information, plans for a full-scale landing were cancelled. Leonov moved his group to Vardo by boat. Although the Germans had destroyed much of the port and its facilities, they also had abandoned large stocks of food and other materiel, including small arms. The detachment turned these supplies over to the Norwegians, and returned to their base at Poliarnyi on 2 November.

Analysis and Conclusions

As the German forces closed on the approaches to Murmansk in the latter half of 1941, the Soviet Northern Fleet was against the wall. The Fleet base was threatened, and there was no alternative base to move to. Apprehensive about the threat of a German amphibious operation around the northern flank that would turn the Soviet defense and lead to the fall of Murmansk, the Soviets discovered a serious gap in their intelligence collection capabilities. Out of dire necessity, the Fleet developed a naval commando force capable of intelligence collection and, as a follow-on, direct action to operational depths in the enemy rear.

The process was evolutionary, with tactical reconnaissance patrolling and clandestine agent operations providing the conceptual basis. The path was full of hard lessons, including those relating to political reliability and physical fitness of personnel, and the dangers of daylight movement in areas of high enemy air threat. The Soviets also tried to find a balance, in the use of this new capability, between collecting intelligence without making enemy contact and engaging in deliberate attacks to throw the enemy off balance and/or support conventional operations. The result, a reconnaissance detachment and a closely related agent platoon, was a special operations force. Analysis of several aspects of their organization, personnel, and combat operations establishes this force as an historical precursor of modern Soviet naval *spetsnaz*.

The name of the reconnaissance detachment is instructive: According to Makar A. Babikov, long-term veteran of the detachment, the Northern Fleet detachment's first official unit designation was 4th Special Volunteer Detachment of Sailors,[67] which in August 1941 changed to 4th Reconnaissance Detachment of Headquarters, Fleet,[68] and ultimately became the 181st Special Reconnaissance Detachment (*osobogo razvedyvatel'nogo otriada*).[69] In current Soviet sources, the organization is referred to by a number of descriptive titles: "Reconnaissance Detachment (Northern Fleet),"[70] "Reconnaissance Detachment of Naval Scouts,"[71] and "Special Purpose Reconnaissance Detachment of the Northern Fleet."[72] The most common elements in these titles are "reconnaissance," and "special purpose" (*osobogo naznacheniya*).

Evolution and subordination of the force provide other indicators: A compartmented force of clandestine agents and commandos, each with overlapping but not identical capabilities for reconnaissance and direct action, was directly subordinated to the intelligence department of the Fleet staff. The force had the full attention of the Fleet commander, Admiral Golovko, who was frequently personally involved in the day-to-day activities of the detachment. Leonov makes several references to personal meetings with Golovko to discuss operational issues. The detachment was also accompanied on many missions by senior staff officers, further emphasizing Command interest. On rare occasions, the reconnaissance detachment was placed under the operational control of a naval infantry unit, but this was only for specific missions and was not a habitual relationship. They always returned to control of the Fleet Headquarters, and were always barracked at the Fleet main base in Poliarnyi, not at the forward base at Pummanki (which was much closer to their area of operations).

Unusual selection, training and intelligence and security practices provide further indicators. Personnel selection stressed political reliability and physical fitness: Leonov, Babikov, and others repeatedly emphasize the high percentage of detachment personnel who were members of the Komsomol or Communist Party, many of whom had participated in underground operations. Both the larger detachment and the mixed Norwegian-Soviet platoon had political officers, whose principal responsibility was to foster and maintain loyalty of the men to the Soviet state, the Communist Party, and most immediately, to the unit and mission. The reconnaissance detachment political officer participated in all combat operations behind German lines. The experience of the joint operation with an Army reconnaissance unit, where a soldier deserted to the Germans near the objective area, reinforced the need for political screening and indoctrination.

Several members of the detachment were superior athletes in their sport, be it cross-country skiing, swimming, boxing, or martial arts. Vladimir Oliashev, for example, was a Champion of the Soviet Union and Merited Master of Sport in skiing.[73] Inzartsev, the physical training director of the Fleet submarine brigade and later commander of the detachment, was the Fleet weight-lifting champion in his class.[74] Ivan Lysenko, a radio operator, was a wrestling champion.[75] Ivan Guznenkov, the detachment political officer in 1944–45, was a competitive rock climber and martial arts fighter.[76] These and other examples illustrate that athletic prowess was an important selection criterion,[77] and gives credence to the belief that Soviet special operations forces recruit among superior (even Olympic-class) athletes.

Another distinctive feature is that the force was exceptionally versatile, and could be flexibly employed by the Fleet staff for rear area conventional and unconventional operations of great military, political and economic significance for which few other conventional forces were capable. Such operations included long-range dismounted patrolling, acquisition and surveillance of critical enemy installations, coast-watching, snatch and field interrogation of prisoners, and direct-action raids as directed by the Fleet staff.

Operational security was stringent, with operators often being briefed on the specifics of a mission only after reaching the immediate proximity of their objective. The reconnaissance detachment also had an unofficial credo that they would not surrender to the enemy alive, or return if they did not accomplish their mission: Some did in fact save their last bullet or grenade for themselves when capture was imminent.[78]

The force also had on-the-ground language capabilities for immediate exploitation of prisoners, documents, and, on at least one occasion, enemy telephone communications. Many of the Russians spoke German, and a few spoke Finnish or Norwegian. The employment of foreign nationals, however, is most significant in this regard: Norwegian communists fleeing the German occupation brought with them a knowledge of the terrain, locales, and customs that few Soviet citizens could possess.

On the conventional side were many of the small-scale reconnaissance and raid operations against German small unit positions and strongpoints along the left (coastal) flank of the German corps facing Murmansk and Poliarnyi. The detachment conducted some of these raids alone, and others in conjunction with naval infantry forces. All were directed toward the detection, disruption, or destruction of German tactical units.

The several attempts to reconnoiter the German airfield at Luostari, the unsuccessful effort to reach the mines at Nikel, and all the raids by the larger detachment along the Varanger Peninsula were unconventional operations. These penetrations went deep into the German corps rear area where the German combat support and logistic infrastructure lay. Luostari airfield was fifty kilometers from the coastline, but since its aircraft were used to bomb Northern Fleet bases, Admiral Golovko authorized its reconnaissance. The mines at Nikel were producing strategic ores for the German munitions factories. Though the attempt to reach this area with a ground reconnaissance element failed, the fact that it was considered a proper target is significant per se. In raids on Varanger, Leonov's men attacked vehicular convoys and isolated shore installations, captured prisoners and destroyed war materiel. Information gained by these frequent penetrations into Norwegian bases kept Golovko apprised of German capabilities for near-term major land and naval operations.

The mixed Soviet-Norwegian coast-watching platoon was used to conduct operational and strategic-depth reconnaissance. Early in the war, the Norwegian subtheater of operations was divided between the British Royal Navy and the Soviet Northern Fleet just to the west of Altafjord, a German naval and air forward operations base. The area north and west of Altafjord was the responsibility of the Northern Fleet, while the Royal Navy had everything south and west.

The Soviets conducted operations to the depth of their area of operations: Arnoy Island, north of Tromso where two Norwegians were put ashore in February 1942 without a radio operator, is about four hundred fifty kilometers straight-line distance from Poliarnyi (twice as far by sea) and almost on the border between the British and Soviet fleets. Information gained by observing German naval traffic along Norway's west coast was used by Golovko for his own Fleet's missions, and was also important to Royal Navy escorts of British and American convoys to Soviet northern ports. It is also likely that the activities of the mixed Soviet-Norwegian platoon were closely monitored by Soviet intelligence organs in Moscow.[79]

Infiltration, resupply, and extraction support for such missions were also out of the ordinary, utilizing submarines, float planes, bombers, parachutes, a variety of small surface ships, motor vehicles, reindeer sleds, skis and feet. In terms of frequency, fast boats (generally torpedo boats but occasionally other small coastal craft) were probably used most often. Leonov's detachment developed a close association with two boat commanders in particular, Senior Lieutenant B. M. Liakh, who commanded a small subchaser (MO-423), and Captain Lieutenant A. O. Shabalin, who commanded a patrol torpedo boat detachment. Some of Leonov's men also jumped into Varanger in October 1944, and one of the three-man teams jumped there in the spring of 1944. Submarines were used, in particular, in conjunction with the three-man teams in Norway: In the course of the war, Soviet submarines alone made fifty insertions of special reconnaissance teams. Thirty-nine of these were conducted in the Far North, mostly in Norwegian territory.[80]

The true measure of the impact of these operations on contemporary Soviet special operations doctrine and force structure, however, may rest with the post-war careers of the key personnel, and the writings they have left in their wake. Twice Hero of the Soviet Union Viktor N. Leonov attended Kirov Caspian Naval School in 1950, and in 1956 was an instructor at the Voroshilov Naval Academy. He retired from active service in July 1956, just before his fortieth birthday. Leonov is known to have played a role in the establishment of Soviet ground forces' *spetsnaz* in the early 1960s.[81] As of this writing, he is seventy-three years old and still living in Moscow.

Hero of the Soviet Union Makar A. Babikov left active service in

1946, and returned to his native Komi region. There he was secretary of a city Party Committee, and then deputy to a member of the autonomous republic's Council of Ministers. After serving in state security, Babikov worked for a time in the bureaucracy of the Central Committee of the Communist Party, and subsequently for the Council of Ministers of RSFSR. His photograph recently appeared in *Morskoi sbornik* (Naval Proceedings), on the occasion of a veterans' conference.[82] Of the other officers, it is known only that in the mid–1950s, Lieutenant Colonel (Ret.) Dobrotin was out of the Navy and living in Moscow, while Inzartsev still served in the Northern Fleet.[83]

Between them, Leonov and Babikov have written about 1,100 pages of memoirs which are freely exploitable by anyone in the West who reads Russian. Much more information in the form of unit records, after-action reports, classified studies, oral histories, and debriefings have likely been used by Soviet analysts to develop contemporary special operations theoretical, doctrinal, and organizational models. Some of these data are accessible to Western analysts, and much more will become available as *glasnost* progresses. Given the direct correlation between past, present and future capabilities, these are invaluable keys to unlocking the questions about Soviet naval *spetsnaz*.

Notes

1. Major portions of this chapter are derived from James F. Gebhardt, "Soviet Naval Special Operations Forces Origins and Operations In World War II," *Journal of Soviet Military Studies*, Vol. 2, No. 4, September 1989, and are used with permission.

2. Robert C. Suggs, "Soviet Subs in Scandinavia: 1930 to 1945," *Proceedings*, March 1986, 100–106.

3. Allen F. Chew, *The White Death* (East Lansing, MI: Michigan State University Press, 1971): 13–14; P. H. Vigor, *Soviet Blitzkrieg Theory* (New York: St. Martin's Press, 1983): 55.

4. John J. Dziak, *Chekisty: A History of the KGB* (Lexington, MA: Lexington Books, 1988): 115.

5. The best description of German operations in this theater throughout the entire war is in Department of the Army Pamphlet 20–271, *The German Northern Theater of Operations* 1940–1945, by Earl F. Ziemke (Washington DC: U.S. Government Printing Office, 1959).

6. Golovko's meeting with Vizgin is described in Makar A. Babikov, *Letom sorok pervogo* (The summer of '41) (Moscow: "Sovetskaia Rossiia," 1980): 67–68, and Vizgin's meeting with his subordinates on 69–70.

7. Babikov, 69. Vizgin is mentioned in a recent article as one of the "leaders and chiefs of intelligence organs" in the Soviet Navy during World War II. See Iu. Kviatkovskii, "Bespokoinaia vakhta razvedki VMF" (Troubled Watch of Naval Intelligence), *Morskoi sbornik* (Naval Proceedings), 10/1988, 13–14.

8. Babikov, 110.

9. Ibid., 111.

10. Babikov, *Otriad osobogo naznacheniya* (Special Purpose Detachment) (Moscow: "Sovetskaia Rossiia," 1986): 135–147.

11. Babikov, *Letom*, 199. According to Babikov, the rank "Intendant" was frequently given to accomplished athletes. Historically, however, holders of this rank generally served in rear support elements. Leonov briefly describes Inzartsev in *Litsom k litsu* (Face to Face) (Moscow: Voyenizdat, 1957): 15.

12. Leonov describes his recruitment in *Litsom*, 4–5.

13. Leonov mentions her in *Litsom*, 21; see also Babikov, *Letom*, 204.

14. Babikov, *Letom*, 200.

15. This mission is described in Babikov, *Letom*, 186–194 and Leonov, 10–14. A German document dated July 24, 1941 briefly mentions this raid, fixing the date of the actual attack as July 22. See *Kriegstagebuch* (War Diary) Nr. 1, AOK 20 (Headquarters, 20th German Army), "Aktennotiz" (Memorandum), microfilm series T-312, roll 1647, frame 001173, National Archives and Records Administration (NARA), Washington DC.

16. The actual raid is described in Babikov, *Letom*, chapter 22, and Leonov, 22–27.

17. Babikov, *Letom*, 219–223.

18. Leonov, already an experienced skier, spent some time at the ski base while recovering from his wounds. Leonov, 32–33. According to Babikov, Leonov was responsible at this time for procurement of the detachment's special winter clothing. Babikov, *Letom*, 253.

19. Babikov mentions parachute training in connection with the Norwegians who were being prepared for coast-watching duty in Norway. Babikov, *Otriad*, 105. As for the personnel of the larger reconnaissance detachment, Leonov clearly indicates that day and night parachute jumping was part of the regular training regime. Leonov, *Gotov'sia k podvigu* (Prepare for An Heroic Deed) (Moscow: Izdatel'stvo DOSAAF, 1985): 25–26.

20. Babikov, *Letom*, 254–74. This action is recorded in German records as follows: "Yesterday evening a deserter appeared south of Luostari Airfield, who declared himself to be a member of a reconnaissance and partisan detachment which was advancing south of Luostari Airfield, and had the mission to attack the airfield and destroy everything." KTB Nr. 1, AOK 20, "Fernspruch Gebirgs Korps Norwegen" (Telephone Message Mountain Corps Norway) Ic 1.9.1941 1745 hours, microfilm series T–312, roll 1013, frame 9209088, NARA. Based on this incident, and the interrogation of the deserter, a reconnaissance detachment was added to Soviet order of battle by German intelligence analysts: "Aufklarungs Abteilung: (Partisanen-Abt.) Gesamtstarke etwa 300 Mann, davon etwa 200 Matrosen." [Reconnaissance Detachment: (Partisan det.) total strength about 300 men, of which approximately 200 are sailors.] KTB 1, AOK 20, "Vermutliche Feindkrafte vor Gesamtraum des A.O.K. Norwegen Stand 5.9.1941" (Probable Enemy Strength in the Operating Area of AOK Norway as of 5.9.1941), microfilm series T–312, roll 1013, frame 9207906, NARA.

21. DA Pamphlet 20–271, chapter 8, contains a good account of this period in English. For a Soviet perspective, see Nikolai M. Rumiantsev, "Oboronitel' nye deistviia 14-i armii v Zapoliar'e v 1941 godu (Defensive Operations of the 14th Army in the Transpolar in 1941)," *Voenno-istoricheskii zhurnal*, 12/1980, 21–33, and Rumiantsev, *Razgrom vraga v Zapoliar'e (1941–1944 gg.)* [Defeat of the Enemy in the Transpolar] (Moscow: Voyenizdat, 1963): chapter 3.

22. Babikov, *Letom*, 305.

23. Babikov, *Otriad*, 6.

24. The account of this operation begins in Babikov, *Otriad*, chapter 5, and concludes in chapter 8.

25. Ibid., 37.

26. Ibid., 32. Babikov makes a veiled reference to "colleagues in Murmansk," implying that another organization besides the Northern Fleet had an interest in this operation. On page 58, Babikov indicates that the planned landing of a follow-on force was cancelled.

27. Ibid., 102.

28. Paul Einar Vatne, *Jeg Var Russisk Spion—Historien om Selmer Nilsen* (I Was a Russian Spy—The Story of Selmer Nilsen) (Oslo: H. Aschenhoug & Co., 1981): 28–29; letter from Robert C. Suggs, March 30, 1989.

29. At least one of the radio operators was involved in an operation with the larger reconnaissance detachment in November, 1941, suggesting some personnel mobility between the two elements. The designation of a platoon commander, a deputy commander for political affairs, a separate communications staff and facility, and the distinct nature of their mission led these authors to conclude that by January 1942 this platoon was not a subset of the larger reconnaissance detachment, but a separate element under the fleet staff intelligence section. A German intelligence assessment from February 1943 supports this analysis. The document describes the "Kundschafter (und Ablenkungs-) Abteilung der Nordmeerflotte" [Intelligence (and Diversionary) Detachment of the Northern Fleet] as containing two separate elements, one for operations in rear areas, the other only for operations in Norway. This document also correctly identifies Vizgin as the chief of the intelligence section of the Fleet and Dobrotin as his deputy. Anlage 3, "Bandentatigkeit und Organisation vor (Geb.) A.O.K. 20" (Band Activities and Organization in Front of 20th Mountain Army), to A.O.K. 20 Nr. 810/43, dated 22.2.1943, microfilm series T–312, roll 1649, frames 001328–29, NARA.

30. Babikov, *Otriad*, 104. According to Babikov, Krymova was a language and area specialist who had lived in Sweden and Norway before the war. She was fluent in all the Scandinavian languages, plus English, French, and German. Leonov, *Litsom*, 82, indicates that Sutiagin also spoke Norwegian.

31. Babikov, *Otriad*, 103–05.

32. Ibid., chapter 25.

33. Ibid., chapter 28.

34. The account of this incident concludes in Babikov, *Otriad*, chapter 21, with no definitive statement of the fate of these men.

35. Ibid., beginning in chapter 18 and concluding in chapter 21.

36. Ibid., chapter 21.

37. Ibid., 171.

38. A German document dated September 27, 1942 notes that two Russian agents with a transmitter were inserted by submarine north of Tromso and subsequently captured. See "Befehl fur den Schutz von Wehrwirtschaftsbetrieben" (Order for the Defense of Military-Industrial Facilities), Annex 1, microfilm series T–312, roll 1648, frame 000903, NARA. Another document, dated

November 19, 1943, describes the mixed Soviet-Norwegian platoon and their activities. It names Capt. 2d Rank Vizgin, as well as several of the Norwegian Communists who belonged to the group. See KTB 2, AOK 20, "Sowjetrussische Spionagetatigkeit im Varanger-Raum" (Soviet-Russian Espionage Activity in the Varanger Area), microfilm series T–312, roll 1651, frames 000682–89, NARA.

39. Babikov, *Morskie razvedchiki* (Naval Scouts) (Syktyvkar: Komi knizhnoe izdatel'stvo, 1966), 12–14. According to Leonov, this team was inserted by parachute and extracted by patrol torpedo boat. See Leonov, *Gotov'sia*, 17–19.

40. Babikov, *Otriad*, chapter 9. Leonov, *Gotov'sia*, 84–88, indicates that this mission was conducted on the night of November 6–7, with a naval infantry reconnaissance company.

41. Several German documents describe this raid, and establish the time of the attack as 0200 hours October 25. See KTB 1, AOK 20, morning reports, evening reports, and teletype messages, series T–312, microfilm roll 1013, frames 9208536–38, 9208836, 9208852, -54, -57, and 59–60, NARA.

42. Babikov, *Otriad*, 83.

43. Ibid., chapter 11.

44. Ibid., 84.

45. Ibid., chapter 12.

46. Ibid., chapter 13.

47. According to a German report, "Russian reconnaissance troops have been repeatedly identified in German uniforms and with German weapons . . . In one action on the Litsa Front, the enemy took the uniforms off of German prisoners and casualties for the purpose of equipping partisans (*banden*)." See Annex 5 to Activity Report for November 1942, "Feindnachrichtenblatt" (Enemy Information Report) Nr. 24, 14 November 1942, microfilm series T–312, roll 1649, frame 000201, NARA.

48. Babikov, *Otriad*, chapter 16.

49. Ibid., chapter 17.

50. Ibid., chapter 19.

51. Ibid., chapter 20.

52. Ibid., chapter 22. A detailed description of this offensive from the Soviet perspective is contained in Rumiantsev, *Razgrom vraga*, chapter 3; and from the German perspective in DA Pamphlet 20–271, 223–28.

53. DA Pamphlet 20–271, map 19, shows the axis of the 12th Naval Infantry Brigade but not the reconnaissance detachment. A better map can be found in Rumiantsev, *Razgrom vraga*, 69. Babikov discusses this action in *Otriad*, chapter 22, and Leonov in *Litsom*, 36–48.

54. Babikov, *Otriad*, chapter 23.

55. Ibid., chapter 24; id., *Morskie*, 14–16; Leonov, *Litsom*, 60–74.

56. Leonov describes this ceremony in *Litsom*, 75–77.

57. Ibid., 82. Leonov does not identify the location, but Babikov does in *Na vostochnom beregu* (On the Eastern Shore) (Moscow: "Sovetskaia Rossiia," 1969): 7. The historical record of the detachment between October 1942 and October 1944 is not well defined. Both Leonov and Babikov wrote about this period, but with less specificity as to dates and locations of combat actions.

58. Neither Leonov nor Babikov indicates when the detachment returned from the training base in the White Sea to their deployment base in Poliarnyi. Leonov discusses these initial operations in *Litsom*, beginning on 82, and in *Gotov'sia*, 57–58.

59. For the German account of this raid, see "Fernschreiben" (Teleprinter) 1.1.1944, microfilm series T-312, roll 1650, frame 000462, NARA. According to the German report, the lighthouse operator was abducted on December 15, and the road ambush was executed against four Luftwaffe vehicles on December 21, 1943.

60. Leonov, *Litsom*, beginning on 87.

61. Ibid., beginning on 90.

62. Id., *Gotov'sia*, 53–55.

63. Ibid., 68–70.

64. Babikov, *Morskie*, 17–18.

65. Leonov, *Litsom*, 94.

66. See ibid., 128–31; id., "Vperedsmotriashchie," 174–78; and Babikov, *Morskie*, 20–40.

67. Babikov, *Morskie*, 4; in Russian *4–i Osobyi dobrovol'cheskii otriad moriakov*.

68. Babikov, *Letom*, 251.

69. I. A. Kozlov and V. S. Shlomin, *Krasnoznamennyi severnyi flot* (Red Banner Northern Fleet) (Moscow: Voyenizdat, 1983): 272.

70. *Geroi sovetskogo soiuza: kratkii biograficheskii slovar'*, 27, entry for S. M. Agafonov.

71. Ibid., 862, entry for V. N. Leonov.

72. In Russian: *razvedotriad osobogo naznacheniya Severnogo flota*, in V. Sadovskii, "Komandir 'chernykh d'iavolov'" (Commander of the 'Black Devils'), *Sovetskii voin* (Soviet Soldier), 3/1985, 36–37.

73. Leonov, *Gotov'sia*, 46; Merited Master of Sport in Russian: *zasluzhennyi master sporta*.

74. Leonov, *Litsom*, 15.

75. Ibid., 79.

76. Ibid., 102.

77. The recruitment of athletes was also important for special operations units of Soviet ground forces during World War II. See F. L. Kurlat and L. A. Studnikov, "Brigada osobogo naznacheniya" (Special Purpose Brigade), *Voprosy istorii* (Questions of History), September 1982, 95–104; and S. Kh. Aganov,

ed., *Inzhenernye voiska sovetskoi armii 1918–1945* (Engineer Troops of the Soviet Army 1918–1945) (Moscow: Voyenizdat, 1985): 459–63, a section that discusses engineer units employed for special operations behind German lines.

78. Leonov, *Gotov'sia*, 36 and 71; id., *Lotsom*, 39 and 68.
79. However, a careful search of the British official history, Capt. S. W. Roskill, *The War At Sea* 1939–1945 (London: Her Majesty's Stationary Office, 1954 and 1956), vols. I and II, does not reveal any sharing of intelligence data.
80. Suggs, "Soviet Subs," 102.
81. Interview with a former Soviet soldier, summer 1987.
82. A. Danilin, "Ne stareiut dyshoi veterany" (The Veterans Are Not Aging in Spirit), *Morskoi sbornik* (Naval Proceedings), 5/1988, 16–18.
83. Leonov, *Litsom*, 150.

CHAPTER 7

The Arctic: Petsamo-Kirkenes, 7 to 30 October 1944

James F. Gebhardt

A typical example of Soviet employment of special purpose forces during World War II is found in the Petsamo-Kirkenes Operation. On 7 October 1944, a Soviet combined arms force of nearly one hundred thousand men launched an offensive against the fifty-seven thousand German troops of XIX Mountain Corps, who were defending prepared positions on Soviet territory northwest of Murmansk. The battlefield was in an obscure sector of the Eastern Front that had seen only local and long-range reconnaissance activities, small-unit actions to achieve local objectives,[1] and one failed Soviet counteroffensive (spring 1942) since the German offensive to seize Murmansk was blunted in October 1941. Despite its limited scope when compared to larger operations on the main front in Eastern Europe, the Soviets nonetheless consider this battle to be one of the ten strategic blows struck against the Germans in 1944. This chapter outlines the use of ground and naval special purpose forces in this battle as described from Soviet sources and corroborated in several aspects by German war diary reports.

The Area of Operations

During World War II, the Murmansk-Kirkenes region had strategic importance to both the Germans and the Soviets. During the three years of the German occupation, from late 1941 to late 1944, German mining engineers and forced laborers extracted ten thousand tons of high-grade nickel ore annually from the mine at Nikel for their armaments industry.[2] The German navy also used the airfields and harbors of northern Norway to interdict and harass Allied convoys carrying Lend-Lease materiel from the United States and Great Britain to Murmansk and Arkhangelsk. The area was important to the Soviets in that the base of the Northern Fleet was located at Poliarnyi, just north of Murmansk, and Murmansk itself was a vital receiving port for war materiel.

The Petsamo-Kirkenes battleground lies on the southern shore of the Barents Sea, between sixty-nine and seventy degrees north latitude, about two hundred miles north of the Arctic Circle. The climate in October is cold and moist, with prevailing winds blown inland from the unfrozen Barents Sea and a normal temperature range of between plus and minus five degrees centigrade. The weather in October is characterized by frequent precipitation as snow or as a mixture of rain and snow, and frequent heavy fog. At this time of year, the sun traverses a low arc across the southern sky, and hours of daylight decrease from 13.5 on 1 October to 10 on 30 October.

Along the coast, the terrain is primarily tundra interspersed with hills of barren rock covered with moss and lichen. Farther inland, steep rock-strewn hills rise to elevations of up to 1,900 feet above sea level. Hundreds of streams flow into scores of swamps and lakes which are drained by northeast-flowing rivers. There are numerous ravines and gullies throughout the region. Vegetation is mostly scrub trees and low bushes. Few trees in the area are thicker than a man's forearm, or taller than twenty-five feet. In October, all deciduous trees are leafless. The ground is not frozen, and cannot support vehicular traffic except on roads. The road net in 1944 was poorly developed, and roads were the focus of combat actions by Soviet special purpose and conventional forces during the battle.

Enemy Dispositions

In October 1944, forces of the German XIX Mountain Corps, commanded by Gen. Ferdinand Jodl, were deployed in three defensive belts. The first belt extended eastward along the Barents Sea coastline, across the Isthmus of Srednyi Peninsula, along the shore of Motovskii Bay to the mouth of the Western Litsa River, then west-southwest to Lake Chapr, and from there across Hill 373 to Hill 237.1. This belt was manned by Divisional Group Van der Hoop in the north, 6th Mountain Division in the center, and 2d Mountain Division in the south. Its density varied according to the terrains from four to six kilometers deep, with fifteen to twenty permanent fortifications per linear kilometer of front. These bunkers were organized into company strongpoints which in turn made up battalion centers of resistance. All strongpoints had trench systems, engineer-prepared minefields, obstacles and barbed-wire, overhead cover bunkers, and provisions of food, water, and ammunition. They were sited for 360-degree observation and fire.[3] General Jodl did not have adequate forces at his disposal to construct a continuous line.

Direct and indirect fire, engineer obstacles, minefields, and patrols with dogs covered the low ground between these company strongpoints and battalion centers of resistance. At night and during periods of limited visibility, guard posts were also used. These sectors between strongpoints

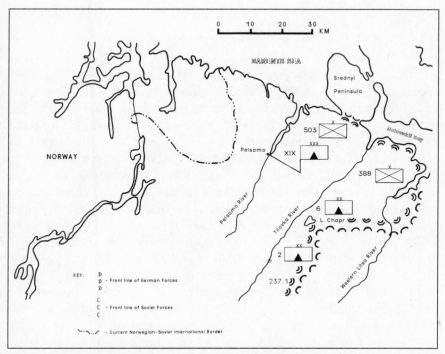

Figure 1. Enemy dispositions at the outset of operations.

varied in width to as much as two to four kilometers, and constituted a major weakness in the first defensive belt.

The second defensive belt lay along the Titovka River, ten to twenty kilometers behind the first belt, and consisted of separate strongpoints and centers of resistance covering approaches to the river. The rear defensive belt lay twenty to twenty-five kilometers farther west along the Petsamo River. Its strongest positions guarded the approaches to Petsamo and Luostari. Additional defensive positions were prepared to guard the approaches to the settlements at Kolosjoki (Nikel), Akhamalakhti, and Kirkenes, the latter being a supply base of the 20th Mountain Army and the principal port in the region. The German right flank positions, south of the Lake Chapr region to Hill 237.1, trailed off into terrain which the Germans considered unsuitable for military operations, even of a limited nature. The nearest German troop positions were some 250 kilometers to the south. The mission of XIX Mountain Corps was to defend in sector until excess supplies stockpiled at Petsamo, Kirkenes and other locations were removed, and then to conduct an orderly withdrawal.

The Plan

The plan prepared by Army General Kirill A. Meretskov, the Karelian Front commander, and approved by Stavka in late September,[4] was straightforward. The 14th Army was to attack with the main effort on the left against the 2d Mountain Division, in the sector from Lake Chapr south to Hill 237.1. The mission of the forces on this axis was to defeat the 2d Mountain Division and seize the Petsamo-Luostari area by frontal attack. To their left, the 126th and 127th Light Rifle Corps would conduct an envelopment of the German right flank in two echelons. Their mission was to lodge themselves on the road junction west of Luostari, to prevent retreat and reinforcement. To the right of the main attack, from Lake Chapr to the north and east, against the German 6th Mountain Division, Soviet forces would continue to defend in an economy of force role. On the Soviet far right, naval infantry forces would attack across the Srednyi Isthmus and along the coastline west of it, with the mission to envelop the German left flank, cutting their path of retreat and reinforcement.

On the main axis, the attacking force was arranged in two echelons, with two rifle corps of five divisions, a light rifle corps of two brigades, tank and artillery units in the first echelon. The second echelon consisted

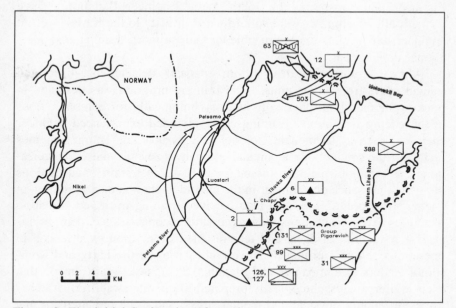

Figure 2. The initial Soviet plan of attack.

of one rifle corps of two divisions, and one light rifle corps of two brigades. The economy of force mission on the Soviet right flank was to be executed by one rifle division, one rifle brigade, and one fortified zone.[5] The Northern Fleet commander would employ one naval infantry brigade to attack across the Srednyi Isthmus, and another naval infantry brigade in amphibious assault to the west of the isthmus. On 6 October, the attack was set to commence at 1035 hours 7 October, to be preceded by an artillery barrage lasting two hours and thirty-five minutes.

Ground Forces Spetsnaz Employment

In July 1944 the Front Commander, General Meretskov, ordered preparation of several *spetsnaz* detachments from an assault combat engineer brigade for operations deep in the German rear.[6] The men came from various engineer units, including the 6th Separate Guards Battalion of *Miners* (OGBM), the 64th and 222d Motorized Assault Combat

Engineer battalions, and the 168th Army Engineer Battalion.[7] Once formed, all detachments were subordinated directly to the Karelian Front engineer staff, which was responsible for their support, training, and operational deployment.

After selection and designation, *spetsnaz* detachments lived and trained apart from other units.[8] The training program was designed to prepare the men both physically and psychologically for combat actions in the enemy rear area.[9] Training cadre included experienced engineer *spetsnaz*, such as Lieutenant Colonel D. S. Krutskikh. Training themes included "the conduct of platoon and company-size ambushes," "organization of a battalion march in mountain and swamp terrain," and "actions of a reconnaissance detachment in the encirclement and destruction of an enemy strongpoint." The men also received training in the coordination of actions between sub-units, how to conduct reconnaissance, demolitions against roads and bridges, and terrain orientation. Men experienced in operations behind German lines were chosen to be the Party and Komsomol leaders in companies and platoons. Their task was to insure that each soldier was psychologically prepared to operate away from friendly forces, to endure physical and mental stress, and to be prepared for any sacrifice in order to accomplish the mission. Physical conditioning emphasized heavy load carrying and hand-to-hand combat skills. All training exercises attempted to foster teamwork and comradeship among the soldiers. In early September, Meretskov met with his Chief of Engineer Troops, General Khrenov, and approved a plan for the utilization of *spetsnaz* detachments in support of the 14th Army's offensive.[10]

The plan called for the insertion of three detachments into the German rear area before the launching of the offensive. The detachments had several missions. They were to reconnoiter the route of the follow-on light rifle corps, conduct uninterrupted reconnaissance of the enemy and terrain, and gain control over the road net. Upon initiation of the offensive, *spetsnaz* troops would assist the main attack by disrupting enemy command, control, and communications, destroying men and equipment, mining roads, and demolishing bridges. General Khrenov personally approved the combat operations plan of each detachment.[11]

The first detachment to deploy was the 6th Separate Guards Battalion of *Miners*, minus one company, commanded by Guards Major A. F. Popov.[12] Most of the 133 men carried submachine guns, with four basic loads (600 rounds) of ammunition, and hand grenades. The detachment additionally carried three light machine guns, three sniper rifles with 600 rounds for each, explosives and fuses, 130 antitank mines, ten delayed action mines, two radios with two supplies of batteries for each, flare guns, medical supplies, and individual rations for seventeen days. The average equipment load of soldiers in the detachment was forty-two kilograms (ninety-two pounds).

The Popov detachment departed their assembly area behind the Soviet left flank at 1400 hours on 18 September, and began the long walk around the German right flank. Major Popov used a reinforced platoon for his advance guard, a squad per company for flank guards, and a platoon for rear guard. He and his command group marched at the front of the main body. Communication between companies was maintained by runners and light signals, within companies and platoons by voice and flags. The formation moved at a speed of two kilometers per hour over the extremely difficult terrain, halting for ten minutes each hour to rest. Until they reached the Titovka River, the men moved during the day and rested at night.

On the fourth day, at 1300 hours on 21 September, the detachment crossed the Titovka River. Moving now at night to avoid detection, Popov and his men waded across the icy cold, chest-deep, fifty-meters-wide Petsamo River. On the night of 23–24 September, they reached the Luostari-Nikel Road, along which flowed a steady stream of German traffic. At 0400 hours on 24 September, the detachment crossed this dangerous obstacle in a rapid rush, and moved quickly away to the north. Popov led his men to a small stream in a wooded area near the Norwegian border, arriving on the morning of 25 September. He reported their arrival to Front headquarters.

From this position, Major Popov's men conducted reconnaissance patrols as far out as twenty-five kilometers, principally to the Petsamo-Tarnet Road, the Luostari-Nikel Road, and the Luostari-Akhamalakhti Road. His men studied traffic patterns, and selected targets and ambush sites for subsequent combat operations. In the base camp, strict noise and light discipline was enforced. Not long after arrival, Major Popov cut rations in half to conserve them. The frequent rain and snow showers kept the men wet and cold, leading also to concern about their health.

While the Popov detachment executed its reconnaissance mission, the remaining company of the 6th Guards Battalion of *Miners* departed its assembly area on 2 October and moved toward its objective area northeast of Nikel. Led by Major Popov's deputy, Captain A. P. Kononenko, the forty-nine-man detachment reached its operating base on the night of 7–8 October, and established communications with the battalion main force.

A third detachment, 108 men of the 222d Motorized Assault Combat Engineer Battalion, commanded by Major G. A. Gradov, also departed its assembly area on 2 October, and on 6 October reached its objective area in the rear of the 2d Mountain Division, between Luostari and the Titovka River. This detachment, which comprised five platoons, deployed along Lanweg and the road between Petsamo and Titovka (Russian Road).

Several hours before the attack on 7 October, all three *spetsnaz* detachments received orders by radio to begin combat operations. A platoon of Major Gradov's 222d Battalion struck the first blow. A German regimental after-action report contains an entry describing an attack on an outpost at 1900 hours on 6 October, fourteen kilometers east of Luostari on Lanweg. [13]

Major Popov's detachment also went into action quickly. His first priority was to destroy the wire communications between the German rear area and front line units, to force enemy units to use the radio, and under the intense pressure of combat use clear text. His second priority was to destroy bridges on all three roads controlled by his battalion. During the night of 6–7 October, Popov's detachment went out in three groups, one

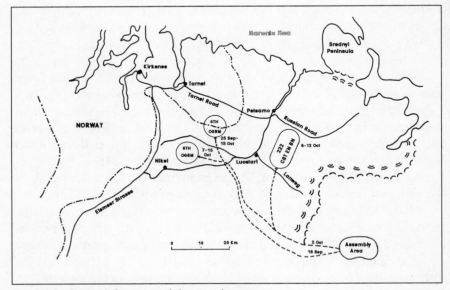

Figure 3. Ground force special operations map.

to each road, and destroyed communications wire, blew up bridges, and planted mines. After all three groups returned to base by dawn on 7 October, Major Popov reported to Front headquarters, then moved his base camp several kilometers to the west.

The weather and terrain were extracting a heavy toll on Popov's men. Forty of them were so weakened by exhaustion, hunger, and cold that they could no longer fight. Popov sent them back toward Soviet lines under the charge of a Captain Vasil'ev. The remaining ninety-plus men continued their nightly raids. The 20th Army morning report for 8 October states that a sabotage group blew up the bridge at Kilometer 28 of Tarnet Road, destroying one truck. The same document reports damage to a bridge and destruction of several powerline poles at Kilometer 486 of the Arctic Ocean Highway (this location is west of Luostari, before the road fork).[14]

Captain Kononenko's men made their first raid on the night of 7–8 October, along the road several kilometers east of Nikel. In this attack his troops took out several hundred meters of telephone line, and planted mines which later destroyed two German fuel trucks. By 10 October, the 20th Army knew the general location of Major Popov's battalion, as well as its identification. A war diary document reports "employment of a 150–200-man element with a sabotage mission in the area between the Eismeer Strasse (Arctic Ocean Highway) and the Tarnet-Kirkenes Road." This group, according to the report, did succeed in disrupting traffic along the main supply routes in the area. The document later specifically identifies one sabotage group as an element of the "6th Independent Guards Detachment (Sabotage)."[15]

Major Gradov and his five platoons of the 222d Battalion continued to attack isolated German units and positions in front of the advancing 99th and 131st Rifle corps, rejoining the main force on 12 October, the day Luostari was captured. According to one Soviet source, Gradov's men conducted six separate attacks, destroyed 3,600 meters of telephone line, blew up two bridges, and killed over 150 German soldiers while suffering only three lightly wounded.[16]

Major Popov's 6th Separate Guards Battalion of *Miners* continued their operations against German columns, mostly now in retreat. On the night of 11 October, a low-flying aircraft (probably a Po–2 night bomber) delivered urgently needed supplies of food, ammunition, and warm clothing to his men. Additional deliveries followed on the next three nights. As the encirclement of the German right flank and the capture of Luostari on 12 October began to force the Germans to withdraw into Norway toward Tarnet, Popov increased his attacks against that road. His men were able to stop traffic at numerous defiles and streams with mines and demolitions, and on more than one occasion they directed air strikes against concentrations of German units. In his report of 5 November 1944, General Jodl wrote that on 13 October the 6th Mountain Division had to deploy combat elements against the Soviet 6th Guards Special Engineer Detachment, which had occupied a sector of road.[17]

After a final successful attack along Tarnet road, in which his troops expended all remaining ammunition, on 15 October Major Popov led his entire force back into Soviet positions, which were by then west of Petsamo-Luostari Road. In eight days of active combat, Popov's battalion destroyed more than eleven kilometers of telephone wire, four bridges, and large amounts of German equipment and troops. His battalion's losses were only four wounded and two missing in action.[18]

In analyzing the employment of *spetsnaz* units by the Karelian Front, several important points emerge. The first is that the use of sabotage troops behind German lines was nothing new or extraordinary. Soviet troops had been conducting raids and reconnaissance in German rear areas since the first weeks of the war back in 1941. By mid-1944 the war in the German rear area was a well-oiled machine which played a significant role in all major Soviet Offensive operations. This employment of *spetsnaz* detachments differed from all the rest in three significant aspects, however. The weather and terrain were much more severe, the terrain provided much less cover and concealment, and there was no indigenous population to provide logistic, intelligence, or partisan support.

Concerning the forces designated and trained for this specific operation, the 6th Separate Guards *Miners* Battalion, the 222d Motorized Assault Combat Engineer Battalion, and others, their combat experience in special operations prior to autumn 1944 is unknown. That they were engineer-based units is, however, significant. They were primarily trained to strike enemy troops and installations. Engineer troops were more likely to have the individual and collective skills necessary for demolitions work, as well as the equipment. Ordinary engineer units could provide a plentiful supply of trained manpower for selection into special purpose units. Reconnaissance skills were important, but mainly for acquiring targets for immediate destruction. These units reported to the Front Chief of Engineer Troops, not the intelligence staff.

Several aspects of the deployment plan deserve attention. The method of insertion—walking—although slow, was probably the most secure, and it served the additional purpose of reconnoitering a route for an important follow-on force, the 126th Light Rifle Corps. The selection of an operating base adjacent to Norwegian territory, and continuous reconnaissance and combat activities on Norwegian territory *prior to* 18 October, when Meretskov received permission to send conventional forces across the border into Norway, indicates that military requirements for special operations took precedence over political sensitivities. It cannot be determined from available sources if Karelian Front had to gain approval from Stavka to deploy *spetsnaz* forces onto Norwegian territory.

Disregarding the time required for the deepest penetrating detachment to reach its position (Major Popov's group), the Soviet *spetsnaz* force was functioning forty to fifty kilometers deep in German-occupied territory for twelve days before the main offensive. Although the Soviet troops moved about only at night and hid during the day, they reported their actions to Front headquarters by regular radio transmissions, two per day before 7 October, and every two hours thereafter. To avoid German detection for such a long period of time, in terrain known for lack of cover, says as much for Soviet camouflage and movement security as for poor German rear area security. To be willing to place one hundred thirty-three men so deep behind enemy lines almost two weeks before an offensive speaks volumes about the Front headquarter's confidence in their military skills and, just as important for *spetsnaz* soldiers, their political reliability.

Finally, in terms of space, the *spetsnaz* detachments operated in a broad zone, extending from regimental rear to corps rear, from eight to fifty kilometers behind the front line. Their reconnaissance and combat activities were directed more at communications and transportation facilities and targets than at combat forces. If they came upon an unsecured artillery battery, though, the *spetsnaz* units did not hesitate to attack. They also, on a few occasions, occupied a piece of key terrain, and then repulsed a German unit which sought use of the same terrain without first conducting reconnaissance.

The *spetsnaz* were effective. In terms of their mission, they did reconnoiter the route for 126th Light Rifle Corps and conduct continuous reconnaissance of the enemy and terrain. Their control of the road net was never total, but certainly adequate. There is not sufficient evidence in German war diary documents to validate or refute the claims made in Soviet sources of quantities of German troops, equipment, and installations destroyed, but that reports of *spetsnaz* actions appear at all in 20th Army records testifies to the concern of the German command for this unanticipated and unwelcome battle in their rear area.

The two Soviet commanders gave high praise to the *spetsnaz* units in their memoirs. Colonel General of Engineer Troops Khrenov wrote the following in 1982:

> Of course, these forms of struggle behind the front line did not determine the success of the offensive. But I have considered it my duty to write about the sapper scouts, in order to more fully expose this little known type of activity of engineer troops, which demanded special moral-combat qualities, and permitted the inflicting on the enemy of great losses with small forces.[19]

Marshal Meretskov expressed similar thoughts in his 1983 memoir:

> From these detachments was gained valuable information which kept the command informed of changes which were occurring in the enemy's defenses. In addition, the sappers controlled the roads, blew up bridges and destroyed telephone lines, causing disorder in the work of German rear services. Finally, on more than one occasion they directed our close air and bomber aviation to concentrations of enemy troops.[20]

Naval Special Operations

During the planning for Northern Fleet support to the ground offensive of 14th Army, naval headquarters in Moscow ordered Admiral Golovko to reestablish a Soviet naval base at Petsamo.[21] Pursuant to this order, Golovko's staff began to plan an amphibious landing at Linakhamari, the small port that lay north of Petsamo on the west shore of Petsamo Bay. Entrance to Petsamo Bay was controlled by a battery of four German 150mm guns, which were positioned on the northern shore of Cape Krestovyi. These guns had to be neutralized in order for the main landing force to succeed.

To accomplish this task the fleet assembled a composite force of sailors and naval infantrymen consisting of the reconnaissance detachment of the Northern Defensive Region, commanded by Captain I. P. Barchenko-Emel'ianov, and the reconnaissance detachment of Headquarters, Northern

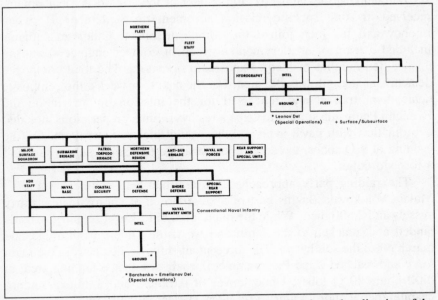

Figure 4. Organization of the Soviet Northern Fleet, showing subordination of the Leonov and Barchenko-Emel'ianov detachments.

Fleet, commanded by Sr. Lt. Viktor N. Leonov. Barchenko-Emel'ianov was an experienced naval infantryman, who had served in reconnaissance units of the 12th Naval Infantry Brigade in the Murmansk area since November 1941. In June 1943 he took command of the Northern Defensive Region reconnaissance detachment, a collection of naval infantrymen who were veteran scouts of many reconnaissance and raid actions against German units and positions along the coast of occupied Finnish and Soviet territory.[22]

Leonov, on the other hand, and most of his detachment were sailors, volunteers from the several surface and submarine units of the Northern Fleet. The detachment had a distinguished combat record dating back to its creation in July 1941 by Admiral Golovko, having participated in many operations behind German lines, on Soviet, Finnish, and Norwegian territory. Leonov, himself a veteran of submarine service, came to the detachment in the late summer of 1941. Courage and leadership displayed in battle earned him promotion to officer rank in late 1942, and to command of the detachment in late 1943.

Barchenko-Emel'ianov, as commander of the composite detachment, received his first specific mission statement on September 11, when Leonov and his men joined the composite unit.[23] Other attachments included a team of artillerymen, a group of combat engineers, and an unspecified number of medics and radio operators. The total composite detachment strength was 195 men. For the next four weeks, the composite detachment trained and rehearsed for the mission on terrain on the Rybachii Peninsula similar to Cape Krestovyi. Final preparations included coordination with naval aviators who would later support them. On the evening of 9 October, the detachment boarded two small subchasers and a torpedo cutter.

The raiding party approached the German-held southern shore of Malaia Volokovaia Bay as part of a larger force of approximately thirty vessels and 2,800 men. While the main force 63rd Naval Infantry Brigade landed and attacked to the south and west, the raiders would land and march off to the southwest. The three small ships broke off from the main force and reached Cape Punainenniemi, their designated landing area, at 0100 hours 10 October. Under cover of darkness and a smoke screen, despite enemy shore battery fire aided by searchlights, the detachments got ashore with no casualties and the loss of one of five radios. Once established ashore, they reported their status to fleet headquarters and began their cross-country march.

The terrain in this region is sparsely vegetated, rocky, mountainous, and interspersed with streams and lakes. Elevations of over 1,000 feet are found two to three kilometers inland from the Barents Sea. On 10 October, 1944, the temperature hovered around freezing, with a strong wind blowing from the sea. The group moved inland that night in a snowstorm which turned to rain in the morning. The men removed their white camouflage smocks in order to blend in with the grey-brown surroundings.

All day on 10 October the men hid in rock caves and only moved again at dusk. At daybreak, 11 October, Capt. Barchenko-Emel'ianov hid his men in a growth of bushes at the southern end of Lake Sisajarvi. In eighteen hours, they had marched over fifteen kilometers. After a rest period, at twilight they continued to move. By nightfall they reached a spur on Petsamo Bay, from which they could view the silhouette of their target, Cape Krestovyi. Beyond the cape they could see the port of Linakhamari across the bay. The men were standing at the top of a vertical cliff from which their descent took six hours.

The plan for the assault on the objective was simple. Leonov's group

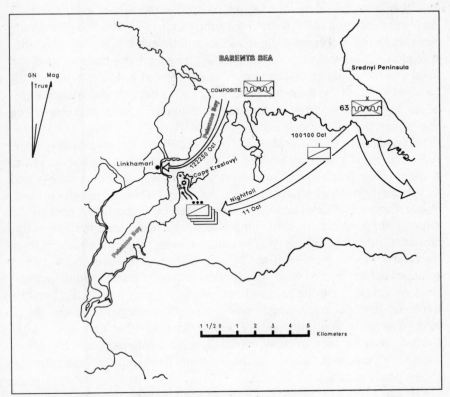

Figure 5. Naval *osnaz* plan of attack.

of ninety-five men would assault the battery of four 88mm antiaircraft guns sited on a gentle slope on the southern portion of the cape. The attached artillerymen went with this group. Barchenko-Emel'ianov ordered two of his own platoons to attack and seize the strongpoint located 300 meters north of the flak battery. This position, in the center of the cape, guarded the landward approaches to the 150mm coastal battery. His remaining platoon would storm this four-gun battery which was located at the water's edge on the northernmost shore of the cape.

After a brief leaders' orientation, which included an oral order, the three elements moved off in the darkness to await the signal for the start of the attack. It is unclear whether the signal rocket that triggered the attack was fired by the attackers or by the startled German defenders.[24]

In either case, the element of surprise was on the Soviet side. Leonov's men were crawling in the barbed wire forty to fifty meters from the 88mm guns when the rocket went up. It was soon followed by German-fired illumination. Leonov and his men quickly breached the barbed wire and assaulted the bunkers, and in hand-to-hand combat killed or drove off the crews and seized the four-gun battery. Leonov's detachment spent the rest of the night fending off numerous German counterattacks, and employing the captured guns against enemy bunkers.

The platoons of Lieutenants Kubarev and Pivovarov also quickly overwhelmed the German defenders in the strongpoint. German survivors from both the flak battery and strongpoint positions withdrew singly and in groups northward along the cape into the 150mm battery positions. While Barchenko-Emel'ianov was establishing his command post in the strongpoint position, his remaining platoon was assaulting the now fully-alerted 150mm shore battery position. Attempts to take the battery from the landward side were repulsed by well dug-in Germans in bunkers and trenches behind barbed wire. The Soviets sent an element around the west flank to attack along the rocky shore, but this group was driven back by the incoming tide. According to one source, the besieged Germans began to destroy their own guns, while Leonov contends that these guns were firing against his men in support of a German counterattack.[25] Unable to capture or destroy the guns, Barchenko-Emel'ianov reported the situation to his headquarters.

At dawn on 12 October, the Germans remaining on the cape regrouped and launched a counterattack. According to German war diary entries, as well as Soviet sources, these counterattacks were supported by German troops sent across the harbor in assault boats.[26] All available German indirect fire support assets were also directed against the Soviet raiders, causing serious casualties. Outnumbered and unable to hold the flak battery positions, Leonov withdrew his men to a nearby hill. The artillerymen removed and took with them the breech blocks of the 88mm guns.

As the counterattacking Germans were approaching the strongpoint position where Barchenko-Emel'ianov and his detachment were holding out, on-call Soviet aviation assets came in and restored the situation. According to the account of Admiral Golovko, his pilots delivered ten air-strikes and dropped several parachute containers of ammunition and provisions in the course of four hours.[27] Soviet ground artillery from Srednyi

Peninsula conducted counterbattery fire throughout the day, helping to defeat several German counterattacks.

By midday 12 October, the Soviet positions in the center of the cape were secure enough that Barchenko-Emel'ianov gave Leonov one platoon plus two squads to bolster his position overlooking the flak battery. With these reinforcements, Leonov and his men counterattacked. By dusk they had retaken the position and the adjacent shore, depriving the Germans of the ability to reinforce on that flank.[28] Some isolated groups of Germans were captured, while others found their way northward to the shore battery position. By nightfall the area was quiet, except for an occasional outburst of gunfire.

At about 2000 hours, Barchenko-Emel'ianov was informed by radio that an amphibious landing force would assault the Linakhamari harbor in three hours. The landing was carried out between 2250 and 2400 hours, 12 October. Approximately six hundred men landed in three waves from eight torpedo cutters and six subchasers.[29] By all accounts, this landing force was detected, illuminated, and fired upon by several German shore batteries. The key battery on Cape Krestovyi did not engage the amphibious landing force, either because of the destruction of the guns or the preoccupation of the crews with Barchenko-Emel'ianov's assaults. All Soviet accounts credit the actions of the raiders for the subsequent success of the landings in the harbor.

During the night of 12–13 October, the raiders were reinforced by a company from the 63rd Naval Infantry Brigade, which had participated in the landing on the night of 9–10 October. These men came in overland from the east. An additional platoon came ashore from a disabled cutter. Before dawn on 13 October, Barchenko-Emel'ianov selected a German officer from among his prisoners and sent him into the shore battery position with a surrender ultimatum. After some delay, the garrison of seventy-eight officers and men surrendered.

The day of 13 October was spent looking after the prisoners and captured equipment. That night the entire detachment was taken across the bay into Linakhamari to assist in mopping up operations which were completed by midday on 14 October. In three days of battle for Krestovyi and Linakhamari, the detachments of Senior Lieutenant Leonov and Captain Barchenko-Emel'ianov lost fifty-three men killed and wounded, or 27 percent of their 195-man force. Barchenko-Emel'ianov, Leonov, and two enlisted men were awarded the gold star and title of Hero of the Soviet Union.

Conclusion

The naval special operation in some ways resembled the ground force's *spetsnaz* operation. The raid on Cape Krestovyi was not the first, but rather the last in a long list of attacks on German installations behind the front line. Concerning the two detachments that combined to execute the raid, by far the most is known about Leonov and his men. But both organizations had extensive combat experience, and this raid fell well within the repertoire of their individual and collective skills.

The insertion of the force onto enemy shores was cleverly masked by the much larger brigade-sized landing to the east. Once ashore, the composite detachment walked the extremely difficult route to the objective area. Although physically demanding and time consuming, it was the only way to reach the target and maintain the advantage of surprise. The naval special operations also employed close air support, both for combat and logistic support.

There were differences in the two operations, as well. From start to finish, the naval special operation lasted only four to five days, compared to the *spetsnaz* operation of twenty-nine days. The chain of command for the naval special operation was not as direct. Leonov was subordinated to Barchenko-Emel'ianov, who reported to the commander of Northern Defensive Region, Maj. Gen. E. T. Dubovtsev. Dubovtsev's immediate superior was Admiral Golovko, commander of the Northern Fleet. The naval special operation was a surgical strike without preliminary, or supplementary, reconnaissance functions.

Taken together, these two examples show a high level of maturity and specialization in Soviet planning, training, organization, and execution of special operations in the later stages of World War II. The Petsamo-Kirkenes Operation was a Soviet success. By the end of October 1944, Soviet troops had cleared all German forces in the area from Soviet territory, and were occupying defensive positions twenty kilometers west of the major Norwegian port of the region, Kirkenes. Lieutenant Colonel Krutskikh and many of his men, and Senior Lieutenant Leonov and over forty of his men, were transferred to the Far East in the late spring of 1945, where in August of that year they conducted special operations against the Japanese forces in Manchuria, discussed at length in Chapter 8.

Notes

1. See Department of the Army Pamphlet 20-269, *Small Unit Actions During the German Campaign in Russia* (Washington DC: U.S. Government Printing Office, 1953), chapter 4, for a sampling of German actions.

2. Waldemar Erfurth, *The Last Finnish War (1941–1944)*, MS # C-073, Historical Division European Command, Foreign Military Studies Branch, 1952. Published in German under the title *Der Finnische Krieg, 1941–1944* (Wiesbaden/Munich: Limes-Verlag, 1977).

3. Information in this section pertaining to German initial defensive positions is from Nikolai M. Rumiantsev, *Razgrom vraga v zapoliar'e* (The Defeat of the Enemy in the Transpolar) (Moscow: Voyenizdat, 1963): 129–137; 2d Mountain Division defensive dispositions are discussed in detail in that unit's war diary records. See KTB 1, 2nd Mountain Division, Folder 77563 (Combat Reports, Attack of the Russians Against the German Defense Line), microfilm series T-315, roll 109, NARA.

4. The document was published in "Osvobvozhdenie sovetskogo Zapoliar'ia" (Liberation of the Soviet Polar Region), compiled by I. V. Iaroshenko and L. I. Smirnova, *Voenno-istoricheskii zhurnal* (Military Historical Journal) (*VIZh*) 6/1985, 33–34.

5. The Russian term is *ukreplennyi raion*, and has two meanings in Soviet military parlance. The applicable definition in this case is "a TO&E troop formation, which is designated for the fulfillment of a defensive mission." Such a formation routinely consisted of several artillery battalions, and units of support and service. See, *Sovetskaia Voennaia Entsiklopediia* 8 (Moscow: Voyenizdat, 1980): 185.

6. K.A. Meretskov, *Na sluzhbe narodu* (In Service to the People) (Moscow: Voyenizdat, 1983), 376. He briefly mentions these detachments, calling them "not simple scouts, but detachments of sappers." Their designation as *spetsnaz* units comes from Maj. Gen. D. S. Krutskikh in "Udary po tylam" (Strikes in the Rear Area), in the book *Eto byla na krainem severe* (It Was In the Far North), (Murmansk: Knizhno Izatdatel'stvo, 1965): 203. Krutskikh was an engineer lieutenant colonel in the Karelian Front engineer staff in 1944, responsible for training the detachments. G. Emel'ianov calls them "detachments of sappers-demolitions men" in "V glubokom tylu vraga" (In the Deep Enemy Rear Area), *VIZh*, October 1974, 55–59. A. F. Khrenov, who in 1944 was Karelian Front Chief of Engineer Troops and Krutskikh's superior, uses the label "sappers of reconnaissance-diversionary detachments" in his memoir, *Mosty k pobedy* (Bridges to Victory) (Moscow: Voyenizdat, 1982): 318.

7. Krutskikh, "Udari po tylam," 203. The 6th Guards Battalion of *Miners* was an extraordinary engineer unit. According to a recently published history of Soviet engineer troops, each Front had such a battalion by October 1942. See S. Kh. Aganov, ed., *Inzhenernye voiska Sovetskoi Armii 1918–1945* (Engineer Troops of the Soviet Army, 1918–1945) (Moscow: Voyenizdat, 1985): 459–63. According to this source, all guards *miners* battalions were specially trained and equipped for reconnaissance and diversionary actions in German rear areas. The Soviets were not alone in using combat engineers as special purpose forces. The first British commandos, organized to raid the Atlantic coast after the German conquest of mainland Europe, were also from combat engineer units.

8. Khrenov, *Mosty k pobede*, 319.

9. Emel'ianov, "V glubokom tylu," 55.

10. Khrenov, *Mosty k pobede*, 317.

11. Ibid., 320.

12. The detailed descriptions which follow came from Krutskikh, "Udary po tylam"; Emel'ianov, "V glubokom tylu"; and Khrenov, *Mosty k pobede*, 319–337. Beginning on 320, Khrenov quotes from written recollections of Guards Major A. F. Popov, who commanded the 6th Separate Guards Battalion of *Miners* in the operation.

13. 2d Mountain Division, KTB 1, "Gebirgsjagerregiment 137, Gefechtsbericht uber die Kampfhandlungen am 7.u.8.10.44 im Abschnitt Isar" (Mountain Rifle Regiment 137, Action Report on the Defensive Battle on 7 and 8 October 1944 in the Isar Sector), microfilm series T-315, roll 109, frame 1089, NARA.

14. KTB 5, 20th Army, Anlage 4, Morning Report, to the entry of 8 October 1944, microfilm series T-312, roll 1063, NARA.

15. KTB 5, 20th Army, Anlage 1, Daily Report, to the entry of 10 October 1944, microfilm series T-312, roll 1063, NARA.

16. Krutskikh, "Udary po tylam," 206.

17. General Ferdinand Jodl, "Kursbericht uber die Kampfhandlungen im Petsamo und Varangerraum" (A Short Report Regarding the Combat Actions in Petsamo and Varanger Area), dated 5 November 1944, microfilm series T-312, roll 1069, item 75034/1, NARA.

18. Emel'ianov, "V glubokom tylu," 59.

19. Khrenov, *Mosty k pobede*, 324.

20. Meretskov, *Na sluzhbe*, 376.

21. A. G. Golovko, *Vmeste s flotom* (Together With the Fleet) (Moscow: Voyenizdat, 1979), 227; N. G. Kuznetsov, *Kursom k pobede* (The Course to Victory) (Moscow: Voyenizdat, 1976), 423.

22. Barchenko-Emel'ianov finished a brief memoir shortly before his death in January 1984, *Frontovye budnyi rybach'ego* (Days at the Front on the Rybachii Peninsula) (Murmansk: Knizhnoe Izdatel'stvo, 1984).

23. Three eyewitness accounts have been used to reconstruct the events of the raid: Barchenko-Emel'ianov, *Frontovye*, 138–54; Leonov, *Litsom*, 106–26, and "Vperedsmotriashchie" (The Lookouts), a chapter in *Cherez fiordy* (Through the Fjords), compiled by V. G. Korshunov (Moscow: Voyenizdat, 1969): 157–78; and A. N. Sintsov, who was an officer in Barchenko-Emel'ianov's detachment, "Shturm krestovogo" (The Storming of Krestovyi), a chapter in *Eto bylo na krainem severe* (It Was in the Far North), edited by S. K. Chirkova (Murmansk: Knizhnoe Izdatel'stvo, 1965): 215–21.

24. Leonov, "Vperedsmotriashchie," 172; Sintsov, "Shturm," 219.

25. Leonov, "Vperedsmotriashchie," 173; Sintsov, "Shturm," 219.

26. KTB 5, AOK 20, Anlage 2, Daily Report, to the entry of 12 October 1944, microfilm series T-312, roll 1063, frame 9265168, NARA. See also, Leonov, "Vperedsmotriashchie," 174; Sintsov, "Shturm," 220; and Barchenko-Emel'ianov, *Frontovye*, 146.

27. Golovko, *Vmeste*, 235. See also, I. G. Inozemtsev, "Sovetskaia aviatsiia v Petsamo-Kirkenesskoi operatsii" (Soviet Aviation in the Petsamo-Kirkenes Operation), *Istoriia SSSR*, No. 2, 1975, 107; and P. I. Khokhlov, *Nad tremia moriami* (Over Three Seas) (Leningrad: Lenizdat, 1988): 223.

28. Barchenko-Emel'ianov, *Frontovyi*, 147, provides the most details on this point; Leonov, "Vperedsmotriashchie," 174, gives the time of the counterattack as dawn on October 13.

29. Golovko, *Vmeste*, 236; Admiral V. I. Platanov, "Pravoflangovye" (The Men on the Right Flank), *Cherez fiordy*, 106; Admiral of the Fleet G. Egorov, "Severnyi flot v Petsamo Kirkeneskoi operatsii" (Northern Fleet in the Petsamo-Kirkenes Operation), *VIZh*, 10/1974, 23. German war diary entries corroborate the fact that at night on October 12 an enemy force under cover of fog and low visibility made a surprise landing in the harbor at Linakhamari, and occupied the port and city. See, KTB 5, AOK 20, Anlage 4, Morning Report, to the entry of 13 October 1944, microfilm series T-312, roll 1063, frame 9265184, NARA.

CHAPTER 8
Manchuria, 1945

William H. Burgess III
James F. Gebhardt

The Manchurian Campaign of August 1945 was the last great Soviet offensive of World War II. In eleven days of often fierce combat, Soviet combined arms forces conquered an area of approximately 1.5 million square kilometers, an area roughly equivalent in size to the state of Alaska.[1]

The area of operations[2] for the campaign was bordered on the east and north by the Soviet Maritime Territory and the Soviet provinces of Khabarovsk and Chita, on the west by Outer Mongolia and the Chinese provinces of Inner Mongolia and Jehol, and on the south by the Bay of Liaotong, the Kuantung Pantao Peninsula, and Korea. At the time of the offensive, a well-developed regional road and rail network connected the major industrial cities of Mukden (Shenyang), Changchun (Ch'angch'un), Harbin (Haerphin) and Tsitsihar (Ch'ich'ihaerh). Cultivated areas predominated in the central valley.

The Soviets fought the Japanese Kwantung Army in numerous border incidents in the years preceding the Soviet invasion, most notably at Lake Khasan in 1938 and Khalkhin-Gol (Nomonhan) in 1939.[3] Tensions were eased somewhat by the Soviet-Japanese Neutrality Pact of April 1941, though the Soviets maintained a force of approximately 1.3 million men, including forty to sixty rifle division equivalents, on the Manchurian border from December 1941 to May 1945.[4]

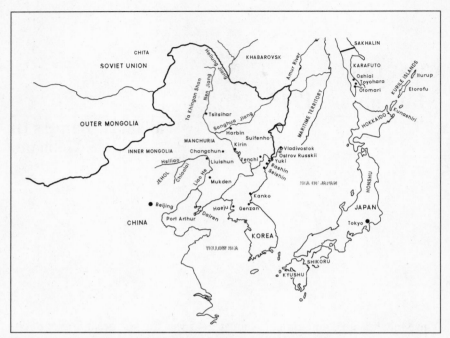

Figure 1. Area of operations of the Manchurian Campaign.

As long as Germany was undefeated, Stalin refused to declare war on Japan.[5] At the February 1945 Yalta Conference, however, Stalin promised that the Soviet Union would assist the Allies in the war against Japan within three months of Germany's surrender.[6] Stalin conditioned the promise on the successful conclusion of a treaty with China, as Soviet troops would operate on Japanese-occupied Chinese territory, and sought Western recognition of Soviet territorial claims in the Kurile Islands, the southern half of Sakhalin Island, and the old Russian bases at Port Arthur (Lüshun or Ryojun) and Dairen (Dalian). In April 1945, preparations for the Far East campaign began in earnest, the Red Army General Staff estimating the campaign would take two to three months. The Soviets planned to launch their campaign in late summer–early autumn to clear the Japanese from Manchuria before winter set in, but their hand was forced on 6 August when the United States dropped an atomic bomb on Hiroshima.[7] On 9 August, the Soviets crossed the Manchurian frontier.

The Soviets employed a variety of special operations (not all involving *spetsnaz*) to support their campaign and, after Japanese capitulation, to consolidate their conquest.[8] Soviet forces conducted approximately twenty airlanding assaults and as many amphibious landings in the Manchurian campaign. Based on information carefully gleaned from open sources, some can be accurately categorized as special operations. This chapter presents detailed and documented evidence of several such operations. Some occurred during the first week of the offensive, and were important to its success. Others were conducted after 19 August, and served to hasten the surrender of already defeated forces. All were important to overall success of the Soviet offensive at the operational and strategic levels.

Strategic Setting

Preparations[9] for the invasion were actually begun the previous autumn, though formal planning did not begin until February 1945.[10] From December 1944 to the end of March 1945, the Soviets sent 410 million rounds of small-arms ammunition and 3.2 million artillery shells to the Far East. From April 1945 until 25 July 1945, the Soviets shipped two fronts, two field armies, one tank army, and associated war materiel 10,000 miles from Europe to the Far East via the Trans-Siberian Railroad in 136,000 rail cars and as many as thirty trains a day. During the period of strategic redeployment, the Soviets regrouped two front and four army command and control systems, fifteen headquarters of rifle, artillery, tank and mechanized corps, thirty-six rifle, artillery and antiaircraft artillery divisions, fifty-three brigades of basic types of ground forces, and two fortified regions, altogether comprising thirty division equivalents.[11]

This redeployment and regrouping was under conditions of great secrecy and deception.[12] Key personnel traveled in disguise and many units moved only at night (staying camouflaged during the day) on their approach march to the Far East. Soviet troops on the frontier built extensive defensive works in an effort to deceive the Japanese into believing that Soviet reinforcements sent to the area were intended to man these fortifications. Regrouping of forces into the 1st Far Eastern Front, the 2d Far Eastern Front and the Transbaikal Front occurred in May to July 1945.[13] On 30 July, the Soviets created the Far East Command under Marshal of the Soviet Union Aleksandr Mikhailovich Vasilevskii.[14]

By August, the Far East Command had just under 1.6 million personnel (1.06 million combat and .5 million rear services), 27,000 guns and
mortars, 1,200 multiple rocket launchers, 5,600 tanks and self-propelled
guns, 3,700 aircraft, and 86,000 vehicles along a 5,000-km frontage. All
forces were tailored down to battalion level for specific tasks.[15] At 1700
hours 8 August (2300 Tokyo time), Soviet foreign minister Vyacheslav M.
Molotov told the Japanese Ambassador in Moscow that a state of war
existed between the two countries.[16] Seventy minutes later, at ten minutes past midnight, Soviet forces crossed the Manchurian frontier.

Enemy Dispositions

The Kwantung Army of August 1945, commanded by Gen. Yamata
Otozo and headquartered at Changchun, was organized into two area
armies (army groups) and a separate combined army. It was supported
by one air army and the Sungari Naval Flotilla. Including forces in Korea,
the Soviets estimated in August 1945 that the Kwantung Army comprised
thirty-one infantry divisions, nine infantry brigades, two tank brigades and
one special purpose brigade. These forces had an aggregate 1,155 tanks,
5,360 guns, and 1,800 aircraft. The army of the puppet state of Manchukuo had an additional eight infantry divisions and seven cavalry divisions with fourteen brigades. The Japanese also had three infantry divisions and one infantry brigade on southern Sakhalin Island. The strength
of the Japanese in Manchuria, Korea, southern Sakhalin Island and the
Kurile Islands numbered about 1.2 million, of whom about 1 million were
Japanese.[17]

The Kwantung Army at the time of the Soviet attack was a shell of
its former self.[18] Although it occupied good defensive terrain and maintained many strongly fortified zones, its better troops had long before been
transferred to other theaters. Only six of its divisions had existed prior
to January 1945. Its troops were generally of low quality and lacked significant quantities of automatic weapons, antiarmor weapons and artillery.
The Japanese 37mm antitank gun was ineffective against Soviet T–34
tanks. Japanese tanks had only 57mm guns and less armor than their
Soviet counterparts. The Japanese considered none of the Kwantung divisions to be combat ready, and considered some divisions to be only 15
percent ready.[19]

When the offensive began, the Soviets had a favorable effective strength ratio over the Japanese of approximately 2.2:1 in personnel, 4.8:1 in tanks and artillery, and 2:1 in aviation assets (which increased to total air superiority when the Japanese ordered its air force out of Manchuria at the outbreak of fighting).[20] Moreover, the Japanese failed to assess the Soviet threat correctly, did not believe that the Soviets would be able to attack before September 1945, and were in the process of a strategic reorientation of their forces when the blow fell.

The Soviet concept of the offensive was a strategic double envelopment conducted on three axes simultaneously, with the objectives of securing Manchuria and destroying the Kwantung Army.[21] The Transbaikal Front, based in Chita and commanded by Marshal Rodion Yakovlevich Malinovsky (formerly commander of the 2d Ukrainian Front), would attack eastward into western Manchuria, delivering its main blow across a four-hundred-kilometer sector. The 1st Far Eastern Front, based in Khabarovsk and under the command of Marshal Kirill Afsans'evich Meretskov (formerly commander of the Karelian Front) would attack westward into eastern Manchuria. The two attacks would converge in the Mukden-Changchun-Harbin-Kirin area. The 2d Far Eastern Front, based in Vladivostok and commanded by General M. A. Purkayev, would conduct a supporting attack into northern Manchuria toward Harbin and Changchun. On-order operations were also planned against southern Sakhalin Island and the Kuriles. The Pacific Fleet under Admiral I. S. Yumashev was ordered to undertake operations against Korean ports and to assist the ground forces on Sakhalin Island and the Kurile Islands.[22]

Special Operations in Support of the Offensive

The first special operation of the Manchurian offensive was the seizure of three key railroad tunnels in the early morning hours of 9 August by elements of the 1st Far Eastern Front on the eve of that Front's thrust into eastern Manchuria.[23] The heavily defended tunnels were one to three kilometers from the Soviet border on the avenue of advance of the 5th Army, with no possibility of bypass. The action was assigned to two detachments of the 20th "Svirsk" Motorized Assault Combat Engineer Brigade.

The 20th Brigade came to the 1st Far Eastern Front from the Karelian Front, where in October 1944 it provided *spetsnaz* detachments for the Petsamo-Kirkenes Operation. The detachments for the tunnel operation

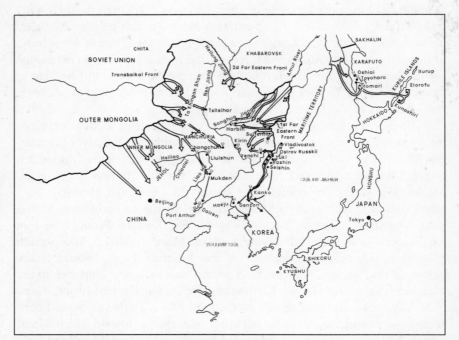

Figure 2. The Manchurian Campaign. From V. I Achksov, ed., *Istoriia vtoroi mirovoy voiny* 1939–1945 (History of the Second World War) (Moscow: Voyenizdat, 1980) 256–257.

were deliberately taken from the 20th Brigade because the men in the brigade "were not sappers in the ordinary sense of the word—they were prepared to conduct all types of combat in the most difficult and unusual situations, and to destroy complex engineer obstacles at the front or in the enemy rear."[24]

Each detachment comprised an assault battalion, a company of flame throwers, two platoons of submachine gunners, and a group of artillery observers. These detachments also had the support of an armored train and two battalions from the artillery brigade in Front reserve. Major V. I. Gurin commanded one detachment and Major Iu. Ia. Iankevich commanded the other. Prior to the operation, both commanders trained their detachments against Soviet tunnels on similar terrain. *Razvedchik*[25] Lt. Col. D. A. Krutskikh, the same engineer officer who organized and trained the ground force *spetsnaz* detachments used in the Petsamo-Kirkenes Operation, actively participated in the preparation of the two detachments.[26]

At 2400 hours on 8 August, sappers began cutting through the barbed wire barriers along the border, and ten minutes later Marshal Meretskov ordered the offensive to begin.[27] The two *spetsnaz* engineer detachments infiltrated into the Japanese defenses under cover of darkness in a driving rainstorm. While one detachment assaulted the tunnels from multiple axes, the other detachment attacked the barracks of the guard force. Supported by well-adjusted artillery fire, they defeated the Japanese forces guarding the tunnel exits, and captured the important road junction between the tunnels and the fortified village and railroad station at Suifenho.[28] With the Japanese tunnel defenses thus neutralized, the forward detachment from the 187th Rifle Division[29] was able to capture all three tunnels intact, and on the morning of 9 August Col. Gen. N. I. Krylov, commander of the 5th Army, committed his main forces into battle.

"Operation Bridge"

All three Fronts experienced stunning successes against the Japanese, and advanced at rates faster than the most optimistic Soviet estimates. On 17 August, General Yamata, Commander-in-Chief of the Kwantung Army, sent a radio message to Vasilevskii requesting the initiation of discussions concerning a cease fire. At the same time, Yamata directed his forces to cease military operations and lay down their arms. Consequently, Vasilevskii sent a message back to Yamata with an ultimatum: The Japanese were to cease military operations by 1200 hours on 20 August, lay down their arms, and surrender; when Japanese forces began to give up their weapons, the Soviet forces would cease military operations.[30] Yamata accepted Vasilevskii's conditions of capitulation on the morning of 18 August, and once again ordered his forces to stop fighting and surrender.[31] During the early evening of 18 August, Vasilevskii ordered his three Front commanders to commit mobile detachments and airborne assault forces (which Vasilevskii had ordered formed sometime prior to the 18th) for the seizure of important cities, bases, railroad crossings, and stations.[32]

The cities of Harbin and Kirin lay within the operational zone of the

1st Far Eastern Front. According to his memoir, General A. F. Khrenov, Chief of Engineer Troops of the 1st Far Eastern Front, approached Meretskov with the idea of airlanding operations to seize the airfields at those cities.[33] After first rejecting the suggestion, citing lack of airborne regiments, Meretskov summoned Khrenov back two days later and approved the concept. Khrenov, apparently confident of Meretskov's approval, had already begun the preparation of two detachments under the command of Lt. Col. Ivan Nikolaevich Zabelin and Lieutenant Colonel Krutskikh.

One source describes these detachments as "specially trained and prepared ahead of time in a special course of tactical preparation and parachute training."[34] The approximately 150 troops who made up each detachment were drawn from the 20th "Svirsk" Engineer Brigade, and for the most part were the same men, according to Khrenov, who had participated in the capture of the three railroad tunnels.[35] The detachments had several missions: capture key bridges, airfields, and other important installations and thus prevent their destruction by the Japanese, while special plenipotentiaries of the Front commander negotiated the surrender of Japanese forces and garrisons.[36] The operation was code-named "Bridge."

Officers from the Front intelligence staff and translators briefed the assault forces, considering all possible contingencies. Particular attention was given to working out the communications plan.[37] Meretskov appointed Maj. Gen. G. A. Shalakhov, the Front deputy chief of staff, as his special plenipotentiary to accompany the Harbin detachment, which was commanded by Lt. Col. Zabelin. Guards Col. V. I. Lebedev was named special plenipotentiary to accompany the Kirin detachment, commanded by Lieutenant Colonel Krutskikh. The engineer soldiers were organized into combat teams, assigned specific tasks, and armed with submachine guns, machine guns, grenades, and demolitions. Each man had 500 to 600 rounds for his submachine gun and four to five grenades. Detachment training included the study of the layout of the target cities, and routes to and from the airfield and objectives.

In accordance with an order from the highest Soviet commander in the theater, Marshal Vasilevskii,[38] on 18 August the detachments went into action. In the early evening, seven Il-2 and C-47 transport aircraft flew into Harbin from Khorol airfield with (approximately) a 120-man assault detachment of Lieutenant Colonel Zabelin.[39] The transports flew across the front line and landed 250 kilometers beyond it in the enemy rear. The detachment's arrival completely surprised the Japanese. Before the aircraft had cut their engines and finished taxiing, the assault force got out and moved toward their objectives. The detachment immediately occupied the hangars, the repair shop, and some stone buildings in the vicinity of the airfield. A short time later, the assault force captured the Japanese legation and took Kwantung Army Chief of Staff General Hata, several generals and other officers, prisoner.[40] General Hata was brought to the Soviet consulate, where Major General Shalakhov gave him an ultimatum to either surrender or Soviet aircraft circling overhead would bomb the immediate area. By this time, Zabelin's men had already captured key bridges, and were moving toward their other objectives. By 2300, the Soviets had occupied the railroad yards, telegraph facility, police headquarters, post office, electric power station, and other critical facilities. On the morning of the 19th, the detachment was reinforced with 158 more men and 800 kilograms of cargo.[41]

That same morning, General Hata and his staff were taken by Soviet transport plane to the command post of the 1st Far Eastern Front, where General Hata agreed to order Japanese forces in Manchuria to cease combat operations not later than 1200 hours on 20 August.[42] On the 20th, an additional 213 men were flown in, and that morning the Red Banner Amur Flotilla arrived in Harbin with an assault force of the 15th Army, which accepted the surrender of the Sungari Flotilla and the Japanese garrison in the city.

The *spetsnaz* assault on Kirin[43] was also scheduled for 18 August, but was delayed because of bad weather. At 1200 hours on 19 August, the 154-man assault detachment of Lieutenant Colonel Krutskikh landed in seven Il–2 and C–47 aircraft. With these troops flew the Front special plenipotentiary Colonel Lebedev. The assault troops deplaned, defeated the airfield defenses in a brief skirmish, and occupied defensive positions around the airfield. At 1800 the detachment organized a reconnaissance into the city using captured trucks. The assault force seized key bridges across the Sungari River, the armory, train station, telephone and telegraph office, radio station, post office, bank, dam, and power station. A Japanese lieutenant colonel, a colonel from the headquarters of the Manchurian forces, and the Japanese brigade located in the city were delivered to the airfield and given the Soviet terms of capitulation. The Japanese officers declared that they did not have the capitulation orders from their higher headquarters. On 20 August, the forward detachment of the 10th Mechanized Corps linked up with the assault force in Kirin.

Similar airlandings took place in many other locations, though the evidence suggests the forces used were of conventional origin. The Transbaikal Front staged an air assault on Mukden on the 19th.[44] The assault force was a 225-man detachment led by Front Plenipotentiary Major General A. D. Pritula. After landing at 1300 hours, the detachment seized the airfield, where they captured the Emperor of Manchukuo, Pu Yi, who was waiting for a special plane to fly him back to Japan. On the same day, the Soviets freed a large number of American and British prisoners of war from a nearby camp. On the second day after the landing, the forward detachment of the 5th Guards Tank Army arrived and the Soviets accepted the surrender of Japanese forces.

The Transbaikal Front mounted several other such operations. For example, at dawn and after a two-hour flight on 19 August the Front Plenipotentiary Colonel I. T. Artemenko[45] landed at Changchun airfield to accept the surrender of the 15,000-man Japanese garrison and other forces in the area. As the plane headed for its destination, Marshal Vasilevskii sent a radiotelegram to General Yamata, Commander in Chief of the Kwantung Army, informing him of the nature of the flight and ordering safe passage for it. One hour after the parliamentary mission took off, an assault force of approximately two hundred fifty soldiers drawn from the 30th Guards Mechanized Brigade, 6th Guards Tank Army, commanded by Hero of the Soviet Union and Guards Major Peter Nikitovich Avramenko,[46] took off on a course for Changchun. Air Force bombers were also launched toward the city. Escorting Artemenko's party of five officers and six privates were several fighters. The assault force landed at 1100 hours, captured the airfield security force, established all-around defense, and disarmed the Changchun garrison. At 1410 hours, General Yamata signed the document of capitulation that had been prepared by the Soviets beforehand. General Yamata and Manchukuo's prime minister, Go Chzhan Tszin-hue, were required to go on the radio and announce the terms of the Japanese capitulation.

On 22 August, the Soviets continued this pattern with airlanded detachments at Liuishun (Liaoyuan) (200 men),[47] Dairen (250 men),[48] and Port Arthur (250 men). There is no available evidence to suggest that any of these were *spetsnaz* forces. At Port Arthur,[49] a 200-man air assault force drawn from the 6th Guards Tank Army, commanded by Major I. I. Belodeda, landed with Lieutenant General V. D. Ivanov, Transbaikal Front plenipotentiary. The assault force was to seize all important objectives as negotiations went on. The assault troops quickly disarmed several units of the nearby garrison and captured approximately two hundred Japanese soldiers and naval infantry. Part of the assault force was dispatched on captured trucks to the western sector of the city, where a large Japanese garrison force was located. At the same time, another part of the assault force occupied telephone and telegraph facilities, the train station, and the port (which still contained many Japanese ships). On 23 August, a tank brigade of the 6th Guards Tank Army arrived in the city. On 25 August, sailors arrived by air to organize the port. In what may have been the last such operations of the war, the Soviets staged air assaults along their now-familiar pattern at Yenchi (238 men) on 23 August, and on 24 August at the Korean cities of Haeju[50] and the rail hub Kanko (Hamhung).[51]

Several important points are apparent in an analysis of these Soviet ground force *spetsnaz* operations: Experienced forces were brought into the theater from the Soviet-German front. In the tunnel operation, the forces were employed in a tactical mission with operational significance. The three tunnels were on the main axis of the 5th Army, which was the Front main axis. Krutskikh, formerly an organizer and trainer, became the commander in the Kirin operation, signifying the importance of the operation, its political-military nature, and the confidence that Meretskov and Khrenov had in him.[52]

Special detachments played a major role in war termination. The Soviet military high command had no confidence in the ability or willingness of the Japanese high command to control its forces at the operational and tactical levels. Their solution was to supplant Japanese military-political authority with Soviet authority, via plenipotentiaries accompanied by special operations forces. Such an approach to the deep insertion of Soviet authority was used, to one degree or another, in the *initial* phase of the invasions of Czechoslovakia (1968) and Afghanistan (1979). This could also be a model for termination of war in Western Europe.

Naval Special Operations

The Soviet Pacific Fleet, commanded by Admiral I. S. Yumashev, conducted a series of amphibious operations to seize the Korean ports of Yuki (Unggi), Rashin (Najin), Seishin (Ch'ongjin), and Genzan (Wonsan), as well as the southern half of Sakhalin Island and the Kurile Islands.[53] Several separate naval infantry battalions, the 13th Naval Infantry Brigade, and the 335th Rifle Division provided the assault forces for these landings.[54] Of particular interest, however, are the special operations conducted by naval forces. These were of two types: airlanding operations on Southern Sakhalin and Iturup islands, and amphibious landing operations by the *spetsnaz* 140th Reconnaissance Detachment of Headquarters, Pacific Fleet.

Military operations against Japanese forces on Southern Sakhalin Island began with a ground offensive on 11 August, supported by amphibious landings on the western and southern shores of the island on August 16, 17, and 19. By 21 August, the Japanese defenders had been driven to the southeast part of the island, into the area around Toyohara. Three assault landings by groups of thirty-five men each were airlanded on Japanese airfields in this area:[55] On 23 August at Oshiai, on 24 August at Toyohara, and on 25 August at Otomari.[56] Little is known about the origin of these small detachments. Some Soviet sources identify them as coming from the Northern Pacific Ocean Flotilla.[57] Another indicates that the men were from a submachine-gun battalion of an airfield supporting unit.[58] In either case, their mission was to prevent the Japanese forces, who by this time had capitulated, from destroying the airfields, aircraft, and other materiel.[59] Even less is known about the airlanding operation on Iturup (Etorofu), a large island in the southern Kurile Islands chain. A force of 130 men from South Sakhalin Island landed on Iturup on 28 August, several days after the Japanese surrender.[60] Although these airlandings resemble similar operations conducted on the mainland, further study is needed before significant lessons can be drawn.

The most significant special operations conducted by forces of the Fleet were the landings along the northern Korean coastline by the 140th Reconnaissance Detachment. The 140th was the Fleet's long-range asset for ground tactical and operational intelligence collection, and was often employed in "reconnaissance by battle" where the situation was uncertain. It was subordinated to the commander, Pacific Fleet, through the intelligence department of the Fleet staff. In August 1945, it was composed of approximately 130 men, one-third of whom were "northerners" transferred from Poliarnyi, Headquarters of the Northern Fleet near Murmansk, in the third week of May 1945. All of the northerners were combat veterans, while the "easterners" had no combat experience and typically had only twelve to eighteen months in service.[61]

The 140th Reconnaissance Detachment was commanded by Hero of the Soviet Union Sr. Lt. Viktor N. Leonov, who had previously commanded the Reconnaissance Detachment of Headquarters, Northern Fleet, and dis-

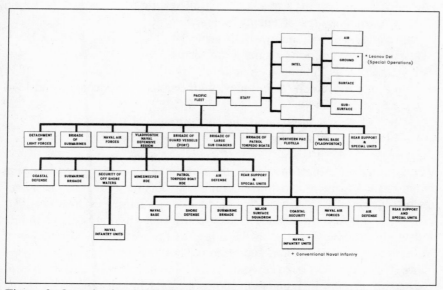

Figure 3. Organization of the Soviet Pacific Fleet, 1945. Rear Adm. G. Iargin, "Sovershenstvovanie organizatsionnoi struktury Voenno-Morskogo Flota," *Voenno-istoricheskii zhurnal*, October 1978, 43–52.

tinguished himself in the Petsamo-Kirkenes Operation. Leonov organized the Pacific Fleet detachment into two line platoons of four squads each and a headquarters/support platoon about half the size of a line platoon. He appointed trusted Northern Fleet combat veterans to all leadership positions and distributed the remainder evenly throughout the squads to teach the "easterners." The headquarters/support platoon contained the command group, communications, medical, and supply personnel, an armorer, bootmaker, cook, drivers, and runners. All support personnel trained together with the line platoons. Many support personnel were former scouts who had been wounded but wanted to remain with the unit, and they participated fully in subsequent combat operations.[62] The majority of the northerners and about half of the easterners were members of the Communist Party.

On 19 June 1945, the 140th moved from Vladivostok to Novik on Ostrov Russkii (Russian Island) and set up a training base. Their training tasks included:[63]

- local topography, especially coastal terrain
- audio signatures of enemy weapons
- employment of enemy small arms
- visual recognition of enemy uniforms
- amphibious landing techniques
- ground movement techniques, with emphasis on distance and load
- urban combat
- use of aerial photographs and topographical maps
- physical conditioning

The intelligence department gave the detachment written materials pertaining to the Korean coastline, including layouts of some of their subsequent objectives, without disclosing their exact names or locations.[64]

The 140th Reconnaissance Detachment's first mission was to conduct a daylight landing directly on the docks of the northern Korean city of Yuki, ascertain the situation, and seize and hold a beachhead on the enemy shore. If the enemy offered resistance, the detachment was to hold on until the arrival of reinforcements. On shore, the detachment was to determine enemy strength and intentions, and report this information to Fleet Headquarters.[65] For this operation, the detachment included interpreters from

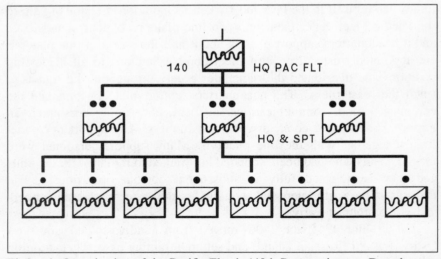

Figure 4. Organization of the Pacific Fleet's 140th Reconnaissance Detachment.

Vladivostok.[66] When Leonov expressed concern over landing on enemy docks in daylight, the Fleet's response was that the enemy would not expect such audacity. Night landings on unfamiliar shores were difficult and more dangerous. Such a deep raid and landing would paralyze the enemy, disrupt his command and control, and induce disorganization and panic, permitting the capture of the port intact.[67]

Leonov and his political officer, Senior Lieutenant Guznenkov, received their orders in person at Vladivostok on 10 August, returned to base, briefed the members of the detachment on the docks, and put to sea during hours of darkness. Two hours later, a second group of 170 machine gunners of the 390th Separate Naval Infantry battalion under the command of Sr. Lt. K. N. Deviatov set out. At sea was a fog, the wind was blowing at force 5, and the waves reached force 4, slowing the ships' progress.[68]

The landing of Leonov's detachment, reinforced by a company of naval infantry submachine gunners, began at approximately 1910 on 11 August, after two days of strikes by aircraft and torpedo boats on the city and the enemy's ships in the port. The landing was unopposed, the Japanese having abandoned the city several hours before the arrival of the assault force. The detachment secured the port, established communications with the 393rd Rifle Division advancing along the coast, and awaited the landing of the main assault force (75th Battalion, 13th Separate Naval Infantry Brigade) the next day.[69] While in Yuki, Leonov and Guznenkov left the detachment for more than an hour to meet with a Soviet agent who had been inserted into Yuki before the outbreak of hostilities.[70] At 0500 hours on 12 August, a column of the 393rd Rifle Division, 1st Far Eastern Front, entered the city from the north.[71] Later that morning, the 140th departed Yuki by boat. Leonov informed his men that their next target would be Rashin, a few miles south of Yuki.[72]

The detachment's role at Rashin was the same—to operate as the forward detachment of the main landing force. Their mission was to land in the port, determine the strength and intentions of the enemy, and seize a beachhead for the follow-on forces.[73] Just as at Yuki, Soviet naval aviation and torpedo boats softened up the harbor with several attacks on the previous day. Leonov's force landed on the docks unopposed at 0900 hours on 12 August, followed two hours later by a company of naval infantry submachine gunners.[74]

The Japanese defenders had abandoned the city, but left behind small groups of rearguards for the destruction of warehouses and the burning of buildings. Leonov's men moved quickly into the city toward their objectives: the railroad station, the military barracks, and an industrial complex. Resistance was light and quickly overcome.[75] An attempt to expand the beachhead along the road south of the city was turned back by Japanese forces.[76] The main assault force, the 358th Naval Infantry Battalion, landed at 0600 hours on 13 August and within a few hours had occupied the entire city and two offshore islands.[77]

Late on 12 August, prior to the final battle at Rashin, the 140th departed that city on torpedo boats. Enroute, one of their boats struck a mine allegedly sown before the battle by an American plane, resulting in the death of two detachment members and a torpedo boat crewman.[78] The detachment reached their base at 2000 hours, where most of the men slept that night on the docks.[79] At 0500 hours on 13 August, the detachment awoke to the news of another mission, this time an amphibious assault on the harbor of Seishin.[80] At 0700 hours the detachment embarked and departed.[81]

Seishin was a large industrial port city, and the most important Japanese naval base in northern Korea. Its rail and harbor facilities were vital to the movement of Japanese troops and materiel. Consequently, the Japanese had four thousand troops garrisoned there and had constructed defensive fortifications facing both landward and seaward.[82] As in the previous two landings, air and surface attacks were used to soften the Japanese defenses. Also, as before, Leonov's detachment was reinforced by a company of naval infantry submachine gunners.

The composite detachment of approximately one hundred eighty men was commanded by chief of the intelligence department of the Fleet staff, Colonel A. Z. Denisin. Acting as forward detachment for the main landing force, their mission was to conduct reconnaissance by combat, determine the strength and intentions of the enemy, and capture a beachhead and hold it until the arrival of the main force.[83] While Leonov's men were making the three-hour crossing from their base to Seishin, a small force of torpedo boats went into the harbor. An eleven-man reconnaissance party (probably sailors from the torpedo boats) went ashore, met resistance from the armed Koreans guarding warehouses, and returned to their boats.[84] The torpedo boats continued their reconnaissance along the shoreline, then went to sea to meet the invasion fleet. These activities may have alerted the Japanese that a landing was imminent.

Despite these activities, however, Leonov and his 140th Reconnaissance Detachment and the company of naval infantry submachine gunners landed unopposed in the harbor a few hours later at 1300 hours on 13 August. Moving on diverging axes, the two forces quickly occupied the docks, but met strong resistance as they began to penetrate into the industrial and commercial areas of the city. Over the next eighteen hours, Leonov and his men fought pitched battles against Japanese forces, and were forced to move several times to avoid encirclement. Due to bad weather, the Soviets had to fight without any air or naval gunfire support.

It was during this period of desperate close-in fighting that the true purpose of Colonel Denisin's presence was revealed. After nightfall on 13 August, taking one of Leonov's platoon leaders and two men with him, Denisin disappeared into the dock area. He reappeared approximately ninety minutes later, having met with clandestine agents he had sent into Seishin some days earlier.[85]

At 0500 hours on 14 August, the first echelon of the main assault force, the 355th Naval Infantry Battalion, landed in the east sector of the harbor, some distance from Leonov's beleaguered detachment. Unable to physically join together, the two Soviet forces defeated all Japanese attempts to drive them back into the sea and held onto a narrow strip of land along the docks until reinforcements arrived just after midnight on 15 August.[86] Two Soviet surface vessels, a frigate and a minesweeper, came into the harbor and approached the docks where Leonov's men were defending. With gunfire support from these ships, the forward detachment held on until the arrival of the 13th Naval Infantry Brigade at 0500 hours on 15 August.[87]

Landing in the beachhead secured by Leonov's detachment and the naval infantry battalion, the 13th Brigade quickly moved into the city. Aided by close air support, which resumed at midday, and attacks by forces of the 25th Army advancing along the coast from the north, enemy resistance was defeated by 1400 hours on 16 August.[88] Despite the intensity of the combat, in which Leonov and one of his platoon leaders earned the title Hero of the Soviet Union, the detachment suffered only three killed and seven wounded.[89] Shortly after the action, the detachment was ordered back to base near Vladivostok by Fleet Headquarters for a well-deserved rest.[90]

On the morning of 19 August, Leonov's detachment departed their base by torpedo boat and returned to Seishin, to the headquarters of the Southern Defensive Region.[91] Its commander, Lt. Gen. S. I. Kabanov, was organizing a major landing operation to seize the port of Genzan (Wonsan). The mission of the landing force was to move quickly and unobtrusively to this Japanese naval base, enter the harbor, capture the port, occupy the city, disarm and intern the large enemy garrison there, capture the nearby airfield, and prevent the departure of enemy vessels from the harbor.[92] On the evening of the 20th, the detachment departed Seishin as part of a 1,800-man assault force bound for Wonsan.

Once again, the 140th was the forward detachment, this time subordinated to the 13th Naval Infantry Brigade. Accompanying Leonov on this mission were two officers from the Fleet intelligence section, the senior of them Lt. Col. N. A. Inzartsev,[93] who in 1941 was Leonov's commander in the Northern Fleet Reconnaissance Detachment. The second officer was the deputy chief of the intelligence section of the Fleet, Capt. 3rd Rank G. P. Koliubakin.[94] Leonov's detachment, this time reinforced with engineer troops equipped with mine detectors, went ashore in the harbor at 0900 hours on 21 August, several hours ahead of the main body.

Meeting no resistance, the detachment split into three groups and headed toward their objectives: the Japanese garrison, the railroad station, post office and telegraph office, and other important facilities. Over the course of the next several hours, Leonov and his men moved back and forth across the city, while the large Japanese garrison force remained in its barracks. Leonov and Inzartsev both conducted negotiations with senior Japanese officers, including an admiral, who were reluctant to give any kind of order to their subordinates.[95] At 1500 hours, both the landing force and the ground force commanders came into the harbor and waited at the docks with Leonov and Inzartsev for the Japanese response to the Soviet surrender demand. The troops of the landing force remained aboard their ship just outside the harbor.

When the Japanese commanders did not appear at the appointed time, Leonov and his men went back into the city and brought them out to the dock, and then aboard ship. While negotiations continued aboard ship, some of Leonov's men went south of the city by patrol torpedo boat and destroyed a rail line the Japanese were using to move troops toward the city. During the night, Leonov's men remained ashore, providing local security for the Soviet vessels tied up at the docks. At first light, Japanese troops began to move out of their garrison, apparently in response to a prearranged plan of their now hostage leaders. Leonov and his men, supported by naval gunfire, forced them to retreat. The detachment was quickly replaced by naval infantrymen, and returned to the dock.

Leonov's next task was to secure the Japanese airfield and disarm its garrison. Accompanied by his political officer and Lieutenant Colonel

Inzartsev, Leonov marched his detachment to the airfield headquarters and demanded its surrender. The Japanese colonel in charge at first refused to negotiate with so junior an officer as Leonov, but finally capitulated under threat of air and naval gunfire bombardment. On 23 August, the detachment landed on one of the offshore islands and accepted the surrender of the shore batteries there. Sometime after 24 August, Leonov and his men sailed back to their base on a Japanese prize vessel, which they crewed themselves. Enroute to Vladivostok, they received word over the radio that they had been designated "Guards" status.[96]

The combat record of the 140th Guards Reconnaissance Detachment of Headquarters, Pacific Fleet, is remarkable given that Leonov had only eight weeks from his arrival in theater in mid-June to the outbreak of hostilities in mid-August to organize and train his force. The detachment's high level of tactical proficiency was clearly demonstrated in the Seishin landing, where it seized and held a beachhead against overwhelming odds, but suffered remarkably low casualties.

The 140th was more than a forward detachment for a naval infantry brigade. It was also entrusted with highly sensitive intelligence-gathering tasks, such as meetings with clandestine agents in Yuki and Seishin. Equally significant was the political-military role of the detachment, and of Leonov personally, in securing the surrender of the garrison at Genzan. Leonov acted much like a Front plenipotentiary, but on behalf of and with the authority of Admiral Yumashev, commander of the Pacific Fleet.

Conclusion

The lack of either sufficient airlift or standing airborne regiments may have forced the Soviets to make greater use of smaller and more specialized forces against critical targets than Soviet planners might have preferred. Similarly, the lack of a viable Soviet-allied fifth column among the Manchurian and Korean populations may have precluded the using of proxies to transform latent incipient resistance to the Japanese into a war of movement prior to the Soviet invasion. Regardless, the record of Soviet special operations during the Manchurian campaign is impressive.

The role of these ground and naval special purpose forces in the Manchurian offensive can be analyzed from several perspectives. At the strategic level, special purpose forces were used for the political-military task of war termination. At the operational level, they captured key terrain which permitted the commitment to battle of larger follow-on forces. At the tactical level they executed the type of combat actions that any commando-type unit would be expected to perform. Just as in Europe, special purpose units were comprised of highly-trained personnel commanded by known special operators with extensive combat experience. These units were subordinated to Front and Fleet staffs, and tailored to accomplish specific tasks. Linguists accompanied the units where appropriate. Organizations and combat techniques that had been developed and proven against the Germans were transferred to the Far East and revalidated.

In the same way that these special operations reflected the past, they also predicted the future. The insertion of special purpose forces by air into Eastern Europe and Afghanistan in our own time reflects this late World War II experience. This linkage of the past with the present is not accidental. A thorough analysis of the postwar careers of the key personnel, were it possible, would probably explain much of Soviet special operations theory and organization in subsequent years. For example, twice Hero of the Soviet Union Viktor Leonov attended the Kirov Caspian Naval School in 1950 and in 1956 was an instructor at the Voroshilov Naval Academy. He retired from active service in July 1956, just before his fortieth birthday. But in the early 1960s, he is known to have played a role in the reestablishment of Soviet ground forces' special purpose forces.[97] The role that others, such as Krutskikh, Babikov, and Inzartsev, may have played in postwar Soviet special purpose force development is unknown at this time, but the rich combat experience of these and other men surely has not been ignored.

Notes

1. Most place names used in this chapter are from the 1945 National Geographic Society Map of China, and the *National Geographic Atlas of the World*, 4th ed. (Washington DC: National Geographic Society, 1975): 133, 140.
2. LTC David M. Glantz, *August Storm: The Soviet 1945 Strategic Offensive in Manchuria* (Fort Leavenworth, KS: Combat Studies Institute, February 1983): 5–24.
3. Ibid., 25.
4. D. F. Ustinov, et al., *Istoriia vtoroi mirovoi voiny* 1939–1945 (History of the Second World War 1939–1945), vol. 11 (Moscow: Voyenizdat, 1980): 183–184; B. V. Sokolov, "O sootnoshenii poter' v liudiakh i boevoi tekhnike na sovetsko-germanskom fronte v khode velikoi otechestvennoi voiny" (Concerning the Correlation of Personnel and Combat Equipment Losses On the Soviet-German Front During the Great Patriotic War), *Voprosy istorii*, 6/1988, 120. See also, MAJ Claude R. Sasso, *Soviet Night Operations in World War II*, Leavenworth Papers No. 6 (Leavenworth, KS: U. S. Army Command and General Staff College, December 1982): 25; Edgar O'Ballance, *The Red Army* (New York: Frederick A. Praeger, 1964): 186.
5. O'Ballance, 187.
6. Malcolm Mackintosh, *Juggernaut: A History of the Soviet Armed Forces* (New York: The Macmillan Company, 1967): 260.
7. O'Ballance, 187.
8. P. H. Vigor, *Soviet Blitzkrieg Theory* (New York: St. Martin's Press, 1983): 115.
9. Ustinov, 187; see also, Sasso, 25–27.
10. Glantz, 1.
11. Ustinov, 193.
12. Sasso, 26–28; Vigor, 105–106.
13. Glantz, 1.
14. Ibid., 3.
15. Ibid., 39–47; Sasso, 26.
16. Vigor, 104.
17. Glantz, 26–34; Vigor, 113; Mackintosh, 261.
18. Sasso, 26.
19. Glantz, 32.
20. Ibid., 33–34; Vigor, 102, 114.
21. Glantz, 73–79; Sasso, 28; Mackintosh, 262.
22. Vigor, 114–115.
23. Arkadii F. Khrenov, *Mostu k pobede* (Bridges to Victory) (Moscow: Voyenizdat, 1982): 336–339.

24. Khrenov, 337–338.
25. A *razvedchik* is a scout or intelligence soldier, from *razvedka*, all-source intelligence.
26. Lt. Col. Krutskikh also subsequently commanded the air assault detachment that seized Kirin on August 19. See Khrenov, 337; V. F. Margelov, et al., *Sovetskie vozdushno-desantnye: voenno-istoricheskii ocherk* (Soviet Airborne Assault Forces: A Military-Historical Outline) (Moscow: Voyenizdat, 1986): 297; Leonid N. Vnotchenko, *Pobeda dal'nem vostoke* (Victory in the Far East) (Moscow: Voyenizdat, 1971): 284. From the available evidence, it is clear that Krutskikh was an important figure in *spetsnaz* operations during World War II.
27. Glantz, 141–142.
28. N. P. Suntsov, et al., *Krasnoznamennyi dal'nevostochnyi: istoriia krasnoznamennogo dal'nevostochnogo voennogo okruga* (Red Banner Far East: The History of the Red Banner Far East Military District) (Moscow: Voyenizdat, 1985): 202; Khrenov, 339.
29. N. I. Krylov, N. I. Alekseev, I. G. Dragan, *Navstrechu pobede: Boevoi put' 5-i armii* (Meeting Victory: The Battle Path of the 5th Army) (Moscow: Izdatel'stvo "Nauka," 1970): 438.
30. A partial text of this message is contained in Vasilevskii's memoir, *Delo vsei zhizni* (A Life-Long Cause) (Moscow: Politizdat, 1983): 521.
31. Kirill A. Meretskov, *Na sluzhbe narody* (In Service to the People) (Moscow: Voyenizdat, 1983): 411; Ustinov, 247–248.
32. Vasilevskii, 521; P. N. Pospelov, et al., *Istoriia velikoi otechestvennoi voiny sovetskogo soiuza 1941–1945* (History of the Great Patriotic War of the Soviet Union, 1941–1945), vol. 5 (Moscow: Voyenizdat, 1963): 578–579.
33. Khrenov, 342–344.
34. Vnotchenko, 283–284.
35. Khrenov, 343.
36. Margelov, 296.
37. Khrenov, 343.
38. Vasilevskii, 521.
39. Margelov, 296.
40. Vasilevskii, 522.
41. Margelov, 283–284.
42. Margelov, 296; Meretskov, 413.
43. Margelov, 297; Vnotchenko, 283–284.
44. Vasilevskii, 522; Margelov, 297; Vnotchenko, 281; Meretskov, 411.
45. An excellent description of the planning and preparation of this mission is contained in Artemenko's memoir, *Ot pervogo do poslednego dnia* (From the First to the Last Day) (Khar'kov: "Prapor," 1987): 151–67.

46. There is no evidence to suggest that Avramenko or his unit had any *spetsnaz* connection. He gained his Hero of the Soviet Union award in fighting with conventional forces in Rumania in August 1944. See *Geroi sovetskogo soiuza* (Heroes of the Soviet Union) (Moscow: Voyenizdat, 1987): 1:25.

47. Col. O. K. Frantsev, "Primenenie aviatsii v Man'chzhurskoi operatsii" (The Utilization of Aviation in the Manchurian Operations), *Voenno-Istoricheskii Zhurnal*, 8/1985, 23.

48. Vnotchenko, 281.

49. Margelov, 298; Vnotchenko, 281; Pospelov, 578–579.

50. Margelov, 299.

51. Ibid.

52. Krutskikh later rose to the rank of Colonel General, and held the position of chief of staff of civil defense of the Russian Federated Republic. Khrenov, 337n.

53. Khafiz Khayrutdinovich Kamalov, *Morskaya pekhota v boyakh za rodinu* (Naval Infantry in combat for the Motherland), 2d ed. (Moscow: Voyenizdat, 1983) (JPRS-UMA-84-011-L trans. chapter six, "Assault Landing Operations of Pacific Naval Fleet Infantry," 151).

54. Vnotchenko, 270.

55. Margelov, 299; V. N. Bagrov, *Iuzhno-Sakhalinskaia i Kuril'skaia operatsii – Avgust 1945* (The Southern Sakhalin and Kuriles Operations–August 1945) (Moscow: Voyenizdat, 1959): 80; S. E. Zakharov, et al., *Krasnoznamennyi tikhookeanskii flot* (Red Banner Pacific Fleet), 2d ed. (Moscow: Voyenizdat, 1973): 229; R. Ia. Malinovskii, *Final* (Final) (Moscow: Izdatel'stvo "Nauka," 1966): 330.

56. Chris Chant, "Eastern Europe," *Airborne Operations* (New York: Crescent Books, 1978): 158.

57. Bagrov and Zakharov.

58. Malinovskii, 330.

59. Margelov, 299.

60. Ustinov, 256.

61. M. A. Babikov, *Na vostochnom berugu* (On the Eastern Shore) (Moscow: Izdatel'stvo "Sovetskaia Rossiia," 1969): 6, 18.

62. Ibid., 20, 24.

63. Ibid., 26–27.

64. Ibid., 28.

65. Ibid., 37.

66. Ibid., 47.

67. Ibid., 38.

68. Zakharov, 278–279.

69. Vnotchenko, 270; Kamalov, 151; Zakharov, 178.

70. Babikov, 52.

71. Ibid., 58.
72. Ibid., 62.
73. Ibid., 62.
74. Zakharov, 179–180.
75. Babikov, 67.
76. Vnotchenko, 271.
77. Zakharov, 179–181.
78. According to the Soviets, from July 12 to August 11, the American air force delivered 780 proximity (influence) mines into the ports of Rashin, Seishin, and Genzan (Wonsan), but did not inform the Soviets until August 21. This "complicated" Soviet operations against these ports. Zakharov, 180; Ustinov, 278.
79. Babikov, 91.
80. The most detailed account of the Seishin operation is in Babikov, 92–192.
81. Ibid., 77–96.
82. Ustinov, 278; Pospelov, 574.
83. Babikov, 97.
84. Zakharov, 184.
85. Babikov, 97–127.
86. Zakharov, 185–191.
87. Ustinov, 280; Zakharov, 191.
88. Pospelov, 574–575.
89. This was Leonov's second award. The second one went to Makar Babikov. Babikov, 166.
90. Ibid., 167.
91. Zakharov, 197. The Southern Defensive Region was a naval ground command similar to the Northern Defensive Region on the Rybachii Peninsula under the Northern Fleet.
92. Babikov, 195; Pospelov, 578–579.
93. For more information on Inzartsev, see Babikov, *Otriad osobogo naznacheniya* (Special Purpose Detachment) (Moscow: "Sovetskaia Rossiia," 1986).
94. Babikov, *Letom sorok pervogo*, 194.
95. Ibid., 200–203.
96. Ibid., 233.
97. Interview with former Soviet soldier, summer of 1987. As of this writing, Leonov is 73 years old and living in Moscow.

CHAPTER 9

Spetsnaz and Soviet Far North Strategy

Kirsten Amundsen

Scandinavia and the Northern Region* is often referred to as "the quiet corner of Europe." The small and stable democracies found here, some in the immediate vicinity of the Soviet Union, manage somehow to maintain correct if not overly friendly relations with powers distant as well as near no matter what the differences in culture, politics, and ideology. These are also highly developed welfare states, apparently shielded from the upheavals and turbulence so characteristic of many other parts of the world.

Yet the swift perusal of the map of the northern areas and the well documented military constellations assembled within it, suggest rather strongly that this vision of a blissfully calm and secure Scandinavia is a mere ephemera. Whatever the prevailing sense of security may be among people living in the area, it is clear that the region is now at the center of strategic concern for both East and West.

The Nordic Balance

In contrast to the benign neglect bestowed upon the Northern Region by most observers and analysts in these parts, it is unmistakably the recipi-

---

*The Northern Region is usually defined as the northern ocean areas between the Norwegian mainland and the Norwegian arctic islands of Jan Mayen, Bjornoya and Svalbard, plus the Norwegian coast and land.

ent of renewed and disturbing attention from the Soviet Union over the past several years. The combination of political moves and pressures vis-à-vis states on the Scandinavian peninsula and the formidable military buildup by the Soviet Union on the Kola peninsula present a challenge to anyone concerned with Western security generally—both for the immediate present and the long-term future. The significance of that challenge is aptly summed up by Adm. Isaac C. Kidd: While a new war may not be won in the Norwegian Sea, it assuredly can be lost there.[1]

For a full understanding of the differing security profiles of the Scandinavian states today, it is essential to first focus attention on the post-World War II developments in the region. Denmark and Norway, subject to a surprise German attack and five years of occupation from 1940 to 1945, were among the first states to join NATO. Both states had learned the bitter lesson so often repeated in human history: Neutrality, conciliatory politics, and low military profiles do not ensure against attack; geopolitical interests override all other concerns for powers with expansionist aims. Sweden, on the other hand, escaped involvement in this devastating Great War, and decided to hold onto the neutrality policy that it, quite mistakenly, presumed had saved it from the bitter fate of its immediate neighbors. Finland, meanwhile, paid the heaviest price of all for its inevitable involvement in World War II. Having joined Germany in the war declared against the Soviet Union in 1941 to regain lands lost in the Winter War following the Soviet attack upon Finland in 1939, this little democracy again became a loser. In the 1945 peace settlements Finland had to cede new territory to its powerful neighbor, thereby giving Norway a rather unwelcome border with the Soviet Union, and was under some pressure to sign a Treaty of Friendship and Mutual Cooperation with the Soviet Union in 1948. While Finland has retained its independence in internal affairs, it has hence been bound to the Soviet Union in a "special relationship" that sets limits and conditions on what the Finns themselves prefer to see as their neutrality policy.

The security pattern described here is often referred to as the "Nordic Balance." It is a possibly illusory designation, implying that a change in the security position of one Scandinavian country will bring about necessary adjustments in the security policies of the rest, thereby assuring the maintenance of the pattern of deterrence and reassurance now in existence. Finland, for instance, is assumed to have some protection against undue pressures from the Soviet Union by the implied threat from NATO partners Norway and Denmark to change their basing policies should their Scandinavian neighbor be forced to join the Soviets in military maneuvers or in an outright military alliance. Sweden, meanwhile, argues that it cannot forfeit its policy of neutrality lest new pressures be brought on Finland. And Norway and Denmark presume that they can still alter the restrictions imposed upon their participation in NATO should the Soviet Union choose to apply new pressures to threaten the independence of either Sweden or Finland.

In terms of the restrictions imposed upon Norway and Denmark's participation in NATO, these have clearly evolved out of Scandinavian concern for the security interests of the Soviet Union and the often belligerent responses from Moscow to any further Western ties or improvements of the Scandinavian security picture. Norway and Denmark's base policy was formulated, in fact, after a sharply critical note from the Soviet government protested their NATO participation. Both countries pledged not to have NATO troops permanently stationed on their soils in 1949. In 1961, both countries also decided not to allow the stockpiling of nuclear weapons on their territories, nor to incorporate tactical nuclear weapons in their defense forces.

Fortress Kola

The military imbalance in the north is documented yearly by London's Institute for Strategic Studies.[2] It is, of course, the dramatic growth and improvement of the Soviet Northern Fleet on the Kola peninsula that is the greatest cause for concern. The Kola also has the heaviest concentration of military installations *and* nuclear weapons found in any region in the world. A September 1986 analysis by the Norwegian Foreign Policy Institute confirmed the building of major new air and naval bases on the peninsula to support ballistic missile submarine operations and long-range bomber forces. A road network extending toward the Norwegian border is also under construction. The significant edge in conventional force strength of the Soviet Union is also evident from these data.

The Kola peninsula provides the Soviets with their one suitable, strategically situated ice-free haven that gives them direct access to the Atlantic and the air and sea lines of communication (ALOCs and SLOCs) over which more than 90 percent of the vital cargoes and reinforcements for NATO would have to pass from the United States to Europe in a long war.[3] In war, the necessity for air and sea superiority, and as extended an early warning net as possible, makes it imperative that the Soviets move beyond Kola to control northern Norway, Svalbard, Jan Mayen Island, Iceland, the Faeroes, and the Shetlands and adjacent waters as soon as possible. The Soviets need these for air bases for their strike, bomber, and radioelectric combat (REC) aircraft, fixed sites for long-range early warning sensors, and harbors for their submarines and surface combatants. Moreover, they must act fast and with as complete strategic, operational, and tactical surprise as possible, lest the Allies reinforce the area, bottle up the Northern Fleet, and contain the Soviet surge.[4] In a fight for Western Europe, the Northern Fleet is the most important of the four Soviet fleets, and the one least likely to be bottled up by NATO forces.[5]

The array of Soviet armed forces in Kola is as shown in chart 1.[6] Severomorsk on the Murmansk fjord (seventy kilometers from the Norwegian border) is the largest of nine main Northern Fleet surface vessel bases and one of seven main naval aviation bases operated by the Naval Aviation of the Northern Fleet. There are at least seven major submarine bases on the Kola peninsula. Nearly 50 percent of the Soviet submarine force is based on Kola. Four Typhoon-class strategic missile boats are

SOVIET ARMED FORCES IN KOLA	
Naval Aircraft	446
Surface Combatants	212
Submarines	133–142
Naval Spetsnaz Brigade	1
Naval Infantry Brigade	1
Motorized Rifle Divisions	2
Main Air Bases	22
Strategic Nuclear Bomber Bases	2
Secondary Airfields	18
Major Bases for Surface Combatants	9
Main Submarine Bases	7
Main Strategic Submarine Bases	2
Strategic Early Warning and Target Acquisition Radar Complexes	2
Strategic Air Defense SAM Systems	70 (approx.)
Theater Nuclear Missile Launch Complex	1

Chart 1. Sources: Skorve and Ries, *Investigating Kola* and "Satellite's View of Severomorsk Base"; Maj. Thomas C. Linn, USMC, "Marines in the Naval Campaign"; and Henry van Loon, "'Arrowhead Express' Underscores Importance of Norway to NATO Defense."

based in Guba Zapadnaya Litsa fjord, forty kilometers from the Norwegian border.[7]

Kola also features twenty-two main air bases with hardened aircraft shelters and runways exceeding 1,600 meters, eighteen secondary airfields, and the prepositioning and deployment infrastructure for one Front-level army.[8] Kola also contains numerous air defense facilities, two motorized rifle divisions (the 54th and 45th), one naval infantry brigade (the 63rd "Kirkenes") at Pechenga, and one six-hundred- to eight-hundred-man naval *spetsnaz*[9] brigade, also at Pechenga.[10] In 1986 the Norwegians also claimed that there was another *spetsnaz* brigade farther south in the Leningrad Military District. Norwegian intelligence sources also estimate that a highly trained naval infantry brigade exists in the area (possibly a mobilization unit), in addition to the standing naval infantry brigade of the Northern Fleet,[11] but this cannot be confirmed.

This is of course most ominous for Norway, which on its side of the border with the Soviet Union has a small population (only 80,000 in the large province of Finmark), only one road linking the three northernmost provinces with central and southern Norway and, in addition to that, only a tripwire force of five hundred men at the border itself. A small military airfield guarded by one thousand men is two hundred miles from the border; other than that, the nearest naval and air bases — both of modest dimensions — are in Troms, about a day's sea travel and nearly two hours by air away. The point to be made here is that the impressive military buildup on the Kola peninsula has taken place in spite of the self-imposed military restrictions and the policy of reassurance followed by Norway.

Given the strategic linkages sketched here and the overriding need for surprise, and the characteristics of climate, terrain, and population, one might expect Soviet special operations and unconventional warfare forces (*spetsnaz*) to figure rather prominently in Soviet war plans for conquest of the region. A sparse population, comparatively small and thinly spread defense forces, extended (in excess of forty-eight hours for the majority) mobilization and deployment times for reserves, long and irregular coast-lines, rugged mountains, and long dark winters[12] make the region well suited for the clandestine infiltration of special operations forces. Their employment against critical targets both for intelligence collection and direct action in the preparatory and execution phases of a conventional invasion may prove to be invaluable. It is this important and often over-looked dimension of Soviet northern strategy that now cries out for analysis.

Whiskey On The Rocks

Not only historical data, but a wealth of indices and reports from recent years suggests the Scandinavian peninsula to be especially sought out for Soviet special operations in the Western Theater of Military Actions. Most strikingly, Soviet submarine operations have been carried out in Swedish and Norwegian territorial waters with a frequency and in a manner provocative enough to gain worldwide media attention. The Soviet Whiskey-class U-boat 137 that ran aground on 27 October 1981 at Gasefjarden, near Torumskar (in a restricted area of the Karlskrona archipelago near the Swedish naval base there) caused an immediate sensation, as most will remember.[13] What is less well known is that this famous "Whiskey on the Rocks" was followed by many other submarines and submersibles of various types in incursions of an even more serious nature in the years that followed. In the late eighties, the record in terms of pattern, characteristics, and numbers demonstrates quite clearly that Sweden has been brought into Soviet contingency war plans (the Swedes admit to having spotted Soviet subs in their waters as early as 1980).[14] Neutral Sweden, in fact, appears targeted in Soviet plans for special forces operations and a surprise attack either in a combined maneuver directed at Norway, or against Sweden itself.

A brief review of the records of these submarine violations and their characteristics with the attendant espionage and/or *spetsnaz* activities carried out in Sweden in the last decade or so will set the background for the analysis to follow. While similar activities in Norway (see chart 2) cannot be neglected, it is clear that here they have neither been as provocative nor as much in evidence in recent years as in Norway's neutral neighbor. Norway, moreover, has little reason to be surprised at the intensive attention it is subject to, legal and otherwise, given the country's NATO membership and pivotal role in the war-fighting strategy of both superpowers. Suffice it to say here, that the geographic pattern of submarine violations in the Norwegian territorial waters confirms suspicions that special operations are planned and prepared for the surprise attack anticipated should war be launched in the North. The districts particularly sought out by intruding submarines all have easy access to the ocean from fjords that lead deep inside the country to traffic centers and vital communication links.[15] There are also reports, some by Norwegians recruited by the Soviets for espionage, of the landing of special agents from subs or surface ships near the Norwegian coast.

	'75	'76	'77	'78	'79	'80	'81	'82	'83	'84	'85	'86	'87	Total
SUBMARINE-LIKE OBJECTS, REPORTS AND CLASSIFICATIONS, 1975–1987														
Probable Submarine	1	2	1	1	1	0	0	1	2	0	0	1	2	12
Possible Submarine	16	9	12	5	5	3	4	7	20	4	9	7	10	111
Own/allied submarine	*	*	*	*	*	*	*	*	*	*	38	44	56	138
Unprocessed reports	19	10	10	4	7	4	4	11	21	64	39	42	32	267
False report	*	*	*	*	*	*	*	*	*	*	*	7	30	37
Total incidents	36	21	23	10	13	7	8	19	43	68	86	101	130	565

Chart 2. Submarinelike objects reported in Norwegian waters, 1975 to 1987.
Source: *Jane's Defence Weekly*, 1 October 1988, 746.

The "Whiskey on the Rocks" affair by itself offers highly instructive suggestions as to what the Soviets were up to in these sensitive Swedish waters, sixteen nautical miles within one of the two most important naval base areas in the country. The older diesel-powered Soviet sub was discovered run aground a skerry by a Swedish fisherman. The Swedish navy did not arrive on the scene until twelve hours after the stranding took place and numerous attempts, also with divers, had been made to extricate the vessel. Interestingly, the sub carried no markings or identifications.

The Swedish government held the submarine for ten days while both Swedish and international media feasted on the amusing, albeit shocking, news that a Soviet sub had managed to "get lost" and go aground in a high security area of a neutral country. As the log book and the hull was examined by Swedish government representatives, Soviet naval units waited in the international waters outside Karlskrona. The tone of the media reports became gradually more serious, especially as the Swedish government announced that it believed the submarine carried nuclear weapons.

The protest issued by Sweden to this disturbing intrusion was a sharp one, but the Soviet government's response was only that of indignant, injured innocence. Sub 137 had been on an ordinary training mission in the Baltic and virtually all navigation aids had failed simultaneously. Political pressures ensued, as Moscow charged Sweden with violating good neighborly relations in its "scandalous" interrogation of Capt. 2d Rank A. M. Gushchin and other Soviet officers on board. The Swedish Ambassador in Moscow, called in to meet a Soviet Deputy Foreign

Minister—with ten Soviet admirals lined up behind him—was issued the demand that the submarine be released forthwith.

In reality, Sub 137 had been inside Swedish waters for three days before it went aground and had to accomplish quite an ingenious feat of navigation to get inside the area of skerries, islands, and shoals it had succeeded in passing. The sub was also taking part in a larger operation, it was determined later, and had aboard a senior Soviet naval officer, a submarine squadron commander. The navigational failures claimed by the Soviets were implausible and intercepted radio communications between the sub and a Soviet destroyer standing by just outside Swedish territorial waters revealed orders from Vice Admiral Kalinin to Captain Gushchin to offer the explanation of navigational error for the intrusion.

The incursion occurred at the time of important Swedish torpedo tests being carried out in the area and immediately before a major Swedish naval exercise. A year later it was discovered that Swedish mine chains had been tampered with in several locations, a likely objective for the Soviet sub, it was suggested by the Swedish Defense Staff. More generally, the conclusion was drawn that the activity was of an intelligence nature and, ominously, involved "direct preparations for an attack against Sweden."[16]

This was not, however, the one and only submarine violation in Swedish territorial waters in 1981. They were in fact continuous. The world and most Swedes were simply unaware of the escalation of these illegal activities and what they were now signalling. Following the U-137 affair, the Soviet response to the embarrassing publicity and sharp Swedish protest note was to send even more subs. The number of detected intrusions in Swedish waters jumped from ten in 1981 (an average for the six previous years) to between forty and fifty in 1982. Four of these were judged by Swedish authorities to be major operations.

The Submarine Defense Commission

In fact, from 1982 on the foreign submarine operations against Sweden became both more frequent and more serious. The embarrassment suffered by the Soviets with the grounding of Submarine 137 outside of Karlskrona in 1981 did anything but cramp the vigor and audacity of the intruders. Quite the contrary.

For example, in October 1982, a number of alien submarines entered Harsfjarden in the Stockholm archipelago and penetrated the main base of the Swedish Navy at Musko with six or more submersibles, three of which were allegedly manned, midget bottom-crawling crafts of a type unknown by Swedish experts.[17] A midget submarine that entered Stockholm harbor a bit earlier was presumed to be part of the Harsfjarden operation. The penetration covered a wide geographical area and appeared very well coordinated. All identifications made—optical sightings, acoustical and ELINT (electronic intelligence) recordings, keel impressions left on the seabed—pointed to Warsaw Pact submarines, in most cases of the Whiskey class.

Following these serious incidents, a Submarine Defense Commission was established by the Swedish government. Its final report came in April 1983.[18] After a careful and exhaustive study, the commission left no doubts about the nationality of the intruder. A grave and important step was taken here, in the words of one commission member, declaring none other than the Soviet Union responsible.

Twenty-five certain and at least an equal number of possible violations of Swedish territorial waters were reported in 1983. In terms of the geographic pattern over the years, the commission clarified that the incursions had punctuated the greater part of the Baltic coast from Skaane in the south to Upper Norrland. Many had taken place in Swedish channels and fjords where sub operations had been repeatedly carried out. The behavior of the intruders was also characterized as increasingly provocative.

There was worse to come. Incursions continued even as the commission issued its remarkable report and Prime Minister Olof Palme verbally attacked the Soviet Union for these disturbing, illegal actions. Both the report and the protest were flatly rejected by the Soviet government, but in January 1984 Palme claimed to have been given assurance by Soviet Foreign Minister Andrei Gromyko that Sweden's neutrality policy would be respected.

Shortly after this, the longest and most provocative submarine incursion to that date took place, right in Karlskrona harbor, Sweden's second largest naval base. Three large submarines, several midget submarines, and small, motorized swimmer delivery vehicles (SDVs)—with visible diver activity—were involved in an operation that lasted thirty days. The Swedish antisubmarine warfare (ASW) unit met this threat with depth charges but had no orders to sink the vessels. The Swedish government also stuck with the policy it had announced in late 1983: that it was impossible to identify the intruder without concrete physical evidence—as in the case of U-137 found aground on a Swedish island in 1981.

The Role of Spies and Spetsnaz

Every year since then, the Swedish defense chief has regularly reported numerous new indications of submarine activities in Swedish territorial waters. While frequency and pattern vary, continued violations and the many indications that *spetsnaz* are involved pose a great challenge to neutral Sweden. A December 1987 government report claims "technical proof" of forty violations of Swedish waters by foreign submarines from April to September that year, including a repeat offense twelve to thirteen miles from downtown Stockholm. "Short of tying up at the Royal landing dock, this is about as outrageous as you can get," said one observer. [19]

While the Swedish government maintains it is unable to determine who the violators are, Swedish military officials have at times broken with the code of silence enforced on this question. Swedish commander-in-chief Bengt Gustafson put it as plainly as possible in December 1987: the Soviet Union is behind the incursions. [20] Another high military official, Col. Lars Hanson, chief of Stockholm's coastal artillery defenses until 1985, charged at the same time that too many restrictions had been imposed on his abilities to stop the sub intruders. He also charged that there must have been leaks from the highest levels of Swedish defense authorities, which informed the Soviets of moves about to be taken. "Many believe as I do," claimed Colonel Hanson. "To claim there are no spies now is to stick your head under the sand. We had Wennerstrom in the '60s and Bergling in the '70s. . . . It could be a Swedish Treholt." [21]

The spies referred to by Colonel Hanson are the most famous cases of Scandinavians caught and convicted for long-term espionage for the Soviet Union. All were classic "moles," placed within political and/or military elites with access to classified materials, and all were recruited by "diplomats" from the Soviet embassy, in Stockholm in the case of the two Swedes, and in Oslo in the case of Arne Treholt. Former Norwegian diplomat Treholt received the maximum sentence possible, twenty years, in 1985. Both Swedes were given life sentences. Bergling, convicted in 1979, managed to escape his Swedish jail in 1987, however, and went via Finland to the Soviet Union.

More serious than these and many other proven cases of espionage, however, are the many indications surfacing over the past few years that *spetsnaz* forces are involved in the sub incursions—and engaged in other missions on land as well. In Sweden, reports of diver activity in locations where foreign subs have been sighted are numerous. Obviously, the midget subs crawling on the bottom of Swedish fjords and inlets, leaving identifiable marks in many cases, had to be manned by specially trained personnel. The suggestion is that these vessels are often left for a relatively long period of time, while the agents aboard surface and go ashore for special missions. Containers with plastic-wrapped food have been found on several sites where submarine activity has occurred. One of the last such reported, near Karlskrona in 1986 (just three miles from the sighting of foreign divers a couple of years earlier), had instructions attached in a foreign language not publicly identified by Swedish authorities. This latter find was kept secret for over two years.[22]

Other finds of a highly revealing nature have been made over the years, and as recently as August 1988. Swedish newspapers have reported the discovery of divers' masks of a foreign origin in the northern part of the Stockholm archipelago. This was in the vicinity of the area where the Swedish navy had launched another major submarine hunt in May 1988, this time trying depth charges that reportedly damaged one of the intruding vessels.[23] Similar finds have been made elsewhere in Swedish waters and beyond. The Finnish marines have determined that diving equipment discovered near the island of Aaland was of Soviet origin. Containers of explosives ("trotyl") have also been found in the waters near Stockholm, wrapped in plastic and with inscriptions in Cyrillic.[24]

Many reports and discoveries that confirm Soviet culpability and suggest the targeting of Sweden for special operations have come from civilians and amateur sleuths. The Swedish government has been reluctant to release information pointing in this direction just as it appears reluctant to pursue the submarine hunt with the vigor and force needed to punish the intruders. Swedish neutrality has become a virtual catechism and Swedish leaders take great pride in their initiatives toward communication and confidence building internationally. For Sweden to sink or catch a Soviet sub after this prolonged period of serious violations and attendant provocative activities would be to admit that Sweden is not just "between the superpowers" but that it has one identifiable potential enemy: the Soviet Union.

So far this conclusion has been avoided by all official representatives. Hopes appear to remain that a political solution to the submarine problem can be worked out without too much publicity. Yet there is much more activity of Soviet-bloc origin beyond submarine escapades for the Swedes to worry about, all of it pointing in the same direction. Apart from more or less "normal" political espionage, with eight major cases of Swedes working for the KGB or GRU since World War II, some unconventional and highly disturbing activities on the part of Polish nationals and other East Europeans have been disclosed.

The sensational story of the Polish art dealers surfaced in 1985. Swedish officers and pilots, it turned out, had been "visited" for years by Polish art dealers who systematically mapped the homes and habits of their Swedish targets. In 1979 and 1981, Swedish police had caught groups of these travelling salesmen and found sixty-six different maps marking airstrips, new roads and bridges, mobilization routes, and localities suitable for airlandings. Clear proofs of espionage, said the chief prosecutor, but still not enough to bring convictions in court, given the uncertainty about who among these "art dealers" were guilty. Eight were expelled from Sweden, and many others were involved.

East European "salesmen" visited 113 Swedish pilots in the following years, and even students of the Air War College were sought out. The art was mass produced but signed as original, and the salesmen often presented themselves as poor art students. The Swedish security police have mapped out their operations, according to newspaper reports.[25] Notably, from 1984 on there was a clear shift in their attention from military installations to key personnel. And as late as 1988, Lieutenant Colonel Hjort, chief of security for Swedish defense, revealed that the foreign dealers were continuing investigative pursuits of Swedish defense.[26]

The increase in Eastern bloc TIR truck traffic in Sweden is also noted with concern, especially as reports have come in of these lingering inexplicably long near sensitive and restricted military areas. These trucks are exempt from conventional customs inspection on the way to or from Finland and the Soviet Union. Drivers and other personnel on the trucks have also been spotted with sophisticated camera equipment, even videocameras, near the same areas.

Hostile intelligence operations directed at Sweden are constant, but increasingly sophisticated, as several representatives of the Swedish security police have confirmed. Foreign agents have reportedly been seeking positions within Sweden's telecommunications system, in Swedish radio, in recent years. In December 1987, a new educational film was prepared by Swedish defense authorities. Titled "Forebudet" (The Warning), it described how Eastern powers sabotage and diversion groups act at the launching of an invasion.[27] A highly uncomfortable reminder of a possibility that the Swedish government itself does not appear to take seriously.

Sweden in Soviet War Plans

"One does not invade with submarines," said Lennard Bodstrom, former Swedish foreign minister, during a bitter exchange over the Soviet sub incursions in 1986. "He's got that backwards," says Col. Bo Hugemark, chair of the Department of Military History at Militara Hojskolan Svenska (MHS, Sweden's military college). "It is precisely invasion [that] it is all about."[28] Submarine operations of the type conducted on the Swedish coast with some frequency since 1981 are one of several ways to make an invasion both cheaper and more secure, according to this noted Swedish defense analyst.

He is not alone in reaching this conclusion. Already in 1983 the Submarine Defense Commission's careful and exhaustive investigation pointed to the Soviet submarine activity in Swedish waters representing "the preparatory phases of military operational planning." The Swedish Parliamentary Defense Committee's report of 1984 confirmed this in a different evaluation. "The motives, which are difficult to determine, can primarily be considered as different forms of preparation for eventual crisis and war situations."[29] A host of other analysts have, sometimes reluctantly, come around to agree to the sobering and startling end note summarized here.

The evidence and suggestions of espionage and *spetsnaz* activity in Sweden in the 1970s and 1980s cited earlier offer ample support for the basic thrust of these theories. While there is little analysis available to inform us how these special operations fit into the overall contingency plans for the invasion of Sweden, followed by or combined with an attack on Norway (that is, exactly *how* they can assist Soviet forces in carrying out a rather massive and risky operation), there is by now a fair understanding of the role played by Scandinavia, in particular Norway, in Soviet conventional war strategy. Norway, at least northern Norway, must be taken, if the war in the Atlantic is to be won for the Soviet Union. With the effective closing of the ALOCs and SLOCs, a capitulation or neutralization of Germany may come within weeks if the nuclear leg of NATO's defense strategy is no longer operative, which appears to be the goal of Soviet-supported peace campaigns, arms control proposals, and diplomatic moves in recent years.

The stakes are formidable, indeed. The use of espionage and special operations by the Soviet Union is not new and certainly not surprising given the significance of the objective suggested here. Yet one is compelled to ask why these continuing and quite provocative operations are undertaken against a neutral country that has gone to great lengths to satisfy the Soviets of its dedication to peace and nonpartisanship in East-West affairs. Can the political fallout possibly be worth the tactical gains potentially scored in the unlikely event that a crisis would prompt a Soviet invasion in the North, in particular Sweden? And what about the Central Front, surely the most important in any military conflict between East and West? Why should the Soviets waste time and resources on the conquest and/or intimidation of a country that is not an integral part of the key area of struggle, against a country that presents neither a military threat nor a likely hindrance to a Soviet military advance on the European continent?

These key questions not only have confounded analysts over the years, they have made many shrug off both evidence and near inevitable conclusions. The implications of Soviet special operations against Sweden thus did not enter the debate about Soviet "new thinking" in foreign and military policy in the 1980s. And yet, it is difficult to conceive of other examples of Soviet behavior so sharply in contrast with the pronounced goals of openness, cooperation, and moving away from regional conflict toward a simply "sufficient" defense.

Targeting Sweden

The conventional evaluation of Soviet military objectives in a European war does recognize the greatly increased strategic value of the Northern Region given the buildup of the strategic bastion of the Kola peninsula. The importance of keeping open the lines of communication for the survival of Europe's Central Front is also conceded and the relative vulnerability of NATO's northern flank was of course what led to the launching of an American Maritime Strategy in the early 1980s.

Yet Sweden has never been ceded any strategic significance in itself except as a possible area of access to northern Norway, or for securing passage through the Danish Straits. This in itself would suggest Sweden to be a likely target for pressures, threats, or limited military campaigns from the Soviet Union in the case of a war, but it does not explain why Sweden is singled out among all countries of the world for special operations of the character and frequency reported earlier—in a period of relative stability and search for East-West reconciliation.

Clearly, contingency war plans and preparations are still taken seriously by Soviet leaders. The submarine incursions and the use of *spetsnaz* in Sweden well into the fourth year of Gorbachev's leadership suggest no change of course for the eastern superpower, but rather the will and daring to proceed with preparations for a possible surprise attack of an unconventional nature. The risk, for that matter, may appear minimal, since so very few have attempted a serious analysis of what is afoot. The Swedish government itself persists in its policy of avoiding a confrontation with the eastern superpower, even refusing to point the finger at the violator of its territorial integrity since 1983.

Regional perspective alone cannot easily explain what is behind the Soviet maneuvers vis-à-vis Sweden. The Baltic Sea is, of course, of great importance to the Soviet Union: Soviet dominance here must be assured and access denied to Western navies in case of war for all the reasons earlier reviewed. But this could surely be achieved without a serious incursion or invasion of Sweden, an operation that *could* become very costly and would draw valuable resources and forces from the suggested key objectives on the Central Front.

Only as the larger strategic perspective can reasonable explanations for the very special attention given Sweden by the Soviet Union be suggested. The Baltic and Sweden must be viewed in the context of a conflict that includes the Kola bastion, northern Norway and the Norwegian Sea, the North Atlantic, *and* the Central Front. Should the battle in Europe ever be launched, or erupt for a whole complex of reasons, there is considerable promise in the use of surprise, special operations, and *spetsnaz* against a country unprepared to deal with such contingencies, against a country whose defeat would give the attacker a definite operational military and ultimately strategic political advantage.

There is, as discussed earlier, the question of access to Norway, which even conventional strategic thinkers concede to be of importance. Here, it must be added that with the prepositioning of heavy materiel for the American Marine Amphibious Brigade (MAB) in Trondelag, swift action is required to take possession not just of key points in northern Norway, but also mid-Norway, to prevent a possible American involvement. Whereas airfields, installations and significant fjords in the North may be taken or put out of function in a matter of days using *spetsnaz*, airborne, air assault and naval infantry *desants*, attack helicopters and aircraft of various types based on the Kola peninsula, it is unlikely that Trondelag could be occupied or the necessary operations here be carried out unless both Soviet troops and planes from the Leningrad Military District can use mid-Sweden for a swift crossover.

Political intimidation of Sweden may be sufficient to obtain the necessary easements for such passage and speculation has surfaced that this may be the main purpose of Soviet submarine operations in Swedish waters over the years. Having tested the Swedes in regard to their will and/or ability to protect the country's territorial integrity, the Soviets can proceed to exploit both the political and tactical advantages gained by presenting the Swedish government at the opportune time with an ultimatum: Allow for necessary overflights and troop transports to Norway for a brief and necessary "defense action," or expect your superpower neighbor to take the measures needed vis-à-vis your own land to assure the safety of its forces.

Unthinkable? The Swedish government allowed the transit of German forces to and from Norway during the Second World War for fear of suffering the fate of its Scandinavian neighbors, invaded and occupied in 1940. If any history lessons are studied and pondered by the Soviet military and political leaders, surely those of the "Great Patriotic War" are. We have, in fact, evidence from captured Soviet contingency plans for an invasion of Scandinavia in World War II that Sweden even then was an important part of the war strategy.[30] The strategic direction was seen by the Soviets to lie across southern Scandinavia, from Stockholm to Oslo, Bergen, and Trondheim, and the operation would have relied heavily on amphibious landings in southern Sweden—where many of the Soviet sub intrusions in recent years have been concentrated.

Yet Sweden has more to offer than possible acquiescence to Soviet domination in the Baltic and transits to Norway. Exercising control over approaches to the Barents, Baltic, and Norwegian seas entails the basing of Soviet naval and air forces in some proximity to the contested areas. Norway offers harbors and anchorages in abundance, but relatively few airfields. Suitable airfields are to be found in Sweden, however, airfields necessary for better protection against NATO air attacks from the Central Front and at the same time immensely useful for Soviet sorties against the same front and against targets in England. Southern Norway has attained a new significance for the same reasons, but again, for airfields in southern and western Norway to be taken, it is essential that Sweden be used, one way or the other.

"Operation Garbo"

Scenarios like these are suggested as possible and likely in the event of conventional war in Europe.[31] Yet another alternative strategy may offer even greater promise in terms of achieving the Soviet objective of putting NATO in disarray, even breaking the U.S./European defense link. A separate military campaign against Sweden, preceded by sabotage and other special operations carried out by the now well-prepared *spetsnaz* forces, could be brought to a successful conclusion before NATO or the U.S. found it possible or desirable to effectively intervene. With Sweden occupied by Soviet forces, Norway's position would be untenable. Soviet demands for cessation of its NATO membership could no longer be resisted, especially so since Denmark, long the weakest political link on NATO's northern flank, would immediately crumble and seek refuge in a new demilitarized neutrality. That would leave the rest of NATO without its flank operation in the north, without the intelligence network, the harbors and airfields so essential for securing of the sea lines. Germany and its remaining allies in Europe would have to contemplate fighting a protracted conventional war with no assured supplies coming in from the United States. In such circumstances the specter of a Soviet dominated, non-aligned Europe may appear less repelling than the assured destruction of either an exhausting conventional war leading to probable defeat, or the holocaust that could follow the entrance of nuclear weapons in the defense of Europe.

Surely a separate attack against Sweden would make no sense unless preparations were made, both of a military and political nature, creating plausible excuses as well as the best possible conditions for a swift victory. It is a rather far-fetched scenario to map out, and yet one that Soviet special operations against Sweden in recent years invite. Some Swedish analysts and writers have, in fact, found the temptation to follow this train of thought irresistible.

Among the most intriguing, and chilling, treatments given the Swedish predicament is the novel *Operation Garbo: A Thriller About A Possible Reality*.[32] Published in Sweden in the spring of 1988, the author or authors (rumored to be three of the sharpest and best known Swedish defense analysts) use the pseudonym "Harry Winter." The book has caused quite a sensation with its detailed and seemingly realistic description of a massive isolated Soviet attack on Sweden in the year 1992. Command of extensive military data, some possibly of a classified nature, insights into operational plans and defense policies, together with a highly sophisticated comprehension of the Soviet decision-making apparatus and its current and post-*perestroika* problems combine to make the frightening story of "Operation Garbo" seem like much more than a work of fiction. Indeed the subtitle suggests the authors intend for it to be far more.

It is against the background of uprisings in the Baltic states spreading to Eastern Europe, together with the failure of economic reforms, that the author(s) see Soviet leaders deciding to move ahead with a war plan carefully developed and prepared over the years. "Operation Garbo" takes full note of the series of submarine intrusions, the use of *spetsnaz*, the espionage and mapping of key personnel and defense sites that for years have been reported in Sweden. The explosive fictional account is fully in accord with what is known and suspected about Soviet special operations in Sweden. The analysis offered of the use of *spetsnaz* and unconventional warfare in this sensational book is, in fact, given substance and to a great part repeated in non-fiction works, written by both academics and defense analysts. [33] Both logic and substance in terms of grasp of the operations concerned impress in every instance. Together they go a long way in explaining the advantage of *spetsnaz* and how special operations make an otherwise costly and risky invasion feasible. It is, in other words, a highly instructive thriller, based on a premise that is regretfully within the realm of reality.

The Spetsnaz Advantage

The problem for the Soviet Union is first to find methods to break Swedish resistance to an attack so swiftly that NATO cannot find a way to go to Sweden's assistance. It must of course be a surprise operation. But even a blitzkrieg of the traditional character takes time and is very costly, in terms of resources used. If the Swedes are given even twenty-four hours' advance notice, their aircraft, coastal artillery, and naval units can be readied. Even though Swedish defense forces may be woefully inadequate to ultimately deal with the Soviet air force and navy, the Swedes could throw Soviet conventional forces off their timetable and perhaps cause a moderation of Soviet plans.

During such a period of delay, Swedish mobilization would be completed or be well under way. More Soviet forces would be required to subdue Sweden and at least a week, in one estimate, would be added to the time needed for the Soviets to establish a bridgehead and to carry out clean-up operations necessary for the attacking forces to move inland and move across mid-Sweden toward Norway. Time enough, very likely, for NATO to make the necessary moves to respond, time possibly for the American MAB to be flown into its prepositioning site in mid-Norway. This would be too risky an operation, when the aim is to achieve the collapse of Swedish defenses *before* a counteroperation is launched from the West. The aim is, of course, to score the necessary gains using conventional force only, thereby keeping the Americans away from triggering the dreaded nuclear war.

How then can *spetsnaz* already placed in Sweden and the minisubs operating in Swedish waters change the picture for the attackers? On land the threat of the Swedish air force can be effectively minimized if the pilots are located and murdered before the mobilization orders have gone out. The Polish "art dealers" have done the essential mapping for this action to proceed, and *spetsnaz* agents can, of course, be infiltrated in advance with both necessary documents and sufficient language capabilities for access. Sabotage can simultaneously be carried out against command, control, communications and intelligence (C3I) centers, bulk electric power facilities, and other targets to blind the Swedes and cause havoc in the rear. Agents in place, e.g., at radio stations, can cause additional distortion or delay in the Swedish response.

Special sabotage teams that have become very familiar with the Swedish coast can be set ashore by submarines that may also serve as launch platforms for a variety of weapons directed at key point targets. Other patrols can cause disarray and destruction of Swedish coastal artillery, minefields, and sensor strings. *Spetsnaz* and submarines may also be used to mine Swedish channels or specific ships in port. Even very simple means and force in this way can seriously degrade much of the Swedish defense.

The success of operations such as those suggested here will of course depend on the effectiveness of Soviet reconnaissance efforts (the "reconnaissance battle") prior to the invasion. As reviewed here, these appear to have been rather systematically pursued over the last decade or so. What has been learned about the *spetsnaz* teams themselves suggests that they are a selected, exceedingly well trained and well rewarded elite. There is every indication that should the Soviets sometime in the future decide to activate contingency plans made for an attack on Sweden, they are ready to do so with the use of their *spetsnaz* units.

Thereby much of the job is done. Swedish defenses may be effectively destroyed, and mobilization efforts disrupted before any massive air attack or invasion is launched from the Soviet Union. Not only will the operation be "cheaper" this way, but it may also by its swift access affect the psychological blow necessary to prompt Norway and Denmark to leave the Western alliance. It is essential now for our strategists to take this threat seriously. Scenarios will have to be adjusted, conventional thinking abandoned if we are to prepare for a contingency that, however unlikely today, could become a reality in times of impending acute crisis for the Soviet Union.

Notes

1. SACLANT Adm. Isaac C. Kidd, quoted in Finne Sollie, *Norge oy de Europeiske Interessene i Nordomaradene* (Oslo: The Norwegian Atlantic Committee, 1986): 5.
2. See especially the Norwegian edition of the *Military Balance in Northern Europe, 1985-1986* (London: International Institute for Strategic Studies). This edition, published by the Norwegian Atlantic Committee, Oslo, adds data and information available from many sources to complement the picture drawn by the IISS.
3. Dexter Jerome Smith, "How SACLANT Surveys the Seas," *Defence*, July 1988, 478.
4. David Fulghum, "Low-Profile A-10 Boosted As Key to Norway Defense," *Army Times*, 20 June 1988, 34.
5. William Tuohy (Los Angeles Times), "Soviets shift naval forces to the Arctic," *Anchorage Daily News*, 17 July 1988, 1, A11.
6. Data derived from Skorve and Ries, *Investigating Kola*, 49, 52; id., "Satellite's view of Severomorsk base," *Jane's Defence Weekly*, 16 July 1988, 68–69; Maj. Thomas C. Linn, USMC, "Marines in the Naval Campaign: Integrating Land/Sea Operations," *Armed Forces Journal International*, April 1988, 80, 82; and Henry van Loon, "'Arrowhead Express' Underscores Importance of Norway to NATO Defense," *Armed Forces Journal International*, May 1988, 32.
7. Rolf Soderlind, "Soviet Sub Developments Prompt Call for More NATO Northern Exercises," *Armed Forces Journal International*, March 1988, 32; "Kola base for 'Typhoon' submarines," *Jane's Defence Weekly*, 6 September 1986.
8. "Kola unveiled," *Jane's Defence Weekly*, 13 September 1986, 538–540.
9. Short for *spetsialnogo naznacheniya*, or "special designation," used by the Soviets to describe a wide variety of non-standard units with unusual missions. The term "spetsnaz" is used here to describe troops of extraordinary selection, training, and expertise, possessing higher than average political reliability, in unique organizations with unusual equipment, used in specialized missions behind enemy lines at all levels of conflict and war.
10. Skorve and Ries, *Investigating Kola*, 49, 52; id., "Satellite's view of Severomorsk base," 68–69.
11. John Berg, "Norway reveals exact locations of Soviet bases," *Jane's Defence Weekly*, 17 May 1986, 865.
12. Dr. Waldemar Erfurth, *Warfare in the Far North*, Department of the Army Pamphlet 20-292 (Washington DC: Headquarters, Department of the Army, October 1951): 7.
13. Kirsten Amundsen, "Soviet Submarines in Scandinavian Waters," *The Wash-*

ington Quarterly, Summer 1985, 113; Cmdr. M. G. M. W. Ellis, Royal Navy (Retired), "Sweden's Ghosts?" *Proceedings*, March 1986, 95–101.

14. "Swedes Identify Soviet Submarines," *Jane's Defence Weekly*, 29 November 1986, 1261.

15. Amundsen, 112.

16. Milton Leitenberg, *Soviet Submarine Operations in Swedish Waters, 1980–1986* (Washington DC: Praeger with CSIS, 1987): 47; see also, Anders Heilberg and Anders Jorle, *Submarine 137: Ten Days That Shook Sweden* (Stockholm: Atlantis, 1984): 246–264.

17. Amundsen, 113; Walter S. Mossberg, *The Wall Street Journal*, 23 June 1983, 1, 24.

18. Submarine Defense Commission, *To Meet the Submarine Threat: The Submarine Incursions and Swedish Security Policy* (Stockholm, 1983).

19. H. B. Jensen, "Sinking Relations With the Soviets," *Insight*, 8 February 1988, 34.

20. *Svenska Dagbladet* (Stockholm), 18 December 1987, 5.

21. *Dagens Nyheter* (Stockholm), 27 November 1987, 5.

22. *Svenska Dagbladet* (Stockholm), 14 September 1986, 1.

23. Ibid., 2 August 1988, 1.

24. Ibid., 19 September 1987, 5.

25. Ibid., 5 September 1985, 5.

26. See, also, Robert L. King, "Swedes Give Away Their War Plans," *Armed Forces Journal International*, July 1986, 32, and Julian Isherwood, "Swedes See Through Transparent Eastern 'Students'," Ibid., March 1989, 42.

27. *Svenska Dagbladet* (Stockholm), 29 January 1988, 5.

28. Bo Hugemark, "Ubatar – finns de?" in *Vaart Forsvar*, No. 6, September 1987, 6.

29. Swedish Parliamentary Defense Committee, *Swedish Security Policy in the 1990s* (Stockholm: 1984): 51–52.

30. Robert P. McQuail, "Khrushchev's Right Flank," *Military Review*, January 1964, 7–23.

31. Stig Lofgren, "Soviet Submarines Against Sweden," *Strategic Review*, Winter 1984; Lyn Hansen, "Soviet Spetsnaz Operations On the Northern Flank," *Stra-Tech Studies*, No. SS84-2, 1984; Wilhelm Agrell, "Hvorfor Ubaat-krenelsene?" *Sikkerhets og Nedrustningspolitiske Utwalg* (Denmark, 1988); Amundsen; Hugemark.

32. Harry Winter, *Operasjon Garbo. En thriller om en mulig virkelighet* (Operation Garbo: A Thriller About a Possible Reality) (Stockholm: Timbro Forlag, 1988).

33. See Hugemark; Agrell; Hansen.

CHAPTER 10
Prague to Kabul

John H. Merritt

Much has been alleged about Soviet capabilities to paralyze Western Europe through the use of *spetsialnogo naznacheniya*, or *spetsnaz*. Western, and in particular American, respect for the gross damage comparatively small units of special forces can do is rooted in historical experience. For example, at a critical point during the December 1944 Ardennes Offensive (the "Battle of the Bulge"), the Germans unleashed the devastating pseudo- (false flag) operations of SS Col. Otto Skorzeny's Panzerbrigade 150 and Stielau Unit, comprised of English-speaking Germans disguised as Americans and used for long- and short-range reconnaissance, sabotage, to spread confusion and initiate combat assaults behind enemy lines.[1] Even though hastily thrown together, marginally trained, and poorly equipped, Skorzeny's commandos took the unsuspecting and conventionally-minded Allies by surprise, caused panic in the Allied command all the way to Paris (where Supreme Allied Commander Gen. Dwight D. Eisenhower became a virtual prisoner of his bodyguard at his headquarters), and otherwise threw the Allied rear into disarray. As a result of the exploits of Skorzeny and several less dramatic experiences, few Western military planners and intelligence personnel are inclined to underestimate the potential of enemy special forces.

The Soviets, moreover, have a long history of varied success in the use of special forces. For the past three decades, they have fielded a large *spetsnaz* force, though the exact magnitude is the object of intense debate.

In this time they have used their special forces on a variety of occasions, most extensively during the invasions of the neighboring socialist states of Czechoslovakia (1968) and Afghanistan (1979). An examination of Soviet employment of *spetsnaz* during these invasions, and in particular in operations against the capital cities of Prague and Kabul is instructive. Through the study and comparison of *spetsnaz* operations against these cities one can gain a measure of knowledge about Soviet modus operandi in special operations and, with such foreknowledge, be forewarned.

The Soviets are careful when it comes to the employment of *spetsnaz* or any other form of military force to settle disputes with neighboring states. Their first and most favored approach in settling disputes (i.e., getting what they want) is through negotiation. They will also attempt to improve the odds of quick Soviet victory, should violence become necessary, through political and military isolation and weakening of their prospective enemy. Once they have decided on military intervention, the Soviets will try to surprise their enemy at the tactical, operational, and strategic levels, and will seek a quick and relatively bloodless victory by suddenly overwhelming their enemy with massive military power projected into the enemy's political-military center of mass on multiple, convergent ground and air axes.[2] Such was the pattern of events culminating in the invasions of Czechoslovakia and Afghanistan.

Czechoslovakia

The Soviets invaded Czechoslovakia to stamp out a counterrevolution known in the West as the "Prague Spring," actually a liberal reform movement that began on 5 January 1968. On that date, the 110-member Central Committee of the Czechoslovak Communist Party meeting in Hradcany Castle overlooking Prague formally ended the fourteen-year reign of First Secretary Antonin Novotny. The man chosen to replace Novotny was the forty-six-year-old Slovak and seemingly unremarkable Party apparatchik Alexander Dubcek.

Despite outward appearances of normalcy, Czechoslovakia was about to attempt a radical political transformation that would seek to reduce autocratic Party controls on the everyday lives of the people of Czechoslovakia. The collective goals of this movement would ultimately become known as "socialism with a human face." Significant change soon followed the election of Dubcek. On 5 March, the ruling Presidium of the Party transferred responsibility for ideology from Novotny associate Jiri Hendrych to reformer Josef Spacek. On 22 March, the Party liberals forced Novotny to resign from the presidency of the Republic, a position he had held for the past eleven years. In April, on the twentieth anniversary of the coup that had brought the Communists to power in Prague, the Party published an "Action Program" calling for a "major experiment in democratic communism."[3]

The Prague Spring not only rankled Soviet ideologues who feared reform would cause loss of Party control, but stirred the hopes of a sympathetic audience in the Ukrainian SSR, part of which has strong ethnic ties to Czechoslovakia. In the seven and one-half months from the election of Dubcek to the invasion, the Soviets attempted to undermine the reform movement through political strong-arming, saber-rattling, and covert action.[4] Initially, the Soviets tried to negotiate the demise of the Prague reforms, the effort culminating in summit meetings with the Czechs in the end of July at Cierna nad Tisou and on 3 August at Bratislava. At the July meeting, the entire Czechoslovak presidium met with all but two members of the Soviet Politburo, and Dubcek is reported to have agreed under intense Soviet pressure to moderate the reformation to make it less offensive to the Soviets. The agreed compromise reached by Czechoslovakia and the Soviet Union was then confirmed at the Bratislava conference attended by the Soviets, Czechs, Poles, Hungarians, Bulgarians, and East Germans.[5]

While negotiations were in progress, Soviet diplomacy sought to isolate the Czech reformers, first by lining up active allies of the Soviet cause within and without Czechoslovakia, and second by persuading other countries, and especially the U.S. and NATO countries, to limit their actions to moral support for the Czechs.[6] In July, the leaders of the Soviet Union, East Germany, Poland, Hungary, and Bulgaria sent a diplomatic note to Prague charging that the Czech reforms endangered Party control, and warning that "the situation in Czechoslovakia jeopardizes the common vital interests of other socialist countries," and that they shared the task of "a decisive rebuff to the forces of anti-Communism."[7] The Czechs stood firm in the face of the Soviet-led opposition in the Warsaw Pact. Only Rumania, among Pact nations, did not join the condemnation of the Czechs. To the south, the independent socialist states of Yugoslavia and Albania actively endorsed the Prague initiatives, and served notice that they would defend their sovereignty by force of arms should the Soviets attempt to intervene in their countries, but offered little more than moral support to the Czechs.

Parallel to the negotiations and diplomatic activity, the Soviets laid the basis for military action. A continuing series of Warsaw Pact and Soviet military exercises were conducted in and around Czechoslovakia during the summer and were accompanied by numerous visits by political and military delegations. Following the Warsaw Pact "SUVAMA" exercise, sixteen thousand Soviet troops remained in Czechoslovakia in a much-delayed withdrawal.[8] As the supreme power within the Warsaw Pact, the Soviets also directed the Czechs to send large quantities of fuel and ammunition to East Germany for an exercise there (thereby depleting stocks that might otherwise be available to resisting Czech forces).[9] From late July until mid-August, the Soviets conducted a massive logistics exercise in the western USSR.[10]

In preparing for the invasion, the Soviets dispatched Army Gen. Ivan G. Pavlovskiy to survey the Czechoslovakian situation under the guise of conducting Warsaw Pact business.[11] The Soviets also in this period succeeded in forcing the Czechs to close down their Military-Political Academy, a hotbed of liberal activism in Prague, possibly as a result of a visit by the head of the Main Political Administration of the Soviet military and advocate of intervention, Gen. A. Epishev.[12] The Warsaw Pact also scheduled a Czech military exercise in western Bohemia for 21–22 August, to divert Czech forces away from invasion crossing points on the Czech frontiers.[13]

The ready access to Czechoslovakia permitted Warsaw Pact representatives, observers, Soviet advisors, and the like, ample opportunity for pre-invasion reconnaissance. Contacts with hardline Czech fifth columnists dispersed throughout the Czech political, military, state security, and media yielded inside information and other assistance. All along, the Soviets orchestrated an intensive propaganda campaign that emphasized the imminent threat from NATO and Western subversion, and tried to rationalize the need for subsequent drastic measures.

After lengthy debate in the Kremlin, the Soviets decided that armed intervention was their only recourse. Author P. H. Vigor suggests that the Politburo reached their decision to use armed intervention after receiving indications that the U.S. government did not consider the Soviet-Czech dispute serious:

[A] prime indicator of the degree of seriousness with which the American government was treating the Soviet-Czech dispute was what the American President did each successive Friday evening. If he stayed in Washington for the weekend it was assumed he was taking things seriously; but if he went off to his ranch in Texas it was assumed that he was not.[14]

On Friday, 2 August, President Lyndon B. Johnson left Washington, D.C., indicating that he would not return until September, except perhaps for an occasional quick visit. To the Kremlin, this signalled that the Americans were not on their guard and were not prepared for swift, momentous decisions.[15] The Soviets also guessed, correctly as it turned out, that a main indicator for the West of the potential for Soviet invasion of Czechoslovakia was the activities of the Group of Soviet Forces Germany (GSFG). They therefore kept most of GSFG in their barracks and used other forces already engaged in a large exercise for the invasion, and thereby facilitated their surprise of Czechoslovakia and the West.[16]

Soviet *spetsnaz* and key elements of *Vozdushno-Desantniye Voiska* (VDV) airborne forces may have been briefed on their respective roles in the invasion as early as Friday, 16 August.[17] The actual decision by the Politburo to intervene militarily was probably made, according to author Robert Littell, over the following weekend and conveyed to the leaders of Bulgaria, East Germany, Hungary, and Poland on 18 August. According to Littell, the final vote of the politburo was seven to four in favor of force, with Aleksei N. Kosygin, Mikhail A. Suslov, Nikolai V. Podgorny, and Gennadi I. Voronov opposed.[18]

At 2000 hours on Tuesday, 20 August, army officers of Warsaw Pact units in East Germany, Poland, Hungary, and the Ukraine assembled their troops and read them a letter written in July by ninety-nine conservative workers at the Auto Praha factory in Prague expressing agreement with Soviet alarm over trends in Czechoslovakia and advocating military intervention by Warsaw Pact forces as a "guarantee of our safety." Two hours later, these units moved out of their cantonments and headed toward the Czech border, crossing at eighteen points in a coordinated maneuver at about 2300 hours.[19] The commander-in-chief of the approximately half-million-man invasion force was General Pavlovskiy. Because of extensive Soviet preparation beforehand, and the surprise, magnitude, and swiftness of the invasion, the Czechoslovaks offered no organized military resistance to the invaders.

The most important and elaborate of the seven Soviet air assault landings in Czechoslovakia was at Prague's Ruzyne Airport. The Prague operation began with a deception. The initial planes to land were civilian, in Aeroflot livery, and carried transponders that indicated civilian, not mili-

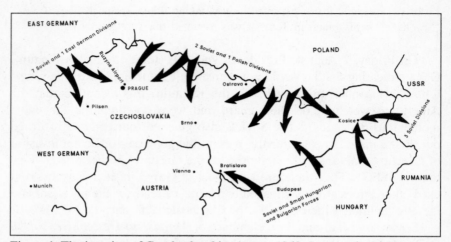

Figure 1. The invasion of Czechoslovakia, August 1968. Source: Colin Chapman, *August 21st: The Rape of Czechoslovakia* (New York: J. B. Lippincott Company, 1968).

tary, presence to electronic interrogators at the airport.[20] Just before 2030 hours, an unscheduled Aeroflot An-24 from Moscow landed, taxied to the end of the tarmac and remained parked. At about 2130 hours (some sources say as late as 2300 hours) a second unscheduled Aeroflot An-24 landed, declaring its departure airfield as Lvov, in the Ukraine. From the second aircraft emerged a number of civilians. The civilians were cordially welcomed at an unusually active customs office by Czech Colonel Elias, commander of the Security Air Squadron of the Ministry of the Interior, and Lt. Col. Rudolph Stachovsky, chief of passport control at Ruzyne. The passengers soon left for Prague and their aircraft returned to Lvov about thirty minutes after its arrival.[21]

Just after 2400 hours, airport dispatchers in the control tower were told by telephone that the airport was closed to all incoming or outgoing traffic. At about 0200 hours, cars belonging to Aeroflot arrived at the airport carrying armed civilians (possibly KGB *spetsnaz*) and Soviet army officers, who took up positions around customs and the foreign departures area and took over the control tower and airport communications. At about the same time, at least one and possibly two unannounced Aeroflot An-12 aircraft landed and taxied up to the airport administration building.

From the aircraft sprang GRU *spetsnaz* who linked up with their counter-parts in civilian clothes and seized the control tower, hangars, and administration building. The several dozen *spetsnaz* entering the main air-port building chased all airport personnel and tourists found therein out into the front of the building. Outside, the Soviets separated the men from the women and children, keeping the men outside and allowing the women and children to sit in the airport waiting room. At about 0530 hours, a Soviet major (possibly wearing the gold star of a Hero of the Soviet Union) arrived and allowed the airport personnel and tourists to leave the airport, but only on foot.[22]

In trail behind the An-12 more GRU *spetsnaz* and paratroopers of the 103rd Guards Airborne Division began landing in military transports at one-minute intervals, reportedly directed either by the An-24 that had landed just before 2030 hours or by a Soviet Air Force general who was with the initial GRU *spetsnaz* assault force at the end of the runway.[23] Within ninety minutes of the arrival of the lead assault An-12, planeloads of GRU *spetsnaz* were moving, allegedly on commandeered transport,[24] the six miles to the center of Prague. Objectives seized in Prague included the presidential palace, Letza Hill (used by the airborne troops to position their artillery), bridges over the Vltava, the radio station on Vinohradska Street, other radio and television stations, railway stations, the post office, telephone central offices, central crossroads, and key leaders of the reform movement.[25]

At about 0300 hours, Czechoslovak Premier Oldrich Cernik was seized at bayonet point by "Soviet airborne troops" (possibly *spetsnaz*) in the government presidium building. Shortly after 0400 hours, three armored vehicles led by a black Volga sedan from the Soviet Embassy pulled up in front of the Central Committee building, headquarters of the Czechoslovak Communist Party (CCP). They were followed by still more armored vehicles.[26] Inside the sedan were Czech Col. Bohumil Molnar, an official of the Ministry of the Interior, and two KGB[27] agents. Moving inside, the sedan's passengers and their military escort captured reformers Dubcek, Josef Smrkovsky (chairman of the National Assembly), Franti-sek Kriegel, Josef Spacek, Bohumil Simon (leading secretary of the city committee of the Party in Prague), and other officials.[28] One of Dubcek's cabinet, Zdenck Mlynar described their capture:

Suddenly the door of Dubcek's office flew open and about eight soldiers and low-ranking officers with machine guns rushed in, surrounding us from behind around a large table, and aimed their weapons at the backs of our heads. Then two officers came into the room. . . . One . . . announced that he was taking us into custody and began to issue various commands.[29]

Later that day, members of Dubcek's cabinet who were considered leading reformers were taken by car to Ruzyne Airport and flown under *spetsnaz* guard in a military transport to Moscow for meetings at the Kremlin. On 26 August, Dubcek and his cabinet signed an agreement that legitimized the presence of Soviet troops on Czechoslovak soil, thereby sealing the Soviet victory and paving the way for the rise of a pro-Soviet regime in Prague and the subsequent cancellation of the reforms that had been the Prague Spring.[30]

Afghanistan 1979

Afghanistan was the first country outside the Soviet Bloc to be invaded by the Soviet Union since World War II. The Soviets and their czarist predecessors, however, had intervened in Afghanistan in 1885, 1928, and 1930 and were well acquainted with Afghanistan's geography, people, and politics. The 1979 invasion was the most pervasive yet, for the Soviets had unprecedented access to Afghan centers of power, allowing them even greater influence over events than they had in Czechoslovakia in 1968. In 1979, Soviet political, economic, and military advisors operated to the very core of the Afghan system.

The modern history of Soviet involvement in Afghanistan dates to 1954 when the Afghan prime minister Mohammed Daoud Khan, frustrated by American intransigence on military aid, turned to Moscow for military assistance. One year later, Daoud convened a *loya jirgah* (assembly of tribal elders) to consider a security relationship with the Soviets. The elders overcame their deep-seated, religiously inspired hatred of communism and agreed. Over the next twenty-five years of Soviet-influenced neutrality, the Soviet connection yielded $2.5 billion in economic and military aid, the education of six thousand Afghan students in Soviet universities, and Soviet indoctrination of four thousand Afghan soldiers.[31]

In 1963 Daoud, by then known as the "Red Prince," stepped down at the request of the royal family, and the country entered a period of constitutional reform. In 1965 a small group of leftist intelligentsia led by

Noor Mohammed Taraki and Barbak Karmal met quietly in Kabul and formed the People's Democratic Party of Afghanistan (PDPA). Within a year, personality conflicts and tactical differences split the PDPA into the *Khalq* (Masses) group led by Taraki and Hafizullah Amin and the *Parcham* (Banner) group led by Karmal. In 1973, failure of constitutional reform, political factionalization, famine, and the temporary absence from Afghanistan of King Zahir Shah provided Daoud the opportune moment to seize power and proclaim a republic.[32]

Daoud's non-ideological, one-party strongman reign was characterized by repression and the improved stature of political fringe parties such as the PDPA. By 1977, although Moscow was Afghanistan's principal benefactor, Daoud's attempts at diversification of foreign support led to a souring relationship between the governments that reached a head in a particularly stormy session between Daoud and Leonid Brezhnev in the Kremlin. Despite subsequent Soviet pressure that resulted in a formal reconciliation of the Khalq and Parcham factions, the Soviets do not seem to have been anticipating fundamental change, and Daoud continued to see the country's three hundred thousand generally dissatisfied right-wing fundamentalist mullahs as his biggest threat.[33]

In April 1978, widespread grievances against Daoud led to mass demonstrations and severe government crackdown on the dissidents. In reaction to harsh government treatment of the demonstrators and other grievances, several hundred military men in Kabul deposed Daoud in a coup and then turned power over to Taraki as president and Amin in charge of the political police. Although the Soviets do not appear to have been in collusion with the perpetrators of the "Great Saur Revolution," the 350 military advisors in Afghanistan did help consolidate the coup.[34]

Intra-party feuding soon erupted. Taraki and the Khalqis quickly and brutally purged the Parchamis through firings, arrests, murders, and exiles. Karmal's exile was to be dispatched as ambassador to Czechoslovakia. Taraki and Amin then embarked on a series of naive and misguided but ruthlessly imposed political and economic reforms that catalyzed the religious fundamentalist *mujahideen* into open, armed rebellion, and forced Afghanistan to become increasingly dependent on Soviet aid. By the end of 1978, there were more than seven hundred Soviet advisors in Afghanistan. In March 1979, an uprising in Herat which resulted in the slaughter of scores of Soviet advisors and dependents, and hundreds of Afghans, caused the Soviets to sharply escalate their military assistance program and, by late November, enter into direct combat with the rebels.

The Soviets became seriously concerned for the continued survival of Afghanistan as a compliant buffer state astride the long-sought entry into the Indian sub-continent. They also knew that a peaceful settlement of the Khalq-Parcham feud was very doubtful and that the growing Afghan resistance forces would move quickly to fill any power vacuum. By late spring and early summer a familiar pattern began to emerge.

In April 1979 General Epishev (still chief political officer of the Soviet military) and six other generals toured Afghanistan on a fact finding mission.[35] In July, Moscow deployed a battalion of paratroops to Bagram Air Base, about sixty-five kilometers north of Kabul, to help secure the facility, free Afghan troops for operations against the resistance, and establish the precedent for introduction of Soviet combat troops.[36] In late August, General of the Army and Commander of Soviet Ground Forces Ivan G. Pavlovskiy (who had commanded the invasion forces in Czechoslovakia in 1968) arrived with a sixty-man General Staff delegation to conduct a detailed on-scene reconnaissance that lasted into October.[37]

Meanwhile, Amin's police-state tactics were galvanizing the resistance and pushing the country deeper into civil war. On his return from Moscow, Taraki attempted (with Soviet complicity) on 14–15 September 1979 to remove Amin, but Amin acted first and emerged as ruler. At about this time, the Soviets deployed a four-hundred-man airborne unit to Bagram air base.[38] On 8 October, Amin had Taraki executed by suffocation. Having failed in their attempts to remove Amin, the Soviets put on a new face, publicly recognized his rule and supported him, but continued to prepare behind the scenes for invasion.

In mid-September an initial call-up of Soviet reserves in the Turkestan and Central Asian military districts (MDs) went out and the 105th Guards Airborne Division at Ferghana was placed on alert. In early November, the General Staff ordered the Southern TVD (Theater of Military Actions) to establish two Fronts in the Afghan border region, with First Deputy Defense Minister Marshal Sergei L. Sokolov as General Staff representative on the scene. The leading formation in the invasion was to be the 40th Army, with its headquarters in the border town of Termez. In the process of preparations, the 105th was reinforced with a regiment each from the 103rd Guards Airborne (Byelorussia MD) and 104th Guards Airborne (Caucasus MD) divisions. The 103rd, by coincidence, had landed in Prague in 1968. A satellite communications link allowed Moscow to supervise operations.

The concept of the operation was that the 40th Army would attack with four motorized rifle divisions (MRDs) plus the reinforced 105th along two land routes (and by air): Termez to Kabul via the Salang Highway, and from Kushka to Herat, Farah, and Kandahar. In reserve would be three additional MRDs. Category "1" (combat ready) divisions on the Chinese border would remain in place to deal with any Chinese response.[39] Soviet doctrinal allocation of special operations-capable military units for this invasion force would have included a diversionary (*spetsnaz*) brigade for each of the two Fronts, a company or battalion-size *spetsnaz* element for the 40th Army,[40] and the airborne division's reconnaissance company. It is reasonable to assume that GRU and KGB *spetsnaz* personnel were among the four thousand to five thousand Soviet advisors, embassy staff, inspection groups, and the like.

In Moscow, Brezhnev's failing health, and improved power projection capabilities served to reduce the level of critical debate in the Kremlin over the merits of direct military intervention. Author Henry S. Bradsher has speculated that the Soviet Politburo formally decided on 26 November to eliminate Amin.[41] Maj. Gen. Viktor Semenovich Paputin of the Soviet Ministry for Internal Security (MVD), second-highest ranking policeman in the Soviet Union, Brezhnev confidant and non-voting member of the Party Central Committee, arrived in Kabul on Wednesday, 28 November for talks with Afghan security officials and was reported to have returned to Moscow on 13 December. His unstated mission was also to "advise" President Amin to make way for Karmal and ensure that the Soviet Union was formally invited to send troops to Afghanistan's aid, in accordance with the Soviet-Afghan treaty of 5 December 1978.[42] Another, unidentified general was reportedly in Kabul at the same time, but without public acknowledgment by the Soviets.[43]

On or about December 8 and 10, the Soviets deployed an airborne regiment of more than fifteen hundred men with tanks and artillery to Bagram. The paratroops were ostensibly landed at Bagram for security duties and by 18 December deployed to secure the Salang highway to the north and its critical tunnel, the most significant chokepoint on the Kushka-Kabul line of communication (LOC).[44] During December 10 through 24, at least a battalion of Soviet troops were moved to Kabul International Airport, only three kilometers from the city. Between December 11 and 15, military aircraft concentrated at bases in the western Soviet Union (Vitebsk, Smolensk, Ferghana, Potshinok, and Sescha).[45]

On 17 December there was an attempt to assassinate Amin at his palace in Kabul. When this last attempt at a solution short of military intervention failed, the invasion became inevitable.[46] About the same time, Soviet advisors down to company level began to exercise virtual command authority in Afghan units. Mobilization of the Category 3 divisions used for the land invasion began on 18 December (individual call-ups had begun in September). Ten days later, on 28 December, they had completed their mobilization, and lead elements began to secure routes into Afghanistan.[47] By 20 December, paratroopers from Bagram had cleared the Salang Pass of rebels who had reportedly held it since September.[48] On 22 December, MRDs from the Turkestan MD moved to the Soviet-Afghan border.[49]

Strategic and tactical deception, begun several weeks earlier, reached a peak on 23 December, when *Pravda* vehemently denied American allegations that the Soviets were about to invade Afghanistan.[50] In Afghanistan, Soviet efforts succeeded in reducing Afghan concerns over the blatant buildup of Soviet combat troops inside Afghanistan. These efforts included the continued dispatch of ministerial level Soviet delegations for formal and informal talks to maintain an atmosphere of normalcy. Many were accompanied by large, athletic staff members, who may have been *spetsnaz* conducting reconnaissance of the political, security, and communications facilities the delegations visited, and which the commandos would later attack. Afghan officers were told, and apparently believed, that the buildup was part of an authorized plan.[51] During the late-December airlift, most Afghans probably thought the arriving Soviets were going to help fight mujahideen guerrillas.[52] Meanwhile, Amin became increasingly isolated from events and, in mid-December retreated into the Darulaman palace complex seven miles southwest of Kabul.[53]

By the eve of the invasion, Soviet troops and civilians had become the backbone of the Amin regime, and Amin had become a non-person in the Soviet media. The regime was politically and militarily isolated, the West was distracted by the Christmas and New Year holidays, and the Americans were particularly preoccupied by the Tehran hostage crisis and election-year politics.[54]

Starting at about 2300 hours on 24 December and running through 27 December, the landing of airborne troops at Kabul airport, Bagram air base, Shindand air base south of Herat, and at Kandahar began in earnest. Approximately 350–380 flights of Il-76, An-12 and An-22 transport aircraft had brought in about five thousand special forces and paratroopers by the evening of 26 December.[55] The first combat troops to land were an advance party of the 105th, which secured Bagram on the first evening

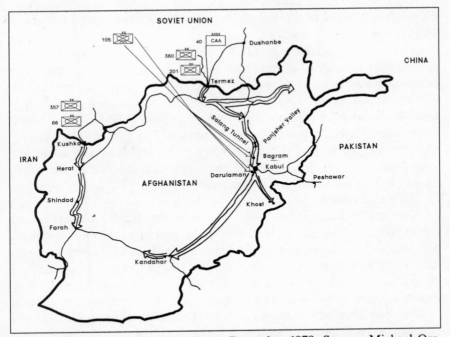

Figure 2. The invasion of Afghanistan, December 1979. Source: Michael Orr, "Invasion of Afghanistan," *War in Peace* (London: Orbis Publishing Ltd., 1981), 289.

of the airlift.[56] On 25–26 December the main body of the 105th arrived in Bagram and Kabul, comprising at least two regiments and supporting troops.[57] At the same time, Soviet advisors began directing Afghan units to turn in vehicle batteries, ammunition, communications gear, and the like, for a variety of contrived excuses—winterizing, inventory, replacement, and so on—thus neutralizing much of the remaining Afghan military in Kabul.[58]

H-hour for the take-down of Kabul appears to have been about 1900 hours on the 27th. On 27 December, Soviet Minister of Communications Nikolai Vladmirovich Talyzin and his entourage held a large reception in Kabul's Intercontinental Hotel for his counterpart and a host of Afghan officials, following a courtesy call on President Amin. During the early evening, the Soviets detained the Afghans in the reception hall by force of arms. At about the same time, other Soviets hosted a cocktail party for Afghan officers of the Kabul garrison, and locked them in at about 1830 hours.[59]

The coup began rolling at 1900 hours with seizure and explosive demolition (possibly by *spetsnaz*) of the central military communications center and killing many of its key officials (it was normally manned by the Afghan air force).[60] At about 1915 hours, a similar Soviet team captured the Ministry of the Interior, possibly in a joint KGB-GRU operation. Elsewhere in Kabul, *spetsnaz* teams captured the Radio Kabul facility after fierce fighting, and seized other key points and facilities. About the same time, author James Adams alleges, Soviet agents broke into armories around Kabul and sabotaged or removed weapons.[61] By late morning on 28 December, Kabul was firmly in Soviet hands.[62]

The centerpiece of the Soviet plan was the attack on Darulaman, where Amin was holed up and defended by part of an armored regiment with eight T-55 tanks and other armored vehicles. Whereas previous Soviet attempts to remove Amin were marked by at least a modicum of guile and deniability, the attack of the 27th was a full-blown assault by a *spetsnaz* unit, possibly combined KGB and GRU, backed up by the two or three battalions of paratroops with BMD infantry fighting vehicles and ASU-85 assault guns. The attack, which began about 1900 hours, destroyed an entire wing of the palace and killed Amin, his family, security force, and entourage.[63] The Soviets suffered about twenty-five killed and 225 wounded in this action. Among the Soviet dead was KGB Colonel Bayerenov, killed in a crossfire by his own troops. Bayerenov is known to have headed the KGB sabotage school at Balashika outside of Moscow.[64]

There is also speculation that General Paputin died in this battle. Subsequently, on the 28th of December, while evacuating their dead and wounded at Kabul airport, one casket was rendered honors appropriate for a general officer.[65] Paputin was officially reported dead of unspecified causes on 28 December. His obituary, published in the 2 January issue of *Pravda*, did not occupy an appropriate place, had no high-level signatories, and exhibited other indications of a less-than-honorable or embarrassing demise. Rumors hold that (1) Paputin had remained in Kabul after 13 December and died in the assault on Darulaman, (2) he had committed suicide on return for having failed to get Amin to step down voluntarily or surrender to the Soviet invaders, or (3) the general killed in Kabul was the mysterious second, unidentified general, possibly of the KGB.[66]

At 2045 hours Radio Moscow, broadcasting from Termez on Radio Kabul's wavelength, carried an obviously prerecorded statement by Karmal that he had taken over the Afghan government and was appealing for Soviet help. At 2130 hours the real Radio Kabul was silenced by Soviet troops. At 2300 hours the fighting stopped. At 2400 hours the coup was a success and Karmal was in the air enroute to Kabul. At about 0200 hours on the 28th Karmal landed and assumed his place as a Soviet-controlled puppet and head of a Parchami-led Afghan government.[67] It is quite possible that he arrived with an escort of Soviet *spetsnaz* troops, such escort/security missions being a known *spetsnaz* mission.

Soviet control was consolidated on the 28th and 29th of December, when the ground phase of the invasion was executed. The 357th and 66th MRDs crossed the border at Kushka and occupied Kandahar and Herat.[68] The 360th and 201st MRDs crossed from Termez, where a pontoon bridge had been built across the Amu Darya (Oxus River), and passed through the paratroopers north of Kabul who had secured the Salang Tunnel.[69] Within a week, Soviet strength in Afghanistan reached eighty thousand personnel, with an additional thirty-five thousand personnel just north of the border. In the same period, the eighty-thousand-man Afghan army was reduced by desertions to less than forty thousand men.[70] Soviet military and political domination of Afghanistan seemed as complete as it had been in Czechoslovakia.

Conclusion

The invasions of Czechoslovakia and Afghanistan were characterized by the use of *spetsnaz*, airborne, and light armored units to quickly seize control of government political and state security infrastructures, communications facilities, and population centers in the early hours of those operations.[71] The invasions were scaled to political and military requirements shaped by phenomenal advance preparation, and were consummated through a combination of guile, subterfuge, and force. The use of *spetsnaz* in these invasions demonstrates the Soviet leadership's faith that a capable and politically reliable advance guard can pay dividends out of proportion to its size and cost. These invasions also illustrate the clear Soviet understanding of the necessity of thoroughly integrating their special operations, cover, and deception plans into their total operations plan.

As illustrated in Prague in 1968 and in Kabul eleven years later, *spetsnaz* come in two varieties. GRU *spetsnaz* serve the interests of army and navy at various echelons. KGB *spetsnaz* serve the national leadership by taking on strategic political and economic targets through assassination, sabotage, and other measures. The KGB appears to have oversight and control over GRU *spetsnaz* operations external to the Soviet Union (except in wartime) due to the politically sensitive nature of such operations and the KGB's political primacy over the GRU.[72] The Prague airport seizure and the assault on Darulaman are examples of this bilateral relationship.

From what evidence is available, it appears that *spetsnaz* at Prague and Kabul played an essential role in facilitating the entry of invasion forces, maintaining the momentum of the offensive, securing and neutralizing their victims' leadership, and conducting politically sensitive missions for the Soviet leadership (e.g., rounding up selected personnel after the invasions had succeeded).[73] All of these missions are well within the responsibilities and capabilities of both GRU and KGB *spetsnaz* units. In Prague and Kabul, their swift and decisive actions may have preempted more effective responses from their victims.

Both invasions demonstrated that a particularly close relationship exists between *spetsnaz* and airborne units, which provides *spetsnaz* with cover, reinforcement, and relief. Relief of *spetsnaz* units at the Prague airport was mutually beneficial, and reinforcement of *spetsnaz* for the assaults in Kabul enabled the lightly armed *spetsnaz* to take on tougher targets. Close association with airborne units in garrison and during deployment serves to camouflage the existence, location, and strength of *spetsnaz* units. It also appears that some airborne units have developed "specialties" such as seizure of airports or other targets, as may be borne out by the attachment of a regiment of the 103d division to the 105th for the Kabul operation. It would reasonably follow that *spetsnaz* units have also developed "specialties" based on contingency plans for wartime employment and may even have a symbiotic operational relationship with specific airborne units.

The Soviets apparently rehearsed for the Czechoslovakian invasion. A possible dress rehearsal for the Afghanistan invasion occurred in August 1978, when ten thousand Soviet troops were airlifted from the Soviet Union to South Yemen and Ethiopia.[74] It is not known for certain whether *spetsnaz* rehearsed for their missions prior to each invasion, but the speed and precision of their actions at their objectives does suggest such. Moreover, even with their long-term familiarity with both countries the Soviets still found it desirable to conduct extensive on-scene reconnaissance of the invasion routes. This may have been simply a brazen exploitation of opportunity, or it may reflect underlying Soviet military conservatism and caution. Conservatism and caution, in the sense of trying to maximize the chances of success, may also account for Soviet willingness to directly involve high officials, such as Minister Talyzin and General Paputin in *spetsnaz* operations.

In Prague and Kabul *spetsnaz* units performed with reasonable competence, but were certainly not supermen. Postulated susceptibilities of NATO to *spetsnaz*-induced chaos, based on a forced comparison with the Prague and Kabul operations, are wide of the mark. Czechoslovakia declined to defend itself against the invaders, Afghanistan was emasculated before the invasion began, and the skills necessary to stab an ally in the back are not the same as those necessary to cripple a strong, well prepared opponent such as NATO. *Spetsnaz* used in Prague and Kabul were probably only moderately more capable than Skorzeny's commandos and operated with considerably more freedom of action. Presently, some competent British analysts rate the best *spetsnaz* units as on a par with Britain's 21 Special Air Service Regiment, a territorial (reserve) unit committed to support British forces in Europe in wartime.

While *spetsnaz* units certainly exploited fully the extremely permissive access to their targets in Prague and Kabul, such access would be difficult to impossible to obtain in a Soviet-NATO confrontation. There is a large difference in infiltration potential between the environments of a neighboring client state and that of the NATO countries. The Soviets have no known special operations aircraft dedicated to supporting *spetsnaz* for insertion, extraction, or resupply. Soviet penetration of NATO airspace in standard troop transports or helicopters would be risky business in any case. Going in prior to D-day under civilian cover would also be chancy, for few (if any) Soviet tourists, sports teams, trade delegations or the like would be expected or welcome in a pre-hostilities period. Nor would official Soviet representations suffice for covering the required number of personnel. Any requirements to live clandestinely in a target country, even with the help of support agents, would be a major undertaking. In addition, the insertion of large numbers of *spetsnaz* prior to D-Day could risk compromising the entire Soviet effort, and could initiate a pre-emptive NATO attack. Large-scale insertion after D-Day would mean *spetsnaz* would miss some of their most critical targets and would in some cases have to fight their way in.

Spetsnaz capabilities have continued to evolve since 1979, and their combat experience in Afghanistan since then will serve them in good stead in future wars. Most reports coming out of Afghanistan credit them with good performance in combat and worthy of respect. Yet, their capabilities against NATO should not be extrapolated from capabilities demonstrated in Prague and Kabul without caveat. As the first enemy soldiers NATO may encounter in an East-West war, *spetsnaz* should be taken seriously but not be overrated.

Notes

1. See Charles Foley, *Commando Extraordinary* (Poole, Dorset: Arms and Armour Press, Ltd., 1987); Charles Whiting, *Ardennes: The Secret War* (New York: Stein and Day, 1985); James Lucas, *Kommando: German Special Forces of World War II* (New York: St. Martin's Press, 1985): 127–135.
2. P. H. Vigor, *Soviet Blitzkrieg Theory* (New York: St. Martin's Press, 1983): 134.
3. Robert Littell, *The Czech Black Book* (New York: Avon Books, 1969): v, vii. Point number four of the August 28, 1968 Resolution of the Functionaries of the Communist Party, Revolutionary Trade Union Movement (ROH), and other National Front organizations of the Telsa Enterprise, Strasnice, reproduced in Littell at 311, was that "We shall bring to life in this country the full scope of the Action Program of the Communist Party adopted at the April session of the Central Committee. We want to realize socialism with a human face."
4. James Adams, *Secret Armies: The Full Story of S.A.S., Delta Force and Spetsnaz* (New York: The Atlantic Monthly Press, 1988): 51.
5. Littell, 23n, 24, 24n, 33.
6. Vigor, 132–133.
7. Littell, 25n.
8. Alex P. Schmid, with Ellen Berends, *Soviet Military Interventions Since 1945* (New Brunswick NJ: Transaction Books, 1985): 31.
9. Jiri Valenta, "From Prague to Kabul—The Soviet Style of Invasion," *International Security*, Fall 1980, 134.
10. H. Gordon Skilling, *Czechoslovakia's Interrupted Revolution* (Princeton, NJ: Princeton University Press, 1976): 713.
11. Thomas T. Hammond, *Red Flag Over Afghanistan—The Communist Coup, The Soviet Invasion, and The Consequences* (Boulder CO: Westview Press, 1984): 97.
12. Schmid and Berends, 32.
13. Skilling, 713.
14. Vigor, 133.
15. Ibid.
16. Ibid., 135.
17. Adams, 51–52.
18. Littell, vii.
19. Ibid., vii–viii, 21, 37n.
20. Vigor, 136.
21. Littell, 16, 18.
22. From *Zemedelske Noviny*, 21 August 1968, and *Letectvi a Kosmonautika*, 27 August 1968, cited in Littell, 16, 18.

23. Beitler, Stephen Seth, *SPETSNAZ: The Soviet Union's Special Operations Forces* (Washington DC: Defense Intelligence College, June 1985).

24. Adams, 52.

25. Alan Kadish, "The Rape of Czechoslovakia," *Airborne Operations* (New York: Crescent Books, 1978): 206.

26. Littell, 22–23, 28–30.

27. Komitet Gosudarstvennoi Bezopasnosti (Committee for State Security), believed to control all Soviet foreign special operations in peacetime.

28. Kadish, 206.

29. Quoted in Adams, at 53.

30. Adams, 54.

31. Senate Committee on Foreign Relations, *The Hidden War: The Struggle for Afghanistan*, 98th Cong., 2d sess., 1984, Committee Print, 5.

32. Ibid., 6.

33. Ibid., 7.

34. Ibid., 8.

35. Valenta, 124.

36. Henry S. Bradsher, *Afghanistan and the Soviet Union* (Durham NC: Duke University Press, 1985): 117.

37. Michael Orr, "Invasion of Afghanistan," *War In Peace*, ed. Sir Robert Thompson (New York: Harmony Books, 1982): 288.

38. Jiri Valenta, 130.

39. Mark Urban, *War in Afghanistan* (London: MacMillan Press, 1988): 38–42; Orr, 288.

40. Beitler, 44–46.

41. Bradsher, 175.

42. Orr, 288; Bradsher, 175–181; *Special Operations: Military Lessons From Six Selected Case Studies* (Centre for Conflict Studies, University of New Brunswick, Fall 1982): 206.

43. Bradsher, 177.

44. The 2.7 km long Salang Pass Tunnel, and its covered corridors at each end with a combined length of two kilometers providing environmental protection for the tunnel approaches, were constructed by the Soviet Union fifteen years before the invasion. It is the world's highest tunnel. It is *the* key chokepoint in the 450 km Termez-Kabul LOC. Graham H. Turbiville, Jr., *Ambush! The Road War In Afghanistan* (Fort Leavenworth KS: Soviet Army Studies Office, 1988): 4.

45. *Special Operations*, 208.

46. Adams, 116.

47. Vigor, 140.

48. Vigor, 138; *Special Operations*, 208–209.

49. *Special Operations*, 208.

50. Ibid., 209.
51. Anthony Arnold, *Afghanistan—The Soviet Invasion in Perspective* (Stanford: The Hoover Institute, 1985): 95.
52. Orr, 288.
53. Arnold, 93.
54. Vigor, 141.
55. *Special Operations*, 209.
56. Arnold, 93.
57. Orr, 289.
58. Arnold, 94.
59. *Special Operations*, 210.
60. Ibid., 210.
61. Adams, 109.
62. Bradsher, 180–182.
63. Orr, 289.
64. Beitler, 36.
65. Bradsher, 177.
66. See David Binder, "U.S. Links Afghan Events And Soviet General's Death," *The New York Times*, 3 February 1980.
67. *Special Operations*, 211.
68. Turbiville, 3.
69. Orr, 289.
70. Ibid., 289.
71. Turbiville, 3.
72. Beitler, 36.
73. Adams, 109.
74. Ibid., 116.

CHAPTER 11

Afghanistan

David C. Isby

> "If the only tool you have is a hammer, treat everything like a nail."
> popular Russian saying

The Afghan resistance (*mujahideen*) call them the "black soldiers," because they darken their faces for night operations. What the Soviets call them is secret even to themselves. *Spetsnaz* (*spets*ialnogo *naz*nacheniya, "special purpose") has become a popular appellation for the whole range of special operations forces (SOF) in the Soviet order of battle. Afghanistan has provided the world with the first demonstration since 1945 of how Soviet SOF function under fire. Many lessons are directly translatable to major conflict in Central Europe and, especially at the tactical level, to potential peripheral conflicts in South Asia and elsewhere.

Standing, mission-specific SOF (*spetsnaz*), such as GRU diversionary brigades described in Western sources, cover a wide range of capabilities. Moreover, Soviet emphasis on centralization and efficient utilization of resources make it probable that the differences between the "branches" of *spetsnaz* (e.g., GRU *spetsnaz* versus naval infantry *spetsnaz*), as well as the differences between standing *spetsnaz* formations and "non-spetsnaz" units such as Guards Airborne Divisions, are less significant than they are in Western forces having comparable special operations (SO) missions. The Soviets are indeed likely to use these forces interchangeably, as much as their mission capabilities permit and as mission requirements dictate, rather than according to any specific division of responsibilities.

In the absence of direct treatment of Soviet SOF in their open sources, actual Soviet views can only be deduced from historical examples, their writing on Western SOF, and their treatment of their own airborne and reconnaissance forces. In Soviet thinking Soviet SOF appear to be "special" because of their potential direct impact at strategic, operational, and tactical levels. The Soviets classify airborne forces' missions as operational-strategic, operational, and tactical and it is unlikely that SOF are more limited. Since 1945, the Soviets have not demonstrated their strategic *spetsnaz* capability, for example, to strike directly at NATO or SAC headquarters. In Afghanistan, Soviet *spetsnaz* were employed in operational missions in support of the 1979 invasion. Thereafter, they largely carried out tactical missions alongside other elite forces in the Soviet Army, filling the role of specialized counter-insurgency infantry.

While it makes some sense to associate *spetsnaz* with strategic or operational SO, especially those associated with operations in the enemy rear, tactically it is irrelevant whether a mission is carried out by *spetsnaz*, airborne troops, naval infantry, air assault troops, motorized rifle troops trained for air assault, or reconnaissance troops of motorized rifle or airborne divisions or echelons above division. What is important is the capability such forces have for SO. Thus, the discussion of Soviet tactical SO in Afghanistan or elsewhere must focus on tactics rather than on specific units. Hard dividing lines between *spetsnaz* and the rest of the Soviet Army are simply not relevant in the Afghan context. In fact, the Afghan resistance could not and did not make such distinctions. When the mujahideen talk of battle with *spetsnaz* or *commandon* — Soviet commandos — they are referring to tactics and not to a specific type of identifiable unit. The air assault battalions of the 66th Motorized Rifle Brigade, headquartered in Jalalabad from 1980 to 1988, were normally identified by the resistance in this way, for example. Nonetheless, the history of the Afghanistan war offers many lessons about overall Soviet *spetsnaz* and SO capabilities.

Kabul and Beyond

The 1979 invasion, accounted in detail by John Merritt in the preceding chapter, was a success for Soviet SOF. Soviet airborne and special forces were able to kill Amin and seize the infrastructure of the central government, as well as the airfields and key choke points. Although *spetsnaz* failed to eliminate Amin "surgically," the Soviet belief in overlapping and redundant capabilities provided a more massive backup in the form of paratroopers and BMDs that successfully carried the day.

Soviet tactics changed during the course of the war, and the use of SOF was a key part in these changes. In 1979–1980, after consolidation of the new regime in Kabul, Soviet paratroopers and SOF were rarely employed outside of defensive, security operations around the capital and major Soviet installations. Large offensive operations were initially left to the rapidly-disintegrating Kabul regime forces, and then to Soviet motorized rifle formations. There was an apparent absence of tactics outside the standard conventional combined-arms framework in the first year of the war, and there may have been a gap in the further deployment of *spetsnaz* to Afghanistan after the 1979 invasion. It was not until 1981 that the Afghans began reporting encounters with *commandon* in the field. In 1981, the Soviets began employing small, often heliborne, attacks. At about this time, reports from the resistance indicated the presence of two separate SO brigades in Afghanistan, one headquartered at Khandahar and one at Shindand. By 1983, there were also reports of special forces in Afghanistan being augmented with special forces from the Central Asia Military District. The trend toward the increasing use of SOF was recorded in an early 1982 report from Kabul:

> Military analysts believe that, to give themselves a first-strike advantage, the Russians are organizing themselves into small, surprise-attack squads with airborne power enabling them to 'drop' onto pockets of Mujahidin resistance. Hitherto the open convoys of Soviet armour were a sitting target for Mujahidin snipers from the shelter of the hills.[1]

The Soviets also continued to stage combined arms operations and sweeps in 1981, typified by the massive Panjsher IV offensive. In 1982, they continued their operational emphasis on these tactics, but in conjunction with the smaller, heliborne units that had first been used in 1981. This combination was also seen in the 1982 Panjsher V and VI offensives, and in fighting in the southwest in early 1983. As Soviet experience increased, such operations became more successful in achieving surprise, encirclement, and destruction of the enemy. Successes in the January 1983 Logar Valley offensive were due to these tactics.

By 1983 the Soviets were stressing the importance of fixed-wing and helicopter air power, although heliborne operations, combined arms sweeps and the use of SOF continued. The resistance noted increasingly effective large operations different from the standard (since 1980) model of combined arms offensives by roadbound mechanized forces. In late

1983 and especially the beginning of 1984, five hundred to fifteen hundred heliborne troops were used independently or in conjunction with ground troops in major offensives. Used in search-and-destroy operations against isolated towns or villages, these operations carried the war to the population and the resistance strongholds.[2]

In 1984, Soviet use of SO tactics, including nighttime commando raids on mujahideen redoubts, became widespread throughout Afghanistan.[3] The more aggressive offensive tactics first seen in the relief of Urgun in January 1984 set the tone for a greater willingness to take the tactical initiative, even with the risk of higher casualties. This had been associated with increased use of SOF. *Spetsnaz* probably returned to Afghanistan in 1984. In that year there was more and better use of twenty-eight- to thirty-two-year-old elite special troops to spearhead major operations in Afghanistan, where eighteen- to twenty-two-year-old conscripts had previously headed such operations. In 1985, use of these tactics increased in conjunction with the Soviet emphasis on interdiction of guerrilla lines of communication (LOCs). Where little attention was paid to guerrilla supply routes in the first few years of the war, the summer of 1984 saw frequent attacks on, and ambushes of, supply caravans by elite Soviet forces.[4]

Reports of tactical improvement and adaptation came from throughout Afghanistan in 1984 to 1985.[5] The widespread nature of these reports suggested that these tactics were not limited to non-divisional *spetsnaz* but that the Soviets were also using a range of forces as specialized (usually heliborne) counterinsurgency light infantry.

Many of the combined arms offensives launched in 1985 were also aimed at interdiction and made extensive use of combined SO and air strikes, especially by attack helicopters and frequently at night. Soviet SOF were reported heavily engaged in both 1985 Kunar Valley offensives of that year. A Western report quoting diplomatic sources stated that of the eight hundred wounded in the spring 1985 Kunar Valley offensive, many were "elite paratroopers and commandos."[6] Another Western source described the forces involved in this offensive as "An entire Soviet Army division of 10,000 men, at least two units of 2,000 'Spetznaz' [sic] commandos each, and 1,000 Afghan troops."[7] The summer 1985 Paktia offensive followed the same basic pattern as the second Kunar Valley offensive. A Soviet and Kabul regime combined-arms force moved down the roads, supported by heavy air and artillery support. Kabul regime forces, including militia, provided flank security and, ahead of the columns, heliborne forces were inserted on high ground. As in Kunar, losses were heavy on both sides.

If U.S. press reports are correct, the Soviets deployed additional *spetsnaz* forces in the Iranian border areas of Afghanistan in mid-1985, possibly to support offensives.[8] This may have been connected with heavy fighting then in progress in the Herat area, but it may also show a Soviet determination to use such forces in the counter-infiltration role on the Iranian border, as they had been used on the Pakistani border. There may also be a connection between the new tactics and the appointment in July 1985 of Gen. Mikhail Mitrofanovich Zaitsev as commander of Southern TVD. Zaitsev, former commander of Group of Soviet Forces Germany (GSFG), has in his writings[9] stressed effective training and placed emphasis on low-level decision making. Believing that more initiative must be given to battalion and company commanders (important to facilitate rapid movement against the mujahideen), he may have placed even greater emphasis on the training and use of SO by Soviet forces throughout Afghanistan. Guerrilla leader Abdul Rahim Wardak described the battlefield impact of the 1984 to 1985 Soviet approach as follows:

The *Spetsnaz* groups' operations are a typical example of the decentralization of command level that is now taking place in the Soviet camp. To a much greater extent than was the case several years ago, the local Soviet leaders make decisions and this delegation of authority gives them the latitude they need for improvisation.[10]

This suggests that the Soviets, needing troops suitable for counterinsurgency offensive operations outside standard combined arms actions, saw their spectrum of SOF as suitable raw material. In 1987, resistance leader Abdul Haq stated:

The Spetsnaz are being employed in counter-guerrilla roles simply because they are the only troops in the whole Soviet Army trained to 'think' on their own and to make autonomous decisions without having to refer to upper commands.[11]

Throughout the first half of 1985, Soviet SOF carried out interdiction, decapitation,[12] and direct action assaults against the guerrillas all across the country. Entire guerrilla formations were surprised and wiped out, and heretofore secure strongholds were seized by SOF.[13] This continued throughout 1985–1986, and until the introduction of "Stinger" and other varieties of man-portable surface-to-air missiles (SAMs) neutralized Soviet air mobility and close air support. Until then, according to Dr. Rony Brauman of the French humanitarian medical organization Medecins Sans Frontieres, the resistance forces "were unable to travel in a single day without encountering Soviet tanks, helicopters and commandos."

While these actions gained the attention of the resistance and Western journalists in 1984–1986, the use of SOF in reconnaissance, target acquisition, and target designation was also important to overall Soviet efforts in Afghanistan. This is consistent with their conventional war tasking. These actions contributed to improved Soviet *razvedka* and target acquisition. The integration of aircraft, mechanized units, dismounted patrols, and the Afghan secret police, the Khidamate Aetilaati Daulati (State Information Service, known as "KHAD," and becoming the State Information Agency, or "WAD," in 1986) by 1986 had further improved the effectiveness of Soviet battlefield tactics. The Soviets in Afghanistan did not lack firepower; the problem was how to apply it to the Afghans.

Throughout 1984–1986, the resistance came to grips with the changing Soviet threat. Reflecting the decentralized nature of the resistance and the wide variation in military skills of the different groups of its fighting men, countermeasures against Soviet SOF were basically local adaptations. Most simply looked to the existing Afghan skills at guerrilla warfare (especially in ambushes) and intelligence provided by a friendly populace and sympathizers within the Kabul regime and Soviet forces. In one report, a resistance group of Jamiat-e-Islami Afghanistan acting on advance information of 9 November 1984 took position in a gorge and ambushed a group of forty Soviet commandos when the latter arrived at the gorge and started preparing an ambush for the people already waiting for them. All the Soviets were killed and their arms and equipment seized.[14] These counter-ambushes became more frequent in the 1985–1986 period.

Other resistance countermeasures were developed through more empirical methods. In 1985, Jamiat sent Mohammed Tahir Mayar to assess Soviet interdiction efforts in Logar Province. Mayar studied the SO unit based at Baraki Barak and found that it was particularly brutal toward the civilian populace, using physical torture to extract information on guerrilla movements and not hesitating to shoot inhabitants of villages suspected of helping the guerrillas. Mayar also determined that this formation operated in platoon-size patrols for up to two or three days in extended dismounted operations. Although he could not identify the designation of this unit, he came to believe that it moved around Afghanistan as a mobile "fire brigade." According to unconfirmed reports, the penal battalion of the Soviet Airborne Forces was operating in this area at this time.[15]

Yet, the necessary skill to counter SOF on the ground was seldom seen in the 1985–1986 period. Jalat Khan, a local Harakat Party resistance commander in Ghazni Province, observed in this period that the *spetsnaz* in his area were "quicker and more courageous" than regular Soviet soldiers, carried silencers on their guns, knew martial arts, and "kill very well."[16] An increased mujahideen understanding of, and ability to cope with, *spetsnaz* by late 1985 was reflected by veteran commander Abdul Haq. In an interview with Edward Giradet of *The Christian Science Monitor*,[17] Haq outlined the Soviet shift in tactics over the preceding ten to twenty months from large-scale, slow-moving operations using tanks and conscripts to smaller operations using lighter, faster paratroopers, airborne troops, and special forces:

> Now they . . . have introduced *spetznaz* [sic] . . . the Soviets are trying harder to cut off our supply routes by ambushing caravans and planting mines along trails and mountain passes. . . . The Soviets began ambushing in earnest 18 to 20 months ago. . . . The helicopters drop *spetznaz* [sic], usually at least 40 or 50 men, who work at night and then set up ambushes along the trails. They are well-equipped with AK-74s [assault rifles], silencers, light mortars, and an RPG [rocket-propelled grenade] team. If the fighting gets hard, they call in helicopters and tanks . . . then have helicopters try to lift them out. . . . The *spetznaz* [sic] are professional soldiers. . . . they are better trained and of course have better equipment. . . .

Haq went on to state that one way his forces were coping with the new threat was by setting up dummy caravans, watching to see where Soviet commandos are put in to ambush these convoys, keeping the Soviets under surveillance to detect their strength and equipment, and then ambushing the Soviets.[18] Thus, the Soviets lost the element of surprise where kept under observation from the time of landing, and where the guerrillas maintained tactical unity and good communications.

Looking back on this period in 1987, Abdul Haq reported that in 1985, " . . . the Spetsnaz were indeed a problem because we did not know how they were operating. But we are now in a position to face them with relative ease." He also stated that the adaptation of SOF as specialized counterinsurgency light infantry was a mistake in Afghanistan.[19] This was certainly a change from resistance statements of the 1984–1985 period, when SOF were a powerful threat. By 1986–1988, it was apparent that the use of SOF was not decisive, for SOF could not compensate for overall limitations to Soviet consolidation in Afghanistan.

The maximum use of SOF was between early 1984 and late 1986, as a relatively cheap and effective element of Soviet combat operations in Afghanistan. Especially useful in interdiction efforts, their widespread use suggested the Soviets had the will and the capability to settle in for the long haul, to wage low-level counterinsurgency conflict into the 1990s. This did not happen. The decline in the utilization and effectiveness of Soviet SOF in Afghanistan between late 1986 and early 1988 stemmed from a broad spectrum of changes. Improved resistance air defense reduced, but did not eliminate, the effectiveness of the Soviet helicopter force on which SOF depend for insertion, mobility, and supporting firepower in independent and combined-arms operations. Long-range operations were particularly curtailed. Once SOF had to depend on artillery for accurate, responsive fire support, their radius of operations was hemmed in to artillery range and, in the offensive, they required the mobility-reducing deployment of artillery. In addition, Soviet withdrawal from a number of their more isolated garrisons in 1987 reduced SOF forward operations bases (FOBs), a trend that continued through 1988.

Large and small defeats led to a cutback in SO in 1986–1988. Counter-ambushes, a risk throughout the war, became more frequent. Improved resistance weaponry and capability made lapses in the context of even "successful" offensives more costly. For instance, in the December 1987 to January 1988 relief of Khost a platoon-sized force of Soviet troopers inserted by helicopter on a forward crest was destroyed. Larger offensives also saw substantial defeats of Soviet SOF, as in the May-June 1987 Jadji offensive.

Soviet Special Operations

The interdiction of enemy lines of supply, especially transportation means, has been a priority of the Soviet concept of the "front in the enemy rear" since partisan operations were supplemented by air-inserted SOF during the Great Patriotic War.[20] The Soviets have always stressed operations in the enemy rear at the strategic,[21] operational[22] and tactical[23] levels. It was, however, over three years after the war began before the Soviets attempted the tactics spelled out in their own tactical literature on the battlefields of Afghanistan.[24]

Some interdiction efforts were carried out independently. Starting about late 1982 and especially after the spring of 1984, Soviet patrols, on foot and in armored vehicles, operated along Afghan infiltration routes. Interdiction was also carried out by SOF as a part of combined arms offensives, especially in the 1984–1985 period. After the introduction of the Stinger to Afghanistan and the greater Soviet sensitivity to casualties that emerged after the pitched battles of 1985 and early 1986, interdiction (along with the whole range of SO) was curtailed. Yet, this did not prevent continued heavy SOF losses in 1986–1987 in offensives with aims including interdiction.[25]

In interdiction, as in other actions throughout Afghanistan, Soviet SOF showed themselves capable of using concealment, camouflage, and tactical *maskirovka*. Soviet ambush forces, in many cases possibly composed of SOF, were sometimes inserted in daylight along roads as Soviet convoys passed. The Soviets would ambush guerrilla convoys running along these same roads at night (or, indeed, in daylight), and then be extracted the next day by returning convoy or by helicopter.[26] Some Soviet SOF have operated in Kabul regime uniforms: Guerrillas frequently have local nonaggression pacts with Kabul regime forces but would detect a Soviet presence. Soviet soldiers have also reportedly dressed as Afghan guerrillas and engaged in "pseudo operations" to burn mosques, destroy food supplies in areas not under Soviet control, and discredit the resistance.[27] Afghan sources also report that Soviet troopers dressed as shepherds have driven herds of sheep up to Afghan positions before attacking.[28] Another way the Soviets attained surprise was by appearing in areas where the resistance thought themselves secure, or where no helicopters had been seen or heard. This was done in many cases by using vehicles to covertly move the ambush forces from the landing zone. Some patrols included the use of armored vehicles flown into remote ambush positions by helicopters,[29] although this was done most often as part of interdiction efforts. Such patrols, like many others, were limited when improved resistance air defense cut back on Soviet helicopter employment. In March 1988 Mohammed Tahir Mayar, then in charge of Jamiat-e-Islami Afghanistan's southern LOC, could report that the Soviets had lost interest in interdiction.

Some ambush patrolling was also done for the protection of airfields. Western reports have mentioned two *reydoviki* (raider) battalions being assigned to airfield protection duties, one each at Jalalabad and Khandahar in the 1983–1984 period. This deployment followed Afghan attacks on Soviet airfields, and these units may be part of the *spetsnaz* brigades alleged to be operating out of these locations. The *reydoviki* were apparently used for aggressive nighttime patrolling and outpost duties rather than static perimeter guard.

Operationally, SO in Afghanistan were essentially all those operations performed outside the context of the basic, mechanized, mode of operations, regardless of the type of troops that carried them out. This means that tactical heliborne operations were among the most widespread Soviet SO in Afghanistan. The Afghans describe helicopter-inserted *commandon* as operating either as part of combined operations with Soviet mechanized units, in surprise raids and sweeps with Kabul regime forces (as in the January-February 1985 Kunar Valley offensive) or independently. Heliborne KGB Border Troops operated effectively as part of a combined operation against guerrillas raiding Soviet territory in 1987.[30] The units used in heliborne assaults varied in strength from squads to multiple battalions. The Soviets were even able to continue the use of heliborne operations despite the introduction of Stingers. In the relief of Khost in December 1987 and January 1988, they mounted a battalion-size heliborne assault by operating at night and using contour flight. Night flying at low altitude allowed the evacuation of the Kabul regime garrison at Barikot in May 1988.

Heliborne operations were also used in conjunction with Soviet decapitation efforts against guerrilla leaders. While use of Afghan assassins in the pay of KHAD/WAD has been the preferred tactic (as in the 1984 attempt to kill Ahmad Shah Massoud immediately before the Panjsher VII offensive, and the December 1984 killing of Zabiollah, Jamiat commander in the Mazar-e-Sharif area by KHAD infiltrators in a competing resistance group), other actions were obviously carried out by the Soviets. Examples include the killing of guerrilla commander Qari Samad at the village of Siachok in Shinwar by heliborne SOF,[31] the February 1985 attempt to kill Abdul Haq in Peshawar, the killing of Captain Mohammed Afghan, a former Kabul regime army officer and National Islamic Front of Afghanistan (NIFA) commander in Kabul Province in March 1985,[32] the unsuccessful 1985 ambush of Wardak Province resistance leader Mohammed Amin Wardak, and the 1987 killing of Kunduz resistance leader Amin Ghulam. In addition, some assassinations of Afghan resistance leaders in Afghanistan and Pakistan may have been carried out by Soviet SOF.[33]

"Soviet commandos" (so described by Afghans, showing the difficulty of associating specific units with SO in Afghanistan) operated with Kabul regime militia in eastern Afghanistan from 1984.[34] Joint *spetsnaz*-Kabul regime militia operations had the potential to be an effective combination, and occasionally were so, especially when being used in the flank protection role during Soviet combined-arms offensives in 1984–1986. Both forces were suited for dismounted operations without large-scale provision of supporting arms, the *spetsnaz* because of their training, the militia because they were armed and operated like the mujahideen. Joint operations allowed the Soviets to take advantage of the militia's knowledge of the local terrain and intelligence capabilities. In much of Afghanistan the mujahideen feared militia patrols more than they did the often-unenthusiastic conscript infantry of the Kabul regime, especially in areas where much of the militia were former mujahideen (e.g., the Kunar Valley in 1987). Soviet sources have described heliborne assault forces cooperating with Kabul regime militia in a battle in an unidentified mountain pass.[35] Soviet offensives in Paktia Province in January to February and August to September 1985 also included extensive cooperation between tribal militia and Soviet paratroopers.

Similar to their cooperation with combined-arms offensives, Soviet SOF also provided the manpower for convoy escort duties. These troops were often dropped by helicopter on crests of hills ahead of the convoy and extracted by helicopter after the convoy passed, although permanent outposts were also created along critical LOCs such as the Salang Pass highway. Western sources have identified two battalions of *reydoviki* used on convoy protection in the area around Herat from mid-1984. Afghans have reported Soviet SOF securing key heights when operating in conjunction with ground operations.[36] These tactics were also seen in the 1985 Kunar and Paktia offensives, and in the 1987–1988 relief of Khost. Additional insight into these tactics may also be offered by a 1984 Soviet description of a four-day convoy protection mission conducted by a reconnaissance company in Afghanistan.[37]

These convoy and flank protection missions required a degree of mountain fighting expertise and commensurate special equipment and training. *Spetsnaz* may thus be used, in conjunction with motorized infantry and airborne troops who have received special training in mountain operations. Soviet sources have described airborne companies capturing objectives "high in the mountains" in Afghanistan,[38] including night attacks foregoing the best conditions for use of air support.[39] Use of these tactics has also been described by Ahmad Shah Massoud to an American doctor who was in the Panjsher in April 1985:

> A few of the more recent and more elite Russian soldiers were better equipped, and he was impressed that these soldiers fighting more recently are much tougher. For example, he found evidence that some of the Russian soldiers had climbed steep mountains, tough even for his troops, carrying packs up to 30 kilograms.[40]

Most of the reporting from the resistance and the journalists who have accompanied them has centered on the use in combat of SOF. But reconnaissance was a critical (if not the most important) mission for them. SOF played a vital part in *razvedka* in Afghanistan. This included short-range and long-range (usually with helicopter insertion) patrols and the manning of observation posts that were often pre-cast concrete structures inserted by helicopter on high peaks.

The Soviets have a centralized command for reconnaissance assets; the chief of *razvedka* not only fills similar staff functions to a U.S. Army G2, but can also exercise operational command over them. A former Soviet *razvedchik* (scout) who served in a non-divisional reconnaissance company in Afghanistan before emigrating reported that his company responded to a centralized higher command, rather than to his regiment. Abdul Haq has seen greater SOF success in reconnaissance than in interdiction: "They are very good at camouflage, map reading, at finding food from nowhere, they are physically strong and good at reconnaissance."[41]

Special Operations and Their Impact, 1978–1988

The Soviet use of SOF in Afghanistan falls into two phases: (1) the operational phase, consisting of the events flowing up to and through the 1979 invasion and (2) the tactical phase consisting of the remainder of the war, during which SOF emerged as specialized light infantry in a broad range of counter insurgency missions. The use of Soviet SOF represented one of a number of successful tactical adaptations, especially in the 1984–1986 period. By mid-1986, they had become a significant component in the apparent trend toward long-term Soviet success. In the summer of 1986, resistance morale had been badly shaken, and the Soviets thought they saw the proverbial "light at the end of the tunnel."

Two years later, the end of the tunnel appeared to be back where they started from, in the Soviet Union. A number of external factors[42] forced the change: (1) The continued failures and divisions of the Afghan communists, (2) Mikhail Gorbachev's[43] larger domestic and international agenda[44] that would not be served by settling in for the long haul in a bloody war of attrition, and (3) tactical problems, as evidenced by the significant but pyrrhic Communist victory at Zhawar in 1986.

The tactical difficulties that flowed from the introduction of Stingers undercut earlier battlefield successes. However effective in 1984–1986, SOF and SO tactics were not used in a comprehensive, sustained, and aggressive operational approach, though the Soviets could claim a number of victories: Panjsher VII, the second Kunar offensive, the 1985 Helmand Valley offensive, and the 1986 Herat-Iranian border offensive are examples. They could also claim interdiction successes, due in large part to the use of SOF. But neither the offensives nor the interdiction ever reached the scope or intensity of, for example, the comparable French operations in Algeria.

The SOF tactics of 1984–1986 were part of the Soviet approach to fight a cheap (in cost and casualties) but nasty war. In 1986–1988, after the introduction of Stingers and the rise of Gorbachev, this was no longer possible. The Soviets had to either escalate the intensity of the conflict or seek a diplomatic solution, rather than pay the costs of settling in for the long haul. The overall Afghan response to Soviet tactics of the 1984–1986 period foreclosed staying the course, as failures in attempts to continue them into 1987 in battles such as Agrandhab and Jadji demonstrated. In mid-1989, while the Soviets had not foreclosed future SOF use (and especially the smaller variant of low-level operations along the Soviet border in north Afghanistan, probably with Mazar-e-Sharif as a capital), their rhetoric was that of diplomatic solution. Even if the Soviets did not choose to further advance their SO tactics, however, one should not assume that their forces and system are not capable of further evolution.

At their height, SOF were only a small percentage—20 percent maximum, using the most liberal definition—of the Limited Contingent of Soviet Forces in Afghanistan, but they were a critical element. SOF of many nations have had a decisive impact on the course of counterinsurgency campaigns in a number of post-1945 conflicts, even when such forces constituted a fraction of the total forces involved. In many counterinsurgency campaigns, the majority of the combat forces involved were unable to undertake effective offensive operations against the guerrillas. Indeed, the service support units required to sustain large conventional combat formations have themselves to be defended. Throughout the war the Soviets apparently chose not to dramatically increase the size of their forces committed to Afghanistan. Escalation consisted instead of upgrading the capabilities of those forces through better weapons and tactics, including the increased use of SOF.

The impact of Soviet SOF was not decisive in the ultimate outcome of the Afghanistan war, but their role was a major one. Yet, the resistance successfully countered overall Soviet diplomatic, political, and military efforts in Afghanistan and limited Soviet SOF successes to only local and temporary impact. Even these successes were muted by the Stingers and improved security and deception. One result was that the resistance often annihilated Soviet SOF in ambushes.[45] While they could not bring overall victory, the Soviet SOF threat to the resistance remained potent to the end of Soviet involvement in Afghanistan.

Notes

1. Karan Thapor, "Afghan Army's Collapse: Russians Fight Losing Battle," *The Times* (London), 2 February 1982, 5.
2. Mohammed Es'Haq, *An Analysis of the Present Situation in Afghanistan* (Peshawar: Jamiat-Islami, November 1984).
3. Julian Gearing, "Evolution of Soviet Military Tactics," *Afghanistan* (London), No. 1, 1985, 5. On the 1984 introduction of spetsnaz see, Paul Quinn Judge, "Soviets Look Back on 'Short War' . . . That Wasn't," *The Christian Science Monitor*, 13 April 1988, 1, 8.
4. Gearing, 5.
5. Drew Middletown, "Russians in Afghanistan: Changes in Tactics," *The New York Times*, 3 November 1985, 21; Gearing, 5; David C. Isby, "Panjsher VII," *Soldier of Fortune*, January 1985, 12; Alexander Alexiev, *Inside the Soviet Army in Afghanistan* (Santa Monica CA: The Rand Corporation, May 1988).
6. Dave Doubrava, "Afghan Rebels Score Major Hit On Air Base," *Washington Times*, 19 June 1985, 6A.
7. "Inside Afghanistan," *The Economist Foreign Report* (London), 20 June 1985, 3.
8. Rowland Evans and Robert Novak, "The Captured Mi-24s" [sic], *The Washington Post*, 31 July 1985, A15.
9. M. M. Zaitsev, "A Creative Approach To Tactics," *Red Star*, 16 March 1982, 2; and M. M. Zaitsev, "They Are Not Born Commanders," *Military Herald*, 2/1976, 20–26 shows his longstanding advocacy of these views. For a Western view of Zaitsev see, C. J. Dick, "Soviet Battle Drills: Strength or Vulnerability?" *International Defense Review*, 5/1985, 665.
10. Albert Henrik Hohn, "Afghan Guerrilla Leader: Our Enemy Has Made Errors and Drawn the Right Conclusions," *Morgenbladet* (Oslo), 3 December 1984 (in undated JPRS translation).
11. "How We Fight the Red Army," *Military Technology*, June 1987, 89–91 (an interview with Abdul Haq).
12. Attacks against key individuals.
13. S. Fazle Akbar, "News From the Battlefield," *Afghan Realities*, No. 32, 1 May 1985, 7–8; Dr. S. B. Majrooh, "Death of a Great Commander," *Afghan Information Centre Monthly Bulletin*, No. 49, April 1985, 8; Dr. Majrooh, "Various News," *Afghan Information Centre Monthly Bulletin*, No. 51, June 1985, 15. The Dr. Brauman quote is from Edward Giradet, "Afghanistan: Bleak Scene For Mujahideen," *The Christian Science Monitor*, 22 December 1986, 1, 10. On the importance of the reconnaissance mission, see the comment by Charles Dick on page 130 in Brian MacDonald, ed., *The Soviet Military Challenge* (Toronto: Canadian Institute of Strategic Studies, 1987).

14. Dr. Majrooh, *Afghan Information Centre Monthly Bulletin*, No. 56, November 1985, 8.

15. Mohammed Tahir Mayar, Washington DC, January 1986. After studying the Western literature on Soviet SOF and consulting with Western and Afghan experts, Tahir Mayar designed and implemented a broad range of anti-SO countermeasures for Jamiat's LOCs in southern Afghanistan in 1986-1987. In March 1988 he reported that these measures had reduced vehicle losses to twenty trucks in the past year. On the unconfirmed use of the airborne penal battalion see, David C. Isby, *Weapons and Tactics of the Soviet Army* (London: Jane's Publishing, 1988): 21. Even the air assault battalions of the 66th Motorized Rifle Brigade regularly committed atrocities. See, Vladislav Naumov, "My War in Afghanistan," *The Washington Post*, 3 January 1988, B5.

16. James Rupert, "Trying to Break a Deadlock," *The Washington Post*, 14 January 1986, A13.

17. Edward Giradet, "Afghan guerrilla leader: Soviets have made significant changes in tactics," *The Christian Science Monitor*, 31 December 1985, 7-8.

18. Ibid.

19. "How We Fight the Red Army." On the loss of a platoon-size force in the 1987-1988 relief of Khost see, Arthur Kent, "The Relief of Khost," *The Observer* (London), 10 January 1988, 9. That the Soviets were still able to undertake heliborne SO even in the face of the Stinger SAM threat is reported in Richard Weintraub, "Flanking Maneuver Credited With Breaking Seige of Khost," *The Washington Post*, 6 January 1988, A15, A18. This is supported by on the scene impressions from two veteran observers who were in combat at Khost: British journalist and former paratrooper Peter Jouvenal, and resistance staff officer and former Afghan army colonel Eshaq Nouri, both of whom were interviewed in Washington DC in February 1988.

20. V. Kazakov, "Gliders In The Skies Of War," *Military History Journal*, February 1983, 43-46; F. L. Kurlat and L. A. Studnikov, "Special Operations Brigade," *Problems of History*, September 1982, 95-104.

21. E.g., operating in the enemy's homeland.

22. E.g., making use of partisans and SOF.

23. E.g., making use of local patrols and infiltration.

24. V. Stakheev, "Reconnaissance Training," *Military Herald*, 3/1975, 4-9; A. D. Sinyayev, *Reconnaissance In Mountain Terrain* (Moscow: Voyenizdat, 1963); S. S. Veshchvnov, *The Motorized Rifle Squad in Reconnaissance* (Moscow: Voyenizdat, 1977); V. Portnyagin, "In Active Opposition," *Red Star*, 8 February 1984, 1.

25. E.g., 120 killed in action in the Jadji offensive, May-June 1987. Richard M. Weintraub and David Ottaway, "Afghan Rebels Said to Hit Foe Hard," *The Washington Post*, 6 July 1987, A1, A4.

26. Maj. V. Yefanov, "In Hand-to-Hand Night Combat," *Red Star*, 4 August 1983, 1; Faziollah, Jamiat-e-Islami commander, Logar Province (Peshawar: February 1985); Paul Christenson, "Trip to Teri Mungal," *The Afghanistan Foundation Newsletter*, vol. 2, no. 3, 22 June 1987, 1–3.

27. Dr. Majrooh, "Difficult Resistance in the Empty Countryside," *Afghan Information Centre Monthly Bulletin*, No. 35, February 1984, 11.

28. Faziollah, op. cit.; and Qari Ramatullah, Peshawar, February 1985.

29. Letter from Ken Guest, British journalist, to David Isby, 1 February 1984; *Al Jehad Hospital News Bulletin* (Quetta), 27 December 1984, 5.

30. "Fired on Soviet Territory, Rebels Say," *The Los Angeles Times*, 25 March 1987, 11. See also, Peter Adams, "Soviet Border Guards Show Mettle Repelling 'Group of Bandits,'" *Army Times*, 27 June 1988, 32.

31. James McManus, "Russian Infiltration of Guerrillas Hits Mujahideen Hard," *Daily Telegraph* (London), 2 March 1985, 8.

32. "Death of Resistance Commanders," *Afghan Information Centre Monthly Bulletin*, No. 47, February 1985, 8.

33. "Afghan Assassins," *Washington Times*, 3 January 1986, 3A; "A Killing in Kunduz," *Defense and Foreign Affairs Weekly*, 20 July 1987, 2; Dr. Edward Luttwak, quoted in Adam Platt, "New Tactics Evolving for Conflicts," *Insight*, 30 December 1985 – 6 January 1986, 47.

34. Dr. Majrooh, op. cit., and Ramatullah Safi (NIFA military advisor), Peshawar, January 1985.

35. Yuri Dmittriyev, "Meetings in Afghanistan," *Zvazda* (Minsk: 26 February 1985): 3, translated at JPRS-UMA-85-035, *USSR Report: Military Affairs*, 22 May 1985, 56–59.

36. David C. Isby, "Resistance in Afghanistan," *Strategy & Tactics*, No. 99, January-February 1985, 11–15.

37. Lt. Col. Igor Ploskonos, "Reconnaissance Officer," *Red Star*, 31 December 1983, 1.

38. Col. Yu. Protasou, "Notes From Afghanistan: Combat Exercise," *Military Herald*, 5/1983, 23; Capt. I. Ploskonos, HSU, "Afghanistan–The Site of Valor. In a Tactical Air Assault," *Military Herald*, 5/1987, 22–23.

39. Guards Col. V. Shishkov, "In Afghanistan, The Airborne Forces Discipline – The Basis of Victory," *Military Herald*, 8/1984, 29.

40. Letter from Dr. J. Preston Darby, MD, to Dr. Robert Simon, MD, 20 May 1985, 3.

41. FM 100-2-1, *The Soviet Army: Operations and Tactics* (Washington DC: Headquarters, Department of the Army, 16 July 1984): 3–8; Isby, *Weapons and Tactics of the Soviet Army*, 369–370; Ian Kemp, "Abdul Haq: Soviet Mistakes In Afghanistan," *Jane's Defence Weekly*, 5 March 1988, 380–381; Sr. Lt. I. Gavrilyuk, Capt. S. Kharenko, "Baptism of Fire," *Military Herald*, 7/1987, 39–41.

42. See, Emily MacFarquhar, Jeff Trimble and Edward Giradet, "Now For the Next All-Afghan War," *U.S. News & World Report,* 30 May 1988, 26–28; Artyem Borovik, "What Kind of War Was This?" *U.S. News & World Report,* 30 May 1988, 32.

43. General Secretary of the Communist Party of the Soviet Union (CPSU) Central Committee.

44. "Statement by General Secretary of the CPSU Central Committee Mikhail Gorbachev on Afghanistan," *Soviet Military Review,* 3/1988, 2–4, reprinted from *Pravda,* 9 February 1988; Charlotte Saikowski, "'New Realism' Seen in Gorbachev's Approach to Soviet Foreign Policy," *The Christian Science Monitor,* 13 April 1988, 1, 32.

45. Dr. Majrooh, "The View of a Resistance Commander," *Afghan Information Centre Monthly Bulletin,* No. 41, August 1984, 4; Gearing, 6; "How We Fight The Red Army," 90.

CHAPTER 12
Spetsnaz and the Deep Operation

William H. Burgess III

The preferred historical Soviet modus operandi since the Bolshevik uprising for dealing with political-military threats to territorial integrity[1] or Party rule has been to strike the enemy rapidly and decisively where he is weakest, on his flanks and in his rear, and throughout the enemy disposition. While commentators give greatest attention to the use of conventional forces (e.g., those engaged in standard battlefield tactics) and, since 1954, to nuclear forces in application of this theory of "deep operation," (though the Soviets have not used this term in their military documents since the 1960s) there are important SO aspects that deserve illumination. Specifically, Soviet state security and military SO can be used across the conflict spectrum against key personnel and installations in enemy rear areas to (1) "decapitate" decision-makers by elimination, incapacitation, or capture; (2) delay, deceive, and disorganize forces in reserve; (3) locate and neutralize special weapons delivery systems and weapons stockpiles; (4) control selected key terrain; (5) disrupt communications; and (6) otherwise expedite and exploit operational and strategic success.[2] Great stress is placed on winning the war in its initial phase, on the use of agents, fifth columnists, and, where quick victory is not possible, revolutionary warfare.

The Soviets have substantial experience in combined-arms "deep battle" (at the tactical level) and "deep operation" (at the operational and strategic levels) spanning almost seven decades,[3] with the greatest efforts being at the operational level. In all of its incarnations — that of the Russo-Polish War period, in the late 1930s, in the latter stages of the Great Patriotic War, and today—deep operation has had a substantial SO component. The SO side of contemporary deep operation is waged at all levels of conflict, including what in Western pluralist democracies is called "peace," and is fought on two fronts. On the political-strategic front, the fight is waged under conditions of extreme secrecy by state security (KGB) against specific targets of great political-military significance designated by the Politburo, Stavka, or other senior authority. Occasional "peacetime" murder and abduction offensives by the KGB, its allies and executive agents, and its predecessors against emigres and defectors across Europe since the 1920s exemplify the state security side of SO deep operation. On the military-operational front, the Ministry of Defense (MOD) uses its forces against specific or generalized targets of operational or theater significance. The seizure of approaches to the tunnels at Suifenho, "reconnaissance by battle" at critical ports in Korea, surprise air assault landings to force the surrender of Japanese garrisons and secure critical facilities in the 1945 Manchurian Campaign, and the seizure of critical but lightly-held objectives in advance of airborne troops in the relatively permissive environments of Prague in 1968 and in Kabul in 1979, illustrate military SO deep operation.

Soviet state security was the first Soviet organ to practice deep operation. In the 1920s and 1930s, state security conducted extensive operations beyond the borders of the Soviet Union to co-opt, disrupt, and destroy centers of anti-Soviet activity.[4] The first recorded overseas assassination by Soviet state security was the OGPU murder of Ukrainian leader Simon Petlura in Paris in 1926.[5] In 1936, the effort reached an organizational peak with the creation of the NKVD Administration of Special Tasks. Through infiltration, deception, abduction, assassination, and other measures, the Soviets effectively neutralized a wide range of external emigre threats until, on the eve of the Great Patriotic War, overseas anti-Soviet activism had ceased to be a significant problem. Similar cross-border campaigns of varied intensity were waged by the KGB and its allies against defectors, hostile emigres, and other political enemies of the Soviet state in the late 1940s, 1950s, and 1960s.

Evolution of Theory

Military deep operation theory emerged at the end of World War I.[6] It drew on prewar concepts frustrated during the war, when technological limits on mobility, firepower, communications, and logistics meant that penetration of the tactical zone (a depth of about thirty kilometers) could not be sustained and continued to an operational depth to put the enemy's reserves and command, control, communications, and intelligence (C3I) at risk and create opportunities for strategic success. In the era of "trench warfare," even the most effective Russian offensives were usually mounted on wide, continuous linear frontages, with reserves used to maintain momentum in difficult areas.

The advent of the tank dramatically changed trench warfare by putting the continuous front in motion, which was logically countered by defense in depth. In May 1918, Brig. Gen. John F. C. Fuller's "Plan 1919" for winning the war against Germany envisioned the concentrated use of armor in a surprise thrust on a ninety-mile front into the enemy's tactical depth (deep *battle*) to isolate German divisions from their army-level headquarters.[7] A contemporary, B. Liddell Hart, advocated the theory of the "expanding torrent"[8] deep *strategic* penetration and envelopment to paralyze and disintegrate the enemy from behind and avoid major, set-piece battles. Where Fuller focussed on armor and tended to ignore the other arms, Hart stressed the use of motorized infantry and dive bombers to accompany the tanks and deal with strongpoints and pockets of resistance.[9] A contemporary of Fuller and Hart, Gen. Billy Mitchell, added another dimension to deep battle theory with his visionary plan to airlift part of the 1st Infantry Division and parachute that force into combat several miles behind the German front line.[10]

In the late 1920s and early 1930s, Soviet military theorists such as Marshal Mikhail N. Tukhachevskiy,[11] V. Triandafillov and B. Shaposhnikov finally put the requisite Soviet combat expertise, ideology, and technology, and leadership traits, and ideas of their Western European counterparts, together to formulate *glubokii boi* (deep battle, later to become deep operation).[12] Their concepts integrated all arms and all services, including tactical air support and airborne forces, for synergistic effects. Maj. Gen. E. Boltin, Soviet military historian, wrote of the Soviet strategy that emerged:[13]

> Soviet strategy . . . was distinguished by harmonious views on modern war and on the means of prosecuting it. This was a strategy avoiding the lopsidedness characteristic of certain bourgeois military theories, such as the Italian Guilio Douhet's doctrine of "air dominance" or the British military writer Major-General John Fuller's theory of "mechanized war" and small

professional armies. The Soviet doctrine called for a rational combination of all the fighting services and combat arms; it attached prime significance to offensive operations. . . . Soviet military leaders of the thirties (M. Tukhachevsky, V. Triandafillov, B. Shaposhnikov, and others) correctly assessed the growing role of such new means of combat as aircraft, tanks, airborne troops, and super-long-range artillery, and they put forward and elaborated the theory of the "deep operation." According to this theory, the fulfillment of operational missions (or the achievement of intermediate strategic aims) required a determined offensive with the delivery of crushing blows throughout the full depth of the enemy operational troop dispositions. . . .

With technological advances in armor, mobile artillery, bombers, automatic weapons, airlift, airborne delivery, and communications, and an expanded industrial base capable in the 1930s of producing large quantities of necessary equipment, the range, lethality, and coordination of Soviet military forces increased the Soviet potential to make deep operation a reality. In a 1930 Soviet field exercise, a small airborne *desant*[14] (assault force) "captured" a corps commander.[15] In the 1934 Byelorussian maneuvers,[16] the Soviets employed another, larger airborne *desant* on a direct action mission to an operational depth, with successful link-up with long-range armored forces.

In a 6 May 1937 article in *Red Star* (appearing just over a month before he was executed) Tukhachevskiy described the state of deep operations at that time:[17]

If the enemy keeps his flanks closed and it is not possible to envelop them, the enemy battle formation must be crushed by a deep strike from the front. . . . Our technical equipment enables us to put pressure on the enemy not only on the line of the front, but also to break through his disposition and attack to the full depth of the battle formation. . . . Modern means of combat permit us to organize the attack in such a way that the enemy is simultaneously hit to the full depth, and his reserves can be contained on their approach to the threatened sector. . . .

Although he was writing about tank warfare in this article, the Soviets then had fifteen airborne combined-arms special-purpose brigades in their order of battle,[18] and a doctrine calling for use of these forces to seize deep objectives (including enemy withdrawal routes) and await link-up within two or three days with armored forces. Tukhachevskiy's postulations of deep operation theory certainly influenced the parallel theoretical development of SO in support of Soviet armored thrusts.

Marshal Matvei V. Zakharov provides a more precise description of the mechanics of deep operation prior to the Russo-Finnish War of 1939–1940:[19]

> The deep operation as a process included several stages; breakthrough of the tactical defense and forming a breach in it by the combined efforts of the infantry, tanks, artillery and aviation; the exploitation of tactical into operational success by means of sending masses of tanks, motorized infantry, and mechanized cavalry through this breach and also by means of making air landings (the destruction of reserves and liquidation of the enemy's operational defense); the exploitation of operational success (operational pursuit) to the complete destruction of the enemy grouping selected as the objective of the operation and seizing a favorable assault position for a new operation. The first stage is the foundation for a deep operation since without a breakthrough of the tactical defense it would not have taken place at all, that is, it would have been frustrated. But its main point was that artillery, tanks (several echelons), aviation and infantry, cooperating among themselves, simultaneously inflict a defeat on the enemy's combat order throughout its whole depth and, as if by a single, surprise, deep and powerful strike, they break his defense, forming breaches in it, and try to reach the operational area. In accomplishing this, all branches of service act in support of the infantry.

With the death of many of the uniformed proponents of deep operation in the Stalinist purges of 1937–39, the military capacity for deep operation was practically destroyed, and even its discussion became taboo.[20] Unmitigated military disasters in Finland (1939–1940) and at the hands of the Germans (1940–1941) were an inevitable result of the lost dimension of personality and expertise. Military deep operation and its use of SOF were subsequently rediscovered as the initiative passed to the Soviets in the midst of World War II, and its embrace by the Soviet military intensified after the death of Stalin.

Modern Combined Arms Theory

Today, deep operation is fundamental to the Soviet perception of combined arms operations and battles.[21] In the past decade, the Soviets have developed the Theater Strategic Operation as an extension of deep operation theory. Theater Strategic Operation is described as follows:[22]

> This concept provides a framework for the integration of forces and strategy designed to wage a rapid nonnuclear or, if imposed by the enemy, nuclear, combined arms campaign in a Theater of Military Operations (TVD) . . . in which enemy strategic objectives located up to a 1,500-kilometer depth must be successfully attacked and neutralized. The Theater Strategic Operation comprises a series of component suboperations designated front, air, antiair, airborne, naval, and nuclear. They are controlled and coordinated by the High Commands of Forces (HCFs) in each continental TVD. . . . The ground maneuver portion is conducted by Soviet fronts. . . . Deep operation has emerged as a primary means to neutralize and seize Soviet objectives deep in an opponent's rear area. The operation consists of deep strikes by aviation, rocket, and artillery forces, as well as attacks into the enemy's deep rear areas conducted by Soviet operational maneuver groups, or OMGs. OMGs can be formed at front- or Army-level. Multiple OMGs would be employed to isolate front-line defending forces; disrupt rear-area logistics; threaten key command-and-control, economic and population centers; neutralize nuclear attack systems; and disrupt the mobilization and reinforcement process critical to a successful . . . defense.

Modern combined-arms deep operation thus entails:[23] (1) the integration of a number of separate but interrelated operations to achieve simultaneous neutralization of the enemy's defenses throughout the entire depth by means of destruction and firepower; (2) rapid breakthrough of the enemy's tactical zones of defense along the main sector of attack; (3) follow-on rapid development of the tactical success into operational success by commitment of additional combined-arms units; and (4) insertion of airborne (air assault) forces to increase the tempo of the operation.

The Soviets do not have a SO doctrine per se. Soviet special political-military action is a variant and subcategory of deep operation that complements the power of infantry, armor, artillery, and aircraft. It comprises unique action taken to prepare the battlefield beforehand, and improve the odds during battle, for victory by conventional force of arms. Moreover, the deeper, more complex, and more sensitive the operation, the greater the political reliability, technical proficiency, and secrecy of the force committed to that operation.[24]

Soviet faith in and commitment to *spetsnaz* and SO has been uneven over the years. During the civil war, the Reds made extensive use of insur-

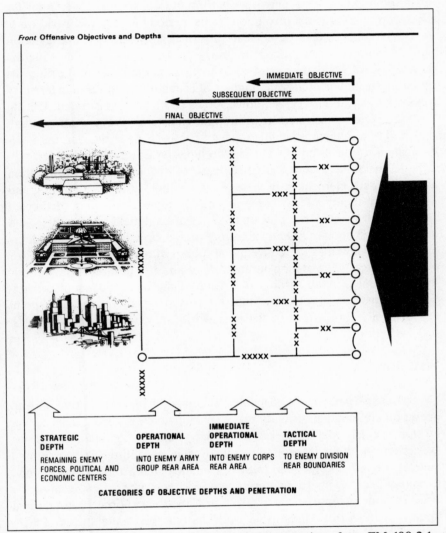

Figure 1. Front offensive objective depths and penetration, from FM 100-2-1.

rectionist, diversionary, and irregular partisan forces against the Whites. After the war, unorthodox combat fell into disfavor with the demise of Trotsky and his followers, who had advocated a proletarian militia in place of a standing army, and the ascent of Frunze and Tukhachevskiy and their allies, who called for a permanent, formally constituted Red Army for the export of communist revolution. In the period between the world wars, the Soviets focussed on large-scale use of armor, artillery, and aviation under high-level, centralized control—the antithesis of SO. With the destruction of Soviet conventional formations at the onset of the German invasion, the Soviets fell back on their SO capabilities in Russian territory to forestall defeat until conventional forces could be reconstituted. During the war, SO demonstrated its utility and came into vogue again (though it proved to be an unpredictable mode of combat). After the war, the Soviets again deemphasized SO. During the 1953–1960 "Revolution in Military Affairs," the Soviets viewed large-scale use of weapons of mass destruction as the decisive element in warfare. Save for their utility in detecting and interdicting enemy preparations to employ atomic weapons, dedicated *spetsnaz* had scant role to play on the nuclear battlefield. In the 1970s and 1980s, Soviet stock in SO and *spetsnaz* rose again with increasing adherence to the view that the conventional phase of a war with the West (or with China) could be of long duration. *Spetsnaz* also became more militarily significant in Afghanistan, as a result of the inadequacies of conventional formations in that war, and this period represents the high point of Soviet SO capabilities in the post-World War II era.

Structures

Soviet *spetsnaz* and SO-capable structures for the prosecution of deep operation are found at virtually every echelon above division. This capacity for special operations often overlaps and is confused (by some Westerners) with Soviet ground reconnaissance capabilities. To compound matters, *razvedchiki* (scouts) in Soviet infantry and armor regiments and divisions bear a superficial resemblance to *spetsnaz*.[25] For example, a Western source reports that many non–Guards Airborne, conventional force *razvedchiki* in Afghanistan wore the blue beret and striped undershirt of VDV airborne forces until ordered to cease by the commander, 40th Army. In the absence of a Guards sleeve insignia on their uniforms, such forces can be easily misidentified as "spetsnaz," though their capabilities fall far short of such. Writ large, Soviet *spetsnaz* and SO-capable forces are as follows:

Division and Regiment. A pseudo-special operations capability is found at divisional and combat arms regimental levels, and is worth mentioning because such troops are sometimes erroneously counted against *spetsnaz* strength figures and because personnel from such units may provide filler for *spetsnaz* or SO-capable units. Every motorized rifle and tank regiment (every such battalion in Afghanistan) in every motorized rifle division (MRD) and tank division (TD) has a motorized reconnaissance or "raiding" company (*reydovaya rota*) that can conduct operations up to twenty-five kilometers forward of the main body using organic vehicles (e.g., motorcycles, infantry fighting vehicles, and tanks). Similarly, every MRD, TD and airborne division has dedicated, motorized, and possibly airborne-capable[26] *razvedchiki* in a long-range reconnaissance company that can conduct tactical reconnaissance and limited strike operations out to one hundred kilometers behind enemy lines. In MRDs and TDs, this company is in the division reconnaissance battalion. In airborne divisions, this is a separate company.[27] All told, the "SO" capabilities of Soviet *razvedchiki* are probably less than those of their counterparts in a standard U.S. mechanized infantry division. For example, the *razvedchiki* are notoriously weak by Western standards in land navigation, map reading, and dismounted patrolling, and tend toward company-size formations where Westerners would use platoons or squads.

VDV Airborne Forces. The seven-division[28] Soviet Airborne Forces (*Vozdushno-Desantniye Voiska* or VDV) may also be considered as quasi-SO capable, with their capabilities for coups de main, seizure of key terrain and facilities, neutralization of special weapons systems and C3I, blocking enemy withdrawal routes, and reconnaissance. They are under the control of the General Staff and are used judiciously for power projection and wartime surprise, deep penetration as forward detachments,[29] and exploitation, as exemplified by their use in Prague (1968) and Kabul (1979).[30]

Army. The long-range reconnaissance company[31] (possibly expanded in some cases to battalion strength) in every combined-arms army (CAA) and tank army (TA), normally depicted as separate from the CAA/TA intelligence battalion, comprises the primary field army-level SO capability. A secondary SO capability is provided by army-level air assault battalions.[32] Although not their primary missions, both are capable of deep strikes and other quasi-SO such as can be performed by U.S. Army ranger companies and battalions and corps long-range surveillance (LRS) companies. These formations also may have radio-electronic combat (REC) capabilities. Army career-term SO professionals (erroneously known as *vysotniki* in some Western sources) may also be integrated into the reconnaissance company and may act as clandestine support agents for especially sensitive missions. The reconnaissance company is composed largely of conscripts (erroneously known by some in the West as *reydoviki*, or "raiders").[33] An Army-level reconnaissance company or air assault battalion can operate more than one hundred kilometers behind enemy lines using Army aviation and ground transport assets.

Front. Front level SO-capable forces and SOF consist of separate air assault, airmobile assault, and SOF *spetsnaz* "brigades" (the Soviet term *brigada* is a formation that varies widely in size and is often smaller than a Western brigade of comparable function).[34] The air assault and airmobile assault brigades each have a separate reconnaissance company similar to those found within the airborne division. These formations normally perform rear attack missions rather than "true" SO, but they comprise important assets in overall Soviet SO potential. Each Front and Fleet SOF *brigada* (among Western sources, there are no publicly reported diversionary forces assigned to separate flotillas) consists of three battalions of SOF "operators" and a SO agent network. The network recruits agents, conducts reconnaissance and target surveillance, provides reception committees, guides, transport, false documentation, and logistics for incoming SOF, and engages in limited sabotage. In addition to having a separate SOF brigade, front structures feature an intelligence regiment, with which at least one source associates a separate SO company.[35] It is not certain whether this company or its association with the intelligence regiment exists, or whether (if it does exist) this company is an addition to the Front SOF brigade. If such a company does exist, it may be composed of professionals who reinforce and support conscripts in the SOF brigade.

Fleet. Naval SOF and SO-capable forces consist of one naval infantry division (Pacific Fleet), three naval infantry brigades (one each for the Northern, Baltic and Black Sea fleets)[36] and four naval *spetsnaz* brigades (one for each fleet). Naval *spetsnaz* are believed subordinate to the intelligence department of their respective Fleet staff. Naval *spetsnaz* brigades are structured similar but on a smaller scale to Front *spetsnaz* brigades, with a core cadre of career-term professionals, two or three combat swimmer battalions (at least one of which is airborne-capable), a miniature submarine formation believed to be of at least company size, support elements, and an agent network. Some analysts maintain that current peacetime strength of each naval *spetsnaz* brigade may be only about company size. Naval *spetsnaz* may be used to stage diversionary landings and/or amphibious, airborne, or airlanding raids and assaults in coastal

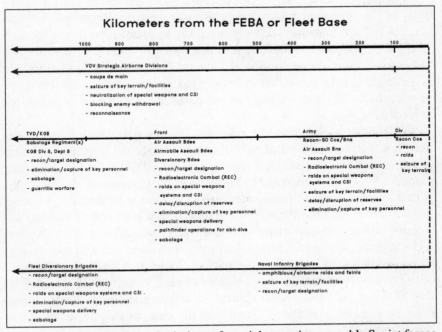

Kilometers from the FEBA or Fleet Base

| | 1000 | 900 | 800 | 700 | 600 | 500 | 400 | 300 | 200 | 100 |

VDV Strategic Airborne Divisions

- coups de main
- seizure of key terrain/facilities
- neutralization of special weapons and C3I
- blocking enemy withdrawal
- reconnaissance

TVD/KGB	Front	Army	Div
Sabotage Regiment(s)	**Air Assault Bdes**	**Recon-SO Cos/Bns**	**Recon Cos**
KGB Div S, Dept 8	Airmobile Assault Bdes	Air Assault Bns	- recon
- recon/target designation	Diversionary Bdes	- recon/target designation	- raids
- elimination/capture of key personnel	- recon/target designation	- Radioelectronic Combat (REC)	- seizure of key terrain
- sabotage	- Radioelectronic Combat (REC)	- raids on special weapons systems and C3I	
- guerrilla warfare	- raids on special weapons systems and C3I	- seizure of key terrain/facilities	
	- delay/disruption of reserves	- delay/disruption of reserves	
	- elimination/capture of key personnel	- elimination/capture of key personnel	
	- special weapons delivery		
	- pathfinder operations for abn divs		
	- sabotage		

Fleet Diversionary Brigades	**Naval Infantry Brigades**
- recon/target designation	- amphibious/airborne raids and feints
- Radioelectronic Combat (REC)	- seizure of key terrain/facilities
- raids on special weapons systems and C3I	- recon/target designation
- elimination/capture of key personnel	
- special weapons delivery	
- sabotage	

Figure 2. Average depths and missions of special operations-capable Soviet forces in the offense.

areas in support of larger conventional forces, sometimes utilizing submarines or high-speed hovercraft for infiltration or extraction.[37] Naval *spetsnaz* is primarily an over-the-horizon force, capable of operating along the flanks of Soviet ground forces and out to several thousand kilometers beyond their Fleet base.[38]

Soviet naval infantry have similar capabilities, but with less range and precision and greater force. In naval infantry reconnaissance, sabotage, or diversionary landings, the force normally employed would be a platoon, company, or battalion.[39] Such landings would likely be made from small surface ships or helicopters. Soviet naval infantry is also believed capable of using airborne or airlanding *desants* of up to battalion strength, including BMD infantry fighting vehicles. It is also possible that on selected missions there is a commingling of *spetsnaz* and infantry, with the former providing the necessary technical expertise and the latter providing the necessary extra firepower and muscle.

Theater/General Staff. The purported highest echelon of military SOF is the so-called Long Range Reconnaissance Regiment.[40] Some sources believe that one such regiment (or brigade) is assigned to each Theater (TVD), while others believe that only one such regiment/brigade exists in the service of the Soviet General Staff. This regiment/brigade can allegedly field more than one hundred groups (action elements), or provide cadre for force-multiplier or partisan missions in occupied or denied territory.

KGB. The KGB reportedly conducts operational planning, coordination, and political control of SOF that operate abroad in peacetime, and for assassinations and wartime sabotage under CPSU Central Committee guidance.[41] KGB Department Eight, within Directorate S (Illegals), generally engages in *aktivnyye meropriyatiya* (active measures, a concept much broader than the Western sense of SO) in hostile and denied territories for subversion and disinformation; target acquisition and sabotage, and *aktivnyye akty* (direct action, including assassinations and abductions) whenever required as an organic part of Soviet foreign policy. Because of the relatively smaller manpower pool of state security SOF, some military SOF are put under KGB control for augmentation and/or reinforcement in selected operations. Such was the case in Prague in 1968 and Kabul in 1979.[42]

Conclusion

Soviet deep operation theory is thus a long spear, with *spetsnaz* at its tip and special operations along its cutting edge. The balance, unity, and integration of the components of deep operation are remarkable, and offer a sharp contrast to the dichotomy between general purpose forces and special forces, and between "conventional" and "special" operations one often finds in Western armies. The Soviets have taken the path that minimizes such distinctions in the interests of maximizing forces capable of fighting to the depth of the enemy dispositions.

At the upper end of their SO capabilities, the Soviets do have dedicated SOF, but the bulk of such capabilities are possessed by forces not seen as "special" by most Western observers. Bound in the seamless web of deep operation theory, *spetsnaz* and SO-capable forces provide the Soviets with the potential to conduct rapid, agile, and synchronized operations of a unique and critical nature from the front line through to the enemy capital. The potential is impressive, even when one considers that the Soviets may yet lack the requisite training, equipment, leadership, and soldier motivation needed to practice deep operation successfully against first-class opposition, such as the armies of NATO can offer.

The Soviet concept of deep operation, and especially its SO dimension, challenges Western military thinkers to reassess the "rear battle" in AirLand Battle and other national operational concepts, to review underlying assumptions about Soviet SO capabilities, and to acknowledge the imprint of deep operation theory on Soviet special political-military activities. The historical employment of SO in the context of deep operation should also prompt Western military professionals to reconsider attitudes and policies that foster the building and maintenance of walls, instead of bridges, between their national armies, services, and branch components thereof.[43] The choice may ultimately be that of waging war as chess rather than as barroom poker.

Notes

1. See, Jiri Valenta, "From Prague to Kabul: The Soviet Style of Invasion," *International Security*, Fall 1980, 114–141.
2. John J. Dziak, "The Soviet Approach to Special Operations," *Special Operations in US Strategy*, Frank R. Barnett, B. Hugh Tovar and Richard H. Schulz, eds. (Washington DC: National Defense University Press, 1984): 105; U.S. Army Field Manual 100-2-2, *The Soviet Army: Specialized Warfare and Rear Area Support* (Washington DC: Headquarters, Department of the Army, 16 July 1984): 5-1 and 5-2; C. N. Donnelly, "Operations in the Enemy Rear: Soviet Doctrine and Tactics," *International Defense Review*, 1/1980, 35–41.
3. The antecedent Russian concept of "deep strike" goes back several centuries. See, Dr. Bruce W. Menning, *The Deep Strike in Russian and Soviet Military History* (Fort Leavenworth KS: Soviet Army Studies Office, undated).
4. See Dziak, *Chekisty: A History of the KGB* (Lexington MA: Lexington Books, 1988): 75–103.
5. John Barron, *KGB: The Secret Work of Soviet Secret Agents* (New York: Reader's Digest Press, 1974): 415.
6. See, Chris Bellamy, "Red Star in the West: Marshal Tukhachevskiy and East-West Exchanges on the Art of War," *Royal United Services Institute Journal*, December 1987, 63–73; *Soviet Battlefield Development Plan*, Vol. 1, "Soviet General Doctrine for War" (Washington DC: U.S. Army Intelligence Agency and Threat Analysis Center, June 1987): 2-28 through 2-32.
7. Hew Strachan, *European Armies and the Conduct of War* (London: George Allen & Unwin, 1983): 155.
8. Strachan, 156.
9. Strachan, 156.
10. John Weeks, *Assault from the Sky* (New York: G. P. Putnam's Sons, 1978): 8.
11. Richard Simpkin, *Red Armour: An Examination of the Soviet Mobile Force Concept* (London: Brassey's Defence Publishers, 1984): 139–143; Scott and Scott, "The Historical Development of Soviet Forward Detachments," *Military Review*, November 1987, 26–35.
12. See Lt. Col. David M. Glantz, "Soviet Operational Formation for Battle: A Perspective," *Military Review*, February 1983, 2-12; id., "The Nature of Operational Art," *Parameters*, Spring 1985, 2-12.
13. Maj. Gen. E. Boltin, "On the Eve of the War," *Soviet Military Review*, February 1967, 46–48.
14. Assault (Landing) Force: Troops which have been specially trained and landed (dropped) or designated for landing (dropping) onto enemy territory for the purpose of conducting combat operations. An assault force may be operational-strategic, operational, operational-tactical, tactical, and special-

purpose, based on number of troops involved, nature of missions performed, and depth to which they are delivered (dropped). Airborne assaults and amphibious landings are differentiated, on the basis of means and modes of troop delivery. Other categories include diversionary assault force, assault landing party, and tankborne assault force. JPRS-UMA-85-015-L, *USSR Report, Military Affairs, Military Encyclopedic Dictionary (Voennyi entsiklopedicheskii slovar')*, vol. III (Washington DC: Foreign Broadcast Information Service, 4 June 1985): 907. See also, Maj. James F. Holcomb, Jr., and Dr. Graham H. Turbiville, Jr., *Exploiting the Vertical Dimension: Continuing Development of the Soviet Desant Force Structure* (Fort Leavenworth KS: Soviet Army Studies Office, May 1987): 1.

15. Weeks, 8–9.
16. Bellamy, op. cit.; Col. David M. Glantz, *The Soviet Airborne Experience*, Combat Studies Institute Research Survey No. 4 (Fort Leavenworth KS: U.S. Army Command and General Staff College, November 1984): 10–11.
17. Scott and Scott, 58.
18. FM 100-2-2, 2-1.
19. M. V. Zakharov, "The Theory of the Operation in Depth," *Voenno-istoricheskiy zhurnal*, October 1970, 16, quoted in Scott and Scott, op. cit., 20. See also, *Soviet Battlefield Development Plan*, 2-30.
20. Scott and Scott, 21.
21. *Soviet Battlefield Development Plan*, vol. 1, "Soviet General Doctrine for War" (Washington DC: U.S. Army Intelligence Agency and U.S. Army Intelligence and Threat Analysis Center, June 1987): 2-31.
22. *Soviet Military Power: An Assessment of the Threat, 1988* (Washington DC: U.S. Government Printing Office, 1988): 69–75.
23. *Soviet Battlefield Development Plan*, 2-32.
24. The Soviets learned this lesson in the Battle of Warsaw during the 1920 Russo-Polish War, when they were blinded and ultimately defeated in large measure because so many of their reconnaissance patrols defected to the Poles.
25. U.S. Army Field Manual 100-2-3, *The Soviet Army: Troops, Organization and Equipment* (Washington DC: Headquarters, Department of the Army, 16 July 1984): 4-8, 4-15, 4-26, 4-33, 4-67, 4-68, 4-69, 4-101.
26. Holcomb and Turbiville, *Exploiting the Vertical Dimension*, 24–27.
27. FM 100-2-3, 4-139.
28. There are eight divisions if one training division is also counted.
29. See Col. David M. Glantz, *Spearhead of the Attack: The Role of the Forward Detachment in tactical Maneuver* (Fort Leavenworth KS: Soviet Army Studies Office, 1988).
30. Turbiville, "Soviet Airborne Operations in Theater War," *Foreign Policy*, vol. XIII, 1985, 160–183; FM 100-2-2, 2-1 through 2-10; FM 100-2-3, 4-134

through 4-144; Graham H. Turbiville, Jr., "Soviet Airborne Troops," *Soviet Armed Forces Review Annual*, vol. 10 (Gulf Breeze FL: Academic International Press, 1987): 146–147; Maj. James F. Holcomb, "Soviet Airborne Forces and the Central Region," *Military Review*, November 1987, 36–47; Holcomb and Turbiville, "Soviet *desant* forces. Part 1: Soviet airborne and air assault capabilities," *International Defense Review*, 9/1988, 1077–1082 at 1081–1082; id., "Soviet *desant* forces. Part 2: Broadening the desant concept," ibid., 10/1988, 1259–1264.

31. FM 100-2-3, 4-114 and 4-115.
32. Holcomb and Turbiville, *Exploiting the Vertical Dimension*, 14–15.
33. Note that the stratification of Soviet SOF personnel into *vysotniki* professionals and *reydoviki* conscripts has not been conclusively established in Western sources. It is safe to assume, given the overall composition of the Soviet armed forces, that SOF comprises a smaller and generally dominant element of career-term soldiers, and a larger and generally subordinate element of conscripts. One can only speculate at this point as to the exact nature of relations between these two elements.
34. FM 100-2-3, 4-123, 4-131, 4-132, 4-133.
35. See, FM 100-2-3, 4-123 and 4-133.
36. FM 100-2-2, 4-1 through 4-8; DDB-2680-170-87, *Force Structure—USSR, Eastern Europe, Mongolia, and Afghanistan* (Washington DC: Defense Intelligence Agency, November 1987): 12–13, 44.
37. Capt. 3rd Rank Oleg Odnokolenko, "The Marines," *Soviet Military Review*, 3/1988, 12–13.
38. Peter Hertel Rasmussen, "Soviet Naval Infantry and Spetsnaz Naval Brigades," *Soviet Armed Forces Review Annual*, vol. 10, 141–145.
39. Holcomb and Turbiville, *Exploiting the Vertical Dimension*, 15–18.
40. Known by some sources as the Sabotage Regiment.
41. *Soviet Military Power 1986* (Washington DC: U.S. Government Printing Office, March 1986): 72.
42. Dziak, "Military Doctrine and Structure," *Hydra of Carnage*, Uri Ra'anan, et al., eds. (Lexington MA: Lexington Books, 1986): 83.
43. For examples of bridge-building, see Maj. Glenn M. Harned, "Special Operations and the AirLand Battle," *Military Review*, September 1985, 73–83; and id., "Bridging the Gap: Special Forces As a Member of the Combined Arms Team," *Special Warfare*, October 1988, 3–9.

CHAPTER 13

Organization, Capabilities and Countermeasures

Jim Shortt

To understand *voiska spetsialnogo naznacheniya* (VSN), one must clearly examine Soviet perceptions of special operations and the *spetsnaz* soldier's place as a citizen and soldier of the Soviet Union. We must see them as they see themselves to understand their unique organizations, capabilities, and vulnerabilities. The Soviet perception of their *spetsnaz* is harnessed to operational role. Central to this role is *diversiya razvedka* (diversionary reconnaissance), achieved through raids, ambushes, prisoner snatching, destruction of vital logistics, and assassination of key enemy personnel. Diversionary reconnaissance is not the sole domain of *spetsnaz*, however, and many types of diversionary-reconnaissance units exist throughout the Soviet military structure at regimental, divisional, Front and Army levels. The tradition of diversionary reconnaissance is seated in Russian history, and was, for example, traditionally the function of Cossack cavalry within the Russian Army as far back as Napoleon's invasion of 1812.

A sense for Soviet special operations is also found in their definition of *spetsialnaya razvedka*, or "special reconnaissance," although this is identified as a foreign term (see Chapter 2). This definition is further refined by certain colloquial terms used within the Soviet Armed Forces to describe those involved in *spetsnaz* operations, e.g., *razvedchiki* are those involved in reconnaissance; *iskatelia* (from the word "seek") are those involved in long-range reconnaissance patrol (LRRP) operations;

vysotniki are personnel inserted by high-altitude, low-opening (HALO) or high-altitude, high-opening (HAHO) parachute operations; *zakhvatchiki* (from the word "to capture") are members of a prisoner snatch group; and *okhotniki* are hunters.

While in the Soviet Union visiting the VDV Airborne Forces Higher Airborne Command School at Ryazan in February 1989, I spoke with numerous *afghanisti* (veterans of the Afghan War), both serving and discharged. I asked them individually what they called *spetsnaz*. They did not use the VSN abbreviation or "spetsnaz": they spoke instead of the *karavan okhotniki*, the "caravan hunters." I also confirmed that the term *reydoviki* (commandos) is not applied to *spetsnaz*. Soviet forces apply that term to NATO special forces assets.[1] Likewise, the Soviet appellation *spetsnaz* is applied to a wide variety of specialist troops such as strategic missile troops or other technically specialized troops unrelated to special operations.

Attempts to positively identify *spetsnaz* soldiers and units on the basis of clothing and uniform accoutrements are futile. There is in fact no known Soviet Armed Forces badge of qualification or unit identity that denotes a *spetsnaz* unit similar to that which exists within NATO special forces. Neither is there any rule of thumb for determining units by dress. It is false to claim, as one writer has, that anyone wearing the Airborne Forces uniform of blue beret* and blue and white T-shirt (*telniashka*) without the Guards badge is *spetsnaz*. All VDV units are Guards units, so a Guards badge is worn on the right breast. However, other airborne units within airmobile brigades, or those at the Ryazan Higher Airborne Command Forces School, are not entitled to wear the Guards badge as a matter of course.

At Ryazan,** for example, I saw a few officers and even some conscript support staff who were not "officially" entitled to, but who nonetheless wore the Guards badge. One captain instructor told me that he continued to wear the Guards badge because he had come from a VDV Guards division and was proud of the honor. This is akin to the way Vietnam-era U.S. Army Rangers wore their "unofficial" scrolled Ranger tab in spite of its lack of official standing. (It is now officially sanctioned.) I also noticed

---

*VDV units now utilize a red flash on the left side of the beret.

**It is not exactly proper to refer to the Higher Airborne Forces Command School as simply "Ryazan," as a separate Army signal school also exists in Ryazan, but that has been done in this chapter for the sake of brevity.

a driver who was qualified but not wearing the Airborne Forces blue shield on his jacket. When asked about this, his reply was that his shield was on his greatcoat, and as it was winter he wore the coat outside all the time. I was also told that in the winter the Airborne Forces wear the *shapka-ushanka** like other troops, reserving the beret for the warmer summer months.

Soviet military publications have also featured photographs of non-Airborne Forces troops wearing VDV insignia (parachute and two air-craft) on the red tabs of the motorized rifle regiment or the black tabs of the tank artillery. I asked about this during my visit and was told that these were not personnel trained by the VDV or Ryazan (conscripts are trained totally within the division to which they are posted). The staff suggested that these might be former Airborne Forces officers posted to non-airborne units Higher Schools who wish to retain their VDV identity. This is possible. However, a photograph has also appeared in the Soviet Union of tank troops with not only the Airborne Forces collar insignia but also the VDV cloth badge on black rather than blue background. These are parachute qualified members of an armored division's diversionary-reconnaissance battalion.

In Afghanistan, everyone including the airborne resorted to wearing the tropical fatigue hat or cap.[2] Videotape and still photographs of Soviet-acknowledged *spetsnaz* units in Afghanistan show them in the same khaki combat utilities worn by the rest of the 40th Army, with the same blue and white T–shirt, lace-up combat boots and the same chest webbing and RD–45 *ryukzak bolshoi*, as normal airborne units. Missing are the subdued Airborne Forces lapel badges, but that in itself is no discriminator, as I discovered at the Ryazan: There I saw some *kursanti* (officer cadets) as well as other ranks wearing them and others that did not. The variation seemed due merely to supply.

Pre-Military Training

All *spetsnaz* (and all other Soviet soldiers) are products of an elaborate state-run system of physical and military technical education and training that has a profound impact on *spetsnaz* capabilities. It is fair to say that

---

*The Russian military winter cap with ear flaps.

the Soviet soldier of the Forces of Special Designation starts his training at the age of ten in a program called the All-Union Sports-Technical Complex Ready for Labor and Defense of the USSR (*Gotov k trude i oborony*) or GTO.

The purpose of the GTO program is to create and maintain a high standard of physical fitness.[3] The program encompasses male and female pre-military and post-military service. It is a civilian program but is overseen and inspected by the Department of Preliminary Military Training at the Soviet Ministry of Defense (MoD). It is conducted in schools, colleges, factories, and on collective farms. The instructors are provided by the local military unit, but final selection lies with the civilian authority. For boys, the purpose of the GTO is to prepare them for their two years' Army conscript service.

From the age of seven, children are eligible to join the Octobrists, the first rung on the ladder to membership in the Communist Party of the Soviet Union (CPSU). Political reliability, i.e., CPSU membership, is a primary requisite for *spetsnaz* service. Membership in the Pioneers (a rule of which is "A Pioneer reveres the memory of fallen fighters and prepares to become a defender of the Motherland") is open to those aged ten to fourteen. Pioneers study the history of the Soviet Army from 1917 to the present, and are given overt military training. This is reinforced through *zarnitsa* (summer lightning) summer camps, where the children learn guard duty, marching drill, tactics, civil defense, first aid, military discipline and regulations.

From the age of fourteen, a youngster is permitted to join DOSAAF (The Voluntary Society for Cooperation With the Army, Air Force and Navy), in addition to his membership in the Pioneers. Between the ages of fifteen and twenty-eight, one can join the Young Communist League (Komsomol), usually on leaving the Pioneers. Komsomolists hold *orlyonok* (Little Eagle) camps where in addition to Pioneer military skills they are taught basic map reading, use of weapons, and grenade throwing.

Thus, there are in effect three "independent" programs to which a youth is exposed to military service (see chart on next page).[4]

The DOSAAF program comprises *orlyonok* camps plus a minimum 140 hours of training spread over two years, exposing the youth to basic military skills, radio procedure and maintenance, driving and vehicle maintenance, and even parachuting. The 1972 DOSAAF regulations state that DOSAAF will provide leadership for the development of military-technical skills. All parachuting, flying and gliding in the Soviet Union is under the control of the Armed Forces.

Stage	Program Name	Age Group
I. GTO	Courage and Skill	10–13
	Young Sportsman	14–15
	Strength and Courage	16–18
(Programs exist for civilians in the 19–60 year range)		
II. CPSU	Octobrists	7–9
	Pioneers	10–14
	Komsomol	15–28
III. DOSAAF		14–45

Conscript Training

Under the 1967 Law of Universal Military Service, young men from the age of eighteen are required to report for military service. There are exceptions — students in higher level schools, or for reasons of health and family, and some even just get left out of the draft. But most young men are drafted. It is not unusual for the GTO program to provide an additional eighty hours pre-callup training.

These eighty hours will provide intensive training in nuclear, biological and chemical (NBC) defense, forced marches, ski races, orienteering and cross-country races in addition to providing refreshers on the military skills already learned. Upon completion, the draftee is given his "Ready for Labor & Defense" certificate. The GTO program has in recent years undergone a vast overhaul following criticism from unit commanders who complained that many of the newly arrived conscripts who had their GTO certificates could not perform even the simplest of military skills.

Once in the Armed Forces, the conscript enters the military physical training program, *voenno-sportivnyi-kompleks*. The VSK was first introduced in 1965 and upgraded in 1973 as a result of military experience in Afghanistan. The program is designed to prepare the soldier for the rigors of combat and to encourage him to take up sport in his off duty period. An incentive system of badges and grades exist to further this, such as the "Athletic Servicemen Award." Physical fitness tests are undertaken several times during the conscripts' service, whereas permanent staff such as warrant officers, commissioned officers and extended service personnel only have to pass them once a year.

The Soviet serviceman is required to participate in daily physical training (PT) during his six-day week. In addition, he is required to (1) have a theoretical knowledge of a number of physical fitness programs operating in the Soviet Union; (2) know how to explain and perform a minimum of two routines from the Soviet physical training manual; (3) participate in at least five Olympic events sports competitions; and (4) participate in the pentathlon and special biathlon of his service unit.

The military pentathlon includes gymnastics, sprinting, cross country running, swimming, and cross country ski racing. The special biathlon centers on events of use to the branch of service. In armored units weight-lifting events are organized for drivers and loaders, while tank commanders and gunners train in speed reaction. Navy and naval infantry units perform swimming and water obstacle events while aircrew and those who will have to operate behind enemy lines will be tasked with orienteering and stress-resistance exercises.

Assault courses are designed for combat realism and include flame[5] and water obstacles and moving at speed from one level of a building to another, entering upper story windows, and jumping between buildings to develop confidence and competence. The obstacles are punctuated with tunnels and barriers over which an ammunition box filled with concrete, or a casualty, has to be transported. Live and blank firing is also organized for entering and leaving particular obstacles in a close-quarter battle (CQB) scenario. The Soviet system CQB is called *rukopashnyi boi* and has two main components, unarmed combat and skill at arms. *Kholodniye oruzhniye* (cold weapons) covers the use of bayonet (*shtyk*), entrenching tool (*shantsevaya lopata*) and knife (*nozh*).

While visiting Ryazan, I was able, as a senior close-quarter battle instructor, to compare training notes with senior *rukopashnyi boi* instructor Lt. Col. Vladimir Panteleev. Panteleev demonstrated protocols for throwing a knife or bayonet, altering the grip on the blade dependent on the distance to be thrown. The unarmed combat section of *rukopashnyi boi* is called *sambo* (*Samo-oborona bez oruzhiya*). *Sambo* was developed by a Russian judo practitioner, Oshchepkov, who having studied judo decided it was not combat efficient and so added to it elements of Japanese jujitsu and Russian wrestling styles. Competitions similar to judo are held on a sporting level, but within the armed forces in addition to Sport Sambo a Sambo Self-Defense system is taught with regular district and national competitions being held.

Sambo Self-Defense, or unarmed combat, has been enlarged to include karate-style techniques. As I witnessed during my visit, a very heavy emphasis is placed on daily training in CQB skill, particularly within the elite units (VDV, *spetsnaz*, etc.). Special *rukopashnyi boi* rooms exist for training which include sound and light controls to enable rhythm training as well to simulate night and battle confusion with strobes and white noise. All Soviet combat training hinges around presenting realistic combat scenarios from unit to personal weapons to bladed weapons to unarmed combat as the lowest common denominator so that the shock of battle is lessened through such simulation and drill.

Officer Training

Officer training takes place at Military Higher Schools or Academies. Ryazan is an example. Quite wrongly, this school was named by author Viktor Suvorov as having a *spetsnaz* facility.[6] Ryazan trains young men between the ages of seventeen and twenty-one (up to twenty-five for those already in the military).[7] The course lasts four years, culminating with a university-equivalent degree in military engineering. There are approximately two thousand *kursanti* attending the school at any particular time.

The purpose of the school, according to its Commandant and Hero of the Soviet Union Lt. Gen. Al'bert Evdokimovich Slyusar'[8] and his deputy Lt. Col. Mikhail Ivanovitch Varentsov, is to provide graduate officers at the rank of lieutenant to the six divisions of the VDV and the Air Mobile/Air Landing units that exist independently of the VDV at Group of Soviet Forces level and within the assets of certain military districts.

The conditions of entry into a Higher School or Academy are: (1) good health and physical fitness; (2) matriculation and good grades in Senior School final exams; and (3) recommendations from DOSAAF, Komsomol, etc. Servicemen who have performed well in Afghanistan as private soldiers or NCOs have been offered places, despite not meeting these criteria.

Each year there are approximately 32,500 applications for the 500 places in the new first-year course. Selection depends on a number of factors. One's record in DOSAAF, the GTO program, school academic record, and Komsomol record are examined. Those not selected from amongst the volunteers, including conscripts who have applied while undertaking their national service, are advised to try elsewhere. But for many it is the airborne or nothing, and as many as 1,000 applicants will live a rough life in the nearby Mischeza Forest when the first year starts each July, hoping for a vacancy to occur.

During the four-year course up to 60 percent of the *kursanti* marry. If they are caught drinking alcohol on or off duty during their four years, they are expelled. The *kursanti* undergo a similar regime of training to the military conscript aimed at making them competent with all the equipment and weapons used by the Airborne Forces. They are then schooled to teach all those skills and be instructors to their troops in their airborne unit. The *kursanti* serve a six-day week with Sundays off. They have a few hours off during the week for personal and family administration but basically serve from 0600 to 2200 hours.

Spetsnaz Selection and Training

I asked General Slyusar' about *spetsnaz* training for officers. His answer was that during the course of the year a special "Spetsnaz Committee" from the GRU visited Ryazan and examined the computer records on each *kursanti*, sought opinions from staff as to physical and academic performance, and scrutinized pre-military preparation as well. Those selected were removed from the school for further *spetsnaz* skills training at designated training centers. The main *spetsnaz* training center, where annual competitions are held, is the General of the Army Sergey M. Shtemenko Higher Military School at Krasnodar (Krasnodarsoye VVU) in the Transcaucasus.[9]

The further training is built on top of the training they have already received at the school in parachuting, CQB, heavy drop (parachute-deployed vehicles), communications and military skills. Field training is carried out in the nearby Oka River training area. The individual and unit skills particular to *spetsnaz* are therefore an extension and adjunct to those skills provided at the Higher School or in his unit, and in pre-service training. There is no comparable system in NATO.

Conscripts for the independent *spetsnaz* units (non-VDV or unit reconnaissance) are selected at the local draft selection point by *spetsnaz* officers. Up to 100 conscripts are selected on the basis of records and interviews, enough for a training company. They then undertake eight weeks of very physical combat-oriented training, at the end of which only about twenty of the original number will be retained in *spetsnaz*. The remainder are sent to airborne or other units.[10]

Special facilities have been built to enable *spetsnaz* groups to practice their role. The *spetsnaz* brigade attached to the Group of Soviet Forces Germany (GSFG) has a special training facility at Letslingerheide Heath. Similar training facilities exist at two training areas in the Carpathian Military District near L'vov and Mukachevo. A center point of all three areas is the assembly of full-size mockups of NATO aircraft, cruise missile TELs, artillery and other equipment, which emphasizes the importance of nuclear weapons delivery systems to *spetsnaz*.[11] Such areas also have museums in which NATO and target force equipment, weapons and literature are available for study, and it is my observation that the Soviets are keenly aware of Western special forces capabilities.

Lessons Learned and Applied

In developing their capabilities the Soviets have learned a great deal from their own special operations battle experience, especially that of World War II. They continue to apply their lessons. To the extensive treatment of *spetsnaz* history and its relevance to contemporary capabilities found in the preceding chapters, I add only a few parenthetical comments. Long before World War II, the Soviet concept of special operations was sophisticated and expansive and, in stark contrast to the resistance modern American special operations forces have experienced from their conventionally-minded overlords, the Soviets were willing to back their concepts with appropriate personnel and other resources.

An example of the scale of pre-World War II Soviet special operations occurred between April and May 1929, when 800 to 1,200 Soviet troops drawn from OGPU divisions were infiltrated across the Afghan border in Afghan Army dress uniforms to operate against the *basmachi*.[12] Soviet thinking in this regard is also underscored by the fact that when in 1933 the first VDV units were placed in the Soviet Armed Forces order of battle they were designated *brigada desantnaya (spetsialnogo naznacheniya)*, or Airborne Assault Brigades of Special Designation.

In addition to their own experience, the Soviets have rapidly absorbed lessons in special operations from their enemies. For example, Soviet forces were badly mauled in the 1940 invasion of Finland by *Jaakan*, independent units that operated in the Soviet rear and were reinforced by Swedish Army volunteers of the Hango Battalions and Svir Company. The experience inspired the Soviet preparation of their first partisan units in the North West Front during World War II.

During World War II, the Soviets were impressed by the activities of the German Abwehr Kampf-Trupps. Originally formed as antisabotage troops, they were made up of predominantly Polish Germans and anticommunist Russians trained at Quenzcut near Brandenburg. They went on to become the Brandenburger Division—arguably the best of the German special forces. The Brandenburgers, Kurfurst Regiment, Bergman and Nightingale battalions, and other German special forces also carried out a series of brilliant surprise attacks in the diversionary mode as the very spearpoint of the blitzkrieg.[13] The Soviets studied their operations during the war, and in several cases individual Germans experienced in special operations, anti-partisan operations, and intelligence worked directly for the Soviets after the war.

SS Col. Otto Skorzeny, a notable leader of German special forces, particularly caught the attention of the Soviets:[14] In 1947, while a prisoner of the United States awaiting trial as a war criminal, Skorzeny was approached in prison by a Polish officer who had been arrested as a Soviet spy. The officer made Skorzeny an offer to liberate him if he would come with him to the Soviet Union. Unfortunately for the Soviets, Skorzeny did not take up the offer, and escaped on his own in 1948.

An examination of East German state security special operations personalities in the 1950s, however, reveals some measure of Soviet success. Along with lifelong Communist underground leaders such as Ernst Wollweber (Minister of State Security for the DDR), one also finds personalities such as Werner Sauerland, former commanding officer of the Hitler Youth weapon training camp. It is perhaps instructive that it was the East Germans under Soviet direction who were held responsible by British intelligence (MI5) for a series of sabotage attacks on installations in Britain and other parts of Europe between 1947 and 1955.[15]

Organization for Diversionary Reconnaissance: Theory and Practice

Principal Soviet diversionary-reconnaissance assets include the following: Six VDV Guards Airborne Divisions (the 7th, 76th, 98th, 103rd,

104th, and 106th); eight air assault brigades at District and Group of Forces level; five *spetsnaz* brigades under control of the GRU Second Directorate; twenty *spetsnaz* brigades under Group of Forces or District control; and four naval infantry (*morskaya pekhota*) regiments/brigades. Two of these naval infantry units, for example, are targeted against Scandinavia, the 63rd ("Kirkenes") Guards NIB at Pechenga and the 36th Guards NIR at Baltysk. They are supported by the 7th *Luzyka Dywizya Desantnowa Morska*, a naval infantry assault division of the Polish Army based at Gdansk, and the East German 29th "Ernst Moritz Arndt" Motor Rifle Regiment at Proro on Rugen Island. The Polish and East German units are supported by attached special purpose units. The Soviets also operate with a brigade of naval *spetsnaz* per NIB, and there may be habitual relations between the two.

The doctrinal role of these naval *spetsnaz* is to secure the hinterland of the landing, guide in the naval infantry and tackle enemy assets that would oppose the landing. The naval infantry would fight out from the beachheads and conventional Army troops would be landed in their wake. The NIB is comprised of four battalions, a tank battalion, an anti-tank battalion and specialist companies, one of which is a diversionary-reconnaissance company that is amphibious and parachute trained.[16] Any full-scale invasion of Scandinavia would also likely be supported by Polish airborne assets and the 76th Guards Assault Division at Pskov.

The twenty *spetsnaz* brigades, one for each military district and Group of Forces, comprise three airborne assault-trained battalions with support and headquarters elements. In certain strategic areas the brigade comprises four battalions, such as the GSFG's brigade based at Neurippen in the 2d Guards Army area. The GSFG's airmobile brigade, the 35th Air Assault Brigade, is based at Cottbus. The 35th, like all airmobile brigades, is comprised of one parachute battalion and two motor rifle battalions plus support and headquarters elements.

During my visit to Ryazan, the Commandant explained the airmobile brigade structure as set out above; he also added that they were deployed at Group of Soviet Forces and District levels at a quota of one, but that not every military district had a brigade. There are believed to be eight Soviet airmobile brigades, one in each of the Group of Soviet Forces and four others situated in the western Soviet Union.

In all, the GRU maintains five *spetsnaz* brigades for deployment in small units from battalion to patrol in support of a TVD and its Strategic Direction. As a result, NATO assets up to 1,000 km from the Warsaw Pact border and even beyond would find themselves under attack from these teams. But the *spetsnaz* brigade and airmobile brigade are not the only reconnaissance-diversionary assets of the GSFG. The GSFG is composed of five Armies, each of four divisions. For example, the 3rd Shock Army at Magdeburg has, in addition to its four divisions, support elements that include a reconnaissance-diversionary brigade in the LRRP role. The 39th Guards Motor Rifle Division based at Ohrdruf within the 8th Guards Army, for another example, has four regiments and a reconnaissance battalion using T64 tanks and BMPs.

Dangerous Offspring

The Soviets have greatly assisted practically all of their allies and clients in the development of special operations (and anti-special operations) capabilities. Soviet *spetsnaz* and special operations thinking has left indelible impressions on the states of the Warsaw Pact and elsewhere in the world, from Latin America[17] to North Korea.[18] This impression is especially visible in Eastern Europe, where training and other contact with Soviet *spetsnaz* is strongest, and the imprint is suggestive of Soviet capabilities.

The Deutsche Demokratische Republik (DDR) Nationale Volksarmee maintains the 40th "Willie Sangar" Fallschirmjager Bataillon at Lehnin, commando troops to be used for operations in the NATO rear. The 40th was formed in 1973 from an airborne company at Cottbus, and is under the direct control of the DDR Ministry of Defense. The DDR Interior Ministry also maintains a special "diversionary" unit, the Felix Dzerzhinsky Wach Regiment, which has a pseudo West German battalion equipped like a Bundeswehr unit. The regiment also has companies equipped as other NATO forces, using U.S. equipment including M113 armored personnel carriers and M48 tanks recovered from Southeast Asia in the post-Vietnam War years. The DDR Volksmarine also includes several airborne-capable *kampfschwimmer* (combat swimmer) companies with missions and capabilities analogous to their Soviet naval counterparts.

Poland's special operations-capable forces include the 6th Pomarska Airborne Division near Krakow and the 4101st Diversionary-Reconnaissance Battalion at Dziwnow.* Czechoslovakia's special-purpose unit is the

---

*The 4101st participated in the 1968 invasion of Czechoslovakia.

22d Vysadkova Airborne Brigade; Hungary's is the 37th Parachute Battalion. Rumania has the 161st Parachute Regiment, and one long-range reconnaissance company for each of its four armies. Bulgaria has at least one airborne assault battalion, possibly based in the Burgas-Plovdiv region.[19]

Spetsnaz training and occasional combat teams have also left their mark in the Middle East, Southeast Asia, and Africa.[20] In the summer of 1982 a long-range patrol of South Africans operating inside Angola ambushed a vehicle and captured a Bulgarian and an East German officer and two Soviet *spetsnaz* officers, one of whom was wounded. Both were immediately flown out on Puma helicopter by military intelligence and later returned to the Soviet Union in prisoner exchanges. Other Soviet *spetsnaz* turned up in Mil 1 (Military Hospital No. 1) in the spring of 1983 after South African special forces raided the Luanda area.

Spetsnaz were involved in Vietnam training North Vietnamese-Vietcong special forces, called "sappers" by the United States military but also known as the Dac Cong. In the January 1968 Tet Offensive, a Vietcong special operations brigade task force played a decisive role in the battle for Saigon and made a major contribution to North Vietnam's efforts to force United States disengagement from South Vietnam.[21] The Saigon operation was commanded by Tran Bach Dang, first secretary of the Party organization in Saigon from 1965 to 1975. Within Saigon, five major urban targets were attacked by an eighty-man special forces unit backed up by 2,500 other troops. Interestingly, the selected targets included the American Embassy, South Vietnamese military headquarters, military radio station, and presidential palace, a targeting profile remarkably similar to that of *spetsnaz* in the 1968 capture of Prague and the 1979 seizure of Kabul.

Now-Colonel Do Tan Phong led a twenty-seven-man force in the attack on the South Vietnamese military headquarters before dawn on 31 January. Fourteen other men captured the military radio station. Another fourteen-man force attacked the presidential palace. At 0247, 18 men breached the wall around the United States Embassy and began a six-and-one-half-hour siege that millions of Americans watched on the evening news. Although not all of their targets were captured, and fifty of the commandos were killed or wounded (only two survived the embassy attack), the American military and American public opinion were badly shaken.

In March 1968, North Vietnamese Army (NVA) special forces attached to the 766th NVA Regiment conducted another operation that showed the influence of *spetsnaz* when they captured the secret United States Air Force (USAF) radar station at Phou Pha Thi, in Laos, used to vector aircraft on raids into North Vietnam. The cliff assault that took the Hmong and Thai mercenaries and USAF personnel completely by surprise, and the ensuing destruction of the radar, were classic *spetsnaz*-type operations.

Actual *spetsnaz* units carried out a remarkably similar operation in May 1987 at Jegdalay in Kabul Province, Afghanistan. A position had been established approximately 3,000 meters above the Saroubi-Kolala road, by National Islamic Front of Afghanistan (NIFA) *mujahideen*, and was used to ambush military convoys. Successive Soviet motor rifle assaults had failed to dislodge the guerrillas, and so special forces were used. I spoke with a *mujahideen* survivor of the assault who told me how three hours into the battle the *spetsnaz* just appeared over the edge of the cliff, having free-climbed straight up with their rucksacks and weapons — a phenomenal feat — and how then, without pausing for breath, they drove the defenders off the mountain in hand-to-hand combat.[22]

The imprimatur of Soviet special operations thinking is also reflected in the operations of thousands of foreign terrorists trained by the Soviets, or their proxies, since the first special purpose training camp for foreigners was created by Lenin in Tashkent in 1920.[23] Since the Cold War, the KGB and GRU have run a series of schools for foreigners staffed by *spetsnaz* personnel at Ksarnovy Vary and at Doupov and Ostravia in Czechoslovakia, Lake Balaton in Hungary, Pankov and Finsterwalds in East Germany, Baku, Tashkent, Odessa and Simerapol in the Soviet Union. The course at Sanprobal near Simerapol on the Black Sea has been described as follows:

> There for six months, the Palestinians — along with activists from Libya, Iraq, South Yemen and Algeria — are given an arduous course of study, including basic military field exercises, communications techniques and lectures in theory. But at the heart of all this instruction comes extensive "engineering classes" . . . The syllabus includes the following: Study of Regular and Electronic Detonators; Production of Incendiary Devices; Preparation of an Electrical Charge by Means of a Detonation; Study of Exploding Metals; Crossing Rivers by Rubber or Wooden Boats; Study of Fuse Types . . . ; Blowing Up of Vehicles, Ammunition Dumps, Petrol Tanks; Preparation of Anti-Personnel Minefields . . . Military training starts out with instruction in the use of a variety of weapons, such as automatic rifles and pistols, bazookas, rockets, mines, and "white weapons" (daggers and bayonets). Tactical training includes simulated individual and group attacks on enemy installations, ambushes, laying mines, crossing minefields, crossing electronic fences, and hand-to-hand combat . . .[24]

During the past two decades, however, the Soviet Union has distanced itself from terrorism and curtailed terrorist training. The most significant camps are now in Libya, Syria and Lebanon,[25] but the imprint of Soviet methodology and capability remains.

Contemporary Capabilities and Countermeasures

Soviet *spetsnaz* are, by all assessments of the direct and indirect evidence, a capable lot. They are well prepared to take on the following assignments in a mid-intensity conflict:

- Neutralization of nuclear weapons and their associated command and logistics by direct action or through terminal guidance or laser designation for aircraft, missile or artillery strikes.
- Neutralization of headquarters and command centers through disrupting lines of communication, destroying bridges, mining roads and ambushing at convoy choke points, and the like.
- Destruction of air defense systems, including demolition of operations centers, early warning radars, aircraft, servicing and fuel facilities and assassination of pilots.
- Assassination of key military and political personnel at national and regional levels.
- Destruction or incapacitation of ports, railways, airports, and other bulk transportation centers.
- Seizure or destruction of critical economic targets such as power stations, bulk petroleum facilities, and bulk water supply systems.
- Intelligence gathering through capture of documents and prisoners.

They are also quite capable of the following operations in a low-intensity conflict:

- Neutralization of remote enemy camps, depots and relatively inaccessible fortifications.
- Interdiction of lines of communication through near and far ambushes and the direction of artillery, air or missile strikes.
- Assassination or abduction of key leaders.
- Psychological (terror) operations.
- Force multiplication through the training and/or leading of host nation or third-party nationals.

Although *spetsnaz* will be aided in the pre-war period and during a war in their attempts to create havoc in the enemy rear by a variety of "useful idiots" and opportunistic terrorist groups, there is small likelihood of any direct coordination between these people and *spetsnaz*. Rather, *spetsnaz* at Army level and above will rely on their own, much more secure and reliable, agent auxiliary for mission support. Nor are they likely to put their operators into the target area too early, so that risk of detection by hostile security services is minimal, stories of "sleeper" *spetsnaz* Amazons at Greenham Common to the contrary. Thus there is a margin for effective defense in almost every case, if the threat is approached intelligently.

A part of the approach is to study how the Soviets combat their own *spetsnaz* in field training exercises. As in NATO, the Soviets use *spetsnaz* to test base and installation security. *Spetsnaz* groups are often parachuted somewhere in the Soviet Union and then ordered to march or ski to a target installation hundreds of kilometers away. Training exercises are very realistic and guards at targeted sites are often injured in the exercises. A favored technique with airfields has been to insert a diversionary force at one point to draw fire and pursuit while attacking another point. The Soviets have stated to me that *spetsnaz* are vulnerable to detection by helicopters and subsequent attack by war dogs.

The KGB and MVD both have *spetsnaz* troops as do the internal security ministries of the non-Soviet Warsaw Pact countries. These are not only used as stay-behind partisan groups in the event of invasion but also as fighting troops against an attack by NATO special forces. They are used against *spetsnaz* in their field training exercises. The local home guard units locate the "enemy" special forces and the MVD or KGB units engage them. Early detection and swift pursuit are the most effective techniques for preventing *spetsnaz* (who usually operate on a very close timetable) from reaching their targets. This is similar to the *Jagdkommando* antipartisan units formed successfully by the Germans in World War II.

Unfortunately, the NATO response (and the response of other states) is to organize home guards of former military who are too old to serve in Regular or Reserve units. These home guards are always the least well equipped and, however well motivated, are invariably not prepared to tackle *spetsnaz*. The solution is the creation of special forces units such as the Sandinista special counterinsurgency battalions or units led by special forces personnel with parallel emphasis on CQB training (unarmed combat and skill at arms) and built around covert observation posts, effective small unit patrolling and the use of centrally controlled light and rapidly mobile Quick Reaction Forces (QRFs) supported by the home guard system.

These rear protection forces should also be highly skilled in the identification of *friendly* as well as hostile forces: The mistake made by the German special forces in the Ardennes Offensive was to pit pseudo-United States forces against United States units. The Soviets are much more cunning and are likely in the confusion of mid-intensity combat in Western Europe to introduce pseudo German forces into the United States, French, Belgian, Dutch and United Kingdom forces and vice versa. If unprepared to meet such a potent, sophisticated Soviet special operations threat to the rear area, the countries of NATO (or any other threatened nation) might be amazed at how swiftly their defenses fail.

Notes

1. *Slovar voennikh terminov* (Dictionary of Military Terminology) (Moscow: Voyenizdat, 1989).
2. The Airborne Forces have now introduced a new camouflage uniform with cold and warm weather issues.
3. David J. Foley and Bill Evans, *Physical Training of the Soviet Soldier* (Washington DC: Defense Intelligence Agency, 1978); U.S. Army Field Manual 100-2-3, *The Soviet Army: Troops, Organization and Equipment* (Washington DC: Headquarters, Department of the Army, 16 July 1984): chapter 3.
4. *The Soviet Soldier* (Sandhurst: Royal Military Academy, Soviet Studies Research Centre, 1982).
5. See Charles E. Pales, "Soviet Flame Training," *How They Fight*, U.S. Army Intelligence Agency and Intelligence and Threat Analysis Center, October–December 1988, 31–35.
6. Viktor Suvorov, *Inside Soviet Military Intelligence* (New York: Macmillan Publishing Co., Inc., 1984) and id., *SPETSNAZ: The Story of the Soviet SAS* (London: Hamish Hamilton, 1987). Suvorov claims to have been a *spetsnaz* officer. During an interview about his books, some journalists identified Suvorov as a low-ranking GRU defector, Vladmir Rezun, who most certainly did not mention anything about having been *spetsnaz* during his debriefing by NATO intelligence. Suvorov's books show a remarkable ignorance of *spetsnaz* history, formations, training and operations. Unfortunately, his works taken at face value have been widely quoted on the subject of Soviet *spetsnaz*.
7. Capt. C. Ros, Royal Dutch Army, *The Training of the Soviet Army Officer* (undated MS).
8. Lt. Gen. Slyusar', born on 10 November 1939, won his Hero of the Soviet Union award on 15 November 1983, at the rank of Maj. Gen., for actions in Afghanistan as Commander of a Guards airborne assault division. "Heroes of the Soviet Union—Afghanistan," *Jane's Soviet Intelligence Review*, March 1989, 111–115.
9. Gen. Shtemenko was chief of the GRU in the late 1950s, and organizer of a "sabotage school" in that period near Moscow. See comments by Mrs. Harriet Fast Scott in Frank R. Barnett, B. Hugh Tovar and Richard H. Shulz, *Special Operations in U.S. Strategy* (Washington DC: U.S. Government Printing Office, December 1984): 121–122; Harriet Fast Scott and William F. Scott, *The Armed Forces of the USSR*, 3rd ed. (London: Arms & Armour Press, 1984): 369.
10. Chris Burton, "The Myth & Reality of the Soviet Paratrooper," *Military Review*, January, 1985, 26–42.
11. A DIA artist's impression (presumably based on satellite photography) has

254

appeared in the U.S. Defense Department's *Soviet Military Power* series, and has been reproduced in several commercial publications. James Adams, *Secret Armies* (New York: The Atlantic Monthly Press, 1987) identifies the site as Furstenburg, DDR.

12. Ian F. W. Beckett, *The Roots of Counter-Insurgency* (Poole, Dorset: Blandford Press, 1988).

13. An excellent Soviet appreciation of German special forces is found in Aleksandr Andrevitch Bogdanov and Ivan Yakovlevich Leonov, comps., *Armiskiye Chekisti* (Army Chekists) (Leningrad: Lenizdat, 1985). See also James Lucas, *Kommando: German Special Forces of World War II* (New York: St. Martin's Press, 1985).

14. Lucas, op. cit.; Charles Whiting, *Ardennes: The Secret War* (New York: Stein and Day, 1985); Blaine Taylor, "Skorzeny," *Soldier of Fortune*, June 1985, 66–69, 96, 98, 99; id., "More On Skorzeny," *Soldier of Fortune*, July 1985, 70–75, 93–95.

15. John Loftus, *The Belarus Secret* (London: Penguin, 1982); John Baker White, *Sabotage is Suspected* (London: Evans Brothers, Ltd., 1957).

16. See *Force Structure Summary—USSR, Eastern Europe, Mongolia, and Afghanistan* (Washington DC: Defense Intelligence Agency, November 1987): 44.

17. DDB–2680–62–86 *Handbook on the Cuban Armed Forces* (Washington DC: Defense Intelligence Agency, May 1986). Note also the Sandinistas' employment of counterinsurgency Special Forces Battalions, composed largely of reservists and stiffened by a cadre of career-term professionals.

18. Joseph S. Bermudez, Jr., "North Korea's light infantry brigades," *Jane's Defence Weekly*, 15 November 1986, 1176–1178; id., *North Korean Special Forces* (Coulsdon, Surrey: Jane's Publishing Company, Ltd., 1988); U.S. Army Field Circular 100–2–99, *North Korean People's Army Operations* (Fort Leavenworth KS: Combined Arms Combat Development Activity, December 1986).

19. See Steven J. Zaloga and James Loop, *Soviet Bloc Elite Forces* (London: Osprey Publishing, 1985).

20. Roberta Goren, *The Soviet Union and Terrorism* (Winchester, MA: George Allen & Unwin, 1984). The Cubans have also employed special Interior Ministry and Ministry of Defense counterinsurgency special forces battalions in Angola: Karl Maier, "A battle that could change the course of Angola's war," *The Christian Science Monitor*, 8 March 1988, 7, 9.

21. Much of the account of Dac Cong special operations against Saigon during the Tet Offensive is drawn from Clayton Jones, "Viet Cong leader recalls blitz that changed the war," *The Christian Science Monitor*, 20 January 1988, 1, 32.

22. The Western view of *spetsnaz* operations in Afghanistan has been badly distorted by Soviet secrecy and by inept and sometimes deliberately false report-

ing from the *mujahideen* side of the battlefield. In some cases, *mujahideen* and their Pakistani Intelligence "advisors" who entered battle without proper preparations have been badly beaten by ordinary motor rifle troops, and have covered their ineptitude by reporting to their higher headquarters that they had been bested by *spetsnaz*.

23. Goren, op. cit.
24. Lt. Col. Shay Avital, Israeli Defense Forces, *Terrorist Suicide Operation Analysis* (Quantico, VA: Marine Corps Command and Staff College, 1985): 10–12.
25. Dr. Ray S. Cline and Dr. Yonah Alexander, *State-Sponsored Terrorism* (Washington DC: Subcommittee on Security and Terrorism of the Committee on the Judiciary, U.S. Senate, June 1985).

CHAPTER 14
Conclusions

William H. Burgess III

The basic conclusions to be drawn from the available historical record of Soviet special operations are:

1. Special operations are important to the Soviets, but not overwhelmingly so, for the quick resolution of strategic and operational political-military conflicts in low- to mid-intensity war.
2. There is no Soviet special operations doctrine per se. Special operations are an integral part of Soviet deep battle (operation) concepts.
3. Political reliability, physical and mental stamina, and operations security are the sine qua non of Soviet special operations.
4. The Soviets have different forces with different capabilities in their state security and military structures for the prosecution of special operations. These forces are routinely task-organized, often with conventional forces. There is no stereotypical *spetsnaz*.
5. Most Soviet special operations-capable forces are not dedicated special forces (*spetsnaz*).
6. KGB *spetsnaz* have primacy in strategic and "peacetime" foreign special operations. Military *spetsnaz* are used mostly for operational, wartime special operations.
7. Some military *spetsnaz* units may have habitual working relationships with certain conventional formations, e.g., with Guards Airborne divisions or air assault brigades.

8. In general, differences in social perspectives and military philosophies make direct comparisons between Soviet and Western special operations forces meaningless.

9. For the most part, *spetsnaz* soldiers are carefully selected, adequately trained, and tough and reliable in the field.

10. In specific instances, uniquely talented personalities such as I. G. Starinov have dramatically advanced the art of Soviet special operations and shaped the modern character of *spetsnaz*. Key individuals such as V. N. Leonov have also been instrumental to the success of specific operations in close-run situations.

11. Most Soviet special operations since the Bolshevik uprising have been remarkably simple and unadorned. The Soviets stick with what works. The greatest changes over time have come from the application of new technologies, but the human element has always been viewed as most important to success.

12. The imprimatur of Soviet thinking and capabilities will be visible in the special operations of Soviet allies and clients, including terrorist groups, well beyond the end of this century.

13. The greatest impediments to a fuller Western understanding of Soviet special operations capabilities are barriers of language and cultural-political bias.

14. There is abundant open-source historical data on Soviet special operations forces that remains to be studied and exploited by Western writers and scholars.

15. The Soviets will stay with the tried and true. Most of the changes that will come in the foreseeable future will result from relatively minor applications of new technologies, e.g., in parachuting, communications, terminal guidance, and night vision, much of it imported from the West.

There are still many unanswered questions about *spetsnaz* order of battle, unit locations, training regimen, logistics, communications, and the like. There is a clear need for more study of Soviet special operations history, particularly by experts in the Western special operations community. More study of KGB *spetsnaz* needs to be done. Western analysts need to review many of their underlying assumptions about Soviet special operations capabilities. "Rear battle" in AirLand Battle doctrine needs to be reassessed by conventional military strategists.

Based on what *is* known about Soviet special operations capabilities, nations faced with such a threat must be prepared to win the crucial, precedent "intelligence battle" before *spetsnaz* are on the ground in the subsequent "tactical battle." There will be a direct correlation between the winning of the former and the winning of the latter. Threatened nations must conduct elaborate intelligence preparation of the battlefield (IPB) to isolate the crucial variables of terrain, weather, and enemy forces. This IPB must be conducted within a comprehensive intelligence and early warning (IEW) system that quickly and accurately identifies the threat and alerts reaction forces. Reaction forces, rather than being built around pensioners, school children, and Walter Mitty types, must be composed of first-line professional paramilitary and combat troops, lest "defense in depth" be a mere illusion.

In the long run, defense will also come through mutual familiarity and a degree of trust between East and West. *Glasnost* offers many opportunities for the exchange of visits by special operations personnel, akin to longstanding ongoing exchanges by senior conventional forces and intelligence personnel, that would help clarify motivations and intentions and promote coexistence. While joint exercises between Soviet and Western special operations forces would be going too far for now, mutual acquaintance through low-level social exchanges and the participation by observers on each side in some events (e.g., in parachuting, survival, or weapons training exercises) might help reduce suspicion and tension, and promote a clearer view of Soviet special operations.

For the present, the Great Spetsnaz Scare of the 1980s is a Cold War misadventure cut from the same cloth as the Bomber Gap and the Missile Gap. Although *spetsnaz* comprise an important aspect of Soviet military capabilities, the threat is far from monolithic, even when one considers their potential as a delivery means for special weapons. The quantity and quality of *spetsnaz* are impressive, but far from overwhelming. Besides, such forces are beset by a host of problems that effectively inhibits their optimum utilization. Beneath the hyperbole, *spetsnaz* are far from being Marxist supermen.

About the Authors

DR. KIRSTEN AMUNDSEN is currently a Visiting Research Scholar at the Hoover Institution, Stanford, California. She started her career as a journalist in her native Norway. She received M.A. and Ph.D. degrees in political science from the University of California, and she is a professor in the Department of Government at California State University, Sacramento. Dr. Amundsen has been a NATO Research Fellow twice and spent one year at the Atlantic Council, U.S.A., as a Visiting Senior Fellow. She has published widely both here and in Europe. Among her recent publications are: *Norway and NATO: The Forgotten Soviet Challenge* (1984), and "Soviet Submarines in Scandinavian Waters," *The Washington Quarterly* (Summer 1985).

WILLIAM H. BURGESS III, Major, U.S. Army, is a Special Forces Branch Officer on assignment to Fort Bragg, North Carolina. Formerly an Infantry and Military Intelligence officer, he served in Special Forces from 1979 to 1985. Duties included working and training with the 10th Special Forces Group (Airborne) and Britain's 22 Special Air Service Regiment. His education includes a B.A. in political science from Southeastern Massachusetts University, an M.P.A. from Clark University, and a J.D. from Washington College of Law, The American University. He is a graduate of O.C.S., the Special Forces Officer Course, the Infantry and Military Intelligence officers advanced courses, and Command and General Staff College. His articles have appeared in *Armed Forces Journal International*, *The Christian Science Monitor*, *Conflict*, *Military Intelligence*, *Military Review* and *Special Warfare*.

DR. JOHN J. DZIAK has served in the Defense Intelligence Agency (DIA) since 1965, specializing in Soviet political-military affairs. He holds a Ph.D. in Soviet/Chinese studies from Georgetown University and is a graduate of the National War College. His current position is Defense Intelligence Officer assigned to the Office of the Secretary of Defense. Dr. Dziak is also an Adjunct Professor of Government, Georgetown University. He is the author of *Chekisty: A History of the KGB* and *Soviet Perceptions of Military Doctrine and Military Power*, and co-author of the *Bibliography of Soviet Intelligence*.

JAMES F. GEBHARDT, Major, U.S. Army, is an Armor Branch officer serving with the Soviet Army Studies Office, Fort Leavenworth, Kansas. He has a B.A. in political science from the University of Idaho, and an M.A. in history from the University of Washington. He is a graduate of the Armor Officer Basic Course, Infantry Officers Advanced Course, Defense Language Institute, Command and General Staff College, and the U.S. Army Russian Institute. He has written for *Armor* and *Infantry*. He is currently preparing the first English-language study of the World War II Soviet combined arms and joint Petsamo-Kirkenes Operation in northern USSR and Norway.

DAVID C. ISBY is a Washington DC-based attorney and foreign affairs analyst. He is the author of a number of books, including *Weapons and Tactics of the Soviet Army, Armies of NATO's Central Front, Russia's War in Afghanistan*, and *War in a Distant Country, Afghanistan: Invasion and Resistance*, and has written more than 150 articles. His research on the war in Afghanistan has included a number of trips with the resistance and extensive interviews with a broad range of participants. He has a B.A. in history from Columbia University and a J.D. from New York University School of Law.

OWEN A. LOCK is Editor-in-Chief, Del Rey Books, where he has been employed since 1974. He is a graduate of the Russian language program of the Defense Language Institute, has an A.B. in Russian literature from Hunter College, City University of New York, and has completed course work toward an M.A. in Chinese Literature. Mr. Lock was a Russian language voice intercept processing specialist with the U.S. Air Force, and served as a Naval Reserve interpreter for the Naval Security Group. He reads Russian, Classical and Mandarin Chinese, and German. Mr. Lock edited the twenty-six volume Ballantine Espionage/Intelligence Library, for which he received special recognition by the National Intelligence Studies Center in 1983. He is currently writing a new book on Soviet military intelligence, *The Chief Directorate for Intelligence: A History of the GRU*.

JOHN H. MERRITT is on leave from the laboratory staff of Sandia National Laboratories where he has been employed since 1979. He enlisted in the U.S. Army in 1958 and spent over fifteen years in Special Forces, including five tours in Southeast Asia. He retired from the Army in 1978 as a Major. He is a graduate of O.C.S., the Infantry Officers Advanced Course, the Intelligence Staff Officers Course, and a variety of special operations courses. He holds a B.A. in Chinese language from the Monterey Institute of International Studies.

JIM SHORTT is a consultant instructor to a number of governments. He specializes in military training and terrorism countermeasures and has lectured extensively to the intelligence communities of NATO and nonaligned countries. Mr. Shortt has an elite unit background and from 1984–1987 was Director of Projects for Special Training Services, based in London, where he organized training and prepared threat analyses for governments throughout Europe, Africa and the Middle East. In 1988 he was with the National Islamic Front of Afghanistan (NIFA) *mujahideen* involved in operations along the Gardez-Khost battlefront. In 1989 he became the first Westerner to visit the Soviet Army Higher Airborne Forces Command School at Ryazan, in the Moscow Military District. Mr. Shortt lectures extensively to military organizations on elite Soviet formations, and is occupied in training military anti-*spetsnaz* teams. He is a prolific writer of books and articles that have appeared in a number of international military journals, and is a consultant deputy editor of *Special Forces* magazine.

ROBERT D. SMITH works as a research specialist with the Air Force at the Pentagon where he specializes in Soviet Ground Forces. Prior to working for the Air Force, Mr. Smith spent seven years on active duty as an Army intelligence officer. While in the Army, he was stationed in West Germany for more than four years, serving in both the 1st Armored Division and Headquarters, VII Corps. Mr. Smith has a B.A. in political science from Western Maryland College.

Appendix

The Players

Soviet special operations history is to a large degree measured by the influences of many unique and very talented individuals. Historically, these critical personalities have been characterized by extraordinary political reliability, technical proficiency, courage, and dedication to mission. It has not been uncommon for such personnel to have special operations careers that spanned several decades and two or more wars, which have influenced events well beyond such careers. A partial inventory is as follows:

Aalto, Bill. Aalto was an American who served as a lieutenant in the 14th Special Corps in Spain and participated in the assault on the fortress at Corchuna. He later served in the OSS during World War II.[1]

Babikov, Makar A. Babikov was one of the earliest recruits for the Reconnaissance Detachment of Headquarters, Northern Fleet, in 1941. He fought with that detachment as a noncommissioned officer alongside Viktor Leonov until the end of the war in Europe. In June 1945, Babikov and about fifty other members of his detachment went to the Far East to reconstitute the Reconnaissance Detachment of Headquarters, Pacific Fleet. By then a senior sergeant, Babikov commanded one of the two platoons of the detachment. Sr. Lt. Leonov was the detachment commander. In August, Babikov was badly wounded in the assault on Seishin, and for his actions there was awarded the title Hero of the Soviet Union. He left active service in 1946 and returned to his home in the Komi region. Since the war, Babikov has served in various Party and government bureaucracies. Over the last thirty years, Babikov has written several books that provide insights into the use of naval *spetsnaz* by the Northern and Pacific Fleets during World War II.

Berzin, Yan Karlovich. Born Peter Kyuzis, Berzin headed the GRU from March 1924 until April 1935. He was an extremely experienced former underground worker and one-time high-ranking KGB military counterintelligence officer. For reasons not entirely clear, Berzin was suddenly reassigned from the GRU in April 1935, to a staff position (possibly chief of staff) under General Bluecher, commander of the Soviet Far Eastern Army. Berzin's intelligence chief in the Far East was Khristofor Salnyn, who may have been reassigned to Spain at the same time as Berzin.[2] In July 1936 Berzin was given the cover name "General Grishin" and appointed head of the military mission to Spain, taking up residence first in Madrid and later (mid-November) in Valencia. After Berzin's recall to the Soviet Union in late May or very early June 1937, he was reinstated as head of the GRU. By December 1937, however, he had become an "enemy of the people" and was purged. He died, probably through execution, in July 1938.[3]

Buitrago, Antonio. Buitrago was the second deputy to Domingo Ungria on Ungria's first operational mission in late December 1936. In mid-1942, Buitrago briefly headed the reformed "14th Corps" that fought in occupied France. He was fatally wounded shortly thereafter.[4]

Eitingon, Leonid Andreyevich. In Spain, Eitingon was covernamed "General Kotov"; possibly also called "General Ivon."[5] He was the first deputy to Orlov, the chief of the KGB mission to Spain, and said to be in charge of the *spetsnaz* activities there.[6] Simultaneously, Eitingon ran an agent network in France.[7] In 1927 he was forced to flee the Harbin rezidency because the Chinese suspected him of espionage activities.[8] Covernamed "Leonid Naumov" in 1929 as the KGB's legal rezident in Constantinople, Eitingon was involved in building the case against Blumkin, for secret meetings with Trotsky (then resident in Turkey).[9] In 1940, Eitingon orchestrated Trotsky's assassination, using Ramon Mercader, a *spetsnaz* during the Civil War and the son of Eitingon's lover, Caridad.[10] In 1942, he was once more the legal KGB rezident in Turkey as Naumov, and may have been involved in the attempted assassination of the German ambassador there, Fritz von Papen.[11] Later, during World War II, Eitingon was deputy chief of the KGB's Fourth (Partisan) Directorate under Pavel Sudoplatov. After the war, Eitingon and Sudoplatov tried unsuccessfully to transform their partisans into agents for illegal *rezidenturas* outside the Soviet Union. Eventually their directorate evolved to coordinate the activity of KGB *spetsnaz rezidenturas* throughout Europe and to conduct assassination operations.[12] Eitingon was purged twice in the early 1950s, once for being Jewish (fall 1951)[13] and, after having been rehabilitated, again for ostensible connection with Beria (September 1953).[14] Eitingon is believed to have been executed after the second purge.

Gerasimov, Peter. Gerasimov was a Soviet advisor to the 14th Special Corps whose detachment carried out a successful long-range penetration behind Franco's lines during the Battle of Ebro in 1938, conducting a nighttime raid on a machinegun battalion quartered at a farmstead, dispersing its personnel, seizing its weapons, and destroying its stores. The detachment returned to its base without loss. Gerasimov died while on a mission behind German lines in Byelorussia during World War II.[15]

Gorev, Vladimir Yefimovich. In 1920 Gorev was chief of *Osobye Otdely* (Special Departments) of the Cheka (precursor of the KGB) dealing with military counterintelligence, and active in Komsomol work. In 1923 he entered the military academy in Moscow, and in 1924 was posted to China. In April or May 1925 he was an advisor on the staff of the Soviet military attache in Beijing.[16] In 1926 Gorev, known then as "Gordon" and "Nikitin," was a Soviet military advisor to Feng Yuxiang's (Feng Yu' hsiang) army, and later senior military advisor to the western column of the New Route Army (NRA). He participated in the storming of Wuchang in October 1926 and was advisor to the NRA 4th Corps.[17] After returning from China, Gorev commanded a tank brigade, possibly in the Leningrad Military District.[18] In 1930 or 1931, Gorev was the GRU resident in New York, and in 1932 was Whittaker Chambers's first Soviet control.[19] In 1932, he returned to Moscow, and in October 1936 was posted as military attache to Spain. Gorev spent the whole campaign in Madrid, with his translator Jose Robles, and working with a "tall Circassian" who was probably Khadzhi-Umar Mamsurov.[20] By January 1937 Gorev also had E. L. Volf (Wolf) on his staff. She was nominally a press attache, but also helped to prepare intelligence reports.[21] Gorev was also assisted by Col. I. O. Ratner, who prepared intelligence reports which were then teletyped to headquarters of the Soviet advisors in Valencia. Also working for him was Colonel Loti, who frequently visited units on the front lines.[22] From 18 August through November 1937, Gorev was cut off with retreating Republican forces in northern Spain, but was able to return to the Soviet Union in November or December. On his return, Gorev was awarded the Order of Lenin by Kalinin, president of the Soviet Union, but was arrested two days later and executed.[23]

Grinchenko, Simone. A former member of a Moscow Komsomol cell, Grinchenko was employed in Spain as an interpreter by Enrique Lister, commander of the 11th Division of the Republican army. During World War II, she fought behind enemy lines in Dmitriy Kuznetsov's partisan detachment. Sometime after the war, Grinchenko worked in Cuba until she fell ill and returned to the Soviet Union. She died shortly thereafter and is buried in Novodevichiy Cemetery.[24]

Inzartsev, N. A. In the summer of 1941, Intendant 3rd Rank Inzartsev was director of the athletic department of the Northern Fleet's submarine brigade and the Fleet weightlifting champion in his class. In July, he was made deputy commander of the Reconnaissance Detachment of Headquarters, Northern Fleet. In early fall, Captain Inzartsev was made detachment commander, a post he held until the next year. In August 1945, as senior representative of the intelligence section of Headquarters, Pacific Fleet, Lieutenant Colonel Inzartsev accompanied Leonov in the assault on Seishin. In the mid-1950s, he was still serving in the Northern Fleet.

Kharish, Ivan. Called "Juan Pekeno" in Spain because of his slight build,[25] Kharish commanded a *spetsnaz* group in Ungria's battalion as early as January 1937. Kharish had been a sailor sometime before the war. He came to Ungria's group with his friend, another former sailor, Ivan Karbovants. Kharish is said to have known English, French, Spanish, and Russian.[26] During World War II, Kharish conducted partisan operations against German forces occupying Yugoslavia. After the war, Kharish was commissioned a brigadier general in the People's Army of Yugoslavia.[27]

Kharitonenko, Grigoriy. In March 1938, Kharitonenko was an advisor in the 14th Special Corps in Spain, serving in the Central Zone, possibly on the Central Front.[28] It is possible that Kharitonenko was a cover-name for Grigoriy Syroezhkin, whose detachment operated near Madrid and whose commander lived there. Syroezhkin probably left Spain in December 1938.

Krutskikh, D. A. In the fall of 1944, Lieutenant Colonel Krutskikh trained the engineer *spetsnaz* battalions used in the Petsamo-Kirkenes Operation. He participated in the preparation of two *spetsnaz* engineer detachments (actually battalion task forces) for the seizure of the approaches to Manchuria's Suifenho tunnels on August 9. Ten days later, he commanded the 154-man *spetsnaz* detachment that seized Kirin. Little is known in the West about Krutskikh's postwar career, except that in 1982 he was a colonel general and held the position of chief of staff of Civil Defense of the Russian Federated Republic.[29]

Leonov, Viktor N. Leonov was recruited into the Reconnaissance Detachment of Headquarters, Northern Fleet in July 1941. He fought with the detachment throughout the war, rising in rank to noncommissioned officer, and then to commissioned officer and commander of the detachment. He was awarded the title Hero of the Soviet Union for his actions in the October 1944 Petsamo-Kirkenes Operation. In the summer of 1945, he and approximately fifty members of his detachment were transferred to the Reconnaissance Detachment of Headquarters, Pacific Fleet. Leonov was given command of this detachment and won a second HSU at Seishin. The entry for Leonov in the *Soviet Military Encyclopedia* merely states that "after the war he worked in the central apparatus of the Soviet Navy," and went into the reserves in 1956,[30] retiring at age forty after nineteen years' service. It is believed that Colonel Leonov was instrumental in the revival of ground and naval *spetsnaz* in the 1950s, and that modern doctrine for the organization and employment of *spetsnaz* bears his imprint. He and Babikov have written more than 1,100 pages in various books and articles about their World War II exploits, a rich mine for the student of naval *spetsnaz* operations during that war.

Mamsurov, Khadzhi-Umar Dzhiorovich. In Spain, cover-named "Sante," Mamsurov was the senior Soviet advisor to the Special Battalion (later upsized and redesignated the 14th Special Corps) from about April through late summer 1937. He was generally known by his given name, Khadzhi, even in Spain. By October 1937,[31] Soviet Army Major Mamsurov was in Madrid, subordinated to Berzin for the duration of the crisis.[32] Mamsurov planned defensive fortifications, trained worker detachments as auxiliary units, prevented infiltration through the tunnels that brought water to the city, and formed a stay-behind guerrilla network to harass Franco's forces should the city be taken.[33] On his return to the Soviet Union in 1937, he would have been purged but for the intercession of President Kalinin.[34] In the summer of 1937 or 1938, Mamsurov supervised the training of GRU illegals in and around Moscow.[35] In 1939, during the Soviet Union's war on Finland, Mamsurov led a *spetsnaz* detachment of about fifty men in an unsuccessful attempt to capture prisoners behind Finnish lines.[36] In 1941, Mamsurov was an instructor at the partisan school of the Western Front with his Spanish Civil War colleagues I. G. Starinov and G. L. Tumanyan.[37] On August 3, 1942, Colonel Mamsurov was named to head the newly formed Southern Staff of the Partisan Movement under the military council of the North Caucasus Front. Among its other duties, the Southern Staff organized a school for the training of partisan cadres.[38] By 1961, Major General Mamsurov was the number-three man in the GRU, in charge of administrative affairs.[39] Lieutenant General Mamsurov died in 1968.

Mamsurov, Polina Veniaminova. In early 1936, Polina, also called "Lina," arrived in Spain to work on what she describes as a progressive Spanish journal, *Europe and America*.[40] In early November 1936, she was assigned to assist as translator for Major Mamsurov, who was eventually to become her husband. During World War II, Mrs. Mamsurov served in the Soviet Army, though her exact assignments are unknown, and rose to rank of major.

Nikolayevskiy, Captain (first name unknown). In 1937 in Spain Nikolayevskiy commanded one of the first Republican detachments to specialize in raiding airfields. He based his attacks on detailed study of his targets. In the summer of 1937, he carried out two raids on enemy airfields within five days. He died when a hand grenade exploded prematurely during an attack on a Nationalist military airfield sixty kilometers from the port of Almeria.[41]

Orlov, Alexander. Born Feldbin, he was generally known in Spain as Orlov, but had many other aliases. In Spain he was a senior Soviet advisor on intelligence, counterintelligence, and partisan warfare. Orlov served in the Red Army during the Civil War and commanded "guerrilla detachments behind enemy lines" on the Southern Front, was a law graduate of Moscow University, served under Dzerzhinskiy as deputy chief of the Economic Directorate of the OGPU, was a brigade commander of border troops in Transcaucasia, and served foreign tours in the OGPU/NKVD in Paris, Berlin, Switzerland, the United States, Austria, Czechoslovakia, and Spain.[42] General Orlov was assigned to the Soviet mission to the Spanish Republic on 12 September 1936 and departed on 12 July 1938. On his departure, Orlov defected to the West rather than return to Moscow and possible death in Stalin's purges. Orlov's first deputy, Leonid Eitingon, is believed to have been directly in charge of guerrilla warfare in Republican Spain.

Orlovskiy, Kirill Prokofyevich. In Spain cover-named "Strik," or "Streak," Orlovskiy was a Soviet advisor in the *spetsnaz* unit commanded by Vasilevskiy. Orlovskiy came to Spain from a border guard unit in the Soviet Union.[43] He fought in World War I, was a member of the Communist Party from 1918, from 1920 to 1925 led partisan groups in western Byelorussia (i.e., eastern Poland), and graduated from Marchlevskiy University in 1930. Orlovskiy fought in the Spanish Civil War from 1936 to 1939, was in the NKVD from 1938, led a partisan detachment behind German lines in 1942 to 1943, and was in the "organs of state security of Byelorussia" from 1943 until 1945. In 1944 he was awarded the title Hero of the Soviet Union. From 1945 until his death in 1968, Orlovskiy headed the Rassvet collective farm. He was a candidate member of the Central Committee of the Communist Party of the Soviet Union from 1956 to 1961, and a deputy of the Supreme Soviet from the 3rd through the 7th

Sessions. In 1958, he was awarded the title Hero of Socialist Labor. Orlov describes him as an expert who was sent, with a squad of experienced Spanish saboteurs, to advise the talented amateurs who were carrying on guerrilla warfare against Franco's forces. Orlovskiy and his Soviet comrade Stephan Glushko parachuted into the Rio Tinto area and spent four months there until control of the operation was assumed by a "Dr. Moro."

Prokopyuk, Nikolay. In Spain called "Nikolas," Prokopyuk was a Soviet advisor probably associated with the Syroezhkin group. He worked with a partisan detachment on the Andalusian front, in southern Spain.[44] He joined the Soviet Army in 1920 and fought in the Russian civil war, then joined the "organs of state security." He participated in the Spanish Civil War from 1936 to 1939. During World War II, Prokopyuk was behind enemy lines from 1942. He commanded large partisan units, from 1944, in the Ukraine, Poland, and Czechoslovakia. From December 1944 through 1946, he took part in the civil war in China. He was a member of the Communist Party from 1944, a colonel from 1948, and was made a Hero of the Soviet Union in 1944.[45]

Rabtsevich, Aleksandr. In Spain called "Viktor," Rabtsevich was a Soviet advisor in Vasilevskiy's unit. He worked behind enemy lines in the 1920 Russo-Polish War, then became a Soviet border guard. During World War II he commanded large partisan forces in Byelorussia. After the war he returned to the border guards, serving until his death in 1956.[46]

Salnyn, Khristofor (Grisha) Intovich. In Spain cover-named "Viktor Jugos," Salnyn was the senior advisor to the 14th Special Corps from summer 1937 to March 1938.[47] Salnyn was born in 1885, joined the Communist Party in 1902, and was on Party assignment outside the Soviet Union until 1920. From 1921 to 1922, he worked behind enemy lines on assignment for the Soviet 2d Amur Army, then the 5th Workers and Peasants Red Army (RKKA), perhaps under the name Zavadskiy. In Harbin in 1922 he posed as a refugee from the Soviet Union. In 1924 he was assigned as an intelligence advisor to Feng Yuxiang in China. In October 1929, Bluecher assigned Salnyn and the Bulgarian Ivan Vinarov to sever road communications in Manchuria, after which Salnyn was ordered to Moscow by GRU chief Berzin to receive an Order of the Red Banner. In the early 1930s, Salnyn was on undercover assignments in Central Europe. In 1935 he followed Berzin to the staff of the Soviet Red Banner Far Eastern Army (OKDVA), where he became intelligence chief (*nachal'nik razvedki*). As early as spring 1937 Salnyn was stationed in Spain. After returning to the Soviet Union in 1938, he was a prisoner in Butyrka Prison.

A "Kh. I. Salnyn" is among those "brave leaders of intelligence groups and rank-and-file intelligence gatherers [who] fought behind enemy lines [during World War II]."[48]

Sprogis, Artur Karlovich. Sprogis joined the Communist Party in 1920, at age sixteen. He fought in the Russian Civil War. In the early 1920s, Sprogis was a military cadet in the Kremlin, and a guard at Kremlin Post Number 27, where he met Lenin. He graduated from the Frunze Military Academy in 1923. In 1928, while the head of a border detachment engaged in "battle with banditry and smuggling along the western border" and tracking border crossers, he met Berzin.[49] He fought in the Spanish Civil War from 1936 to 1939. About November 1936, Sprogis was attached as advisor and instructor to the guerrilla band led by Jose Munoz Gomez in the Malaga area. In late January and early February 1937, their detachment was engaged in the defense of Malaga, mining roads and destroying bridges leading from Malaga to Nationalist-held Granada.[50] He was an organizer and leader of the partisan movement in Byelorussia and Latvia in World War II, reaching the rank of colonel in 1943. During the early years of the war, Sprogis headed a school for partisan intelligence and demolition personnel, then became a partisan leader. In 1943 to 1944, he headed the Latvian staff of the partisan movement. After the war, he was engaged in Party and "instructional" work.[51]

Starinov, Ilya Grigorevich. In October 1917, Starinov joined a paramilitary workers unit that sabotaged the Petrograd rail line without access to explosives and yet impeded the movement of "counterrevolutionaries." Later, he joined the Red Army, was captured, escaped, and ended up in the 20th Rifle Regiment fighting Deniken. For the rest of the Civil War, he fought with a variety of infantry units. In 1919 he was badly wounded in the leg, but recovered. In 1922, he transferred to a railroad regiment and began to demonstrate a talent for demolitions. In 1924 he became a member of the Communist Party. From about 1926 to 1929, Starinov was part of a task force in the Ukrainian Military District that worked out demolition procedures and obstacles to be used in the event of an invasion of the Soviet Union. Among the task force's duties were the development of demolition technology, the establishment of hidden stores of explosives, and the training of more than sixty demolition units (about 1,400 personnel in all) to carry out the destruction of railway bridges, track beds, and rolling stock to prevent their falling into enemy hands.[52] From January 1930 through 1932, Starinov worked under the supervision of Latvian A. I. Baar, chief of the intelligence department of the Ukrainian Military District, to train personnel who, in the event of an invasion of the Soviet Union, would form the cadre of stay-behind partisan networks. These cadre were taught demolitions, parachuting (Starinov participated in night drops), and partisan tactics, were familiarized with foreign weapons, and the like.[53] In 1933, he was assigned to the Moscow apparatus of the GRU, under the supervision of *otdel* (section) head Mirra Sakhnovskiy.[54] Although at a desk job, Starinov taught "partisans," probably foreign agents undergoing training prior to deployment outside the Soviet Union, military personnel directly subordinate to the GRU, and/or cadre meant to train units subordinate to the military districts. In the fall of 1935 his Party credentials were challenged, but he was cleared. Starinov and his translator, Anna Obruchev, arrived in Spain sometime after early November 1936 and were immediately assigned to train fledgling *spetsnaz* for the Republic. In Spain called "Rodolfo" and "Rudolf," Starinov was a Soviet advisor to the first formal Spanish Republican *spetsnaz* group from November or December 1936.[55] Military Engineer 3rd Class Starinov returned to the Soviet Union in November or December 1937.[56] There he was interrogated by the NKVD, but no action was taken against him. On 17 February 1938, he was promoted to colonel.[57] On 20 March he was appointed chief of the Central Scientific-Experimental Railroad Proving Ground of the Red Army, a vast complex that included an eighteen-kilometer section of track used to test railroad demolitions and the recovery from such attacks. He also spent a lot of time at the proving ground working on experimental mine technology. In the Winter War, Starinov evaluated mine/countermine operations in the field and was severely wounded in the arm by a sniper on one of his field trips. In July 1941, Colonel Starinov was reassigned from his position as a department head of the Chief Military-Engineering Directorate of the Soviet Army to head the Operational Training Center of the Western Front, where at least two other of the school's instructors (Mamsurov and Tumanyan) were experienced *spetsnaz* from the Spanish Civil War.[58]

Syroezhkin, Grigoriy Sergeyevich. Called "Grisha Grande" in Spain, Syroezhkin was a senior advisor on partisan matters to the 14th Special Corps.[59] He was a specialist in paramilitary counterintelligence. In 1924, he was awarded the Order of the Red Banner for participating in the capture of anti-Soviet revolutionary Boris Savinkov. In 1924 to 1925 he helped put down a "counterrevolutionary uprising" in Chechinya, and in 1928 was in Verkhoyansk as leader of the KGB's Northern Operations Group.[60] In 1929, Syroezhkin commanded a detachment that fought in

Mongolia and Oirotiya.[61] In 1936, just before being posted to Spain, he was engaged in counterintelligence in the Leningrad area.[62] From fall 1936 to December 1938 (about one month before the 25 January 1939 fall of Barcelona), he was posted as liaison officer between Eitingon and KGB headquarters and the *spetsnaz* detachment commanded by Vasilevskiy at Las Vegas,[63] screening and recruiting personnel for, and advising, Vasilevskiy's detachment.[64] In August 1937, he and Vasilevskiy were ordered by Soviet senior military advisor General Shtern to leave for Paris to avoid trouble with the anarchists, who claimed that Vasilevskiy's detachment had attacked a brigade of the 14th Anarchist Division without reason (possibly to prevent the anarchists from retreating).[65] In late December 1938 Syroezhkin was recalled to the Soviet Union, where he may have been executed.[66]

Tumanyan, Gay Lazarevich. Tumanyan was a Soviet military advisor on *spetsnaz* operations who in the latter half of April 1937 accompanied Mamsurov on a tour of *spetsnaz* camps in Jaen, Villanueva de Cordoba, and the clandestine base near Adamuz.[67] Prior to departing for Spain, he was either a *kombrig* or a colonel, probably on the GRU staff in Moscow, and saw to the briefing and outfitting of I. G. Starinov before the latter's departure for Spain.[68] Tumanyan left Spain on 2 May 1937.[69] During World War II, Colonel Tumanyan taught at the Western Front Operational Training Center's school for partisans along with colonels Starinov and Mamsurov.[70]

Ungria, Domingo. Ungria was a former Republican army cavalry officer who commanded the 14th Special Corps and its predecessors from November or December 1936 until February or March 1939, rising from captain to lieutenant-colonel. During World War II, Ungria was one of three hundred former *spetsnaz* of the 14th who served under I. G. Starinov in the Operational Training Center of the Western Front and in the 5th Separate Spetsnaz Engineer Brigade.[71]

Vasilevskiy, Lev Petrovich. From about March 1937[72] until February 1939,[73] Vasilevskiy was commander of a *spetsnaz* group supervised by Syroezhkin.[74] In 1936, Vasilevskiy had been commander and/or commissar of an aviation unit stationed along the Soviet-Chinese border ("Eastern border okrug"), near Sinkiang.[75]

Vaupshasov, Stanislav A. In Spain cover-named "Alfred," Vaupshasov was a *spetsnaz* advisor associated with Syroezhkin. In 1918 he joined the Soviet army, and in the 1920s and 1930s was on "intelligence assignment." While in Spain he was responsible for the combat employment of *spetsnaz* and for the personal bodyguard of Spanish Communist Party leader Delores Ibarra. In late 1938, after the fall of Catalonia, Vaupshasov was tasked to assess the martial spirit of Republican forces at large in the central-south zone. If it seemed sufficient, he was to remain, as senior advisor to the 14th Special Corps; otherwise he was to exfiltrate to friendly territory. He remained in the cut-off area, even establishing partisan leadership courses, until the final surrender in spring 1939.[76] He became a Communist Party member in 1940. In the fall of 1941, Vaupshasov was ordered to form and lead a seventy-man "reconnaissance-sabotage operational group" for insertion behind enemy lines. Original plans for employment of the detachment were scrapped at the time of the battle for Moscow, and the group was resubordinated to the NKVD *spetsnaz* OMSBON and given a new mission. During World War II, he was, or became, a colonel. In the spring of 1942, as a member of an OMSBON unit, he led thirty-two men through German lines west of Moscow westward into the forests of Minsk oblast where from 1942 to 1944 he organized, trained, and commanded a partisan unit. He was declared a Hero of the Soviet Union in 1944, and died in 1976.[77]

Notes

1. Landis, Arthur H., *The Abraham Lincoln Brigade* (New York: The Citadel Press, 1967): xx, 490.

2. M. Korenevskiy and A. Sgibnev, "Zhizn' i podvig Khristofora Salnynya" (The Life and Exploits of Christopher Salnyn), in Vasilevich, comp., *Vernost' Dolgu* (A Faithfulness to Duty) (Moscow: Voyenizdat, 1985): 411–413.

3. Ilya Grigorevich Starinov, *Miny zhut svoego chas* (The Mines Await Their Hour) (Moscow: Voyenizdat, 1964): 158; N. V. Ogarkov, et al., comps., *Voyenno-entsiklopedicheskiy slovar'* (Military Encyclopedic Dictionary) (Moscow: Voyenizdat, 1983): 78.

4. I. G. Starinov, 86; Anna Kornilovna Starinov, "V tylu y myatezhnikov" (In the Rebels' Rear), in Aleksandrovskaya, et al., *My–internationalisty* (We Are Internationalists) (Moscow: Politizdat, 1975): 115.

5. I. G. Starinov, 77–78.

6. Orlov's testimony before the Senate Subcommittee on Internal Security, February 14 and 15, 1957, cited in Isaac Don Levine, *The Mind of an Assassin* (New York: Farrar, Straus and Cudahy, 1959): 32.

7. Nikolai I. Khokhlov, *Pravo na sovest'* (The Right to a Conscience) (Frankfurt-Main FRG: Possev-Verlag, 1957): 42; Levine, 34.
8. Georges A. Agabekov, *OGPU: The Secret Russian Terror* (New York: Brentanos, 1931): 208. It is not known if Eitingon was the "Naumov" who served as a "political worker" in Guangzhou during 1925. A. I. Cherepanov, *Zapiski voennogo sovetnika v kitae* (As Military Advisor in China) (Moscow: Progress, 1982): 234.
9. Agabekov, 207–208.
10. Levine, 16, 34–35; *The New York Times*, 5 January 1988, A6.
11. Ismail Gusseynovich Akhmedov, *In and Out of Stalin's GRU* (Maryland: University Publications of America, 1984): 162–164.
12. Khokhlov, *In The Name of Conscience* (New York: McKay, 1959 and London: Muller, 1960): 125, 193.
13. Khokhlov, *Pravo na sovest'*, 264.
14. Khokhlov, *In the Name of Conscience*, 181–183.
15. Vasiliy Avramovich Troyan, "Chetyrnadtsatyy spetsial'nyy" (The 14th Special Corps), in Aleksandrovskaya, et al., *My–internationalisty*, 249–250.
16. Y. V. Chudodeyev, *Sovetskiye dobrovoltsy v kitae* (Soviet Volunteers in China) (Moscow: Progress, 1980): 89.
17. Ibid., 192.
18. E. L. Volf, "Nezabymoye" (The Unforgettable), in Aleksandrovskaya, *My internationalisty*, 177, 178ff; Whittaker Chambers, *Witness* (New York: Random House, 1952): 281; Aleksandr Orlov, *The Secret History of Stalin's Crimes* (New York: Random House, 1953): 235; Nadezhda and Maya Ulanovskiy, *Istoriya odnoy semi* (One Family's Story) (New York: Chalidze Publications, 1982): 101, 131–133.
19. Ulanovskiy, 101.
20. Nikolay Gerasimovich Kuznetsov, *Na dalekom meridiane: Vospominaniya uchastnika natsional'no-revolyutsionoy voyny v Ispanii* (On a Distant Meridian: Memoirs of a Participant in Spain's National-Revolutionary War) (Moscow: Nauka, 1972): 26, 32; Aleksandr Orlov, *Handbook of Intelligence and Guerrilla Warfare* (Ann Arbor: University of Michigan Press, 1963): 235; Fischer, 395, 425, 669. Robles disappeared and was rumored to have been killed, in December 1936 or early 1937.
21. Volf, 179.
22. Volf, 179.
23. Orlov, *The Secret History*, 235–236; Ulanovskiy, 101.
24. Lev Petrovich Vasilevskiy, *Ispanskaya Khronika Grigoriy Grande* (The Spanish Chronicle of Gregory Grand) (Moscow: Molodaya Gvardiya, 1974): 47.
25. I. G. Starinov, 100.
26. Ibid., 100–101.
27. A. K. Starinov, 107.

28. Troyan, 243.
29. Arkadii F. Khrenov, *Mostu k pobede* (Bridges to Victory) (Moscow: Voyeniz-dat, 1982): 337n.
30. *Soviet Military Encyclopedia*, vol. 4 (Moscow: Voyenizdat, 1977): 622.
31. E. Vorobyev, "Starik i ego ucheniki" (The Old Man and His Students), in I. Vasilevich, comp., *Vernost' Dolgu* (A Faithfulness to Duty) (Moscow: Voyenizdat, 1985): 28.
32. Ibid., 28.
33. Polina Veniaminova Mamsurov, "Boyevoe zadaniye" (Combat Mission), in *My—Internationalisty*, 48–49.
34. Peter Deriabin, conversation with Owen Lock, 24 August 1988.
35. "Ruth Werner" (Ursula Kuczynski), *Sonjas Rapport* (Sonya's Report) (Berlin: Verlag Neues Leben, 1977): 215.
36. Dr. John J. Dziak, *Chekisty: A History of the KGB* (Lexington MA: Lexington Books, 1988): 135, citing an interview with Ismail Akhmedov, June 1985.
37. A. T. Kuzmin, et al., *Vsenarodnaya bor'ba v Belorussii protiv nemetsko-fashistikh zakhvatchikov v gody velikoy otechestvennoy voyny* (The National Battle in Belorussia Against the Fascist German Bandits During World War II), vol. 1 of 3 (Minsk: Belarus', 1983): 107.
38. Andrey Antonovich Grechko, *Gody Voyny: 1941–1943* (The War Years: 1941–1943) (Moscow: Voyenizdat, 1976): 195.
39. Oleg Penkovskiy, *The Penkovskiy Papers* (New York: Ballantine Books, 1982): 62.
40. P. Mamsurov, 46.
41. Orlov, *Handbook*, 179, 180.
42. Orlov, *Secret History*, ix–x.
43. Vasilevskiy, 53.
44. Ibid., 54.
45. Ogarkov, 594.
46. Vasilevskiy, 54.
47. Korenevskiy and Sgibnev, 407–408.
48. Zakharov, et al., 467; Korenevskiy and Sgibnev, 406–408.
49. Vorobyev, 32.
50. Ibid., 56.
51. Ogarkov, 700.
52. I. G. Starinov, 17–30.
53. Ibid., 30–46.
54. Ibid., 46–48.
55. A. K. Starinov, 103–116.
56. Ibid., 151, 162.
57. Ibid., 162.
58. Kuzmin, et al., 107.

59. Vasilevskiy, 14.
60. Ibid., 132, 212.
61. Ibid., 139.
62. Ibid., 213.
63. Ibid., 213.
64. Ibid., 14.
65. Ibid., 112.
66. Ibid., 187–189.
67. I. G. Starinov, 132.
68. Ibid., 65–66.
69. Ibid., 135.
70. Kuzmin, 107.
71. A. K. Starinov, 115.
72. Vasilevskiy, 39.
73. Ibid., 213.
74. Ibid., 14.
75. Ibid., 8.
76. Vasilevskiy, 55.
77. Ogarkov, 113.

Bibliography

Abwehr (Ostfront). *Organisation und Aufgaben des sowjetischen Geheimdienstes im Operationsgebiet der Ostfront, 1944* (Abwehr manual from German archives, declassified 15 August 1946).

Adams, James. "Special Forces in America: The Day Before." *ORBIS* (Spring 1988): 199–215.

————. *Secret Armies: The Full Story of S.A.S., Delta Force and Spetsnaz*. New York: The Atlantic Monthly Press, 1987.

Adams, Peter. "Soviet Border Guards Show Mettle Repelling 'Group of Bandits'." *Army Times*, 27 June 1988, 32.

Adams, CPT Tom. "Special Operations Forces of the Soviet Union." *Military Intelligence*, October–December 1982, 17–18.

Adriashenko, V. I. "Na severe" (In the North). In Aleksandrovskaya, et al., comps., *My—Internatsionalisty*, 227–241.

"Afghan Assassins." *Washington Times*, 3 January 1986, 3A.

Agabekov, Georges A. *OGPU: The Secret Russian Terror*. New York: Brentanos, 1931.

Aganov, S. Kh., ed. *Inzhenernye voiska sovetskogo armii 1918–1945*. Moscow: Voyenizdat, 1985.

Agrell, Wilhelm. "Hvorfor Ubaatkrenelsene?" *Sikkerhets og Nedrustningspolitiske Utwalg*. Denmark: 1988.

Airborne Operations. New York: Crescent Books, 1978.

"Airborne Troopers Carry Out Reconnaissance." *Soviet Military Review*, 6/1985, 16–16.

Akbar, S. Fazle. "News From the Battlefield." *Afghan Realities*, No. 32, 1 May 1985, 7–8.

"A Killing in Kunduz." *Defense and Foreign Affairs Weekly*, 20 July 1987, 2.

Akhmedov, Ismail Gusseynovich. *In and Out of Stalin's GRU*. Bethesda MD: University Publications of America, 1984.

Aleksandrov, P. A., et al., eds. *Partiya voglave narodnoy bor'by v tylu vraga, 1941–1944*. Moscow: Izdatel'stvo "Mysl'," 1976.

Aleksandrovskaya, Sofya Mikhailovna, et al. *My—internationalisty* (We Are Internationalists). Moscow: Politizdat, 1975.

Alexiev, Alexander. *Inside the Soviet Army in Afghanistan*. Santa Monica CA: The Rand Corporation, May 1988.

Amundsen, Kirsten. "Soviet Submarines in Scandinavian Waters." *The Washington Quarterly*, Summer 1985, 111–122.

Anlage 1, Daily Report, to the entry of 10 October 1944, KTB No. 5, AOK 20, roll 1063, T-312, National Archives and Records Administration (NARA), Washington DC.

277

Anlage 2, Daily Report, to the entry of 12 October 1944, KTB No. 5, AOK 20, Frame 9265168, microfilm roll 1063, series T-312, NARA, Washington DC.

Anlage 3, "Bandentatigkeit und Organisation vor (Geb.) A.O.K. 20" (Band Activities and Organization in Front of 20th Mountain Army), to AOK 20 Nr. 810/43, dated 22.2, 1943, microfilm series T-312, roll 1649, frames 001328–29, NARA, Washington DC.

Anlage 4, Morning Report, to the entry of 8 October 1944, KTB No., 5, AOK 20, microfilm roll 1063, series T-312, NARA, Washington DC.

Anlage 4, Morning Report, to the entry of 13 October 1944, KTB No. 5, AOK 20, frame 9265184, microfilm roll 1063, series T-312, NARA, Washington, DC.

U.S. Army Field Circular 100-2-99. *North Korean People's Army Operations*. Fort Leavenworth KS: Combined Arms Combat Development Activity, December 1986.

U.S. Army Field Circular 100-20. *Low Intensity Conflict*. Fort Leavenworth KS: U.S. Army Command and General Staff College, 30 May 1986.

U.S. Army Field Manual 7-93. *Long-Range Surveillance Unit Operations*. Washington DC: Headquarters, Department of the Army, 9 June 1987.

U.S. Army Field Manual 100-2-2. *The Soviet Army: Specialized Warfare and Rear Area Support*. Washington DC: Headquarters, Department of the Army, 16 July 1984.

U.S. Army Field Manual 100-2-3. *The Soviet Army: Troops, Organization and Equipment*. Washington DC: Headquarters, Department of the Army, 16 July 1984.

Department of the Army Pamphlet 20-240. *Rear Area Security in Russia: The Soviet Second Front Behind the German Lines.* Washington DC: U.S. Government Printing Office, 31 July 1951.

Department of the Army Pamphlet 20-244. *The Soviet Partisan Movement, 1941–1944*. Edgar M. Howell, auth. Washington DC: U.S. Government Printing Office, 30 August 1956.

Department of the Army Pamphlet 20-269. *Small Unit Actions During the German Campaign in Russia*. Washington DC: U.S. Government Printing Office, 1953.

Arnold, Anthony. *Afghanistan: The Soviet Invasion in Perspective*. Stanford CA: Stanford University Press, 1981, rev. ed. Hoover Institute Press, 1985.

Artemenko, I. T. *Ot pervogo do poslednego dnia* (From the First to the Last Day). Kharkov: "Prapor," 1987.

"ASW funds boost for Sweden." *Jane's Defence Weekly*, 14 May 1988, 919.

"Athletes in War." *Soviet Military Review*, 4/1981, 62–63.

Avital, Lt. Col. Shay. *Terrorist Suicide Operation Analysis*. Quantico VA: Marine Corps Command and Staff College, 1985.

Babikov, Makar A. *Morskie razvedchiki* (Naval Scouts). Syktyvkar: Komi knizhnoe izdatel'stvo, 1966.

————. *Na vostochnom berugu* (On the Eastern Shore). Moscow: Izdatel' stvo "Sovetskaia Rossiia," 1969.

————. *Letom sorok pervogo* (The Summer of '41). Moscow: "Sovetskaia Rossiia," 1980.

————. *Otriad osobogo naznacheniya* (Special Purpose Detachment). Moscow: "Sovetskaia Rossiia," 1986.

Bagrov, V. N. *Iuzhno-Sakhalinskaia i Kuril'skaia operatsii—Avgust 1945* (The Southern Sakhalin and Kuriles Operations—August 1945). Moscow: Voyenizdat, 1959.

Barchenko-Emel'ianov, I. P. *Frontovye budni rybach'ego* (Days at the Front on the Rybachii Peninsula). Murmansk: Knizhnoe izdatel'stvo, 1984.

Barnett, Frank R. and B. Hugh Tovar, *Special Operations in U.S. Strategy* (Washington DC: U.S. Government Printing Office, December 1984).

Barron, John. *KGB: The Secret Work of Soviet Secret Agents*. New York: Reader's Digest Press, 1974.

————. *The KGB Today: The Hidden Hand*. New York: Reader's Digest Press, 1983.

————. "Double Agents in a Secret War." *Reader's Digest* (May 1985): 181–182, 184–186, 188, 190.

————. "Ambush at Silk Gorge." *Reader's Digest*, February 1988, 74–78.

————. "The KGB's Deepest Secret." *Reader's Digest*, November 1988, 94–99.

Bates, Tom. "Red Rumors Rising: SOF Staffer Teams With Eskimo Scouts to Track Soviet Spetsnaz in Alaska." *Soldier of Fortune*, January 1989, 50–59, 93–94, 96–101.

Batov, P. I., et al. *Solidarnost' narodov c Ispanskoy Respublikoy: 1936–1939* (International Solidarity With the Spanish Republic, 1936–1939). Moscow: Nauka, 1972.

Baxter, William P. *Soviet AirLand Battle Tactics*. Novato CA: Presidio Press, 1986.

Beckett, Ian F. W. *The Roots of Counter-Insurgency*. Poole, Dorset: Blandford Press, 1988.

Bedard, Paul. "On Siberian Border, Eskimo Scouts Search for Clues of Soviet Plans to Invade Alaska." *Defense Week*, 8 September 1988, 8–9.

"Befehl fur den Schutz von Wehrwirtschaftsbetrieben" (Order for the Defense of Military-Industrial Facilities), Annex 1, microfilm series T-312, roll 1648, frame 000903, NARA, Washington DC.

Beitler, Stephen Seth. *SPETSNAZ: The Soviet Union's Special Operations Forces*. Washington DC: Defense Intelligence College, June 1985.

Belikov, I. G., et al. *Imeni Dzerzhinskogo*. Moscow: Voyenizdat, 1976.

Bellamy, Chris. "Red Star in the West: Marshal Tukhachevskiy and East-West Exchanges on the Art of War." *Royal United Services Institute for Defence Studies*, December 1987, 63–73.

Belov, G. A., et al., eds. *Iz istorii vserossiyskoy chrezvychaynoy komissii 1917–1921gg. Sbornik dokumentov*. Moscow: Gospolitizdat, 1958.

Berg, John. "Norway reveals exact locations of Soviet bases." *Jane's Defence Weekly*, 17 May 1986, 865.

Berkowitz, Marc J. "Soviet Naval Spetsnaz Forces." *Naval War College Review*. (Spring 1988): 5–21.

Bermudez, Joseph S., Jr. "North Korea's light infantry brigades." *Jane's Defence Weekly*, 15 November 1986, 1176–1178.

———. *North Korean Special Forces*. Coulsdon, Surrey: Jane's Publishing Company, Ltd., 1988.

Bidwell, Brig. Gen. Shelford, et al. *Russian Military Power*. New York: St. Martin's Press, Inc., 1980.

Bildt, Carl. "Submarine incursions: Sweden fights back." *Jane's Naval Review*. 135–141. London: Jane's Defence Publishers, Ltd., 1985.

Binder, David. "U.S. Links Afghan Events and Soviet General's Death." *New York Times*, 3 February 1980.

Bodansky, Yossef. "Soviet Net Closes In On Afghan Resistance." *Jane's Defence Weekly*, 2 August 1986, 173–176.

———. "The New Generation of Soviet High Command." *Jane's Defence Weekly*, 31 October 1987, 1010–1012.

Bogdanov, Aleksandr Andrevitch and Ivan Yakovlevich Leonov. *Armiskiye Chekisti* (Army Chekists). Leningrad: Lenizdat, 1985.

Boltin, Maj. Gen. E. "On the Eve of War." *Soviet Military Review*, February 1967, 46–48.

Bonesteel, CPT Ronald M. "Soviets' 'Other' Forces." *Infantry*, November-December 1988, 25–28.

Borovik, Artyem. "The Hidden War." *Life*, February 1988, 100–106.

———. "What Kind of War Was This?" *U.S. News & World Report*, 30 May 1988, 32.

Boyd, Robert S. "SPETSNAZ: Soviet Innovation in Special Forces." *Air University Review*, November-December 1986, 63–69.

Bradsher, Henry S. *Afghanistan and the Soviet Union*. Durham NC: Duke University Press, 1985.

Brandt, Joseph C. "Soviet Military Grapples With the Language of Command." *Armed Forces Journal International*, July 1988, 38, 41.

Brown, F. C. "Soviet Cong: Ivan in Indochina." *Soldier of Fortune Magazine*, November 1985, 70–74.

Bruins, Berend D. "Understanding the Soviet Union." *Proceedings*, September 1984, 66–71.

Burton, Chris. "The Myth and Reality of the Soviet Paratrooper." *Military Review,* (January 1985): 26–42.

Burtt, LTC David A., II. *Soviet Use of Spetsnaz Forces.* Maxwell AFB AL: Air War College, March 1986.

Campbell, CPT Erin E. "The Soviet SPETSNAZ Threat to NATO." *Airpower Journal* (Summer 1988): 61–67.

Cappacio, Tony. "Killers or Infiltrators." *Defense Week,* 24 August 1987, 1, 10–11.

Casteel, MAJ Burton A., Jr. *SPETSNAZ: A Soviet Sabotage Threat.* Maxwell AFB AL: Air Command and Staff College, Air University, April 1986.

Chambers, Whittaker. *Witness.* New York: Random House, 1952.

Chaney, Otto Preston, Jr. *Zhukov.* Norman OK: University of Oklahoma Press, 1971.

Chapman, Colin. *August 21st: The Rape of Czechoslovakia.* New York: J. B. Lippincott Company, 1968.

Cherepanov, A. I. *As Military Advisor in China* (Zapiski voennogo sovetnika v kitae). Moscow: Progress, 1982.

Chew, Dr. Allen F. *The White Death: The Epic of the Soviet-Finnish Winter War.* East Lansing MI: Michigan State University Press, 1971.

————. *Fighting the Russians in Winter: Three Case Studies.* Leavenworth Paper No. 5. Fort Leavenworth KS: U.S. Army Command and General Staff College, December 1981.

Christiansson, Lars. "Sweden and Her Armed Forces." *Defence,* November 1987, 701–705.

Christenson, Paul. "Trip to Teri Mungal." *The Afghanistan Foundation Newsletter,* vol. 2, no. 3, 22 June 1987, 1–3.

Chudodeyev, Y. V. *Soviet Volunteers in China* (Sovetskiia dobrovoltsy v kitae). Moscow: Progress, 1980.

Cline, Dr. Ray S. and Dr. Yonah Alexander. *State Sponsored Terrorism.* Washington DC: Subcommittee on Security and Terrorism of the Committee on the Judiciary, U.S. Senate, June 1985.

Collins, John M. *Green Berets, SEALs & Spetsnaz: U.S. & Soviet Special Military Operations.* Washington DC: Pergamon-Brassey's, 1987.

Collins, CAPT Joseph J. "The Soviet Invasion of Afghanistan: Methods, Motives and Ramifications." *Naval War College Review,* November 1980.

————. "Soviet Military Performance in Afghanistan: A Preliminary Assessment." *Comparative Strategy,* vol. 4, no. 2, 1983, 147.

————. *The Soviet Invasion of Afghanistan—A Study in the Use of Force in Soviet Foreign Policy.* Lexington MA: Lexington Books, 1985.

Conine, Ernest. "Submarine offensive against Swedes spoils Soviets' new image." *New Haven Register* (30 March 1988): 17.

Coox, Alvin D. *Nomonhan: Japan Against Russia, 1939.* 2 vols. Stanford CA: Stanford University Press, 1985.

Cordevilla, Angelo. "The Challenge of Special Operations." *Journal of Defense & Diplomacy* (June 1985): 18–27.

Czechoslovakia, A Country Study. Washington DC: U.S. Government Printing Office, 1982.

Danilin, A. "Ne stareiut dyshoi veterany" (The Veterans Are Not Aging In Spirit), *Morskoi sbornik* (Naval Proceedings), 5/1988, 16–18.

Deutscher, Isaac. *Stalin: A Political Biography.* New York: Vintage Books, 1962.

Dewitt, Kurt. "The Role of Partisans in Soviet Intelligence." *War Documentation Project.* Research Study No. 6, Vol. 1. Maxwell AFB AL: Air Research and Development Command, 1954.

Dick, C. J. "Catching NATO Unawares: Soviet Army Surprise and Deception Techniques." *International Defense Review,* 1/1986, 21–26.

Dmittriyev, Yuri. "Meetings in Afghanistan." *Zvyazda* (Minsk), 26 February 1985, 3, translated at JPRS-UMA-85-035. *USSR Report: Military Affairs.* 22 May 1985, 56–59.

Domaik, A. "Vzaimobeistvie partizan s eoiskami v Roven-Lutskoi operatsii" (Coordination of the Partisans With the Forces in the Roveno-Lutsk Operation), *Voenno-istoricheskii zhurnal* 11/1979, 22–26.

Donnelly, C. N. "Operations in the Enemy Rear: Soviet Doctrine and Tactics." *International Defense Review,* 1/1980, 35–41.

————. "The Development of Soviet Military Doctrine." *International Defense Review,* 12/1981, 1589–1596.

Dorman, William A. and Mansour Farhang. *The U.S. Press and Iran: Foreign Policy and the Journalism of Deference.* Berkeley CA: University of California Press, 1987.

Doubrava, Dave. "Afghan Rebels Score Major Hit on Air Base." *Washington Times,* 19 June 1985, 6A.

Drea, Edward J. *Nomonhan: Japanese-Soviet Tactical Combat, 1939.* Leavenworth Paper No. 2. Fort Leavenworth KS: U.S. Army Command and General Staff College, January 1981.

Dupuy, COL T. N. *A Genius for War: The German Army and General Staff, 1807–1945.* Fairfax VA: Hero Books, 1984.

Dziak, Dr. John J. "Soviet Intelligence and Security Services in the 1980s: The Paramilitary Dimension." *Intelligence Requirements for the 1980s: Counterintelligence.* Roy Godson, ed. Washington DC: National Strategy Information Center, Inc., 1980.

————. "The Soviet Approach to Special Operations." *Special Operations in U.S. Strategy.* B. Hugh Trovar and Richard H. Schulz, eds. 95–120. Washington DC: National Defense University Press, 1984.

————. "Military Doctrine and Structure." *Hydra of Carnage.* Uri Ra'anan, et al., eds. Lexington MA: Lexington Books, 1986.

————. *Chekisty: A History of the KGB.* Lexington MA: Lexington Books, 1988.

Egorov, Adm. G. "Severnyi flot v Petsamo-Kirkenesskoi operatsii" (Northern Fleet in the Petsamo-Kirkenes Operation) *Voenno-istoricheskii zhurnal.* 10/1974, 23.

Ellis, John. *Cavalry: The History of Mounted Warfare.* New York: G. P. Putnam's Sons, 1978.

Ellis, Cmdr. M. G. M. W. "Sweden's Ghosts?" *Proceedings*, March 1986, 95–101.

Emil'ianov, G. "V glubokom tylu vraga" (In the Deep Enemy Rear Area), *Voenno-istoricheskii zhurnal*, October 1974, 55–59.

Emelyanov, A. *Sovetskiye podvodnye lodki v Velikoi otechestvennoi Voine.* Moscow: Voyenizdat, 1981.

Endzheyak, V. and A. Kuznetsov. *Osobaya partizansko-diversionaya.* Kiev: Politizdat Ukrainy, 1977.

Engle, Eloise and Lauri Paananen. *The Winter War: The Russo-Finnish Conflict, 1939–1940.* New York: Charles Scribner's Sons, 1973.

Erfurth, Waldemar. *The Last Finnish War (1941–1944).* MS # C-073, Historical Division European Command, Foreign Military Studies Branch, 1952. Published in German under the title *Der Finnische Krieg, 1941–1944.* Wiesbaden/Munich: Limes-Verlag, 1977.

———. *Warfare in the Far North.* Washington DC: U.S. Army Center of Military History, facsimile edition, 1982, 1987.

Erikson, John. *The Soviet High Command.* London: St. Martin's Press, 1962.

Es'haq, Mohammed. *An Analysis of the Present Situation in Afghanistan.* Peshawar: Jamiat-Islami, November 1984.

FBI Letter. SAC New York to Director FBI (105-22869), 8 June 1954.

"Feindnachrichtenblatt" (Enemy Information Report), Nr. 24, 14 November 1942, microfilm series T-312, roll 1649, frame 000201, NARA, Washington DC.

"Fernschreiben" (Teleprinter) 1.1.1944, microfilm series T-312, roll 1650, frame 000462, NARA, Washington DC.

"Finnish airline rejects air force pilots." *Jane's Defence Weekly*, 21 May 1988, 1000.

Fischer, Lewis. *Men and Politics: An Autobiography.* New York: Duell, Sloan and Pierce, 1941.

"Fired on Soviet Territory, Rebels Say." *The Los Angeles Times*, 25 March 1987, 11.

Foley, Charles. *Commando Extraordinary.* Poole, Dorset: Arms and Armour Press, Ltd., 1987.

Foley, David J. and Bill Evans. *Physical Training of the Soviet Soldier.* Washington DC: Defense Intelligence Agency, 1978.

Force Structure — USSR, Eastern Europe, Mongolia, and Afghanistan. DDB-2680-170-87. Washington DC: Defense Intelligence Agency, November 1987.

"Forts to Loom Beneath Norwegian Horizon." *Armed Forces Journal International*, July 1988, 37.

Fowler, William, "Mobilisation in Norway." *Defence*, October 1988, 731.

Frantsev, Col. O. K. "Primenie aviatsii v Man'chzhurskoi operatsii" (The Utilization of Aviation in the Manchurian Operations). *Voenno-istoricheskii zhurnal*, 8/1985.

Fulghum, David. "Low-Profile A-10 Boosted As Key to Norway Defense." *Army Times*, 20 June 1988, 34.

"Further Details Released on SS-20 Saber Missile." *Jane's Defence Weekly*, 30 January 1988, 182–183.

Fyodorov, A. *The Underground R. C. Carries On.* 2 vols. Moscow: Foreign Language Publishing House, 1949–1950.

Gander, Terry. "Sweden's powerful anti-invasion force." *Jane's Defence Weekly*, 20 December 1986, 1458–1459.

Garcia, CPT Rudolf N. "Finland's Small Stalingrad: The Battle of Suomussalmi." *Military Intelligence*, April-June 1985, 28–32.

Garfield, Brian. *The Thousand-Mile War: World War II in Alaska and the Aleutians.* Garden City NY: Nelson Doubleday, Inc., 1983.

Garthoff, Raymond L. *Soviet Military Doctrine.* Glencoe IL: The Free Press, 1953.

———. *Soviet Military Policy: A Historical Analysis.* New York: Frederick A. Praeger, 1966.

Gavrilyuk, Sr. Lt. I. and Capt. S. Kharenko. "Baptism of Fire." *Military Herald*, 7/1987, 39–41.

Gearing, Julian. "Evolution in Military Tactics." *Afghanistan* (London), No. 1, 1985.

Gebhardt, Maj. James F. *Soviet Naval Special Operations Forces: Origins and Operations in World War II.* Fort Leavenworth KS: Soviet Army Studies Office, unpublished MS, March 1989.

Gerassi, John. *The Premature Antifascists: North American Volunteers in the Spanish Civil War 1936–1939.* An Oral History. Westport CT: Praeger, 1986.

Giradet, Edward. "Afghan Trek." *The Christian Science Monitor*, 5 December 1984, 30–31.

———. "Afghanistan: Soviets Get Tougher." *The Christian Science Monitor*, 27 December 1985, 1, 8.

———. "Afghan Guerrilla Leader: Soviets Have Made Significant Changes in Tactics." *The Christian Science Monitor*, 31 December 1985, 7, 8.

———. "Behind New Soviet Tactics in Afghanistan." *U.S. News & World Report*, 20 January 1986, 30–31.

———. "Afghanistan: Bleak Scene for Mujahideen." *The Christian Science Monitor*, 22 December 1986, 1, 10.

Glantz, Col. David M. *August Storm: The Soviet 1945 Strategic Offensive in Manchuria.* Leavenworth Paper No. 7. Fort Leavenworth KS: U.S. Army Command and General Staff College, February 1983.

———. "Soviet Operational Formation for Battle: A Perspective." *Military Review*, February 1983, 2–12.

————. *August Storm: Soviet Tactical and Operational Combat in Manchuria, 1945.* Leavenworth Paper No. 8. Fort Leavenworth KS: U.S. Army Command and General Staff College, June 1983.

————. *The Soviet Airborne Experience.* Combat Studies Research Institute Research Survey No. 4. Fort Leavenworth KS: U.S. Army Command and General Staff College, November 1984.

————. "The Nature of Soviet Operational Art." *Parameters*, Spring 1985, 2–12.

————. *Deep Attack: The Soviet Conduct of Operational Maneuver.* Fort Leavenworth KS: Soviet Army Studies Office, April 1987.

————. *Soviet Operational Intelligence [Razvedka] in the Vistula-Oder Operation (January 1943).* Fort Leavenworth KS: undated MS c. 1988.

————. *Soviet Operational Intelligence in the Kursk Operation (July 1943).* Fort Leavenworth KS: Soviet Army Studies Office, August 1988.

————. "Spearhead of the Attack: The Role of the Forward Detachment in Tactical Maneuver." *Journal of Soviet Military Studies*, October 1988.

Goerlitz, Walter. *Der zweite Weltkrieg, 1939–1945.* Stuttgart: Steingrubon-Verlag, 1952.

Gogg, I. N. "Pod Teruehlem" (At Truel). In Aleksandrovskaya, et al., *My—internationalisty* (We are Internationalists). Moscow: Politizdat, 1975.

Goldhurst, Richard. *The Midnight War: The American Intervention in Russia, 1918–1920.* New York: McGraw-Hill Book Company, 1978.

Goldshteyn, Pavel I. *Tochka opory.* Jerusalem: MS, 1982.

Golovko, Adm. A. G. *Vmeste c flotom* (Together With the Fleet). Moscow: Voyenizdat, 1979.

Goodrich, Lawrence. Review of *Spetsnaz: The Inside Story of the Soviet Special Forces*, by Viktor Suvorov. *The Christian Science Monitor*, 19 December 1988, 18.

Goren, Roberta. *The Soviet Union and Terrorism.* Winchester MA: George Allen & Unwin, 1984.

Gradelius, Lt. Cmdr. Erik, Swedish Navy (Retired). "Nobody asked me, but. . . ." *Proceedings*, March 1988, 168.

Grecho, Andrey Antonovich. *Gody Voyny: 1941–1943* (The War Years: 1941–1943). Moscow: Voyenizdat, 1976.

"Greenham Defences 'copied for Spetsnaz training.'" *Jane's Defence Weekly*, 25 January 1986, 84.

The Hale Foundation. *Conference on Spetsnaz, Soviet Special Purpose Forces.* Washington DC: The Hale Foundation, 11 December 1986.

Hamilton, Henry W. *The Aftermath of War: Experiences of a Quaker Relief Officer on the Polish-Russian Border, 1923–1924.* Dayton, OH: Morningside House, Inc., 1982.

Hammond, Thomas T. *Red Flag Over Afghanistan—The Communist Coup, The Soviet Invasion, and The Consequences.* Boulder CO: Westview Press, 1984.

Handbook on the Cuban Armed Forces. Washington DC: Defense Intelligence Agency, May 1986.

Hansen, James. "Soviet Vanguard Forces – Spetsnaz." *National Defense*, March 1986, 28–32, 36–37.

Hansen, Lynn. "Soviet Spetsnaz Operations On the Northern Flank." *Stra-Tech Studies*, No. SS84–2, 1984.

Harned, MAJ Glenn M. "Special Operations and the AirLand Battle." *Military Review*, September 1985, 73–83.

――――. "Bridging the Gap: Special Forces as a Member of the Combined Arms Team." *Special Warfare*, October 1988, 3–9.

Hart, B. H. Liddell. *Strategy.* New York: The New American Library, 1974.

――――. *The Red Army.* New York: Harcourt, Brace, and Company, 1956.

Heilberg, Anders and Anders Jorle. *Submarine 137: Ten Days That Shook Sweden.* Stockholm: Atlantis, 1984.

"Heroes of the Soviet Union – Afghanistan." *Jane's Soviet Intelligence Review*, March 1989, 111–115.

Hohn, Albert Henrik. "Afghan Guerrilla Leader: Our Enemy Has Made Errors and Drawn the Right Conclusions." *Morgenbladet* (Oslo), 3 December 1984 (undated JPRS translation).

Holcomb, MAJ James, Jr. *Soviet Special Operations: The Legacy of the Great Patriotic War.* Fort Leavenworth KS: Soviet Army Studies Office, April 1987.

――――. "Soviet Airborne Forces and the Central Region." *Military Review*, November 1987, 36–47.

Holcomb, MAJ James F., Jr., and Dr. Graham H. Turbiville, Jr. *Exploiting the Vertical Dimension: Continuing Development of the Soviet Desant* Force Structure.* Fort Leavenworth KS: Soviet Army Studies Office, May 1987.

――――. "Soviet *desant* forces, Part 1: Soviet airborne and air-assault capabilities." *International Defense Review*, 9/1988, 1077–1082.

――――. "Soviet *desant* forces, Part 2: Broadening the desant concept." *International Defense Review*, 10/1988, 1259–1264.

"How We Fight the Red Army." *Military Technology*, June 1987, 89–91 (interview with Abdul Haq).

Howard, Peter. "The Norwegian Home Guard." *Jane's Defence Weekly*, 20 December 1986, 1460–1461.

Hugemark, Bo. "Ubatar – finnes de?" *Vaart Forsvar*, No. 6, September 1987, 6.

Huitfeldt, Tonne. "Soviet naval exercises more 'unpredictable'." *Jane's Defence Weekly*, 31 January 1987, 139.

――――. "West Germans firm on Norway offer." *Jane's Defence Weekly*, 14 May 1988, 937.

――――. "Norway to revamp coastal artillery." *Jane's Defence Weekly*, 17 September 1988, 658.

Hulen, David. "Some Wonder if Soviet Troops Occasionally Visit St. Lawrence." *Anchorage Daily News*, 23 December 1987, 1, A8.

Hussain, Alvi and Rizvi. *Afghanistan Under Soviet Occupation*. Islamabad: World Affairs Publications, 1980.

Hyman, Anthony. *Afghanistan Under Soviet Domination*. 1964–81. London: Macmillan Press Ltd., 1982.

Iaroshenko, I. V. and L. I. Smirnova. "Osvobvozhdenie sovetskogo Zapoliar'ia" (Liberation of the Soviet Polar Region), *Voenno-istoricheskii zhurnal*, 6/1985, 33–34.

"Increased Spetznaz [sic] Incursions Into USA." *Special Forces*, August 1988, 4.

"Inside Afghanistan." *The Economist Foreign Report* (London), 20 June 1985, 3.

Inozemtsev, I. G. "Sovetskaia aviatsiia v Petsamo-Kirkenesskoi operatsii" (Soviet Aviation in the Petsamo-Kirkenes Operation). *Istoriia SSSR*, No. 2, 1975, 107.

Isby, David C. "Afghanistan, the Unending Struggle." *Jane's Military Review*, 1982–1983. London: Jane's Defence Publishing Co., Ltd., 1982.

––––––. "Spetznaz [sic] Suppressor Captured in Afghanistan." *Soldier of Fortune Magazine*, August 1984, 70–71, 92, 94, 96.

––––––. "Panjsher VII." *Soldier of Fortune*, January 1985.

––––––. "Resistance in Afghanistan." *Strategy & Tactics*, No. 99, January-February 1985, 11–15.

––––––. "Soviet Special Operations Forces And The War in Afghanistan: Organization and Capabilities for Combat." *Special Forces*, December 1987, 34–38.

––––––. *Weapons and Tactics of the Soviet Army*. London: Jane's Publishing Company, Ltd., 1988.

Iseman, Peter A. "Lifting the Ice Curtain." *The New York Times Magazine*, 23 October 1988, 48–51, 59–62.

Ivanov, S. P., et al. *The Initial Period of War: A Soviet View*. Moscow: Voyenizdat, 1974. English translation, Washington DC: U.S. Government Printing Office, 1986.

Jodl, General der Artillerie F. "A Short Report Regarding the Combat Actions in Petsamo and Varanger Area." 5 November 1944, item 75034/1, roll 1069, T-312, NARA, Washington DC.

Jones, Clayton. "Viet Cong leader recalls blitz that changed the war." *The Christian Science Monitor*, 20 January 1988, 1, 32.

Judge, Paul Quinn. "Soviets Look Back on 'Short War' . . . That Wasn't." *The Christian Science Monitor*, 13 April 1988, 1, 8.

Kadish, Alan. "The Rape of Czechoslovakia." *Airborne Operations*. 206. New York: Crescent Books, 1978.

Kadishev, A. B., ed. *Voprosy Taktiki v Sovetskikh Trudakh 1917–1940* (Questions of Tactics in Soviet Military Works 1917–1940). Moscow: Voyenizdat, 1970.

Kamalov, Khafiz Khayrutdinovic. *Morskaya pekhota v boyakh za rodinu* (Naval Infantry in Combat for the Motherland), 2d ed. Moscow: Voyenizdat, 1983.

Kaza, Juris. "Sweden targets mystery frogmen off coast." *The Christian Science Monitor*, 1 February 1984, 1, 10.

————. "Foreign sub still eludes Sweden's net." *The Christian Science Monitor*, 7 March 1984, 7.

————. "Sweden's hunt for underwater intruders begins to come under political attack." *The Christian Science Monitor*, 13 March 1984, 16.

————. "Can Swedes keep subs at bay?" *The Christian Science Monitor*, 14 May 1984, 13.

————. "Swedish worry over Soviet submarines resurfaces." *The Christian Science Monitor*, 11 January 1988, 9.

Kazakov, V. "Gliders in the Skies of War." *Military History Journal*, February 1983, 43–46.

Kazokins, MAJ J., RA. "Nationality in the Soviet Army." *RUSI Journal*, December 1985, 27–34.

Kelly, Ross. "Spetsnaz: Special Operations Forces of the USSR." *Defense & Foreign Affairs*, December 1984, 28–29.

————. "Soviet Low-Intensity Operations: Moving to Center Stage." *Defense & Foreign Affairs*, January 1985, 28–29, 37.

Kemp, Ian. "Abdul Haq: Soviet Mistakes in Afghanistan." *Jane's Defence Weekly*, 5 March 1988, 380–381.

Kennan, George F. *Russia and the West*. New York: The New American Library, 1960.

Kennedy, COL William V., et al. *The Intelligence War*. London: Salamander Books, Ltd., 1983.

Kent, Arthur. "The Relief of Khost." *The Observer* (London), 10 January 1988, 9.

Khenkin, Kirill. *Okhotnik vverkh nogami* (A Hunter With His Feet In the Air). Frankfurt-Main: Possev Verlag, n.d.

Khokhlov, Nikolai I. *Pravo na sovest'* (The Right to a Conscience). Frankfurt-Main: Possev Verlag, 1957.

————. *In the Name of Conscience*. New York: McKay, 1959 and London: Muller, 1960.

Khokhlov, P. I. *Nad tremia moriami* (Over Three Seas). Leningrad: Lenizdat, 1988.

Khrenov, Col. Gen. (Res.) Arkadii F. *Mostu k pobede* (Bridges to Victory). Moscow: Voyenizdat, 1982.

————. "Petsamo-Kirkenesskaia Operatsiia." *Voenno-istoricheskii zhurnal* 10/1984, 10–16.

King, Robert. "Swedes Give Away Their War Plans." *Armed Forces Journal International*, July 1986, 32.

Kipp, Dr. Jacob W. *Conventional Force Modernization and the Asymmetries of*

Military Doctrine: Historical Reflections on AirLand Battle and the Operational Maneuver Group. Fort Leavenworth KS: Soviet Army Studies Office, 1988.

————. *The Soviet Far Eastern Buildup and the Manchurian Campaign. February-August 1945: Lessons and Implications.* Fort Leavenworth KS: Soviet Army Studies Office, 1988.

Kirkwood, R. Cort. "Soviet Sabotage and Assassination Teams Operate in America." *Conservative Digest*, April 1988, 71–80.

Kohler, LCDR David R. "Spetsnaz." *Proceedings*, August 1987, 47–54.

"Kola base for 'Typhoon' submarines." *Jane's Defence Weekly*, 6 September 1986.

"Kola unveiled." *Jane's Defence Weekly*, 13 September 1986, 538–540.

Kolibernov, E. "Inzhenernoe obespechenie proryva oborony protivnika po opytu voiny" (Engineer Support of the Penetration of Enemy Defenses Based on War Experience). *Voenno-istoricheskii zhurnal*, August 1980, 42–50.

"Komandir 'chernykh d'iavolov" (Commander of the Black Devils). *Sovetskii voin*, 3/1987, 36.

Korenevskiy, M. and A. Sgibnev. "Zhizn' i podvig Khristofora Salnynya" (The Life and Exploits of Christopher Salnyn), in Vasilevich, comp., *Vernost Dolgu* (A Faithfulness to Duty). Moscow: Voyenizdat, 1985.

Korshunov, V. G., comp. *Cherez fiordy* (Through the Fjords). Moscow: Voyenizdat, 1969.

Kostylev, Lt. Gen. V. "Combat Activeness of Paratroopers," *Military Herald*, 1/1985, 72–77.

Kournakoff, Capt. Sergei N. *Russia's Fighting Forces*. New York: International Publishers, 1942.

Kriegstagebuch (War Diary) Nr. 1, AOK 20 (Headquarters, 20th German Army), "Aktennotiz" (Memorandum), microfilm series T-312, frame 001173, NARA, Washington DC.

Krivitskiy, Walter G. *I Was Stalin's Agent*. London: Hamish Hamilton, 1939.

————. *In Stalin's Secret Service*. Westport CT: Hyperion Press, 1985, reprint of 1939 edition.

Krutskikh, D. A. "Udary po Tylam" (Strikes in the Rear Area). *Eto byla na krainem severe* (It Was in the Far North). Murmansk: Knizhno Izdatel'stvo, 1965.

Krylov, N. I., et al. *Navstrechu pobede: Boevoi put' 5-i armii* (Meeting Victory: The Battle Path of the 5th Army). Moscow: Izdatel'stvo "Nauka," 1970.

KTB 1, AOK 20. "Fernspruch Gebirgs Korps Norwegen" (Telephone Message Mountain Corps Norway) Ic 1.9.1941 1745 hours, microfilm series T-312, roll 1013, frame 9209088, NARA, Washington DC.

KTB 1, AOK 20, morning reports, evening reports and teletype messages, series T-312, microfilm roll 1013, frames 9208536-9208538, 9208836, 9208852, 9208854, 9208857, and 9208859-9208860, NARA, Washington DC.

KTB 1, AOK 20. "Vermutliche Feindkrafte vor Gesamtraum des A.O.K. Norwegen Stand 5.9.1941 (Probable Enemy Strength in the Operating Area of AOK Norway as of 5.9.1941). Microfilm series T-312, roll 1013, frame 9207906, NARA, Washington DC.

KTB 1, 2d Mountain Division, Folder 77563. "Combat Reports, Attack of the Russians Against the German Defense Line." Microfilm roll 109, series T-315, NARA, Washington DC.

KTB 1, 2d Mountain Division. "Gebirgsjagerregiment 137, Gefechtsbericht uber die Kampfhandlungen am 7.u.8.10.44 im Abschnitt Isar" (Mountain Rifle Regiment 137, Action Report on the Defensive Battle on 7 and 8 October 1944 in the Isar Sector), microfilm series T-312, roll 1063, NARA, Washington DC.

KTB 2, AOK 20. "Sowjetrussische Spionagetatigkeit im Varanger-Raum" (Soviet-Russian Espionage Activity in the Varanger Area). Microfilm series T-312, roll 1651, frames 000682-000689.

KTB 5, AOK 20, Anlage 1, Daily Report, to the entry of 8 October 1944, microfilm series T-312, roll 1063, NARA, Washington DC.

KTB 5, AOK 20, Anlage 4, Morning Report, to the entry of 8 October 1944, microfilm series T-312, roll 1063, NARA, Washington DC.

KTB 5, AOK 20, Anlage 4, Morning Report, to the entry of 13 October 1944, microfilm series T-312, roll 1063, frame 9265184, NARA, Washington DC.

KTB 5, AOK 20, Daily Report, to the entry of 12 October 1944, microfilm series T-312, roll 1063, frame 9265168, NARA, Washington DC.

Kukiel, Gen. Marian. *The Polish-Soviet Campaign of 1920*. Scottish-Polish Society Publications. Edinburgh: Oliver and Boyd, Ltd. Undated reprint of a 1928 article in *Slavonic Review*.

Kukiela, Pulk. Marjana (Marian Kukiel). *Studja Taktyczne: z historji wojen polskich 1918-1921*, Tomy 1-5 (Tactical Studies: The History of the Polish Army, 1918-1921, vols. 1-5). Warsaw: Wojskowy Instytut Naukowo-Wydawniczy, 1923.

———. (Marian Kukiel). *Studja Taktyczne: z history wojen polskich 1918-1921*, Tomy 1-10 (Tactical Studies: The History of the Polish Army, 1918-1921, vols. 1-10). Warsaw: Wojskowy Instytut Naukowo-Wydawniczy, 1925.

Kurlat, F. L. and L. A. Studnikov. "Brigada osobogo naznacheniia" (Special Purpose Brigade). *Voprosy istorii*, September 1982, 95-104.

Kuzichkin, Maj. Vladmir. "Coups and Killings in Kabul." *Time*, 22 November 1982, 33.

Kuzmin, A. T., et al. *Vsenarodnaya bor'ba v Belorussii protiv nemetsko-fashistikh zakhvatchikov v gody velikoy otechestvennoy voyny* (The National Battle in Belorussia Against the Fascist German Bandits During World War II). Vol. 1 of 3. Minsk: Belarus', 1983.

Kuznetsov, Nikolay Gerasimovich. *Na dalekom meridiane: Vospominaniya uchastnika natsional'no-revolyutsionoy voyny v Ispanii* (On a Distant Meridian: Memoirs of a Participant in Spain's National-Revolutionary War). Moscow: Nauka, 1972.

————. *Kursom k pobede* (The Course to Victory). Moscow: Voyenizdat, 1976.

Kviatkovskii, Iu. "Besokoina vakhta razvedki VMF" (Troubled Watch of Naval Intelligence). *Morskoi sbornik* (Naval Proceedings), 10/1988.

Landis, Arthur H. *The Abraham Lincoln Brigade*. New York: The Citadel Press, 1967.

Lang, Walter N., et al. *The World's Elite Forces*. New York: Military Press, 1987.

Larabee, F. Stephen. "Gorbachev and the Soviet Military." *Foreign Affairs* (Summer 1988): 1002–1026.

Lee, Asher. *The Soviet Air Force*. New York: The John Day Company, 1962.

Leggett, George. *The Cheka: Lenin's Political Police*. Oxford: Oxford University Press, 1981.

Leitenberg, Milton. *Soviet Submarine Operations in Swedish Waters*, 1980–1986. New York: Praeger, 1987.

Leonov, Viktor N. *Litsom k litsu* (Face to Face). Moscow: Voyenizdat, 1957.

————. "Vperedsmotriashchie" (The Lookouts). *Cherez fiordy* (Through the Fjords). Moscow: Voyenizdat, 1969.

————. *Gotov'sia k podvigu* (Prepare for An Heroic Deed). Moscow: Izdatel'stvo DOSAAF, 1985.

Lettlander, Erik. "Sweden's report on submarine incursions names no names." *The Christian Science Monitor*, 23 December 1983, 10.

Levine, Isaac Don. *The Mind of an Assassin*. New York: Farrar, Straus and Cudahy, 1959.

Lincoln, W. Bruce. *In War's Dark Shadow: The Russians Before the Great War*. New York: Simon & Schuster, 1983.

Linn, MAJ Thomas C. "Marines in the Naval Campaign: Integrating Land/Sea Operations." *Armed Forces Journal International*, April 1988, 80, 82.

Lisov, I. I. *Desantniki—voyduzhnye desanty* (Airlanding Troops—Airlandings). Moscow: Voyenizdat, 1968.

Lister, Enrique. *Nasha voyna (iz istorii natsional'no-revolyutsionnoy voyny)* (Our War: From the History of the National-Revolutionary War of the Spanish People). Moscow: Politizdat, 1969.

Littel, Robert, ed. *The Czech Black Book*. New York: Avon Books, 1969.

Livingstone, Neil C. and M. K. Pilgrim. "Spetsnaz Invades America." *Soldier of Fortune*, January 1988, 56–61.

Lofgren, Stig. "Soviet Submarines Against Sweden." *Strategic Review*, Winter 1984.

Loftus, John. *The Belarus Secret*. London: Penguin, 1982.

Lucas, James. *Kommando: German Special Forces of World War II*. New York: St. Martin's Press, 1985.

Luttwak, Edward N. *The Grand Strategy of the Soviet Union*. New York: St. Martin's Press, 1983.

MacDonald, Brian, ed. *The Soviet Military Challenge*. Toronto: Canadian Institute of Strategic Studies, 1987.

MacFarquhar, Emily, Jeff Trimble and Edward Giradet. "Now For the Next All-Afghan War." *U.S. News & World Report*, 30 May 1988, 26–28.

Macintosh, Malcolm. *Juggernaut: A History of the Soviet Armed Forces*. New York: The Macmillan Company, 1967.

Macksey, Kenneth. *The Tank Pioneers*. New York: Jane's Publishing Company, Inc., 1981.

Maier, Karl. "A battle that could change the course of Angola's war." *The Christian Science Monitor*, 8 March 1988, 7, 9.

Majrooh, Dr. S. B. "Difficult Resistance in the Empty Countryside." *Afghan Information Centre Bulletin*, No. 35, February 1984, 11.

———. "The View of a Resistance Commander." *Afghan Information Centre Monthly Bulletin*, No. 41, August 1984, 4.

———. "Death of a Great Commander." *Afghan Information Centre Monthly Bulletin*, No. 49, April 1985, 15.

Malinovskiy, Rodion Ia. "Gnevnye vikhri ispanii" (Angry Whirlwinds of Spain). In Voronov, et al., *Pod zamenem Ispanskoy respublikoy* (Under the Flag of the Republic of Spain). Moscow: Nauka, 1965.

———. *Final* (Final). Moscow: Izdatel'stvo "Nauka," 1966.

Mamsurov, Khadzhi-Umar Dzhiorovich. "The First Days of the War." Polina Mamsurov, ed. *Moscow News*, 29/1988, 12–13.

Mamsurov, Polina Veniaminova. "Boyevoe zadaniye" (Combat Mission). In Aleksandrovskaya, et. al. *My-internationalisty* (We Are Internationalists). Moscow: Politizdat, 1975.

Manayenkov, A. L., et al., eds. *Partizanskie formirovaniya Belorussii v gody Velikoy Otechestvonnoy, 1941–1944*. Minsk: Izdatel'stvo "Belarus," 1983.

Margelov, V. F., I. I. Lisov, Ya. P. Samoylenko, and V. I. Ivonin. *Sovetskiye vozdushno desantnye: voyenno-istoricheskiy ocherk* (Soviet Airborne Forces: A Military-Historical Sketch). Moscow: Voyenizdat, 1980, 1986.

Matthews, Mervyn, ed. *Soviet Government: A Selection of Official Documents on Internal Policies*. New York: Taplinger Publishing Co., 1974, 237–238.

Marx, Karl and Friedrich Engels. *The Communist Manifesto*. Trans. Joseph Katz. New York: Washington Square Press, Inc., July 1968.

McDermott, CPT David F. "The Invasion of Afghanistan" *Infantry*, January-February 1985, 19.

McManus, James. "Russian Infiltration of Guerrillas Hits Mujahideen Hard." *Daily Telegraph* (London), 2 March 1985, 8.

McQuail, Robert P. "Khrushchev's Right Flank." *Military Review*, January 1964, 7–23.

Medred, Craig. "Investigation Draws Bead on Alaska Guide." *Anchorage Daily News*, 27 February 1988, B1, B3.

Menning, Dr. Bruce W. *The Deep Strike in Russian and Soviet Military History*. Fort Leavenworth KS: Soviet Army Studies Office, undated.

Meretskov, MSU K. A. *Na sluzhbe narody* (In Service to the People). Moscow: Politizdat, 1968.

Middleton, Drew. "Russia's 'Twilight' War Poses Greatest Threat." *The Salt Lake Tribune*, 29 March 1985, A15.

Miller, Marshall Lee. "Airborne Warfare: A Concept the USSR Can Actually Claim It Invented First." *Armed Forces Journal International*, October 1986, 48–51.

Military Balance in Northern Europe, 1985–1986. London: International Institute for Strategic Studies.

Mossberg, Walter S. "Sweden Says It Believes That Soviet Sub Visits Reflect War Planning." *The Wall Street Journal*, 23 June 1983, 1, 24.

"Mountain Rifle Regiment 137, Action Report on the Defensive Battle on 7–8 October in the Isar Sector." Frame 1089, microfilm roll 109, series T-315, NARA, Washington DC.

Murphy, Paul J., ed. *The Soviet Air Forces*. Jefferson NC: McFarland & Company, Inc., 1984.

Myagkov, Aleksei. "Soviet Sabotage Training for World War III." *Soviet Analyst*, 20 December 1979, 2–6.

Naumov, Vladislav. "My War in Afghanistan." *The Washington Post*, 3 January 1988, B5.

O'Ballance, Edgar. *The Red Army*. New York: Frederick A. Praeger, 1964.

Odnokolenko, Capt. 3rd Rank Oleg. "The Marines." *Soviet Military Review*, 3/1988, 12–13.

Odom, William E. "Soviet Military Doctrine." *Foreign Affairs*, Winter 1988/89, 114–134.

O'Dwyer, Gerard. "Swedish Army reductions planned for the 1990s." *Jane's Defence Weekly*, 26 March 1988, 561.

———. "Swedes plan training savings." *Jane's Defence Weekly*, 23 April 1988, 777.

———. "Finland's role on the northern front." *Jane's Defence Weekly*, 14 May 1988, 956, 959.

Olcott, Martha B. "The Basmachi or Freeman's Revolt in Turkestan, 1918–1924." *Soviet Studies*, July 1981, 362.

Orlov, Aleksandr. *The Secret History of Stalin's Crimes*. New York: Random House, 1953.

———. *Handbook of Intelligence and Guerrilla Warfare*. Ann Arbor: University of Michigan Press, 1963.

Orlov, Viktor. "When Spies Fool Themselves." *World Monitor*, March 1989, 42–46.

Orr, Michael. "Invasion of Afghanistan." *War In Peace*, Sir Robert Thompson, ed. New York: Harmony Books, 1982.

Pales, Charles E. "Soviet Flame Training." *How They Fight*, U.S. Army Intelligence Agency and Intelligence and Threat Analysis Center, October-December 1988, 31–35.

Penkovskiy, Oleg. *The Penkovskiy Papers* Trans. Peter Deriabin. Garden City NY: Doubleday & Company, Inc., 1965.

Pilsudski, Jozef. *Year 1920* and *Battle of Warsaw*. New York: Pilsudski Institute of America, 1972.

Platonov, Adm. V. I. "Pravoflangovye" (The Men on the Right Flank). *Cherez fiordy*. Moscow: Voyenizdat, 1969.

Platt, Adam. "New Tactics Evolving for Conflicts." *Insight*, 30 December 1985–6 January 1986, 47.

Polskonos, Capt. Igor, HSU. "Reconnaissance Officer." *Red Star*, 31 December 1983, 1.

———. "Afghanistan–The Site of Valor. In a Tactical Air Assault." *Military Herald*, 8/1984, 29.

Pomeroy, William J., ed. *Guerrilla Warfare and Marxism*. New York: International Publishers, 1968.

Pope, Victoria, with Marcus W. Brauchli. "Soviet-Bloc Troops Prowl in West Europe: Spetsnaz Commandos Are Said to Spy by the Thousands." *The Wall Street Journal*, 7 March 1988, 14.

Poretsky, Elizabeth. *Our Own People*. London: Oxford University Press, 1969.

Portnyagin, V. "In Active Opposition." *Red Star*, 8 February 1984, 1.

Pospelov, P. N., et al. *Istoriia velikoi otechestvennoi voiny sovetskogo soiuza 1941–1945* (The History of the Great Patriotic War of the Soviet Union, 1941–1945). Moscow: Voyenizdat, 1963, published in English by Progress Publishers, 1974.

"Pride of the Guard." *Soldier of Fortune*, January 1989, 54–55.

Protasou, Col. Yu. "Notes From Afghanistan: Combat Exercise." *Military Herald*, 5/1983, 23.

Quinley, John. "Soviets Sighted Off St. Lawrence Island." *Anchorage Times*, 11 February 1988, B1, B3.

Radkey, Oliver H. *The Unknown Civil War In Soviet Russia*. Stanford CA: Hoover Institute Press, Stanford University, 1976.

Ranft, Bryan and Geoffrey Till. *The Sea in Soviet Strategy*. Annapolis MD: Naval Institute Press, 1983.

Rasmussen, Peter Hertel. "Soviet Naval Infantry and Spetsnaz Naval Brigades." *Soviet Armed Forces Review Annual*, vol. 10, 141–145.

Riasanovsky, Nicholas V. *A History of Russia*. 4th ed. New York: Oxford University Press, 1984.

Richelson, Jeffrey T. *Sword and Shield: Soviet Intelligence and Security Apparatus*. Cambridge MA: Ballinger Publishing Company, 1986.

Ries, Tomas. "Soviet Submarines in Sweden: Psychological Warfare in the Nordic Region?" *International Defense Review*, 6/1984, 695–696.

Ries, Tomas and Johnny Skorve. *Investigating Kola: A Study of Military Bases Using Satellite Photography.* New York: Brassey's Defence Publishers, 1987.

————. "Satellite's view of Severomorsk base." *Jane's Defence Weekly*, 16 July 1988, 32.

Roskill, Capt. S. W. *The War At Sea 1939–1945*, vols. I and II. London: Her Majesty's Stationary Office, 1954 and 1956.

Rumiantsev, Nikolai M. *Razgrom vraga v zapolier' e* (The Defeat of the Enemy in the Transpolar). Moscow: Voyenizdat, 1963.

————. "Oboronitel'nye deisrviia 14-i armii v Zapoliar'e v 1941 godu" (Defensive Operations of the 14th Army in the Transpolar in 1941). *Voenno-istoricheskii zhurnal*, 12/1980, 21–33.

Rupert, James. "Trying to Break a Deadlock." *The Washington Post*, 14 January 1986, A13.

Sadovskii, V. "Komandir 'chernykh d'iavolov' " (Commander of the "Black Devils"), *Sovetskii voin* (Soviet Soldier), 3/1985, 36–37.

Saikowski, Charlotte. " 'New Realism' Seen in Gorbachev's Approach to Soviet Foreign Policy." *The Christian Science Monitor*, 13 April 1988, 1, 32.

Samoylenko, Col. (ret.) Ya. "Airborne Raid," *Military Herald*, 1/1985, 42–48.

Sasso, MAJ Claude R. *Soviet Night Operations in World War II.* Leavenworth Papers No. 6. Fort Leavenworth KS: U.S. Army Command and General Staff College, December 1982.

Savich, Ovidiy Gertsovich. *Dva goda v Ispanii* (Two Years in Spain). 4th ed. Moscow: Sovetskiy Pisatel', 1981.

Schmid, Alex P., with Ellen Berends. *Soviet Military Interventions Since 1945.* New Brunswick NJ: Transaction Books, 1985.

Scott, Harriet Fast. "The Politburo." *Air Force Magazine*, March 1988, 54–59.

Scott, Harriet Fast and William F. Scott. *The Armed Forces of the USSR.* 3rd ed. Boulder CO: Westview Press and London: Arms & Armour Press, 1984.

————. *The Soviet Art of War: Doctrine, Strategy and Tactics.* Boulder CO: Westview Press, 1982.

Scott, John. *Behind the Urals.* Bloomington IN: Indiana University Press, 1973.

Scott, William F. "Another Look at the USSR's 'Defensive' Doctrine." *Air Force Magazine*, March 1988, 48–52.

Seaton, Albert and John Seaton. *The Soviet Army: 1918 to the Present.* New York: The New American Library, 1986.

Selections from Operations on the Vistula in August, 1920. Trans. from Polish into Russian by the Military Publications Division, 1931, trans. from Russian into English. Washington DC: The Army War College: November 1934.

Senate Committee on the Judiciary. *The Legacy of Alexander Orlov.* 93rd Cong., 1st sess. Washington DC: Government Printing Office, 1973.

Serebryannikov, V. "Gotovyy byt' ryadovym" (Ready to Serve as a Private). *Kommunist*, 17/1979, 106–114.

Sherfey, MAJ Lloyd W. *Operational Employment of Airborne Forces: The Soviet Approach and Implications for NATO.* Fort Leavenworth KS: U.S. Army Command and General Staff College, 22 April 1987.

Shishkov, Guards Col. V. "In Afghanistan, The Airborne Forces Discipline—The Basis of Victory." *Military Herald*, 8/1984, 29.

Shortt, Jim. "Rebuffing the Bear: Swedish Rangers Prepare for Soviet Invasion." *Soldier of Fortune*, December 1987, 84–87.

Sidorenko, A. A. *The Offensive.* Moscow: Voyenizdat, 1970. Trans. U.S. Air Force Washington DC: U.S. Government Printing Office, 1976.

Sikorski, Gen. L. *The Russo-Polish War, 1920.* Fort Leavenworth KS: The Command and General Staff School, 1936.

Simes, Dimitri. Review of *Inside the Aquarium: The Making of a Top Soviet Spy,* by Viktor Suvorov. *The Washington Post,* 11 May 1986.

Simpkin, Richard. *Red Armour: An Examination of the Soviet Mobile Force Concept.* London: Brassey's Defence Publishers, 1984.

Sintsov, A. N., et al. *Eto bylo na krainem severe* (It Was in the Far North). Murmansk: Knizhnoe izdatel'stvo, 1965.

Sinyayev, A. D. *Reconnaissance in Mountain Terrain.* Moscow: Voyenizdat, 1963.

Skilling, H. Gordon. *Czechoslovakia's Interrupted Revolution.* Princeton, NJ: Princeton University Press, 1976.

Smith, Dexter Jerome. "How SACLANT Surveys the Seas." *Defence,* July 1988, 478.

Soderlind, Rolf. "Soviet Sub Developments Prompt Call for More NATO Northern Exercises." *Armed Forces Journal International*, March 1988, 32.

———. "Norway to Accept German Troops on Its Soil." *Armed Forces Journal International,* April 1988, 30.

———. "East Meets West in Finland's 'Blizzard 88' Exercise." *Armed Forces Journal International,* June 1988, 22, 24.

Sofinov, P. G. *Ocherki istorii vserossiyskoy chrezvychaynoy komissiy* (1917–1922gg.). Moscow: Gospolitizdat, 1960.

Sokolov, B. V. "O sootnoshenii poter' v liudiakh i boevoi tekhnike na sovetsko-germanskom fronte v khode velikoi otechestvennoi voiny" (Concerning the Correlation of Personnel and Combat Equipment Losses On the Soviet-German Front During the Great Patriotic War). *Voprosy istorii*, 6/1988, 120.

Sollie, Finne. *Norge oy de Europeiske Interessene i Nordomaradene-Oslo:* The Norwegian Atlantic Committee, 1986.

Soskov, COL. A. A. "Sovershenstvovanie organizatsionnoy struktury inzhenernykh voysk v gody velikoi otechestvennoi voyny" (Improvements in the Organization of Engineering Troops During World War II). *Voenno-istoricheskii zhurnal*, 12/1985, 66–70.

Sovetskaia voennaia entsiklopedicheskii slovar' (Soviet Military Encyclopedic Dictionary). Moscow: Voyenizdat, 1977, 1978, 1979, 1980, 1983, 1986.

Soviet Battlefield Development Plan 1. "Soviet General Doctrine for War." Washington DC: U.S. Army Intelligence Agency and U.S. Army Intelligence and Threat Analysis Center, June 1987.

"Soviet Break-ins?" *Newsweek*, 9 November 1987, 6.

Soviet Military Power, 1986. Washington DC: U.S. Government Printing Office, 1986.

Soviet Military Power, 1987. Washington DC: U.S. Government Printing Office, 1987.

Soviet Military Power: An Assessment of the Threat, 1988. Washington DC: U.S. Government Printing Office, 1988.

"Soviets Buy Deep-Diving Subs from Finland," *Armed Forces Journal International*, March 1988, 30.

"Soviet ship carries torpedo boats," *Jane's Defence Weekly*, 27 September 1986, 661.

The Soviet Soldier. Sandhurst: Royal Military Academy, Soviet Studies Research Centre, 1982.

Special Operations: Military Lessons from Six Selected Case Studies. Centre for Conflict Studies, University of New Brunswick, Fall 1982.

Stakheev, V. "Reconnaissance Training." *Military Herald*, 3/1975, 4–9.

Stanglin, Douglas and Rene Riley. "Soviet Saboteurs: On-Site Training." *U.S. News & World Report*, 30 March 1987, 46.

Starinov, Anna Kornilovna. "V tylu y myatezhnikov" (In the Rebels' Rear). In Aleksandrovskaya, et al. *My-internationalisty* (We Are Internationalists). Moscow: Politizdat, 1975.

Starinov, Ilya Grigorevich. *Miny zhdut svoego chasa* (The Mines Await Their Hour). Moscow: Voyenizdat, 1964.

"Statement by General Secretary of the CPSU Central Committee Mikhail Gorbachev on Afghanistan." *Soviet Military Review*, 3/1988, 2–4, reprinted from *Pravda*, 9 February 1988.

Storvik, Olav Trygge. "Norway Faces Reduced Budget in '88." *Defence*, December 1987, 746.

Strachan, Hew. *European Armies and the Conduct of War*. London: George Allen & Unwin, 1983.

Submarine Defense Commission. *To Meet the Submarine Threat: The Submarine Incursions and Swedish Security Policy*. Stockholm: 1983.

"Submarine sighting under investigation." *Jane's Defence Weekly*, 30 August 1986, 347.

Suggs, Dr. Robert C. "Soviet Subs in Scandinavia: 1930–1935." *Proceedings*, March 1986, 100–106.

Suntsov, N. P., et al. *Krasnoznamennyi dal' nevostochnuii: istoriia krasnoznamennogo dal' nevostochnogo voennogo okruga* (Red Banner Far East: The History of the Red Banner Far East Military District). Moscow: Voyenizdat, 1985.

Suvorov, Viktor. *The Liberators: My Life in the Soviet Army*. New York: W. W. Norton & Company, 1981.

————. *Inside the Soviet Army.* New York: Macmillan Publishing Co., Inc., 1982.

————. "Spetsnaz: The Soviet Union's Special Forces." *International Defence Review,* 9/1983, 1209–1216.

————. *Inside Soviet Military Intelligence.* New York: Macmillan Publishing Co., Inc., 1984.

————. "Soviet special forces at work in the Baltic?" *Jane's Naval Review.* 142–149. London: Jane's Defence Publishers, Ltd., 1985.

————. *Inside the Aquarium: The Making of a Top Soviet Spy.* New York: Macmillan Publishing Co., Inc., 1986.

————. *SPETSNAZ: The Story of the Soviet SAS.* London: Hamish Hamilton, 1987. Published in the U.S. as *SPETSNAZ: The Inside Story of the Soviet Special Forces.* New York: W. W. Norton & Company, 1988.

"Sweden should speed up airfield dispersion." *Jane's Defence Weekly,* 2 May 1987, 808.

"Sweden Warns: 'Blood Could Flow' Over Subs." *Defense Week,* 4 January 1988, 5.

"Swedes Hope to Sight Sub, Sink Same." *U.S. News & World Report,* 11 January 1988, 42.

"Swedish ASW operation fruitless." *Jane's Defence Weekly,* 25 June 1988, 1281.

Swedish Parliamentary Defense Committee. *Swedish Security Policy in the 1990s.* Stockholm: 1984.

Taylor, Blaine. "Skorzeny." *Soldier of Fortune,* June 1985, 66–69, 96, 98, 99.

————. "More On Skorzeny." *Soldier of Fortune,* July 1985, 70–75, 93–95.

Temple, LTG Herbert R., Jr. Interview, "Newsmakers," WTUU. Anchorage AK, 15 February 1988.

Terekhov, P. V. *Boevye deistviia tankov na severo-zapade v 1944g.* Moscow: Voyenizdat, 1965.

Thapor, Karan. "Afghan Army's Collapse: Russians Fight Losing Battle." *The Times* (London), 2 February 1982, 5.

Thomas, Hugh. *The Spanish Civil War.* Rev. ed. New York: Harper and Row, 1977.

Toth, Robert C. (*Los Angeles Times*). "Success of 'Finlandization' outlives past scorns." *Anchorage Daily News,* 29 May 1988, A8.

Troyan, Vasiliy Avramovich. "Chetyrnadtsatyy spetsial'nyy" (The 14th Special Corps). In Aleksandrovskaya, et al. *My—internationalisty* (We Are Internationalists). Moscow: Politizdat, 1975.

Tsvigun, S. K., et al. *V.I. Lenin i VChK: Sbornik dokumentov* (1919–1922 gg.). Moscow: Politizdat, 1975.

Tuohy, William (*Los Angeles Times*). "Soviets shift naval forces to the arctic." *Anchorage Daily News,* 17 July 1988, 1, A11.

Turbiville, Dr. Graham H., Jr. "Soviet Airborne Operations in Theater War." *Foreign Policy,* vol. XIII, 1986, 160–183.

————. "Soviet Airborne Troops." *Soviet Armed Forces Review Annual*, vol. 10. Gulf Breeze FL: Academic International Press, 1987.

————. "Ambush! The Road War in Afghanistan." *Army*, January 1988, 32–42.

Turbiville, Dr. Graham H., Jr. and Charles G. Pritchard. "Soviet Airborne Assault." *Marine Corps Gazette*, October 1987, 52–53.

Ulanovskiy, Nadezhda and Maya. *Istoriya odnoy semi* (One Family's Story). New York: Chalidze Publications, 1982.

"Unidentified submarine hit, Sweden says." *Anchorage Daily News*, 23 June 1988, A9.

"Units of Special Designation (1917–1925)." *Voenno-istoricheskii zhurnal*, 4/1969, 106–112, trans. James F. Gebhardt.

UPI. "Soviet Soldiers Detected on Remote Alaskan Island." *New Haven Register*, 11 February 1988, 24.

Urban, Mark. *War in Afghanistan*. London: Macmillan Press, 1988.

U.S. Congress. Senate. Committee on Foreign Relations. *The Hidden War: The Struggle for Afghanistan*. 98th Cong., 2d sess., 1984. Committee Print.

USSR Report, Military Affairs, Military Encyclopedic Dictionary (Voennyi entsiklopedicheskii slovar'). Vol. III. Washington DC: Foreign Broadcast Information Service, 4 June 1985. JPRS-UMA-85-015-L.

Ustinov, D. F., et al. *Istoriia vtoroi mirovoi voiny 1939–1945* (History of the Second World War, 1939–1945). Vols. 2 and 11. Moscow: Voyenizdat, 1980.

Valenta, Jiri. "From Prague to Kabul: The Soviet Style of Invasion." *International Security*, Fall 1980, 114–141.

van Loon, Henry. "'Arrowhead Express' Underscores Importance of Norway to NATO Defenses." *Armed Forces Journal International*, May 1988, 32.

Vasilevich, I., comp. *Vernost' Dolgu* (A Faithfulness to Duty). Moscow: Voyenizdat, 1985.

Vasilevskii, A. M. *Delo vsei zhizni* (My Life). Moscow: Politizdat, 1983.

Vasilevskiy, Lev Petrovich. *Ispanskaya Khronika Grigoriy Grande* (The Spanish Chronicle of Gregory Grande). Moscow: Molodaya Gvardiya, 1974.

Vatne, Paul Einar. *Jeg Var Russisk Spion—Historien om Selmer Nilsen* (I Was A Russian Spy—The Story of Selmer Nilsen). Oslo: H. Aschenhoug & Co., 1981.

Vaupshasov, Stanislav Alekseyevich. *Na trevozhnikh perekrestakh. Zapiski chekista* (Troubled Crossings. Notes of a Chekist). Moscow: Izdatel'stvo Politicheskoy Literatury, 1971.

Veshchvonov, S. S. *The Motorised Rifle Squad in Reconnaissance*. Moscow: Voyenizdat, 1977.

Vigor, P. H. *Soviet Blitzkrieg Theory*. New York: St. Martin's Press, 1983.

Vishnyakova-Akimova, Vera Vladimirovna. *Two Years in Revolutionary China: 1925–1927*. Trans. Steven I. Levine. Harvard East Asian Monographs No. 40. Cambridge: East Asian Research Center, 1971.

Vnotchenko, L. N. *Pobeda na dal 'nem vostoke* (Victory in the East). Moscow: Voyenizdat, 1971, 1980.

Volf, E. L. "Nezabymoye" (The Unforgettable). In Aleksandrovskaya, et al. *My-internationalisty* (We Are Internationalists). Moscow: Politizdat, 1975.

Volkogonov, D. A. *Marksistsko-leninskye ucheniye o voyne i armii.* Moscow: Voyenizdat, 1984.

von Clausewitz, Carl. *On War.* Trans. J. J. Graham. Ed. Anatol Rapoport. Baltimore: Penguin Books, 1968.

Vorobyev, E. "Starik i ego ucheniki" (The Old Man and His Students). In Vasilevich, I., comp. *Vernost' Dolgu* (A Faithfulness to Duty). Moscow: Voyenizdat, 1985.

Wachtmeister, H. Alarik. "Sending political signals beneath the Baltic Sea?" *Washington Times*, 10 October 1988.

Watt, Richard M. *Bitter Glory: Poland and Its Fate, 1918–1939.* New York: Simon and Schuster, 1979.

Weeks, John. *Assault from the Sky.* New York: G.P. Putnam's Sons, 1978.

Weintraub, Richard. "Flanking Maneuver Credited with Breaking Seige of Khost." *The Washington Post*, 6 January 1988, A15, A18.

Weintraub, Richard and David Ottaway. "Afghan Rebels Said to Hit Foe Hard." *The Washington Post*, 6 July 1987, A1, A4.

"Werner, Ruth" (Ursula Kuczynski). *Sonjas Rapport* (Sonya's Report). Berlin: Verlag Neues Leben, 1977.

Whaley, Barton. "Guerrillas in the Spanish Civil War." Cambridge MA: Center for International Studies, MIT, September 1969.

White, John Baker. *Sabotage Is Suspected.* London: Evans Brothers, Ltd., 1957.

Whiting, Charles. *Ardennes: The Secret War.* New York: Stein and Day, 1985.

Williams, Air Commodore E. S. "Morale, Motivation and Leadership in the Soviet Armed Forces." *RUSI Journal*, 14 September 1984, 3–7.

"Winged Guard." *Soviet Military Review*, 6/1987, 14–17.

"Winter, Harry." *Operasjon Garbo. En thriller om en mulig virkelighet* (Operation Garbo: A Thriller About a Possible Reality). Stockholm: Timpbro Forlag, 1988.

Yefanov, Maj. V. "In Hand-to-Hand Night Combat." *Red Star*, 4 August 1983, 1.

Yudin, N. F. *Pervaya partizanskaya.* Moscow: Izdatel'stvo "Moskoviskiy Rabochiy," 1983.

Zaitsev, Mikhail Mitrofanovich. "They Are Not Born Commanders." *Military Herald*, 2/1976, 20–26.

———. "A Creative Approach to Tactics." *Red Star*, 16 March 1982, 2.

Zakharov, Matvei V., et al. *50 let vooruzhennykh sil SSR* (50 Years of the Armed Forces of the USSR). Moscow: Voyenizdat, 1968.

————. "The Theory of the Operation in Depth." *Voyenno-istoricheskii zhurnal*, 10/1970, 16.

Zakharov, S. E. *Krasnoznamennyi tikhookeanskii flot* (Red Banner Pacific Fleet). 2d ed. Moscow: Voyenizdat, 1973.

Zaloga, Steven J. and James Loop. *Soviet Bloc Elite Forces*. London: Osprey Publishing, Ltd., 1985.

Zaloga, Steven J. and Victor Madej. *The Polish Campaign 1939*. New York: Hippocrene Books, 1985.

Zeigler, David W. "Yellow Rain: An Analysis That Went Awry?" *International Journal of Intelligence and Counterintelligence* (Spring 1988): 91–113.

Ziemke, Earl F. *The German Northern Theater of Operations, 1940–1945*. Department of the Army Pamphlet 20-271. Washington DC: Headquarters, Department of the Army, 15 December 1959.

Index

Abakumov, Gen. Viktor 38
Afghanistan xiv, xv, 2, 4, 6, 20, 37, 42, 43,
    48, 67, 182, 188–95, 196–98, 203–220,
    222, 228, 229, 232, 238, 239, 241,
    245, 249, 250
  Darulaman Palace complex 4, 4n. 25, 192,
    194, 196
  Kabul takeover 4, 193–95
  Mujahideen 4, 6, 20, 189, 192, 203, 206,
    213
  Murder of Pres. Amin 4, 194
  Salang Tunnel complex 191, 191n. 44, 192,
    195
  Soviet advisors in 188, 189, 192, 193
  Soviet counterinsurgency operations 189,
    191, 195, 204, 205–16
  use of *spetsnaz* in xiv, 4, 37, 182, 192,
    194–98, 203, 204–16, 228
    reydoviki battalion at Jalalabad 212
    reydoviki battalion at Khandahar 212
    special operations brigade at Khandahar
      205
    special operations brigade at Shindand
      205
    special operations unit at Baraki Barak
      208–09
  1979 Soviet invasion of 188–95, 203, 204
Aganov, S. Kh. 74n.9, 75
Airborne Combined Arms Special Purpose
    Brigades (Airborne Assault Brigades of
    Special Designation) 34, 37, 224–25
  special purpose battalions 34–35, 37
Airborne Forces xv, xvi, 2, 34, 37, 43, 142,
    153, 185, 187, 190–91, 192–93, 194,
    195, 203–04, 214, 222, 223, 224, 228,
    229, 231, 238–39, 242–44, 245, 247
AirLand Battle 233, 258
Alaska 4, 22–23, 22n.12
Amin, Pres. Hafizullah 189, 190, 191, 192,
    194, 204
  murder of 194, 204
Artemenko, Col. I. T. 144
Avramenko, Guards Maj. Peter Nikitovich 144

Babikov, Makar A. 102, 103, 105–106, 263,
    267, 279
Balashika, KGB sabotage school at 194

Barchenko-Emilianov, Capt. I. P. 124–26,
    128–30
Basmachi xix, 2, 32, 42
  Afghanistan 2
  Freeman's Revolt 2
  Soviet Central Asia 2, 32
Bayerenov, Col. 194
Beria, Lavrentyi Pavlovich 35, 39, 42
Berzin, Yan Karlovich (Peter Kyuzis and
    "General Grishin") 35–36, 51–52, 54,
    58–61, 263–64, 267, 269
Boltin, Maj.Gen. E. 223–24
Boyarskiy, Pavel 58, 59
Breshnev, Leonid 43, 189, 191
Butriago, Antonio 66, 264

Central Scientific-Experimental Railroad Prov-
    ing Ground of the Red Army 271
Central Staff of the Partisan Movement 37–41.
    See also Partisan Warfare; SMERSH.
Chambers, Whittaker 51, 265
Chasti osobogo naznacheniya (ChON) xvii,
    1–2, 31
Cheka (VChKa) xvii, 2, 3, 29, 30, 31, 32–33,
    265
  Administration of Special Tasks 2, 32–33
  formation 29–30
  Kronstadt uprising 31
  See also NKVD; KGB; MGB.
Combined Arms Theory 225–28
Communist Party
  of Czechoslovakia (CCP) 182–83, 187
  of Norway 84, 88, 103, 104
  of the Soviet Union (CPSU) 29–32, 37, 40,
    41, 75, 84, 86, 103, 106, 118, 147, 191,
    221, 232, 240, 268–71, 273
  of Spain xv, 54, 273
  See also Komsomol.
Czechoslovakia 4, 41, 48, 182–88, 190, 195–98,
    222, 229, 232, 248, 249, 250, 268
  arrest of Czech leaders 187–88
  seizure of Government Presidium 187
  seizure of Presidential Palace 187
  seizure of Ruzyne Airport 4, 185–87, 196
  use of *spetsnaz* in 4, 185–88, 195–98
  1968 Soviet invasion of 4, 182–88, 190,
    191–95

Deep Battle (Operation) xvi, 73, 79, 221–33
    origins 222–25
    See Combined Arms Theory.
Denisin, Col. A. Z. 150, 151
Denmark 160–61, 175, 178
Dobrotin, Maj. L. V. 84, 97, 106
Domozhirov, Capt. 84
Dubcek, Alexander 182, 183, 188
Dzerzhinskiy Division 31, 32
Dzerzhinskiy, Feliks Edmundovich 30, 268.
    See also NKVD; KGB.

Eisenhower, Gen. Dwight D. 181
Eitingon, Leonid Andreyevich (General Kotov)
    35, 36, 38, 42, 43, 52, 264, 268, 272
    in Spain 35, 36, 52, 268
Engineering xvi, 1, 3, 71, 74, 270–71
    Great Patriotic War 71–79
    Guards *Miners* xviii, xix, 3, 74–77, 118,
        119, 121, 122
    Manchuria 77–79
    Petsamo-Kirkenes 76–77, 117–24
    pre-World War II 71–73
    See also I. G. Starinov; D. A. Krutskikh.
Epishev, Gen. A. 184, 190
Explosive Demolitions 1, 53, 54, 56, 57, 59,
    60, 62–63, 64, 71–73, 74, 75, 118,
    121–22, 194, 270–71

Far North 2–3, 4, 40, 41, 81–82, 159–78
    agent operations 40, 41, 81, 102, 168, 170
    Kola Peninsula 161–63, 172, 173
    spetsnaz operations in 2–3, 37, 76–77,
        81–106, 117–30, 164–78
    See also Finland; V. N. Leonov; Norway;
        Petsamo-Kirkenes; submarine opera-
        tions; Sweden.
Finland 2–3, 35, 37, 81–82, 83, 125, 160, 161,
    169, 170, 225, 245, 267
    Winter War (1939–1940) 2–3, 37, 81–82,
        86, 160, 225, 245, 267, 271
    World War II 82, 83, 85, 160
Franco, Generalissimo Francisco (forces of)
    47, 53, 55, 56, 57, 60, 61, 62, 64, 65,
    264, 267, 269
Fuller, Brig. Gen. John F. C. ("Plan 1919") 223
Frunze, Mikhail Vasilevich 227

"General Grishin" 52, 263. *See* Y. K. Berzin.
"General Ivon" 52, 54, 264. *See* L. A.
    Eitingon.

Gerasimov, Peter 264–65
Glushko, Capt. Stepan 58, 269
Golovko, Adm. A. G. 82–83, 85, 86, 87, 91,
    92, 93, 94, 102, 104, 105, 124, 125,
    128, 130
Gomez, Jose Munoz 59, 270
Gorbachev, Mikhail 173, 215
Gorev, Gen. Vladmir Yefimovich 50–51, 52,
    265
Gradov, Maj. G. A. 120, 121
Grinchenko, Simone 265
GRU xvii, 1, 2, 3, 4, 21, 35, 37, 38, 40, 42,
    43, 50, 71, 73, 82, 170 , 187, 191, 194,
    196, 244, 247, 250, 263, 264, 265,
    267, 269, 271, 272
    Spain 2, 35–36, 50–51
    spetsnaz 3, 4, 21, 43, 73, 82, 187, 191, 194,
        196
    training of terrorists 4, 250–51
Gurin, Maj. V. I. 140

Haq, Abdul 207, 209–10, 214
Hart, B. Liddell, theory of the "expanding
    torrent" 223
Hemingway, Ernest 57, 61

Iankevich, Maj. Iu. Ia. 140
Ibarra, Delores 273. *See* Communist Party of
    Spain.
Internationalists (Interbrigadists) 47, 55, 58,
    62, 67
Inzartsev, Lt.Col. N. A. 85, 91, 92, 93, 95–97,
    106, 152–53, 154, 265–66
IPB (Intelligence Preparation of the Batt-
    lefield) xvii, 9–10, 259

Jodl, Gen. Ferdinand 114–15
Johnson, Pres. Lyndon B. 185

Kachanov, Gen. Kuzma Maksimovich 52, 64
Kalinin Front 72, 74, 75
Karelian Front 76, 116, 117, 123, 139. *See*
    K. A. Meretskov.
Karmal, Barbak 189, 191, 195
KGB xvii, 1, 3, 4, 19, 20, 30, 33, 36, 42, 43,
    48, 49, 50, 51, 52, 53, 59, 63, 67, 71,
    170, 186, 187, 191, 194, 196, 212, 222,
    232, 250, 252, 257, 258, 263, 264,
    265, 271
    Department 8, Directorate S 3–4, 19, 33,
        232

spetsnaz 3–4, 19, 33, 67, 186, 191, 194, 196, 252, 257, 258, 264.
  See also Cheka; MGB; NKVD.
Khan, Mohammed Daoud 188–89
  overthrow of 189
Kharish, Ivan 266
Kharitonenko, Grigoriy 62, 206. *See* G. S. Syroezhkin.
Khorezm Group 32
Khrenov, Gen. Arkadii F. 118, 124, 142
Khrushchev period 43
Kidd, Adm. Isaac C. 160
Kobulov, Gen. 39, 42
Koliuabakin, Capt. 3rd Rank G. P. 152
Komsomol xvii, 75, 84, 86, 103, 118, 240, 241, 243, 265. *See also* Communist Party of the Soviet Union.
Kononenko, Capt. Aleksandr P. 119, 121
Kovalev, Lt. I. P. 76
Krutskikh, Lt.Col. D. A. 118, 130, 140–41, 141n. 26, 142, 143, 145, 154, 266
Kunslich (Cunslich), Alex 55
Kyuzis, Peter 51. *See* Y. A. Berzin.

Language Capabilities xv, 2, 8, 50, 54, 59, 62, 65, 82, 85, 88n. 30, 92, 99, 103, 104, 142, 148, 154, 177, 266, 267, 271
Lapchinskiy, Aleksandr N. 2
Lebedev, Guards Col. V. I. 142
Leonov, Viktor N. 85, 95, 97, 99–103, 105, 106, 125, 126–29, 130, 146–47, 149–54, 258, 263, 266–67
  writings by 291
Long Range Reconnaissance Regiment 232

Malinovsky, Marshal Rodion Yakovlevich 139.
  See Transbaikal Front.
Mamsurov, Gen. Khadzhi-Umar Dzhiorovich 2–3, 35, 36–37, 40, 56, 57, 58–59, 61, 67, 265, 267, 271, 272
  Spanish Civil War 35, 36–37, 56, 57, 58–59
  Winter War with Finland 2–3, 37, 82
  World War II 267
  See also P. V. Mamsurov.
Mamsurov, Polina Veniaminova 56, 267–68
Manchuria 3, 53, 130, 135–54, 222, 269
  airlanding of *desants* 3, 77–79, 137, 141–45, 146, 222
  deception 137
  engineer *spetsnaz* in 77–79, 139–41, 142–43
  Japanese capitulation 143, 144, 146
  Japanese forces in 138–39

Korean operations 139, 145–53, 222
Kurile Islands operation 3, 136, 138, 139, 145–46
Kwantung Army 135, 138–39, 144
  naval *spetsnaz* in 3, 130, 145–53
  preparations for invasion of 136–38
  Sakhalin Island operation 3, 136, 138, 139, 145, 146
  Soviet declaration of war 138
  Suifenho Tunnels operation 77, 139–41, 142, 145, 266
Mannerheim, Field Marshal Carl Gustav Emil 82
Maskirovka xix, 4, 72
Media 4–6, 10, 17, 21–22, 25, 57, 81, 165, 184, 192, 194
  James Adams 5, 194
  Yossef Bodansky 5
  Christian Science Monitor 23, 209
  Edward Giradet 209, 284
  Lawrence Goodrich 23
  Jane's Defence Weekly 5
  Neil C. Livingstone 22
  M. K. Pilgrim 22
  Viktor Suvorov 23
  Wall Street Journal 23
Meretskov, Gen. Kirill A. 116, 117, 118, 124, 139, 142, 145
Merkulov 42
Miners (Guards Miners, OGBM) xviii, 3, 74–77, 117–23
Ministry of State Security (MGB) xvii, 33, 42–43. *See also* Cheka; KGB; NKVD.
Ministry of Internal Affairs (MVD) xvii, 20, 191, 252
Mitchell, Gen. Billy 223
Molotov, Vyacheslav M. 138

NATO (North Atlantic Treaty Organization) 18, 24, 42, 160, 161, 162, 164, 171, 172, 174, 175, 176, 177, 183, 184, 197, 198, 204, 223, 238, 244, 245, 247, 248, 252, 253
Naval *Spetsnaz* 3, 81–106, 113, 124–30, 145–53, 203, 230–31, 247, 263, 267
  coastwatching 40, 88, 103
  See Manchuria; Northern Fleet; Norway; Pacific Fleet; Petsamo-Kirkenes.
Nikolaev, Lt. F. 85–86
Nilsen, Selmer 88
NKVD xviii, 2, 3, 31, 32, 33, 35, 36, 37, 38–40, 41, 42, 71, 241, 268, 273

Administration of Special Tasks 2, 32–33
Separate Motorized Rifle Special Purpose
  Brigade (OMSBON) 3, 3n. 18, 273
special groups in World War II 3, 39
"wet affairs" 3, 32–33, 43
See also Cheka; KGB; MGB; Nikolay I.
  Yezhov.
Northern Fleet 3, 81, 82, 83, 84, 88n. 29, 95,
  101–02, 103, 104–05, 106, 114, 117,
  124–30, 152, 161–63, 263, 265, 266
Northern Pacific Ocean Flotilla 146
Norway 40, 41, 81, 82, 84, 85, 88–91, 93, 99–101,
  104, 105, 113–14, 123, 125, 159–63,
  164, 165, 168, 173, 174, 177, 178
  Kirkenes 82, 85, 93, 101, 113, 116, 130
  Varanger Peninsula 82, 87, 91, 99, 101, 105

Obruchev, Anna K. 54, 271. See A. K.
  Starinov.
OGBM (otdelnyy gvardeyskiy batal'on minerov)
  xviii, 74–77
OKDVA (Soviet Red Banner Far Eastern
  Army) 51, 269
OMSBON. See NKVD Separate Motorized
  Rifle Special Purpose Brigade.
Operations Security (OPSEC) xiv, xv, xviii,
  36, 67, 84, 86, 93, 104, 119, 123
Operational Training Center of the Western
  Front 53, 66, 73, 271, 272
"Operation Bridge" 141–45
"Operation Garbo" 175–76
Orlov, Gen. Aleksander 35–36, 49, 52–53,
  268–69
Orlovskiy, Kirill Prokofyevich 58, 59, 268–69
osnaz (osobogo naznacheniya) 40, 102, 127.
  See also spetsnaz.
OSS (Office of Strategic Services) 66, 263
Ozolin, Lev 53

Pacific Fleet 3, 139, 146, 148, 152, 153, 263, 266
Paputin, Gen. Viktor Semenovich 20, 191,
  194, 197
Parachuting xv, 2, 4, 7, 72, 75, 76, 82, 86,
  86n. 19, 91, 101, 105, 128, 141, 142,
  153, 173, 223, 224, 229–32, 238, 239,
  240, 247, 249, 252, 258, 259, 269, 271
Paraeva, Olga 85
Partisan (Guerrilla) Warfare xiv, 3, 19, 34, 35,
  36, 38, 39, 40, 41, 42, 47, 48, 50, 52,
  53, 54, 56, 58, 61, 63, 66, 71–73, 75,
  76, 88, 122, 211, 211n. 22, 213, 227,
  232, 246, 251, 252, 263–73

Central Staff of the Partisan Movement
  37–41
SMERSH 37, 38, 41
See spetsnaz; NKVD.
Patrakhaltsev, Nikolay Kririllovich 62
Pavlovskiy, Gen. Ivan G. 184, 185, 190
PDPA (People's Democratic Party of
  Afghanistan) 189
  Great Saur Revolution 189
  overthrow of King Zahir Shah 189
  See B. Karmal; N. M. Taraki.
Penkovskiy, Col. Oleg 37
Peregrin, Galarsa 58
Petlura, Simon, OGPU murder of 222
Petsamo-Kirkenes Operation 76–77, 101,
  113–30, 141, 147, 266
  Cape Krestovyi raid 124–30
  engineer spetsnaz in 76–77, 117–24, 266
  naval spetsnaz in 124–29
Politburo xviii, 48, 52, 67, 183, 184, 185, 191
Ponomarenko, Gen. P. K. 38
Popov, Guards Maj. A. F. 118–22, 123
Pritula, Maj. Gen. A. D. 144
Prokopyuk, Nikolay 61, 269
Purkayev, Gen. M. A. 139. See 2d Far Eastern
  Front.

Rabtsevich, Aleksandr 269
Radioelectronic Combat (REC). xviii, 162,
  229. See Signals Intelligence
Reydoviki xx, 212, 213, 230, 230n. 33, 238
Razvedka xx, 1, 1n. 1, 20, 47, 71, 79, 140n.
  25, 214, 237, 269
  razvedchiki (scouts) xx, 53, 94, 96, 97, 98,
  101, 102, 125, 140, 140n.25, 214, 228,
  229, 237
Reconnaissance xiv, 1, 3, 4, 20, 25, 54, 60,
  67, 71, 74, 77, 79, 81, 82, 84, 85, 86,
  87, 88–91, 92, 95, 96, 98, 99, 102,
  103, 104, 105, 118, 119, 123, 124, 125,
  130, 143, 146, 150, 153, 170, 177, 181,
  184, 191, 192, 197, 204, 208, 214, 229,
  230, 237, 239, 244, 246, 248, 249, 273
  by battle (combat) 3, 146, 150, 222
Red Army (Soviet Army) 2, 30, 31, 32, 34,
  38, 39, 40, 41, 71, 73, 82, 204, 207,
  228, 240, 268, 269, 270, 271, 272
Red Banner Amur Flotilla 143
Russian Civil War 1–2, 30, 31, 32, 34, 62,
  71, 226
  special Red cavalry in 1
  See Chasti osobogo naznacheniya (ChON).

Russo-Polish War 1–2, 52, 58, 71, 221, 268, 269
  insurgent Cossack cavalry 1–2
  partisan forces in 1–2, 269
  Red Polish cavalry in 1–2, 2n. 3

Salnyn, Brig.Gen. Khristofor (Grisha) Intovich 61–62, 263, 269–70
Serov, Ivan 37, 42
Shalakhov, Maj.Gen. G. A., 142, 143
Shaposhnikov, B. 223
Shtemenko, Sergey M., Gen. of the Army Higher Military School at Krasnodar 244, 244n.9
Shtern (Stern), Gen. Grigoriy Mikhailovich 52, 272
Signals Intelligence (SIGINT) xv, xviii, 4, 41, 162, 229
Simes, Dimitri 23
Skorzeny, Col. Otto 181, 197, 246, 253
Sokolov, First Deputy Defense Minister Marshal Sergei L. 190
Spanish Civil War xv, 2, 35–37, 42, 47–67, 71, 73, 82, 263–72
  Anarchists 36, 272
  Nationalists 35, 37, 47, 60, 67, 268
  Republicans (Loyalists) 35, 36, 47, 49, 50, 51, 52–53, 54, 56, 57, 61, 62, 64, 65, 66, 67, 265, 268, 271, 273
  Special Battalion 56–57, 61
  spetsnaz operations in 35, 47–48, 50, 52–65, 268, 271, 272, 273
  See Gen. F. Franco; Internationalists; 14th Special Corps.
Special Operations Targeting 2–4, 5, 6, 20, 32–33, 34, 36, 47–48, 62–63, 67, 71–72, 75, 78, 104, 118, 141, 142, 163, 173, 177, 196, 204, 215, 221–22, 230–31, 249, 251–52
  airfields, aircraft and pilots 2, 5, 56, 67, 86, 88, 91–92, 97, 104, 142–45, 146, 152, 170, 174, 177, 185–87, 191, 196, 245, 268
  banks 78, 143
  bridges 53, 54, 56, 59, 61, 74, 75, 76, 77, 78, 118, 120, 121, 122, 124, 142–45, 170, 187, 251, 270
  caravans 6, 206, 258
  coastwatching 40, 83, 89, 91, 105
  command, control, communication and intelligence (C3I) 6, 36, 62–63, 76, 164, 172, 177, 206, 251
  economic targets 56, 92–93, 104, 251

  electric power 53, 143, 177, 251
  ground transportation 6, 36, 53, 54, 56, 59, 62–63, 74, 76, 99, 104, 118, 121, 124, 164, 170, 187, 206, 209, 211, 251, 270
  military installations 85, 87, 91, 92, 93, 96, 98–99, 100, 104, 118, 124–29, 130, 143, 152, 153, 165, 170, 177, 224, 249, 251, 252, 264–65
  munitions and supplies 62, 64–65, 74, 76, 91, 104, 122
  political/military leadership 3–4, 20, 32–33, 34, 38, 39, 42–43, 72–73, 82, 143, 144, 152, 181, 187–88, 191–92, 194, 221, 222, 224, 232, 249, 251, 264
  ports and waterways 2, 83, 144, 145–53, 164, 174, 222, 251
  post offices 143, 152, 187
  prison camps 144
  prisoner snatching 54, 60, 67, 82, 85, 93, 99, 100, 101, 103, 104, 222, 238, 251, 267
  pseudo operations 1–2, 211, 248, 253
  radars 6, 249–50
  radio and television stations 143, 177, 187, 194, 249
  railroads 53, 54, 56, 62, 72, 75, 76, 78, 143, 145, 152, 187, 251, 270, 271
  security forces 143, 192, 194
  telecommunications targets 54, 76, 77, 78, 85, 120, 121, 122, 124, 143, 145, 152, 170, 187, 194, 221
  tunnels 3, 56, 77, 78, 139–41, 191, 222, 266
  underwater sensors 177
  VIP escort/security 195, 273
  water supply 143
  weapons systems 6, 75, 221, 228, 229, 245, 251
spetsnaz
  agents 5, 8, 20, 41, 51, 53, 54, 81, 85, 88–91, 91n.38, 102, 149, 151, 164, 170, 177, 194, 197, 221, 246, 252, 354–58
  capabilities xv, 1, 4, 5–9, 10, 19–20, 24–25, 73–79, 89–90, 101–06, 203, 204, 209, 213–14, 221, 229–32, 245–46, 250–52, 259
  close quarter battle (CQB) 118, 242–43
  combat engineers in xvi, 1, 3, 71–79, 117–24, 244–52
  communications 6, 9, 89–90, 91, 94, 95, 96, 97, 100, 119, 120, 121, 123, 126, 149, 170, 244, 258
  countermeasures against 9–10, 91, 93, 94, 208–09, 210, 252–53

defined xiii-xiv, xviii, 1, 19
equipment xiii, 6, 8, 53, 54, 75, 77, 84, 86,
    90, 92, 92n.47, 93, 97, 99, 118-19,
    126, 152, 209, 239
females in xv, 5, 54, 59, 72, 85, 132,
    132n.30
foreigners in xv, 7-8, 23, 41, 50, 55, 56,
    57-58, 67, 85, 87, 88, 90, 104, 263,
    264, 266, 272
foreign terrorists, training of 4, 250-51,
    258
identification xiii-xiv, 238-39
infiltration xv 8-9, 23-24, 40, 75, 76, 82,
    84-94, 96-101, 105, 119, 123, 126-28,
    130, 142, 143, 144, 146, 149, 150, 151,
    152, 164, 177, 185-87, 192-94, 197,
    211, 214, 230-31, 252
influence on allies 248-51, 258
interface with conventional forces xv, 8-9,
    32, 34, 77, 79, 86, 196, 203, 224-25,
    231, 257
missions of xiii, 1-4, 20-21, 39, 40, 47,
    71-72, 73-74, 82, 99, 102, 104-05,
    118, 123, 124, 139, 141, 145-46, 148,
    149, 150, 151-52, 153-54, 163, 195,
    196, 204, 214, 221, 228, 229-32,
    237-38, 251-52
myths about 4-5, 4n.32, 10, 17-18, 23-24
name xiii
non-Slavs in xv, 7-8
organization 6, 17, 71, 72, 73, 95, 105, 140,
    142, 146, 148, 154, 228-32, 246-49
patrolling 206-08, 209, 211, 212, 237
personalities xiv, 50, 258, 263-73
personnel selection xiii-xiv, xvi, 6, 84, 86,
    89, 103, 103n.77, 118, 124-25, 244-45,
    257-58, 272
planning 130, 163
political reliability xiii, xiv, 6, 29, 32, 67,
    75, 84, 85, 88, 93, 103, 240, 243, 257,
    263
press treatment of. See Media.
resupply 86, 87, 90, 92, 105, 121, 128
security xiv, xv, xviii, 36, 67, 84, 86, 93,
    119, 123
subordination of xiv, 21, 35, 36, 37, 74, 77,
    84, 95, 98, 118, 125, 146, 147, 196
surprise 6-7, 86, 94, 130, 142-43, 173, 176,
    181, 205, 209, 211
training xiii-xiv, 7, 50, 53, 54, 71-74, 84,
    85, 86, 89, 90, 99, 103, 118, 130, 140,
    141-42, 147-48, 177, 233, 239-45,
    250, 267, 270-71, 273

weapons 6, 49, 52, 53, 54, 56-57, 63, 74,
    77, 84, 86, 92, 92n.47, 97, 99, 118-19,
    128, 140, 142, 148, 209, 211, 244, 250,
    271
Western perceptions of 4n.32, 17-18
Sprogis, Artur Karlovich 35, 52, 58-61, 270
Stalin, Josef 33, 34, 35, 38, 43, 47, 48, 50,
    73, 82, 136, 225, 268
    purges 34, 35, 36, 38, 48, 50, 62, 73, 224,
    225, 264, 265, 268, 269, 272
Starinov, Anna Kornilovna 49-50, 54, 61. See
    A. K. Obruchev.
Starinov, Ilya Grigorevich 53-54, 56, 59, 66,
    71-73, 267, 270-71, 272
Stavka Verkhovnoe Glavnokomandovaniye
    (Stavka or VGK) xiv, xviii, 4, 41, 74,
    116, 123, 222
Submarine Operations 4, 40, 41, 81, 81n.2,
    87-91, 100, 105, 164-69, 171, 177, 230
    U-137 ("Whiskey on the Rocks") Incident
    164-66
    World War II 87-91, 100, 105
Sudoplatov, Gen. Pavel 35, 38, 42, 264
Sutiagin, Sr.Lt. P.G. 88, 99
Suvorov, Viktor (Vladimir Rezun) 21, 23,
    23n.22
Sweden 81, 160-61, 164-78, 246
Syroezhkin, Grigoriy Sergeyevich 53, 57, 266,
    271-72

Talyzin, Soviet Minister of Communications
    Nikolai Vladmirovich 193-97
Taraki, Noor Mohammed 189-90
Transbaikal Front 139, 144
    See R.Y. Malinovsky.
Triandafillov, V. 223, 224
Trotsky, Leon 32, 36, 38, 42, 43, 227, 264
    NKVD murder of 38, 42
Troyan, Vasily Avramovich 62, 63, 64, 66
Tukhachevskiy, Marshal Mikhail N. 2, 34, 37,
    223, 224-25, 227
    concept of the "nonstop" offensive 34
Tumanyan, Gay Lazarevich 271, 272

Ungria, Domingo 54-57, 61, 62, 266, 272

Vasilevskii, Marshal of the Soviet Union
    Aleksandr Mikhailovich 137, 141, 142,
    144
Vasilevskiy, Lev Petrovich 56, 57-58, 60, 63,
    64, 268, 272

Vaupshasov, Stanislav A. 59, 63, 66, 272–73
Vinarov, Ivan 269
Vizgin, Capt. 3rd Rank P. A. 83–84, 83n.6,
    83n.7, 85–87, 88–89, 92–94, 95
Vladivostok 139, 147, 149, 150, 151, 153
Voiska spetsialnogo naznacheniya (VSN). *See*
    spetsnaz.
Vozdushno-Desantniye Voiska (VDV). *See* air-
    borne forces.
vysotniki xx, 229, 230n.33, 238

Wardak, Abdul Rahim 207

Yezhov, Nikolay I. 32, 33
Yumashev, Adm. 145, 153

Zabelin, Lt.Col. Ivan Nikolaevich 142–43
Zaitsev Gen. Mikhail Mitrofanovich 207
Zakharov, Marshal Matvei V. 225

MILITARY UNITS

XIV Special Corps. *See* 14th Special Corps.
1st Far Eastern Front 77, 137, 139, 140, 142,
    143, 149
    See Karelian Front; K. A. Meretskov.
1st Guards Special Purpose Engineer Brigade
    76
1st Partisan Regiment, 3rd Partisan Brigade 76
2d Far Eastern Front 137, 139. *See* Gen.
    M. A. Purkayev.

4th Reconnaissance Detachment of Headquar-
    ters, Fleet 102
4th Special Volunteer Detachment of Sailors
    102
5th Separate Spetsnaz Engineer Brigade 66,
    72, 73, 74, 75, 272
6th OGBM 76–77, 117, 118–22
9th OGBM 76
10th OGBM 75–76
13th OGBM 76
14th Special Corps 36–37, 50, 56–57, 61–65,
    66, 73, 263, 264, 267, 269, 272, 273.
    See Spanish Civil War.
20th Motorized Assault Combat Engineer Bri-
    gade 77–78, 139–43
22d Spetsnaz Battalion 6n.36
63rd OGPU Division 32
64th Motorized Assault Combat Engineer Bat-
    talion 117–18
103rd Guards Airborne Division 4, 187, 190,
    196, 246
104th Guards Airborne Division 190, 246–47
105th Guards Airborne Division 190, 192–93,
    196
140th Guards Reconnaissance Detachment,
    Headquarters Pacific Fleet 146–53
160th Engineer Obsta le Battalion 74
166th Engineer Obsta le Battalion 74
168th Army Engineer Battalion 118
181st Special Reconnaissance Detachment 102.
    See Northern Fleet.
222d Motorized Assault Combat Engineer
    Battalion 77, 117–18, 120, 121, 122